TIBET
THE HIMALAYAN REGION
Religion, Society and Politics

TIBET
THE HIMALAYAN REGION
Religion, Society and Politics

DR. GIRIRAJ SHAH

KALPAZ PUBLICATIONS
Delhi-110052

TIBET: THE HIMALAYAN REGION
Religion, Society and Politics
(Religion, Sociology, Tourism)

Rs. 890

ISBN : 81-7835-092-0

Published in 2003 in India by
Kalpaz Publications
C-30, Satyawati Nagar
Delhi-110 052

e-mail: kalpaz@hotmail.com

Lassertypesetting at: A.A. Computer
Printed at : Mehra Offset Press

Contents

5. Treaty between Tibet and Nepal—1856 Translation.
6. The Convention of Chefoo (between the British Government and the Government of China, 1876).
7. Convention Relating to Burma and Tibet July 24th, 1886 (Between the British Government and the Government of China).
8. Convention of March 15th 1890 between Great Britain and China Relating to Sikkim.
9. Regulation Regarding Trade, Communication and Pasturge, to be Appended to the Convention between Great Britain, and China of 7 March 1890 Relating to Sikkim and Tibet, signed at Darjeeling, December 5, 1883.
10. Convention between Great Britain and Tibet Signed at Lhasa September 7th, 1904.
11. Convention between Great Britain and China Respecting Tibet. Signed at Peking, April 27, 1906 (Ratification exchanged at London July 23, 1906).
12. Convention between Great Britain and Russia Relating to Persia, Afghanistan and Tibet signed at St. Petersberg August 31, 1907.
13. Agreement between Great Britain, China, Tibet amending Trade Regulation in Tibet, of December, 1893, signed at Calcutta, April 20, 1908 (Ratification Exchanged in Peking October 14, 1908. Article 6 of this treaty is of Great Significance which was Later on was Surrendered by Government of India in 1954.
14. Treaty between Tibet and Mangolia, January, 1913 (Said to have been signed at Urga in January 1913).
15. India—Tibet Frontier 1914—Exchange of Notes between the British and Tibetan Plenipotentiaries—This is the Most Important Agreement between two governments.
16. Convention between Great Britain, China and Tibet Simla 1914. This was a very-very important Agreement which is quite often quoted.

Preface

India has always looked upon Tibet, "the roof of the world" with traditional reverence and an autonomous buffer state. For more than five centuries, the Chinese have attempted to subjugate Tibet, though with no success, till the huge People's Liberation Army (PLA) finally overwhelmed the resistance put up by Tibetan chieftains and finally occupied in October 1950. As a result thereof the Dalai Lama and lakhs of Tibetans migrated to India as refugees and settled in several states.

The author has done a scholarly work, weaving the whole theme into fourteen chapters including as many as twenty Treaties and Agreements signed from time to time. He has commenced with the early history of Tibet, beliefs and practices of Tibetans, the Dalai Lama as the Seal of authority, Chinese control over Tibet, British Missions to Tibet, Indo-China dispute on Tibetan frontier, Nehru's meeting with Dalai Lama, Tibetan refugees and developmental schemes for them, Dalai Lama's consistent efforts to regain his position in Tibet and the future status of Tibet.

Dr. Giriraj Shah has meticulously covered religion, society and politics in Tibetan region and has given several details having deep bearing on this Himalayan region which is the 'worst victim' of political circumstances since 1950s. The solution, if any, in favour of Tibetans, appear to be dim in the present circumstances.

This work is useful for social scientists, teachers, researchers and students interested in the history, culture and political developments in this Himalayan region.

Dr. Giriraj Shah

Introduction

Both history and geography have conspired to create a cockpit of conflict to the north of the subcontinent, in the 'Pamir Knot', the junction of China, Russia, Afghanistan and India on the one side and the Himalayan region that separates India from Chinese-occupied Tibet on the other. Fierce territorial disputes overlap one another in the western sector—those between India and China, India and Pakistan, and between China and Russia, now open and now concealed battlelines are drawn.

Background

Way back in 1896 the Chinese in Sinkiang has protested to the British against the inclusion of Aksai Chin as part of British-held Ladakh—a claim dismissed as absurd by the Britishers. Its absurdity, if proof is needed, is evident in the inconsistency that the Chinese at the time claimed Aksai Chin was part of Tibet, while in the context of the Sino-Indian boundary dispute the Chinese now maintain that this barren plateau always formed part of Sinkiang

India has always looked upon Tibet, 'the roof of the world' or 'Meru' to early Aryans, with traditional reverence, as a natural barrier or as an autonomous buffer state, to use modern geo-political jargon. But for more than five centuries the Chinese have attempted to subjugate Tibet, though with little or no success, till the vast People's Liberation Army (PLA) finally overwhelmed the resistance put up by Tibetan chieftains and finally occupied Tibet in October 1950.

The state was now set for the next phase—the Chinese thrust further south, both in the west and east, which took India almost unawares. It is interesting to observe how the heightening of tension in Sino-Soviet relations in 1962 coincided with the Chinese aggression against India. Because, reduced to its essentials, this conflict reveals the contours of a tussle between Moscow and Beijing for the ultimate dominance of Asia.

The foreign office in London had perhaps foreseen the Chinese itch for expansion. The tripartite meeting of India, China and Tibet at Simla in 1913, was a sagacious move by the British to circumscribe Chinese authority in Tibet on the one side and on the other, to commit the Chinese to accepting the Himalayan crest as the boundary between India and Tibet.

The convention tabled as statement describing the Tibetan boundaries thus: 'Well authenticated records, both Chinese and Tibetan, including the China-Tibet treaty of 822 AD and the Chinese maps of the Tang dynasty, indicate historic Tibetan frontiers such as are shown by the red line on the skeleton map' (McMohan Line) attached to Article 9 of the convention. Though their representative Ivan Chen initiallled the draft agreement, the Chinese did not ratify the convention ultimately. This was not because of the Indo-Tibetan boundary demarcation but due to the inability of China and Tibet to agree to the demarcation (of outer Tibet) between them.

India-Checkmated

This historical background to Chinese expansionist designs provided a body of experience which the political leadership of free India lost sight of in the paranoid euphoria for world peace and Afro-Asian solidarity. The tragic drama of comic bunglings in our Himalayan policy unfolds with the invasion and occupation of Tibet by the Chinese army on October 7, 1950. Ambassador Panikkar presented an 'aide-memoire of concern' to Beijing on October 21. Instead of protesting for the rights of Tibetans for freedom and self-determination, and for the sake of world peace—values which free India so loudly proclaimed—the note peevishly stressed that India's interest was 'only to see that the admission of the people's government to UN is not against postponed'! When at last realism dawned, India argued with Beijing for Tibetan rights, using the expression 'suzerainty' to describe the status of Chinese relations with Tibet. But in the Chinese translation of the Indian note somebody treacherously replaced 'suzerainty' with the word 'sovereignty', which only strengthened the Chinese claim for Tibet!

It has to be recorded that the then Governor-General, C. Rajagopalachari, and Sardar Patel disagreed with Prime Minister Nehru and cautioned him against the recognition of Tibet as Chinese territory. Somewhat prophetically, Acharya Kripalani thundered in Parliament: "China has demolished a buffer state; in international politics when a buffer state is abolished by a powerful nation, that nation is considered to have aggressive designs on neighbours."

Comedy of Errors

Nehru scoffed at such warnings in his self-centred righteousness. The comedy of errors was compounded when India signed the 1954

agreement with China on 'Trade and intercourse between the Tibet region of China and India'. The whole exercise was designed by the Chinese to secure India's formal recognition of Tibet as a part of China under the garb of a trade pact. While de facto recognition was inescapable, why should India have ratified the Chinese absorption of Tibet? In 1914, even a weak China had refused to ratify the Simla convention mentioned earlier. How did Nehru ratify the absorption of Tibet into China before defining the territorial limits of Tibet or seeking Chinese recognition of the McMohan Line in return?

The Dalai Lama's flight to India was followed by two ominous incidents. On August 25, 1959, Indian and Chinese forces clashed over possession of Longju, a small village in the eastern sector. We said it was on the McMohan line and, therefore, ours, the Chinese said it was two miles north of it and, therefore, theirs.

There were a few casualities on both sides. On October 20 the same year, an Indian patrol sent to probe the Aksai Chin was ambushed by the Chinese at Kongka La. Nine Indian frontier policemen were killed and seven taken prisoners, with this, Indian public opinion was inflamed. But public opinion, even when not inflamed, is quite often ill informed. The Indian public never really understood the historical background of the dispute.

Failed China Policy

We claimed that what the Chinese were disputing was ours and that was accepted by almost all except the doctrinaire Marxist Communists, who may have done this for different reasons altogether. The Indian government knew better, but it put itself out on a limb and now the opposition got to work to saw off that limb. The influence of the domestic imperative in the international politics of democratic countries must never be underestimated. It is also an inherent characteristic of democratic societies that very little flexibility is given to the decision-makers in choosing a policy from a wide spectrum of options. If for instance, Nehru accepted Chou-en-lai's offers of a settlement on a give and take basis, he would have been accused of giving up our "sacred" territory. As it is the opposition was having a field day exploiting Nehru's discomfiture over his failed China policy.

In the highly partisan atmosphere that characterised our politics then, as it is even now, any stick is good enough for the opposition to beat the government with and vice versa. The opposition, small in number, then as it now, made up for lack of quantity by quality, eminent leaders, known for their incisive views like Ram Manohar Lohia, Acharya Kripalani, Asoka Mehta, Deendayal Upadhyaya, Minoo Masani and C. Rajagopalachari, all smarting at their electoral inconsequence tore into the government in Parliament and outside.

Many of Nehru's colleagues, upset by his "loftiness" and his fondness for Krishna Menon, often preferred to be bemused. Observers enjoying these blistering attacks. China was treated as Nehru's problem. To be fair to them Nehru for long had kept the problems with China to himself as he did with most matters pertaining to external relations. To get over this uncomfortable "debating" situation in Parliament, Nehru often had to sound tough and uncompromising. This would have been fine, if he had the military strength to back him up. Unfortunately for the country, this was not so.

Ill Prepared

The Indian Army then was poorly-equipped, short-staffed and generally in a bad way. Krishna Menon as defence minister, squabbled with the generals in public and wrought havoc with the morale of the brass. Aiding him in good measure was a Nehru Kinsman, Lt. Gen. B.M. Kaul, a soldier with no combat experience, who in his bid to be one up over his peers, would agree to do things the politicians wanted done, but the general staff baulked at.

The press in those troubled days was not very helpful either. The major English language papers almost in unison shrilly demanded that the Chinese be expelled and often accused the government of not doing its duty. The influential English language media with few notable exceptions, being still conditioned by their pro-British past and current indigenous capitalist ownership was generally pro-Western and thus found this a good opportunity to needle the government on its policy of non-alignment seen by them in Dullesian terms as being pro-Soviet. The editors and pundits, never comfortable with Nehru's non-alignment went hammer and tongs at him. Given this atmosphere, partisan political interests took precedence over national interests. This is not unfamiliar even today. The need to develop a non-partisan national consensus based on a rational survey of facts and events never was greater, yet was as far as it often seems even now.

Against this surcharged backdrop, Nehru had to come up with something. This something was the Foreward Policy. This policy called for establishing posts in the disputed areas often behind the Chinese line of forward posts. Thus, a number of small forward posts were set up with meagre resources, poor communications and extremely vulnerable supply lines. Most of these posts had to be supplied by air drops and quite a bit of the supply would end up in Chinese hands and often the PLA would hand these over to our men to derive a psychological advantage.

Nothing describes the Forward Policy better than the words of an Indian Army Officer. "We thought it was a sort of game. They would stick up a post and we would stick up a post and we did not think it would come to much more". It came to much more as it had to and the consequences were felt in 1962 when a full-scale border war broke out. The Forward Policy was against all sound military advice.

Lt. Gen. Daulat Singh, GOC, Northern Command in a memo to the government bitterly criticised this policy. He wrote: "It is imperative that political direction is based on military means." Daulat Singh's warning like those of many other senior officers was ignored. Defence Minister Krishna Menon, Intelligence Bureau Director B.N. Mullick and Lt. Gen. B.M. Kaul who between themselves had conjured up this policy, had Nehru's ear and that was what mattered. If Nehru had learnt a little from the much publicised Bay of Pigs fiasco the new American administration of John Kennedy had landed itself into in 1961, he would have been very wary of this threesome. In Kennedy's case, he let the legendary CIA director of operations, Richard Bissell, awe him, his cabinet and his military chiefs into approving an operation that was based on little hard intelligence and a lot of wishful thinking. Also in Kennedy's case the pressures of the domestic imperative was overwhelming. The planning of the operation had begun in Eisenhower's time with Richard Nixon playing a leading part in it.

If Kennedy aborted the plan he would have been accused of being "soft on communists" and what greater crime can there be in that bastion of "freedom and liberty" than this? He succumbed to the pressures of public opinion just as Nehru was to do later. In both cases, the policies ended up in unmitigated disasters and almost irretrievably hardened positions and thus shaped the future course of national direction and domestic politics.

Continued Chinese Belligerency and Our Lukewarm Response

In the 40 years that followed the debacle of 1962, little has changed. We in India have not yet been able to get together a non-partisan consensus on crucial issues such as this. We do not seem to have as yet grasped the real and futile nature of the border dispute. On the other hand, there are signs that the old Forward Policy has been dusted up and put into effect again. Already in the Somdurong Chu valley, an area that should be well within Indian territory if one had to go by accepted cartographic conventions even if we agree that the McMohan Line is a thick ink line on paper not clearly demarcated on the ground, Indian and Chinese posts now lie within yards of each other. There have been news reports in the Western press of border aggrandisement and troop movements on the Tibetan side.

The official Chinese tone has had a more belligerent edge in recent days and some of our own rhetoric has had a pre-1962 tenor to it. The Defence Minister's of India have been stating that we will not give up even an inch of our territory and will throw out those occupying our land. This was exactly the language Krishna Menon used when confronted with criticism but we draw a flak even when facing Pakistan.

In an overpopulated, overcrowded and primarily agricultural country with a relatively small land mass to share, the concern and obsession with land is understandable. Land is our primary economic resource and hence it is an ingrained national characteristic to be possessive about land. Our leaders, notorious for their land grabbing ways, not surprisingly have acquired an estate agents mentality as far as territory goes. It seems that to us country no longer means people but land. Or else why would we care so little about our people and their interests and honour, and care so much for an uninhabitable terrain.

The India-China Confrontation Strategy

There seems absolutely no chance that the Chinese could be persuaded to cede Aksai Chin to us. There also seems an even remoter chance that we might be able to retrieve it from the Chinese by military means. Even if we summon the political will, the physical costs will be enormous!

Consider going on an offensive against the largest land army in the world? The Chinese are said to have almost 70 infantry division in Tibet and Sinkiang. They are as well-equipped as us. Though their air force consists mostly of obselete aircraft, they have the advantage in numbers. Our supply lines are extremely tenuous and often the only means of supply is by air. The only highway linking Ladakh to the rest of the country remains closed in the winters and runs uncomfortable close to Pakistani Military positions.

The Chinese have an excellent network of roads linking their forward positions to their cantonments. On the other hand, their main population and industrial centres are thousands of kilometres away from our forward bases. Delhi, Calcutta, and much of north and east India are within range of Chinese aircraft and Nuclear Missiles. One cannot also be sure that in a large scale war that Nepal and Bhutan's neutrality will be inviolate. The temptation for the Chinese, if the strategic situation so demands, to go through these countries would be enormous.

The von Schlieffen plan of the German army in World War I called for an attack on France through a "neutral" Belgium and so did the German strategy in World War II. If this happens here, the risks to us become even greater as beyond these countries lies the Indian heartland—the Gangetic plain—that over the ages backoned many an invader to our country.

When push comes to shove we can be sure that 1962 will not be repeated. Our generals are less politicised, our men better trained and provided for, with superior equipment and our overall military position is far better than it ever was. In a short border war we can hold our own and most likely beat the Chinese. But longer wars call for greater resources and resilience, and a total mobilisation of society. It needs a different attitude and thinking. For instance, long wars call for an ability to give up space to lure the adversary into unfavourable terrain to cut him up, Vietnam, even in its short border war with China, did this to great effect when it gave up a large swathe of territory including provincial capital of Lang Son. The Chinese, who wanted to "teach the Vietnamese a lesson", were then encircled by Gen. Le Dung's army and mercilessly hammered.

In our open society it is in conceivable than we can pull back to more favourable positions to ensure military success. Given our mentality, success is holding or taking territory. In 1962, if our troops were pulled back from the Thagla ridge to positions nearer Sela, as suggested by several generals, it is possible that our defensive line in the Tawang sector would have held. But would the Parliament, the media and all those other ill-informed people who constitute our informed public opinion have accepted this? It is unlikely they will do so even now.

Vying for Leadership

It is not being suggested that we capitulate before the Chinese and settle our problems entirely on their terms. This is hardly likely to ensure permanent friendship and amity. The differing nature of our two societies is such that we will for long be competitive. Behind its Marxist facade there lurks a fierce and aggressive Chinese nationalism that motivates it to seek predominance in world affairs. We can thus never flag in our military preparations and we must not.

A great India must necessarily be militarily powerful and a tenacious and resilient adversary if the situation so demands. We must raise our forces to match the largest of our adversaries present and future. If there is another conflict with the Chinese we cannot afford not to face them. There can be little argument about this. But must we continue to play the imperialist Great Game still?

It is possible for us to settle our border disputes with China on the basis of a clearly demarcatated McMohan Line. On the western sector the Chinese line of actual control now lies west of the Karakorum range. This is hardly a defensible line from their point of view. The Karakorum range would be the ideal border for both of us. This means the British foreign office line of 1873, midway through the Karakorum range till the Galwan river, be extended up till the Karakorum pass. We could negotiate for this with the Chinese, whose only aim in this sector seems to secure the Sinkiang-Tibet highway through the Aksai Chin. While this will not entirely dissipate the rivalry between the two countries it will remove a cause of frequent tension that only serves to underline our unfavourable position.

The challenge now for our national leadership is to harmonise reality with sentiment; pragmatism with unhistorical belief and national aspirations with imperalistic legacies. To be able to do this we first need to extricate such sensitive and critical issues from the ambit of partisan politics.

The responsibility for this lies with the government of the day which alone can orchestrate such an exercise. By doing this, we can once again bring into alignment our political objectives with military means and reality. We can then negotiate from a position of strength and give ourselves secure, defensible and natural boundaries in the north at least. And who knows this may even lead to lasting good relations between the two great countries.

Chinese Checker

As a great civilisation, China needs to think cooly and maturely, and not portion itself on the wrong side of India, another great civilisation. An unfortunate factor in India, China Relation since the end of World War II was Nehru's naive handling of these relations. At one stage, when Chinese troops entered Tibet only after India had recognised the new regime in Tibet. In 1949, whatever police and postal personal war in Tibet, were all Indian's and between 1912-1950 there was not a single Chinese in Tibet, in the name of Authority. Thus, losing valuable initiative of introducing Tibet in the United Nations, India thoughtlessly conceded Chinese suzerainty over Tibet and Chinese interpreted and exploited 'Suzerainty' for "Sovereignty" and gobbled up Tibet. Unfortunately, notwithstanding, Sardar Patel's advice to the contrary, Nehru went one step further by recognising Chinese claim on Taiwan without getting anything in return, even a formal acceptance of established border and support for Kashmir.

When China progressed India was happy and when China stabbed India in 1962, India was sad. When China went Nuclear India did not utter a word but when India had its first Nuclear Explosion and then Pokhran II was materialised by India, Chinese reaction crossed all limits of decency by asking India to stop immediately. The development of all Nuclear weapons and came out stubbornly with following four demands—

Firstly—that Indias action reflected "on outrageous contempt for the common will of the International community" in favour of the CTBT.

Secondly—India is using the "China Threat" as an excuse for the Development of its own Nuclear weapons.

Thirdly—India is seeking "Hegemony" in South Asia, and

Fourthly—The International community should adopt a common position in strongly demanding India to immediately stop it's Nuclear development programmes."

Right now Pakistan is China and United States hubby and they are arming it to the teeth out of sheer competation or zealousy—that who gets the bride. Pakistan is happy but it must see for itself the latest history after 1950-1962 between India-China where "Bhai-Bhai" became "Nak-Katai". I can only say "ख़ुदा खैर करे" and let the Pakistanese see the reality. They must realise that they are nearer to India in culture, traditions and history. And we must remember that if Tibet is an integral part of China (Which it is not neither by history nor by tradition), Pakistan is an artificial creation of British Imperialists design of dividing India and leaving it into two states so that they permanently fight for separate existence and a nation which had separate existence is now part of China merely due to military power and diplomatic manoeuvering.

Dr. Giriraj Shah

1

Tibet: Frontiers, Area and Population

When we talk about Tibet, it is better to know properly what is the exact meaning of that term. Do we talk of a country which is inhabited by free citizens or the one in control of China? Actually it has become very difficult to specify the name Tibet for any of the two. The political Tibet is considerably smaller than its ethnographic counterpart. While attempting to define the former, let us not neglect the latter, for national sentiment in Tibet, so long in abeyance, is now a growing force. It may be that the Mongol countries at present linked up with the British Government in India may draw back into closer relationship with Tibet or China. The separation movement is strong in Burma and is also present in the Himalayan district of Darjeeling. There are indications that the demand of separation may grow in Bhutan, Sikkim, and those other Himalayan territories which are inhabited by men of the Mongol races.

Geography

The territory under Tibetan rule extends approximately between the 78th and the 103rd degree of east longitude and between the 27th and the 37th degree of north latitude. The frontiers, especially on the north and east, are often ill defined because the country is large and difficult of access ; the population is sparse, and Governmental control in Tibet and China is loose and shifting. Even in the more settled portions of their country, Tibetans do not necessarily take mountain ranges or rivers as their boundaries. In 1904, the boundary between Bhutan and Tibet at the trijunction of Tibet, Bhutan, and Sikkim was what the Tibetans called an 'upland-tree lowland-tree' boundary? that is, the pine forests belonged to Tibet and the bamboo forests to Bhutan, which means in effect a contour of about 11,500 ft. above sea-level. It is really a good and practical boundary undoubtedly because it serves the agricultural and general needs of both countries, for the Tibetans need the higher lands for grazing their yaks and upland sheep, while the Bhutanese make great use of the bamboo. But it is a boundary not easily recognized by the other people, who look for frontiers along high mountain ranges, which are defended easily and can be demarcated on maps. The same type of boundary line may well account in part for the former Tibetan claim to north Sikkim, an early source of dispute between Great Britain and Tibet ; and may possibly have influenced the Tibetans in their claim to Lingtu which led to the Sikkim Expedition of 1888.

In the north-west, the frontier between Tibet and Sinkiang, or Chinese Turkestan, begins on the Kuenlun range north of Lake Lighten, in about 35° 30' north latitude and 80° 30' east longitude, and thence approximately follows the watershed eastward to a point about 90° 30' east, where it leaves the Kuenlun range and strikes in an irregular line northward, west of the Tsai-dam basin, till it reaches the watershed of the Altyn-tagh. This it follows again eastward through the intricacies of the Nan-shan mountains to about 101° east, where it strikes south, passing just west of Donkyr (Tangar), between Kokonor lake and Sining. From somewhere near the northernmost point of the frontier (94° 30' east), eastwards the Koko-nor district marches no longer with Turkestan but with Kansu, though here again the line of demarcation is defined very ill. The Tsai-dam and Koko-nor are the disputed areas between Tibet and China.

From the neighbourhood of Donkyr the boundary runs generally southwards or in south-eastern direction to near the 28th parallel, separating Tibet successively from Kansu, Szechuan, and Yunnan. Der-ge, Cham-do, Tra-ya, and Mang-kam are under complete Tibetan control ; Am-do, Go-lok, Nya-rong, Ba-tang, and Li-tang comprise the disputed areas.

Turning westward and crossing the Salween river at a point about 28° 20' north, the southern boundary, between Tibet and Burma, is at first hardly more clearly defined. Farther west, the borders of Tibet are determined by those of Assam as far as where the Dihang or Brahmaputra breaks through the mountains from the north. After this, the frontier follows the Himalaya range in a general manner. Here Assam is bounded on the north by a district inhabited by wild tribes of Mishmis, Abors etc. which appear to be as free of Tibetan as of British Indian control. Westwards again is Bhutan, lying between the Indian plain and the Himalayan divide, along which the Tibetan frontier here for the most part runs, to stretch south once more down the Chumbi valley between Bhutan and Sikkim. Teesta, the main river of Sikkim, forms the Sikkim frontier of Tibet. Farther west, the boundary between Tibet and Nepal appears to run mainly along the principal ridge of the Himalayan range, but the watershed here lies in general farther to the north, and Tibet maintains posts some distance down the southern valleys.

Tibet's western frontier may be said to begin where the Kumaon district is reached beyond Nepal. Here, in Almora and Garhwal, the boundary continues to follow in general the main divide in a north-westernly direction along the Zaskar ridge. On reaching the Hill States of Tehri and Bashahr, it takes a more northernly course, crosses the Sutlej at Shipki, and continues in an irregular northern direction, leaving Dankar in the Spiti district of the Panjab, Karak in Tibet and Hanle in Kashmir. The frontier crosses the Indus about 25 miles below Demchok (33° north), and cuts the Pangong chain of lakes about midway (79° east), and skirts the basins of the western rivers in a north-easterly direction to the borders of Turkestan.

The possession of Chumbi valley was claimed by Sikkim till the Chinese invasion of Nepal in 1792. But little Sikkim has lost land on all its sides. The State Chronicle sadly records, it has been shorn by

> Powerful hordes of elephants from the south,
> Active hordes of monkeys from the west,
> Cunning hordes of foxes from the north.

There is no doubt that the British elephant, the Gurkha monkey, and the Tibetan fox have devoured large slices of Sikkim.

It is noteworthy that Tibet is entirely surrounded by the lands of the British and Chinese Commonwealths. To Britain and China falls naturally the duty of helping the Tibetan people along the path of progress and self-realization.

Ladakh, in the north-east of Kashmir, and Bhutan in the eastern Himalayas are also Tibetan from the ethnographic standpoint. So too the State of Sikkim, originally under Tibetan rule, though three-fourths of its inhabitants are now Nepalese, yet its Ruler and most of its leading men are still Tibetan. Along the northern border of Nepal and, westwards, along the Indo-Tibetan frontier to Kashmir, we find many Tibetan settlements on the Indian side, but no Indian settlements on the Tibetan side of the frontier. The district of Darjeeling was originally in Sikkim and Bhutan, and therefore, ethnographically a part of Tibet, but many years of British administration have changed it so completely that it is now inhabited mainly by Nepalese and is a centre of Indian interests.

Ethnographic

The ethnographic Tibet extends somewhat between seven and eight hundred thousand square miles. The population may be estimated at four or five millions, of whom the majority live in the districts between Lhasa and the Chinese border. The western half of Tibet supports a population of only about one human being per square mile, for even the plains and valleys lie mostly over 15,000 ft. above sea-level which are too high for crops to ripen. The general slope of the country is from west to east. The south-eastern districts descend in places to below 5,000 ft., and here grow not only barley, wheat, and peas, the staple crops of central Tibet, but maize, and occasionally even rice also. So, it is in eastern and south-eastern Tibet that the population is chiefly found.

The lofty altitude of Tibet and its great size have formed the best possible barrier to India on the north. They have, at the same time, prevented us from learning much of Tibetan history in days gone by. Very few foreign travellers penetrated the country until comparatively recent years, when the European instinct for exploration asserted itself. The devastating hordes of Mongol conquest, that ravaged Asia and reduced the Russian Tsar and half Europe to vassalage, never crossed Tibet, though it lay at their doors and they themselves were habitual of a cold climate. Their robust vigour did indeed enable them successfully to invade India and to impose their will on the softer races of this country, but they came to India only after passing round Tibet through the easier mountains of Afghanistan. Hardly ever have invading forces crossed the vast northern plains of Tibet, where even the hardy Tibetans with difficulty find the means of subsistence. The Chinese pilgrims who have furnished us with such valuable side-lights on Indian history in the fifth and seventh centuries avoided Tibet, winding round through Chinese Turkestan and the mountain ranges to the north-west of India.

2

Physical Characteristics

The physical features of Tibet have enough variations. Lying at significantly high altitudes, Tibet falls naturally into three great physical divisions. Its northern face is covered by the Chang Tang, the 'Northern Plains', a tangled mass of plains and valleys, lying at an elevation of more than 16,000 feet above the sea-level, rising several thousand feet higher in its mountain peaks and ridges. Bounded on the north by the Kuen Lun range and the Mongolian steppes of Tsaidam, the Chang Tang falls away in the south to the great river of southern Tibet the Tsang Po. The chief rivers rising from its northern part are the Kiria, which breaks through the Kuen Lun to the north-west, flows past Polu and ends in the Takla Makan desert. Some 300 miles further east, the Cherchen Daria, rising from the Arka Tagh, flows past Cherchen and is lost in the marshes of Lob Nor.

Many Lakes and Rivers

The Chang Tang is studded with many lakes which are fed by the waters from surrounding mountains and valleys, but have no outlets. The great majority of the streams in the Chang Tang are lost in these lakes. But their utility is great since they give fresh water to a country where the lakes are mostly salty. There are no trees, because it is too cold and too high. The grass, though scanty, is sufficient to maintain large numbers of wild yaks, wild asses, wild sheep, wild goats, antelopes, wolves and other animals. Here and there, herds of yaks and flocks of sheep are tended by the nomads, whose daily allowance of grain is not more than a quarter of the normal amount, because the barley has to be brought laboriously over the mountains from southern Tibet. Since the barley is ground by hand, instead of by water-power, which is plentiful in the settled lands of the south Tibet, the barley flour is of poor quality. Radishes are grown and potatoes on the southern face of the tableland. No grain grows in this part not even the stunted barley, that is found at an elevation of fifteen thousand feet on the plains of southern Tibet. The southern and western ranges of the great plateau form the water-parting of India. To the east and north of this, the rivers of Tibet find their way through Myanmar, Siam, China proper, Mongolia and Chinese Turkestan.

Some fifteen hundred miles from east to west, four or five hundred miles from north to south, 16,000 feet above the sea and almost uninhabited, this inhospitable tableland is the true barrier of India to its north.

Tibet's second natural division comprises the valleys of the Indus and Sutlej to the west, and the valley of the Tsang-po, the Brahmaputra of India, to the south and south-east. These three large rivers rise in the same region near the sacred Manasarowar lake. The Indus and Sutlej rise on the slopes of the sacred mountain, known to Indians as Kailash, the Paradise of Siva in Sanskrit literature. They move towards northwest and then south through the Punjab to the Indian Ocean. The Tsang-po runs placidly from west to east through the heart of southern Tibet.

'Tsang-po' in the Tibetan language means the 'Purifier', and is applied to any of the large rivers. This river is known by different names on different parts of its course. Interestingly, the tributaries, as a rule, flow in a direction contrary to that of the main river, raising the presumption that, in earlier times, the Tsang-po flowed from east to west. It is interesting to think how these lesser streams tended to curve backwards towards the course of the Tsang-po.

Down long stretches of the great river go the boats of the country, even during the floods of the rainy season. From Lhatse, near the 88th meridian, to one day's journey below Tse-tang, near the 92nd, a distance of some 400 miles down its winding course, we have the unique spectacle of a navigable river flowing at more than 12,000 feet above the sea level. The boats, or coracles, are made from the hides of yaks and other cattle, stretched on a framework of withes. These latter are sometimes of willow, but preferably sliced from the tougher wood of the thorny scrub, known in Lhasa as *la*, which grows profusely along the river banks in the uplands of central Tibet. A Tibetan boatman, carries his coracle ten or twelve miles a day upstream, accompanied by a solitary sheep, which carries his food and other essentials.

Fragile as they seem for the task before them, and, when empty, drawing only a few inches of water, it is, nevertheless, remarkable what these coracles will carry. At Shi-ga-tse large family was seen in its little 'hide-boat'; as the Tibetans call them, after their donkey has clambered in beside them, paddle across the broad river to its northern bank. And down the river that flows by Lhasa one may see daily a succession of these coracles carrying not only loads of passengers and light goods, but long, heavy logs of walnut and poplar.

On the banks of the Tsang-po and its tributaries lie Lhasa and Shi-ga-tse, the two chief towns in Tibet, and Gyantse, also one of the largest. Prosperous monasteries minister, more than amply, to the religious needs of the countryside. And hither converge trade routes from Turkestan, Siberia, Mongolia, China and India. This part is Tibet proper, the seat of the Dalai Lama and his Government. It contains the districts controlled by the Government most closely. The people know it as *Pö* (pronounced same as the French word *peu*) in contradistinction to the Chang Tang on the north and the districts of Kham, which embrace the eastern Tibet.

The word 'Tibet' is not used by the people themselves. It seems to be a corruption of the Tibetan words *Tö Pö* (Upper Tibet) and was first applied to the elevated regions of western Tibet. The earliest mention of the word 'Tibet' is found in the Arab Istakhri's works (c. 590 A.D.) where it is written 'Tobbat'.

Mountains and Valleys

Tibet's third great division consists of the mountains and valleys of eastern Tibet between the Chang Tang and the border of China. On the eastern slopes of these northern plains rise the great rivers of China, Siam and Myanmar. The Hwang Ho and the Yangtse flow eastward through China, the Mekong and Salween south through Siam and Myanmar respectively. In south-eastern Tibet, we find the Yangtse, the Mekong, and the Salween, three of the largest rivers in Asia, flowing in deep, parallel troughs close to each other. The Mekong is only 28 miles from the Yangtse on one side, and even less from the Salween on the other. The Irawadi rises in the tribal territory in the north of Myanmar between China and the north-eastern corner of Assam.

The third division of Tibet contains many lesser districts and States, some of which acknowledge the Government at Lhasa, while others fall easily under Chinese control, though all respond, in greater or lesser degree, to the religious influence of the Dalai Lama and the Lhasa priesthood. Some States, like Der-ge, are comparatively advanced in civilization ; other live by highway robbery and brigandage in large measure. Still others are these who live chiefly by brigandage during part of the year, and bring salt for sale to southern Tibet at other times; an arrangement readily tolerated by the Tibetan Government, which is unable to exercise a complete control over its wide and difficult territory.

Eastern Tibet, by all means, is a country with a future. The lands on the whole lie at more reasonable elevations. Agriculture is possible on a large scale. Grazing is abundant and there are extensive forests. For its mineral wealth—gold, silver, copper, iron, and lead—hitherto almost untouched, may well prove of great value when developed on modern lines.

It is noteworthy that the limit of perpetual snow, which is about 17,000 feet in the Sikkim Himalaya, is about 20,000 feet in central Tibet. This large difference is due mainly to the fact that the southern slopes are exposed to damp winds from the Indian Ocean, which drop much of their moisture before crossing the range. Since Tibet is very dry, its snow-line is higher than those of mountains situated in the same latitudes but in other continents. In eastern Tibet, the line falls considerably, ranging between 15,000 and 16,000 feet.

Usually, the Tibetans do not give names to their mountain peaks, unless these are objects of especial worship. Chomolhari, 'The Mountain of the Goddess', which dominates the plains round Tuna and Phari for 50 miles, is devoutly worshipped like many others. But it does not seem to have been considered worth while to name those peaks of which no use is made. Passes always receive names, for they are used and, therefore, discussed about. The different grazing grounds on mountain slopes are fully named, and the rights in them are safeguarded zealously. When winter covers the plain with a mantle of snow, the Tibetan drives his yaks and sheep up the mountain slopes, which are cleared of snow, at any rate in patches, by the violence of the winds. The scanty stunted grass found here, is far more nutritious than the long, lush growth of the plains and valleys below.

It is, probably, necessary to note that the Tibetan names on our maps are often awfully incorrect, perhaps because the surveyors who recorded them had inproper knowledge of Tibetan. Thus Gye-mo Chen, 'The Great Queen', at the tri-junction point of Tibet, Bhutan, and Sikkim, is recorded as Gipmochi. Cho-mo Yum-mo, 'The Mother of the Goddess', a lofty snow nountain in the north of Sikkim, is demarcated our maps as Chumiumo. It is to be hoped that somebody who has the necessary time and experience may correct such map names. But before this is done, an international system of spelling should, if possible, be agreed upon.

3

Lakes, Climate and Trade Routes in Tibet

The rivers of Tibet have been given in the paragraphs above which relate to the three physical divisions of the country.

Lakes

But a little must be said about the lakes, that are studded about the country in great numbers, particularly Chang Tang and southern Tibet. These lakes have probably been formed in one of the following ways :

(a) by the damming of a main valley by the material bring down through its tributaries ;

(b) by the rise of a river bed at a rate more than the rate of erosion of the river, due to which a barrier is formulated and ultimately a dam accumulates across the valley ;

(c) due to the filling of a rock-basin earlier scooped out by a glacier.

The greater portion of the Chang Tang forms a great basin in that rivers flow and empty themselves into lakes, but never reach the sea.

The biggest Tibetan lake is that of Koko Nor, to the north-east of the Tibetan plateau and outer area of the basin. It has an area of 1,630 square miles. The Tengri Nor in the centre of Tibet is about 1,000 square miles in area, and many others are of more than 100 square miles.

These lakes were in past ages much bigger than are now. We may still see salt-covered flats and old beaches on the hill-sides, sometimes several hundred feet higher than the existing levels. The Himalaya mountains have risen within recent geological ages. They have thus intercepted more and more the rain-currents from India and made Tibet drier and more drier. Evaporation from the lakes has been increased ; their sorrounding areas have been shrunk and their waters become more saline.

The Ne-sar monastery in the broad valley of the Nyang River, 13,000 feet above the sea, near about thirty miles from Shigatse, is reputed to be more than 1,200 years old, and is definitely one of the oldest monasteries in Tibet, as is proofed by its tiled roof as well as by the reference to it in Tibetan histories. Though now the walls are of sun-dried brick, these were at first built of cypress wood. Even though, at present, the original pillars of cypress are standing, black with age. The priests said me that in earlier days there were various kind of cypress trees in Tibet, for the climate was then more humid and more snow used to fall. This convention is at any rate worthy of mention. Tibetans generally believe that there were more trees and fuller crops in prior ages, though, characteristically, they attribute those advantages to greater kindliness and truthfulness among the male and female of olden times.

The suddenness and violence with which storms sweep through the Tibetan lakes have been pictorially described by Dr. Sven Hedin after his dareful journeys through the Chang Tang. In these wide, blank spaces, there is nothing to break its force.

It may very well considered that Tibet, the world's highest country possesses an exceptionally severe climate. And the severity is still further enhanced by the winds, that blow aggressively during the greater portion of the year, and should be analysed to be appreciated. Nothing but good skin and fur keeps them out, and visitors in Tibet in autumn and winter frequently find it advisable to commence marches in the keen frosts of sunrise, in order to escape as much as possible the biting winds of midday and matinee.

In the lower lands, those below 12,000 feet, like Chumbi Valley, the weather is agreeable and, despite of the cold, is healthy, for it is dry, bracing, and free from most of the diseases that infest the Indian plains. Here Europeans can live and thrive, though a citizen of many years is generally usually found to try the heart, nerves, and digestion, the last-named suffering from the difficulty of cooking food at an altitude on problem which the boiling-point of water is more lowered. My Tibetan friends, returning to Tibet after four or five years in England, expressed to me his appreciation of our English winters, but found the English summers much relaxing.

But in Tibet some Tibetan women find the winters trying. 'During winter', a Tibetan nobleman intimated me, 'our ladies do not leave their houses much. They usually exchange visits with their close friends, but do not usually go too far. They have to think of their complexions, that will turn blue if they go out in the winter winds.'

When going out to visit friends and relatives during the winter—and they are too crasy in visits and entertainments—their faces and gorgeous head-dresses are muffled up with little meticulous care. And still more is this so, when riding out to go their estates. To these precautions are due the well-preserved complexions of so many of the women of the Tibetan Royalty.

But when they attend the ceremonies and shows in which all delight, these wrappings are eliminated. It doesn't matter that the hour is dawn on an ice-bound winter morning, and that the wind from the north is sweeping over the Lhasa plain. Clad as warmly as may be, each vies with the other in the display of silks, ornaments and precious stones. Human nature is after all human nature.

All the time when one crossed the main axis of the Himalaya into Tibet, one could not fail to be struck by the contrast between the deep, rocky gorges and the moisture-laden air in Sikkim and Bhutan on the one hand ; and the vast plains, the wide valleys, the yellow, round-topped mountains and the dryness of Tibet on the other. Clear as is the air of Sikkim, that of Tibet is more clearer. We travel on our sturdy Tibetan ponies, now cantering, now roaming, and now at the favourite Tibetan amble, for mile after mile, but our target seems to draw but little nearer, as the wind grows stronger and the clouds roll up for the afternoon storm. What looked four or five miles distant is really twenty. In the year 1904, when the British Expedition to Tibet was encamped on the plain of Phari, our one mountain guns—so it has been said—do practice for the edification of the king of Bhutan. But the distance estimated at a mile proving to be a mile and three-quarters, His Highness had to depend upon his well-known skill and courtesy in framing his appreciation of the marvel showed to him.

Sikkim as well as Darjeeling has varying rainfall Is annually according to locality, from about eighty to two hundred and fifty inches, but once above the head of the Phari plain, the rainfall averages only 20 cms in the year. Its my observation that 12 cms was, the lowest and 30 cms is the highest annual rainfall recorded at Gyantse in ten or twelve years of observation. The year's fall of 30 cms was enough to cause flood-damage. As one penetrates farther into central Tibet, the rainfall tries to increase. At Lhasa it averages about 35 cms anually. Sixty miles north of the capital, observing by the vegetation, it is again little bit heavier, perhaps forty five to fifty centimeters.

Trade Routes

The Tibetans are keen businessman, and that's why we find that

Tibet is well supplied with trade-routes, that run to India on the south, to China on the east, and to Mongolia on the north.

From Kashmir capital that is Srinagar, a route runs to Leh, the capital of Ladakh, and hence through southern Tibet to Shigatse and Lhasa. From Lhasa a much-used route goes to Chamdo. Here breaks in two parts. The southern road passes via Batang and Litang to Tachienlu ; the northern comes at the same destination via Kanze and Dango. Tachienlu, the ethnographical boundary between China and Tibet, is the main entrepot of trade between the two countries. The wool from the Tibetan sheep is exchanged by the teas of China, that find its way along the rough mountain tracks around the whole length of Tibet, which also found in the villages of Ladakh. Tibetans aver that the Chinese tea, mixed according to their convention with butter and soda, is more nutritious than the Indian, and suits their constitutions in better manner.

From Lhasa another great trade-route strikes north, past Nag-chu-ka across the Chang Tang to Urga, which is the capital of Mongolia, and thus, connects with the plains of Siberia.

Once in summer, and a gain in winter, the caravans come together near the great lake of Koko Nor, the borderland of Tibet, Mongolia, and China. So united for mutual security against robber bands, the merchandisers and pilgrims cross north-eastern Tibet and the northern plains, coming in Lhasa during August or January. Climate-scarred, even in August, were the parties which we met fifty miles north of Lhasa, their religious fervour growing daily as they neared the Holy City. Camels and yaks are used for riding and transport across the northern plateau. The camels are left at Nag-chu-ka, ten days journey north of Lhasa ; it is not allowed to bring them nearer the city. From Nag-chu-ka to Lhasa the travellers come in small parties ; between these places there is not much danger from brigands.

Shimla is the starting-point of an marvellous road, that becomes rougher as it nears the Tibetan frontier at Shipki and joins the first route, the road from Leh. Though elaborated grandiloquently as the Hindustan-Tibet road, its trade with the latter country is nevertheless insignificant. The roads from Almora, across various Tibetan passes, carry a enough traffic. The two main routes through Nepal are one that passes by Kirong Dzong on the upper waters of the Gandak river, and another one is that crosses near Nya-nam Dzong, on the upper waters of the Arun.

The most important of all the trade-routes between India and Tibet takes off from Kalimpong in the district of Darjeeling, crosses south-eastern Sikkim, and enters the Chumbi Valley by the Jelep La. Hence it goes up the Chumbi Valley to Phari. From Phari many of the caravans take a track along the eastern side of the Hram Tso to Lhasa—a line that is shorter and affords good grazing—while a few follow the more round about road via Gyantse Half the whole trade between Tibet and India traverses this Lhasa-Kalimpong route.

The most direct and most natural route from Lhasa to India is that one which goes via Tse-tang and Tso-na Dzong to Ta-wang. We may expect much from this route, between Tibet and Assam, in the future, as well as from one which will be start from the north-east corner of Assam, run along with the Lohit valley to the fertile lands of south-eastern Tibet, and connect with China via Ba-tang and Tachienlu—a trunk road from India to China, though a highly mountainous one.

It will be easily understood that the word 'trade-route' does not connote a well-made road. The tracks, along which the trade goes are sometimes very rough. But it takes a broad deal to daunt the perseverance of the baggage animal, be it yak, broad, mule, or sheep. The small, stocky Tibetan mule will climb up and down the mountain sides like a cat. I have known one, when carrying its load of a hundred and fifty pounds, drop seven to eight feet through the flooring of a broken bridge, and after being dug out of the rocks and mud at the bottom, resume and complete his journey, none the worse for this trifling misadventure.

The mule is better than the yak on slippery grass, but the yak is unsurpassed in carrying either goods or passengers over clearly apparently impossible rocks and boulders. Though seemingly of awkeward build, it clambers over these with but little difficulty, playfully prodding at man or beast in front with its massive horns.

The muleteers are always to be seen riding on sturdy, shaggy ponies behind their caravans, but dismounting to walk down the steep hills. For the old Tibetan saying tells us,

If you do not carry him up the hill, you are no pony ;
If you do not walk down the hill, you are no man.

4

Early History of Tibetans

The early history of Tibetans, like any other people, is interesting. We must start with it which as follows.

Mangolian Trade

The Tibetans anticipated Darwin by claiming descent from a monkey. Darwin who is known as an incarnation of the Compassionate Spirit, met an evil who addressed him thus : 'By reason of my actions in my former life I have been born in a demon race, but, being in the power of the god of lust, I love you greatly.' After much hesitation and after getting help with his spiritual guide the Compassionate One married her and they had six children. The father fed these on sacred grain, with the result that by degrees the hair on their bodies got reduced and their tails became smaller and finally disappeared. So says the Tibetan chronicle. Another chronicle adds, 'Those who took after their father were full of love and piety and were eloquent and meek ; those who took after their mother were full of sin, contention, and jealousy, and were greedy and mischievous. But all possessed strong bodies and courage.' The above traits, good and bad, have thus come to the Tibetans as inherited from their first ancestors.

Thus far their own custom. Western science places the Tibetan race among the Mongolian family of nations, that with their allied Turkish tribes, inhabited high Asia from time immemorial. This is usually thought that the Tibetans came partly from the north-east, and partly from Assam and Burma in the south-east. Philologically the Tibetans hail to the same linguistic family as the Burmese. And, as far as appearance goes, it is even now difficult to differentiate a Tibetan from a Mongol, until he speaks. The early Tibetans would appear to have led an whole pastoral life. That is among the shepherds and the yak-herdsmen which we still find the cleanest type of the race.

Early History

The earlier history of Tibet is ambiguous. The number of historical works written by Tibetans are not small. I have got from my Tibetan friends most of them are held in good repute. They deal mainly with religious happenings, many of which looks trivial to us. They abound in myths and miracles, in dreams and religious discussions. For Buddhists, like Hindus, lack the historical sense, as the Hindus is understood by Europeans, Chinese, and Mahomedans. It is to be noticed that, even at the present time, Tibetan monks are not permitted to read histories. 'Otherwise', as I was intimated in Lhasa, 'they would be regularly reading them, and ignoring works on religion and philosophy that are more difficult and less attractive subjects.' It must not, however, be considered that Tibetan histories are worthless. They give most of the information on the growth of Tibetan Buddhism and a few also on the common life of the people. But lack of space will allow only a limited reference to them here.

Tibet did not free the notice of the Father of History. Writing some around two thousand four hundred years ago, Herodotus tells us of a rumour about a race of many ants which delved for gold in a country to the north-west of India. From time to time travellers tried to steal the gold and to ride away with it, but the ants caught them and killed. An clarification that has found credence with some, is furnished by the gold diggings at Thok Jalung in western Tibet. The too much cold of this lofty tableland, aggravated by the violent winds that sweep unceasingly over it, insist the Tibetan layman to dig hunched up in their back yak-hair blankets. They are assisted by their watchdogs. These too are generally black ; ferocious and fast they would definitely follow and attack the robbers after the manner explained by Herodotus.

Blue Record

The 'Blue Record' which is the best Tibetan histories, referring to the visits to Tibet of an Indian saint, who had got the power of living a very long time, mentions a convention that says, 'The first time when he came, he saw Tibet under water. The second visit displayed the water receding, patches of brushwood, and a few deer roaming about'. It brings to attention also 'a custom which says that Tibet at first comprised a group of twelve States, but, as they were not important and none of their emperor served the trust, their history ends there.' History, until it centres on religion, does not appeal to the Tibetan mind.

Passing by the legendary kings, who lived between the first century B.C. and the seventh century A.D., and during whose reigns charcoal was made, reservoirs and irrigation introduced, mules imported and mining further developed, we come in the seventh century to King Song-tsen

Gam-po and the beginning of Tibetan civilization. Buddhism had entered Tibet some two hundred years back but got only a little hold on the country. The new king acceded to the throne at the age of thirteen and ruled for many years. His armies surmounted Upper Burma and Western China. The King of China was compeled to yield a princess in marriage to the conqueror, who also took to wife a princess from Nepal. The two queens, being Buddhists, translated the young king to their trust and he used all his influence to spread Buddhism in Tibet. A part of the Buddhist Scriptures was brought from India. Tibetan had hitherto been a verbal language only, but, in order that the sacred books might be converted, a written character was discovered. This was depend upon the Indian alphabet as then used in Kashmir. Considerable opposition was aroused, but the work was delayed on and Buddhist monasteries were rectified. For the Chinese queen had invented by astrology that Tibet was 'like a female demon lying on her back.' So the monasteries were built in those parts of Tibet that corresponded with the arms and hands, and with the legs and feet of the demon, whose authority was thereby decreased. We are told of this King that he retired into seclusion for four years, to learn reading and writing.

We are also said that 'he established laws for the punishment of murder, robbery, and adultery. He appreciated learning and the practice of the sixteen righteous duties. He got the priesthood, ordaining some priests as a beginning. And in other manner also he gave a strong religious impulse to the all of Tibet.

Other account refers to the order introducing the new laws as follows : The high should be pressed down by law, the poor should be governed according to a appropriate system. Establish measures, fertile land and teach the people to read and write. Establish good manners. Fine those who abused ; compensate for murder ; make thieves pay eightfold the amount of the stolen goods. Banish one who promise rape to another country and cut off one of his limbs. Cut out the tongue of the liar, make the people to worship God, to respect and repay the liberal of its parents, the loving mother, the old father and the uncle.

'Return commodity for commodity. Do not quarrel with liberal people. Read the manuscripts and get them. Trust in Karma, forsake everything that is not religious, help your neighbour. Drink in moderation. Be modest. Pay your debts swiftly and do not use wrong measures. Do not hear to your friend's wife. If there be a "yea" and a "nay", take the gods as siteness.'

The law was introduced with music and dance. Eighteen girls sang and offered flowers. The people held races and sports, and hoisted flags on trees. It is noticed that the holy doctrine spread over the whole land as the sun and moon cover the earth.

Introduction of Buddhism

The form of Buddhism which availed in the neighbouring hill-country of Nepal was got as the State religion. We may presume that it was strongly mixed with natureworship, as is the Hinduism of Nepal at the present day. And in any case the Pön religion, which then prevailed in whole country and was itself mostly animistic, was too strong to be ousted altogether by the new principles.

The Buddhist missionaries, who came actually from Nepal, Kashmir, and China, introduced arts and convention from India and China. The Chinese queen introduced butter, cheese, and barley-beer, and the people were learnt how to make pottery works and water-mills. The king himself built a palace by Lhasa, on the 'Red Hill', where the Dalai Lama's mansion which is known as the Potala, now stands. By his successive conquests he extended his power over Nepal, as well as over Upper Burma and western China. As a conqueror, a law-giver and a religious and educational reformer, Song-tsen Gam-po has set an undying name in Tibetan annals. To this day his chapel in the great Temple in Lhasa is thronged with worshippers, who sing songs of prayer and praise, and bring enormous jugs of barley-beer as offerings to the great emperor. And in his first mansion four or five miles outside Lhasa, religious services are still held whenever there is peril of war.

His grandson started tea from China, and this in time became, and still is, the national liquor. The well-to-do Tibetan of modern times drinks fourty to eighty cups of tea in a day.

In the years that followed, many works on astronomy, astrology, and medicine were converted from Sanskrit and Chinese. We may actually say that the present civilization of Tibet was taken mainly from China, and only in a lesser degree from India. The religion was brought down partly from India and rest from Nepal and Kashmir, but developed by the Tibetans according to their own lights. In this connexion it should be given that the population of Nepal is Mongolian, and has thus always formed a appropriate channel of communication between India and Tibet. Moreover it is possible that Buddha, who was born in what is now Nepalese territory, was, partially or wholly, of Mongolian origin. The general appliances of civilization apart from religion—and in a lesser degree religion also—have been brought China. It should be noticed fewer that in the early days of Tibetan Buddhism the Indian influence was moderable, while during the last five or six centuries it has been but slight, that of China and Mongolia predominating. The common kinship—partial though not fulfill of Chinese, Mongolians, and Tibetans asserted itself against outside emphasis.

Coming of Padma Sambhava

During the last half of the eighth century another famous emperor Ti-song De-tsen, ruled over Tibet. He summoned the Tantrik Buddhist, Padma Sambhava, from Udyayana in north-western India. Padma Sambhava suppressed demons, performed miracles, and settled Buddhism efficiently. Among other monasteries that he built was the great monastery at Sam-ye, fifty miles south-east of Lhasa. It is the oldest of the large monasteries in Tibet, and is still a flourishing institution. Padma Sambhava is one of the patron monk of Tibet, and the main saint of the Red Hat sect, the followers of the original Buddhism of Tibet. Among the Red Hats his inpression occupies the place of honour on Tibetan altars as usually as that of Gotama Buddha himself. For the people say that Buddha would be helpless without the priests who spread his principles and the books in which those principles are expounded.

The historian of this period insist the difficulty that the monarch encountered in summoning teachers from the south, for the ministers urged the perils of sorcery, remarking that the Indians and Nepalese were noted for their knowledge of the black arts. By this period the main teaching of Buddha had been wellnigh eliminated in India and changed by the Tantrik principles with their charms and mystic meanings. It was this later phase of Buddhism that penetrated Tibet. We are again told that many holy books were changed from Chinese, as well as from Nepalese, into Tibetan, and thus the religion was made as clear as daylight to the people.

King Ti-song De-tsen also instituted codes of civil and criminal justice. He was a witty and powerful monarch, one of the landmarks in last Tibetan history.

The Tibetans have several democratic traits in their nature character. One of these was left in the next emperor. Mu-ni Tsem-po, who ordained that people must share equally in the wealth of the country. An equal portion was made, but the equality soon disappeared. Even twice again all were made to share and share same. But the inequalities became worse than earlier for it has been seen that the poor, who had become indolent during their time of ease, became poorer than before. After the third attempt the king was poisoned by his mother.

The principle of the western world is 'equal opportunities for all', either in educational or other advantages, is held by many. But the hundreds of millions who believe in the Hindu or Buddhist religions cannot reconcile such a principle with their creeds. For both believe in interexchange of the soul, or mind, through successive worldly existences. And the Law of *Karma*, one of the main foundations of their religion, could never allow that all should start equal in this life, however good or bad their earlier lives had been. Thus it was that the Tibetan priesthood ascribed the failure of the scheme to the deeds, good and bad, of previous lives working out their inevitable outcomes.

During the reign of Ral-pa-chan, in the latter half of the ninth century, standard weights and measures were started from India. The priesthood was consulted and increased, temples built, and Buddhism zealously enhanced throughout the country. Many Indian teachers came to the country and translated religious books.

Tibetan priests also went to India to study the religion there, halting on the way in Nepal to learn the Indian languages. Some of these passed on to India, though their death-roll was heavy. Out of a party of ten or twelve not more than three or four would return to Tibet. It is not without reason that the Tibetan fears the Indian weather.

Of Ral-pa-chan we read that 'Fastening to his clotted hair a sheet of silk, he request the priests sit on it. He allocated seven lay households to the assist of each of the priests, and paid great homage to the priesthood.' The enthusiasm of the king seems to have been too much for his people, for when only forty-six years old, he was killed at the instigation of his brother, Lang-dar-ma, who was at the head of the anti-Buddhist party. As soon as the Lang-dar-ma succeeded to the throne, he did what he could to destroy Buddhism in Tibet.

'The religious law broke like a rotten rope. The peace of Tibet looked like a lamp without oil. Devil increased like a storm ; the good feelings were forgotten as a dream. The monks, finding none to serve them, returned to their homes ; the evil ministers destine the power. These appointed as emperor Lang-dar-ma, an incarnate fiend.'

Tibetan Conquests

From the time of Song-tsen Gam-po to that of Ral-pa-chan, Tibet and China were constantly at war, with varying feeling. Tibetan convention records that after the death of Song-tsen Gam-po, that occurred about A.D. 650, the Chinese conquered Lhasa. During the reign of Ti-song De-tsen, Tibet was at the acme of her power, and was really one of the great military powers of Asia. Her king touched those of the Arabs and Turks across the Pamirs. Turkestan and Nepal look to have been subject to her, and her victorious armies had overrun the western parts of China. The horrified Chinese paid tribute to Tibet to save their capital, Changan. But when, with the assist of a new Emperor, they failed to pay this tribute, the Tibetans attacked again, and in A.D. 763 or thereabouts took over the Chinese capital.

It was possibly during the reign of this king that the Tibetans and Nepalese attacked India. This incident occurred after the death of Harsha, who was king of northern India during the visit of the Chinese pilgrim Hiuen Tsiang in the seventh century of our era. One of the histories of western Tibet records of Ti-song De-tsen's reign, 'All the countries on the four frontiers were subdued. China in the east, India in the south, Baltistan and Gilgit in the west, and Kashgar in the north were elaborates under his power.'

Another chronicle describes the extent of the Tibetan kingdom during the reign of Ral-pa-chan thus :

'During the time of king Ral-pa-chan, the Lord of Power, the frontiers held with the Kings of the four borders were as follow : The range of the Sro-long-shen mountains, looking a curtain of white silk, was the frontier with the Chinese King of Astrology ; near the great river, Ganges, there was an iron pillar, that was the frontier with the Indian King of Religion : the gate of Pa-ta Sha-dung was the frontier with the Persian King of Wealth ; and the ridge of sand, which seems like the back of Nya-mang-ma, was the frontier with the King of Be-ta.'

Twenty years after, Tibetan armies again captured western China. A treaty was finalised by which the Koko Nor lake was fixed as the north-eastern boundary of Tibet. The Tibetan king cancelled his conquests in China, but hold the mountainous lands, the homes of his race. Tibetans have never dreaded the hot countries. The fear of disease should often have saved India from the incursions of their hardy neighbours on the north.

The Bhutanese, living in a little bit warmer climate, have periodically invaded Bengal and Assam. They would carry men, women, and goods back to their mountain fastnesses, a former Raja of Kuch Bihar having been one of their victims. It was not till the establishment of British power in north-eastern India that the Bengalis and Assamese could feel safe from raids.

The important conquests of the Tibetan kings and their treaties with China are made known to us, partly by the Chinese and Tibetan histories, and rest by two stone pillars at Lhasa. The writing on these has been obliterated in parts, both by the passage of time and by the Chinese during their later occupation of Lhasa. But more remains, when read with the references in the Tibetan and Chinese books, to give us an outline of what happened.

Song-tsen Gam-po, Ti-song De-tsen, and Ral-pa-chan are the renounce figures, both in war and peace, among the kings of Tibet. They are known to Tibetans as 'The Three Religious Kings, Men of Power.' The development of Buddhism, that forbids the taking of life and preaches peace and renunciation, checked if it did not sap, the martial ardour of a race akin to the conquering and destroying hordes of Jenghiz Khan. It is noticed that, when in recent years the Russians re-introduced the arts of war into Mongolia, the Mongols periodically proved themselves more than a match for the Chinese troops so too with the Tibetans. Poor trained but having few thousand modern rifles with only twenty or thirty rounds per rifle, they have expelled the regular forces of China from large areas of their country. The fighting spirit is still alive in Mongol or Tibetan.

End of Empire

Lang-dar-ma was himself shotted after a reign of only three years by a Lama. Smearing his white pony with charcoal—so the custom runs—the priest donned a black robe with white lining and rode into Lhasa. He saw the king examining the inscription on one of the stone pillars given above. Dancing a marvellous dance, which he had discovered for the occasion he came slightly closer to the royal presence. Lang-dar-ma called him to come near and do the dance. While making the twofold prostration which the occasion demanded, the lama drew a bow and arrow from his broad-sleeved robe and kill the king. Then mounting his steed he galloped off. The crossing of a river washed the charcoal from his pony. He himself turned his robe inside out and, thus transformed fleed into security.

At present this dance, is known as 'The Black Hat Dance', is still celebrated in whole Tibet in commemoration of the revengers exploit. But the set-back to Buddhism continued for seventy years.

With Lang-dar-ma the long line of Tibetan kings comes to an end. The country became full of petty chiefs, who built forts on hills and ridges overlooking their subjects on the plains mentioned below. So came into use the Tibetan saying :

The fort on the hill,

The fields on the plain.

The fort secured the villages below and the villages fed the fort.

When a head died, his widow or daughter would sometimes block the reins of government and rule the little kingdom with vigour and wisdom. There are records of many of these chieftainesses in old times, and to this day are pointed out the forts in that they held sway. For the position of women in Tibet has usually been a good one ; they also have shared in the control of their country's destiny.

Indian pandits, the chief of whom was Atisha, continued to travel Tibet published the religion and were well-received. The cave where Atisha lived, sixteen miles east of Lhasa, is still procured. High up on the sunny mountainside, surrounded by stunted junipers and bushes of wild currant and wild rose, it looked a fitting home for a religious reformer in this land of ice and snow.

We have tremendous glimpse of Tibetan life at this time, the period of the Norman conquest of England, in the autobiography of the Tibetan poet-saint, Milarepa. We knew how he lived in caves as Tibetan hermits do at the present he was poor-treated by robbers, who were further caught by the prefect of the district and had their eyes put out ; and how shells were then the admitted currency of the country. To aid him in his meditation he resorted to turning and breathing exercises. Life in Tibet does not seem to have changed very greatly during the last eight hundred years.

At the time of twelfth and thirteenth centuries the priests of the new religion, Buddhism in its Lamaistic form, were constantly extending their influence among a people always prone to trust in spirits and mysticism. The grandson of Jenghiz invited the High Priest of the large Tibetan monastery at Sakya to his Court. In A.D. 1270 Khublai Khan, the first Mongol Emperor of China, having similarly invited the Sakya Hierarch of the period, became a convert to Lamaism, and gave the sovereignty of Tibet to his visitor. Thus began in Tibet the rule of the priest-kings. This first instalment of it lasted for seventy-five years, from about 1270 to 1345. During this tenure many Indian priests found their way to Tibet, and the religion in its Tantrik form got a firmer hold. It is recorded also of the chief to these Hierarchs that he 'was very lenient as regards religious opinions. He appreciated every one to do his best and to be earnest in his creed, whatever it might be.'

The power of Sakya was broken by King Chang-chub Gyal-tsen, who brought almost all Tibet under his sway and started the Second Monarchy of Tibet. He continued to promote the religion, but eliminated many of the Chinese and Mongolian creations introduced by the Sakya priest-kings. But the martial vigour of the Tibetans was not what it had been. Chinese and Mongolian influence continued to be realised in Tibet. The Sakya Hierarchs had depended on the Mongol kings. The new dynasty, which is known as the Sitya, was, in some measure at any rate, dependent on China.

The Sitya dynasty ruled in Tibet for three hundred years, till 1635, when the king of the Tsang province of Central Tibet ousted it, but was himself after few years subdued by Gushi Khan, the chief of the Oelöt Mongols. It was on the whole a time of peace and prosperity.

It was obvious that Mongolia should adopt the religion of her Tibetan cousins, for the relation between the two races has always maintained strong. Even at the present day the Tibetan Government regards the two countries as bound together by a close understanding, if not by a true alliance. But the advent of Buddhism has centred the views of both on religion, so that the two nations, even if allied, would be infinitely less powerful for the purposes of war than anyone standing alone before Buddhism obtained a hold.

5

Beliefs and Practices of Tibetans

Tibet belongs to religious people. It is a land where religion is given first priority. The religion shows the great knowledge gives clear understandings to each and all. Tibetans, have faith in one supreme being, i.e., Buddha. In fact the Dalai Lama being the important man in the Tibetan land.

Religion

Tibet's religion, as we all know, is Great Vehicle (Māhāyana) Buddhism. And this religion deeply affects the country's every institution and inhabitant. It has taken a distinct and peculiar form, which is not shared by the Mahāyāna found elsewhere in the Far East—except for that of Mongolia, Sikkim and Bhutan. This form is often called 'Lamaism' from the important part played by the Lama (*blama*), a term not denoting just any monk, but a person's spiritual master or teacher (*guru*) alone. We shall find that his role is indeed extraordinary even from a doctrinal viewpoint. So I do not feel it necessary to depart from this name.

There can be no question of giving even the most incomplete overall account. The entire world, is immensely complex, embracing many aspects such as a rich and subtle philosophy, with its own dialectics and metaphysics; a very advanced depth-psychology usually linked to techniques of meditation and the control of psycho-physiological functions *(yoga)* ; an enormous temple for all gods ; countless rites and rituals ; popular practices ; cosmological speculations ; systems of divination. The Tibetans have devoted thousands of volumes to all these sides of their religion, which is further complicated by the fact that their conceptual bases derive from India (and slightly from China). In consequence I shall only be able to go over a few topics, attitudes and modes of behaviour that to me hold significance.

To embark on a complete account is all the more impossible in that it is essential not to neglect two other religions which have contributed to

Tibetan civilization. The first is Bon (with its adherents, the Bonpos), Buddhism's predecessor. The second being of the native ideas and customs belonging to the tradition : a religious, but an unorganized, churchless, doctrineless, priestless and almost nameless, whole. Not that we could lay hands on such a religion in its pure state. Buddhism's influence can be seen everywhere, as Christianity did in Europe, we can discriminate the early evidences concerning the Lamas vestiges of it.

European authors have frequently confused this nameless religion with Bon, describing both as 'primitive'. The Tibetan historians contributed to the confusion for they believed everything that is not Buddhism is necessarily barbarous and demonic. They did, however, preserve a vital distinction between the 'religion of the gods' (*lha-chos*). and the 'religion of men' (*mi-chos*). The first means, or has successively meant, Bon and Buddhism, whilst the second denotes folklore. Historians have given us an important glimpse on these subjects.

Lamaism

The Gist of the Doctrine

Hard as the task may be we must first give some account of the doctrinal groundwork or the main foundation.

Two Indian schools dominate Lamaic thought and have been officially accepted in Tibet regardless of divergences of school or order. They are the Madhyamika (Tibetan *dBu-ma*, 'middle way') of Nagarjuna second to third century?) and the Yogacara ('practice of yoga') or Vijhaptanatra (*Sems-tsam*, 'consciousness-only') of Asanga (fourth century).

To simplify the complex situation, it is tempting to see in the relative importance these two systems have in Tibet a further instance of the study-and-practice polarity we noted earlier. The first-named school may be thought to carry more weight with the 'reformed' Geluk-pas, the second with the Nyingma-pa 'ancients' and associated orders. At first sight, the Geluk-pas, are more classified by philosophy (*mtshan-nyid* : literally 'characteristics', Skt. *laksana*) and theoretical discussion, the others more by meditation and psychic experiences. But the Madhyamika school recognizes swift, direct experience (sudden enlightenment or purification) too ; whilst the Yogacara, conversely, accepts the simple and steady path to perfection and excellent philosophy. Atisa and Tsongkha-pa, the two masters of the reformation, stressed on harmony of the two systems. Meditations and tantric ritual are prevalent among Geluk-pas, and the Nyingma-pas are no strangers to theoretic study.

What both schools are concerned with is the nature of the *Noumenon*, that which is beyond *phenomena*—which I shall in future refer to, for convenience, as 'the Absolute' : it is this very thing that must be attained to ensure salvation. Reason cannot entirely bring us there, but it can prepare the way by destroying appearances and conventional concepts : it has a negative aspect. Psychical technique, on the contrary, can lead to the goal through an indiscribable realization, not to be grasped by discursive thought, but positively experienced by avarious means.

For both schools 'things', the elements, however minute of our phenomenal world, have no reality of their own, in themselves (*nihsvabhava*). The only true Reality is 'the Absolute' and its' a fact. It cannot be defined but, for want of a better name, it is called Emptiness (*sunyata*), Own Nature (of phenomena, *svabhava*), That which is Thus ('Suchness' or Quiddity, *tathata* : Tibetan *de-bzhin-nyid*), etc. For both schools this 'Absolute' can only be attained through yoga experience. Besides, this there is no another option. The Madhyamika has something of a negative cast : nothing can be affirmed of the 'Absolute', which is neither this nor that, and 'things' are 'empty', have no reality of their own. The Yogacara has a more positive aspect : the inmost reality of the 'Absolute' is characterized as Thought (consciousness, *citta*) which penetrates everywhere, like space, and is likened to a pure, bright mirror reflecting nothing but its own light ; it is mere Consciousness-only, where there is no two fold between subject and object. The relative phenomenal world of 'things', on the other hand, is merely the projection of thoughts which are subject to causal laws and preserved in potential form, like seeds, in a kind of underlying psychic receptacle (*alayavijnana*, Tibetan *kun-gzhi'i rnam-par shes-pa*). The passage from the 'Absolute', Thought-in-itself, to the Relative of thoughts or associations, or the linkage between one and the other, is too complex to be stated here as it isn't going to make sense but in a way they are only different aspects of the same thing. Return to the 'Absolute', the condition of salvation, is brought about by the kind of meditation that eliminates thinking (subject)—thought (object) duality from deep in the psyche. That is the 'consummation' (*nispatti*, Tibetan *rdzogs-pa*) which leads to 'whole' or 'perfected' (*parinispanna*) own-nature. We shall come across these terms again in meditation procedure and in the name of the principal Nyingma-pa order.

The Madhyamika had to be defended from heresies. In asserting Emptiness, it had to steer a middle course between overstrong denials which would lead to nihilism (nothing exists, everything is over when the body dies) and a too restricted, purely theoretic negation, which would tend to allow something to remain (immortality of the soul) : the just mean being to assert nothing about 'things', except that they have no reality of their own. The artful solution was to put in place two kinds of truth. One is 'really true' (*paramartha,* Tibetan *don dam-pa*), and from that point of view 'things'—the phenomenal world—have no existence at all. It corresponds to the 'Absolute', which is indefinable and beyond understanding : 'the silence of the saints'. The other truth is 'relatively true', based on truth (*samvrti*, Tibetan *kun-rdzob*), the relative reality of appearance. From that point of view 'things' exist. In other words the constituents of our world are empty of inherent reality, simply in every sense illusory ; but the illusion itself exists and is perfectly real, at any rate as long as one has not attained 'the Absolute' (*snang-stong*, the existence of phenomena or appearance—*snang*—which have no own-nature, are empty—*stong*—of substance). Our world exists, as an illusion does therefore what one sees it not actually what he is seeing. Someone suffering from an eye-disease sees hairs in his food : there are no hairs, but his illusion is real, and he can only realize this when he has been completely cured. And the illusion is dangerous, for it leads the victim to abnormal behaviour : seeing hairs, he refuses to eat as long as they are there and tries to remove them but in vain.

This theory is crucial, since it allows to hold back morality and religious works for the common believer. Since these half-seemingly scientific laws remain valid within relative truth, ordinary Buddhist concepts as to the consequences of action (*Karma*) must continue to govern religious life, in all respects. This is the side that appealed to the 'reformers' deeply faced with the outlandish behaviour to which practical experience of the non-reality of phenomena could lead (such as eating faeces, killing, etc.).

It is also worth getting two other aspects of Lamaist thought into our heads straight away. 'True' (*paramartha*) truth corresponds to the 'real', or certain, meaning (*nges-don :* equivalent to the Sanskrit *nitartha*, 'proven meaning') which is derived from it. 'Conventional' (*samvrti)* truth corresponds to the 'alleged meaning' (*drang-don :* Skt. *neyartha*, 'that which has to be proved or interpreted') which is derived from it. Even within this 'straightforward meaning', the Tibetans further distinguish between ordinary (*thun-mong*) conduct and that which is not so (*thun-mong ma-yin-pa*). The former belongs to the lay believer who worships Lamas and thinks how hard it is to obtain a human body (in the chain of rebirths), that life is temporary and that bad or good actions have their fruits. The second course is that of an ordinary monk who takes refuge in the Buddha the Dharma and the Sangha, makes the vow of producing *bodhi* within himself, purifies himself of sins by confession, and makes an offering of his 'two accumulations' (stocks of knowledge and merit). As for the 'real meaning', it is reserved for those who practise meditation by means of the 'guru's yoga' (*bla-ma' i rnal-'byor*) of which we shall be speaking later.

Accordingly the seeker should rely on meaning (*don* : Sanskrit *artha*) and not words ; on the doctrine (*chos* : *dharma*) and not on men ; on absolute knowledge or gnosis (*ye-shes* : *jnana*) and not on perceptions (*rnam-shes* : *vijnana*) ; on the 'real meaning' sutras and not the 'straightforward meaning' sutras. But it is quite impossible for one to grasp both or even one of these truths ; different levels of spiritual capacity are recognized.

Men are grouped into three categories, each capable of understanding three of the paths to liberation, or 'vehicles' (*theg-pa* : *yana*), in the most usual Nine Vehicle classification. Not that anyone is excluded, in principle, from supreme enlightenment : we all have the buddha-nature within us, in a potential, latent state, and can, in theory, realize it. 'The inherent nature (*rang-bzhin*) of thought (*sems*) is (everywhere and in everyone) the same, but its characteristics (*mtshan-nyid*) are different.' According to their stage of development, after innumerable past lives, men have differing intellectual capacities or power of grasping knowledege which are grouped into three levels—upper, middle and lower. For the lower minds are intended the three vehicles of the 'listeners' (*nyan-thos,* Sanskrit *sravaka,* Buddhist laymen), the buddhas for/by themselves (*rang-rgyal*, Sanskrit *pratyekabuddha*, i.e. the Hinayana) and the *bodhisattvas* (*byang-chub sems-dpa'* : ordinary Mahayana). They were all taught by the historical buddha Sakyamuni.

The two other categories correspond to the *tantras*. The middle group is still enternal it consists of the *kriya-tantras* (*bya-ba'i rgyud* : chiefly magic), the *Upaya-tantras* or *Carya-tantras* (*spyod-pa'i rgyud* : mainly ritual), and the *Yoga-tantras* (*rnal-'byor rgyud*). The first were revealed on the Himalayas to human and divine 'knowledge-bearers' (*rig-'dzin* : Sanskrit *vidyadhara*) ; the second to gods in the heaven or paradise of Tusita (*dGa'-ldan* in Tibetan) and the last to gods and bodhisattvas in the heaven of the Thirty-three and the Akanistha ('*og-min*) paradise. In spite of this relatively exalted status, it is only the third category that is internal. According to the source we are following here, of *Mahayoga*, *Anuyoga* and *Atiyoga*. A tenth vehicle (*sPyi-ti yo-ga*) is sometimes added, or even a fresh series of three vehicles (*sPyi-ti*, *Yang-ti* and *mTha'-chen*). It is impossible to go into the details here, but it is worth noting that the upper and medium vehicles are associated with the ten 'lands' (*bhumi*) or stages of progress of the bodhisattva. The three middle vehicles (Kriya, Upaya and Yoga) are taught to the saints of the third, fourth and fifth 'lands', and so on.

'Relative Truth' which accepts the world and its laws is not just useful in that it encourages moral conduct in the 'lower' class of personality. It is also necessary as the bodhisattva's field of activity when he operates in this phenomenal world, out of compassion and love. The enlightened saint who has attained 'the Absolute', Emptiness, does not remain in that condition, but returns to the conventional world to help others.

But if, for some, acceptance of the phenomenal world carries the binding agreement of pure moral behaviour with the object of a slow, gradual ascent to sainthood (*lam-rim*), for others the discovery that things are void, and empty and no other than Emptiness and Absolute Reality, leads to identification of the Absolute and the Relative and being free from the restraints of common rules. This is the swift and instantaneous path, the 'deep doctrine' (*zab-chos*). For the saint dwelling in the state of Absolute Reality, *nirvana* and *samsara* (Tibetan '*Khor-'das*) are just one. For him, there can be on difference between good and evil and goes hand in hand. To make it quite plain that, all things being empty, there is no difference between them, he indulges in all kinds of unconventional behaviour. To attain 'the Absolute' it is, in fact, necessary to get rid of the major obstacle, namely our rational thought based on the misleading impression of an acting and thinking I (*bdag-'dzin*, *ngar-'dzin*). Dialectics can be of some use to this end, through the destruction of conventional ideas it brings about and the puzzle it arouses. But this technique is not truely applied ; religious behaviour, for instance faith, on which we shall have more to say, is more effective.

Tantrism

Tantrism went a step farther and flourished in India at the time when Tibetans went there in search of their religion : a Buddhist Tantrism, its techniques shared with Shivaite Tantrism and yoga in general. In this system, 'the Absolute' involves two positive characteristics, not subject to proof by reason, but revealed by the psychic experience of meditation, usually accompanied by control of physiological functions. They are perfect happiness or Great Bliss (*bde-chen*, Sanskrit *mahasukha*), and Compassion (*snying-rje* : *karuna*). The former is inherent in 'the Absolute'. But the Absolute is regarded on two planes, as it were, partly as a unity and partly as embracing two complementary principles. Regarded as one, 'the Absolute'—perfect purity, the *dharma-kaya*, *tathata*, the All—is the Mother (*yum*). But from another point of view a passive female principle, Wisdom (*shes-rab*, Sanskrit *prajna*), needs, to become evident an active male principle, 'Means' or 'Method' (*thabs* : *upaya*). Method's sphere of activity is the phenomenal world when it withdraws, so to speak, from Wisdom, but its contrary tendency leads to mystical union (it should be noted that this is the opposite of Shivaite Tantrism where the passive principle is masculine, Siva, and the active principle feminine, Sakti : but there too Siva is realized through Sakti). Thus, in symbolic representations, the same word 'mother' (*yum*) also denotes the wife or spiritual consort. The union of the two yields Great Bliss or the Bodhicitta (*byang-sems*, 'thought of *bodhi*', but also likened to a 'drop', a sort of psychic counterpart of the semen).

This system tells us about the process of meditation or, contrarywise, is explained by it. The extraordinary world has a kind of usefulness. Emptiness (*sunyata*) has no place without active Compassion (*Karuna*) ; Absolute Reality and phenomenal existence goes hand to hand. In fact existence itself cannot exist without Emptiness or Absolute Reality. The world of appearances can be compared to the bridegroom. Without him the bride Sunyata would be as if dead. But conversely, if the bride were separated even for an instant from her groom, he would be left in permanent bondage.

Meditation

So meditation is a technique of actualization (*sgrub*, Sanskrit *sadhana*) a beginningless relationship between Emptiness or 'the Absolute' and phenomenal existence. It consists essentially of two parts : the phase of (mental) 'creation', coming out from Emptiness, which goes along with phenomenal existence (*bskyed-rim* : *utpanna-krama*) ; and that of 'completion' or return to the unity of 'the Absolute' (*rdzogs-rim* : *nispanna-krama*). The first phase is (relatively) easy to understand and perform, at least in the purely Tibetan system. The second dwells with psycho-physiological yoga practices (especially in connection with 'breath' and sexual energy).

The value of meditation, therefore, is that it allows a kind of experimental demonstration, a living experience not only of Supreme Reality, Emptiness, 'the Absolute', but also of the nature of phenomenal existence which is only the latter's mental creation. The aim of the exercise, especially its second phase is to attain Great Bliss, is salvation, liberation. But it happens to have a side-effect as well—especially through its first phase of mentally creating phenomenal existence—a sort of by-product, viz. supernatural powers (*dngos-grub* : *siddhi*). They are useless but the saint may make use of them to convert people with miracles, to protect the religion against human or non-human enemies, and in general to 'benefit beings'. For realization of Emptiness through meditation is brought about for one's own benefit, but also for others' : by means of active compassion (*karuna*), the resultant forces are placed at the service of all beings.

It is easy for us to guess how, starting from this doctrinal basis and proceeding to logical conclusions, certain teachers or schools could have been led to very unconventional magical and ritual practices. But the fact is that even 'reformers' such as Atisa and Tsongkha-pa studied and accepted these doctrines. To be sure, there are great Geluk-pa scholars, like Sumpa Khenpo in 1748, who look upon them with discontentment. Even he, however, closes his critical account of Nyingma-pa Tantric doctrines with the remark that the Second and Third Dalai Lamas (1475-1542 and 1542-1588) had not studied them minutely and what is more, the Great Fifth (1617-1682) had taken a special interest in them 'owing to the fact that he had become the general Lama of all Tibet' (from the viewpoint of political power). And sure enough, the second half of his Collected Works is entirely devoted to Nyingma-pa systems. It is true that this part was afterwards kept secret and became hard to be possessed by anyone.

Religious Practices

So far we can make a sketch about the characteristic of Lamaism that proceeds from all this. Its central religious activity is the concern for monks and hermits. It is unapproachable to ordinary believers. Their deep faith depends entirely upon the members of the monastic community. Lay Buddhists do not take part in rituals and religious services after themselves just by being save mere spectators. They do not hear sermons and do not indulge in private prayers. Since they belong to the class of those whose grade of intellectual faculties does not permit them to escape 'conventional truth', they can only hope to improve their karma, the fruit their actions will bear in a next coming life. That is why their religious activity consists essentially of piling up merit (*bsod-nams*) : by making gifts to monasteries or lamas and to the poor, and 'needly by lighting lamps before the images of gods deities, by making pilgrimages or walking round sacred objects, and by asking lamas for blessings or charms. They know the ultimate source of action and its rewards which leads to rebirth in one of six possible states : gods, titans, men, animals, hungry ghosts or hells.

These spheres of rebirth are portrayed in the 'Wheel (of transmigration) of the World' (*srid-pa'i 'khor-lo*), the so-called 'Wheel of Life', paintings of which are seen every now and then. The punishments in the hells and the judging of the dead are popularized by strolling story-tellers who are supposed to have been to hell and come back alive (*'das-log* : known since the fifteenth century at least). Lastly, some of the masked dances present, for the mental or moral improvement of the faithful, the deities met within the intermediate state between death and the next life (*bar-do*).

Laymen and illiterate monks can also have recourse to the recitation or visual representation of certain formulae, the *mantras*, which shorten as it were, a corresponding deity. Recitation may be actual or performed by mechanical means : wheels turned by hand, water or wind ; models for shaping images. The most famous formula is *om mani padme hum*, invoking Tibet's patron Avalokitesvara, but there are others. In Tantrism, such formulae are looked upon as having a power of evoking and materializing divinity which works in a almost automatic fashion—provided they are pronounced correctly and joined along with suitable meditation. For the mass of Tibetan Buddhists, it is the act of faith which chiefly counts in recitation ; and this faith makes possible a species of meditation and an destruction of the ego. Though saying or writing the mani has become standard practice for the Buddhist masses in modern Tibet, formerly (twelfth century) this practice was, like everything else in the religion the business of experts—in this case the *ma-ni-pa*, who were experts equipped with Avalokitesvara's initiation (that is, in Tibetan, the 'power' (*dbang*) to recite the formula). Nowadays the *ma-ni-pa* are strolling story-tellers who recite improving tales whilst showing the episodes on a painting, but they also perform rites (smashing a heavy stone on their chest, lying on the points of two swords) which show their unusual powers.

Otherwise, whenever religious interference is necessary, the ordinary believers turn to specialists—for healing or exorcism in the event of illness or possession, help to the dead during the *bar-do* intermediate period, summoning good luck (*g.yang-'gug*) or long life (*tshe-'gug*) at weddings and other occasions, protection of livestock or crops, evoking or putting a stop to rain or hail—and yet other natural operations. Certain beliefs will concern us later : though all fully integrated in Lamaism, they have retained features that are not specifically Buddhist, in nature and can be treated separately.

Faith and the Teacher

There is one religious display that ordinary believers share with even the most distinguished men of religion. It is faith, whose absolute necessity countless texts declare. This might at first surprise us, given the absence of a God and the illusory character of all the divinities, who are only mental creations like any other phenomenon. But the reason for this need is clearly stated. It is that through the unconditional impulse of faith we can escape our ego and stop, at least momentarily, the activity of discursive thought which provides the illusion of this ego and is the chief to obstruction the path of enlightenment. Of course, one can set up a distinction according to the object of this impulse. For all who move in the world of relative reality, faith can be directed at a 'deity'—buddhas, bodhisattvas, gods or goddesses. It hardly matters what fulcrum is used as the springboard. The divinities of the pantheon are only mental projections emanating from Emptiness, 'the Absolute', and representing it in an individualized form, so to speak. The power of meditation can create them, but that is a difficult process and requires a lot of time. Faith can take its place by producing an analogous concentration : it can produce a deity through intense emotion, and this deity will then be as objectively real and effective as if it had come forth from Emptiness through meditation done.

It is said that the Fifth Dalai Lama had once, from the top of his Potala, seen the goddess Tara regularly making a ritual circuit of that palace, a common devotional practice among Tibetans. After noting the accurate times at which she went by and ordering an inquiry, he inferred that her movements corresponded to those of a certain poor old man. He sent for him and asked whether he knew that Tara was accompanying him regularly on his circumambulations. Frightened, the old man replied that he did not do so. Questioned further, he disclosed that he had learnt Tara's text by heart and had been reciting it consistently for 40 years while making his daily circuit. When was asked to recite the text, he was found to have got it wrong. He was then made to learn the correct text. But as soon as the old man had learnt and recited it in place of the other, Tara ceased to appear. He was then authorized to recite the text as he had been used to, and Tara showed herself again as before. When he recites the faulty text, the Dalai Lama concluded, his mind is concentrated on Tara, and she comes to bless him. But when he recites the right text his mind is attached to it and not to Tara. That is the difference. The concentration of mind play a vital role for the vision of gods and goddesses.

No matter what focus is used, the concentration that results from faith, not only creates and brings before us faith's object, the deity, but generates the beneficent power of blessing which automatically ensues. By willpower and constant training, the meditator functions in the same way and gets the same results.

To the devotee in search of sainthood and enlightenment, true faith can equally well bring about a sudden insight (here we must recall the remnants of Chinese Ch'an (Zen) doctrines which have been noted in Tibet). And a feature of Tantrism which we have not so far had the chance to emphasize as it deserves, may be added—utilization of the emotions. Despite the extraordinary discipline and iron will that meditation training implies to experts, they are often seen to dissolve in tears from the emotion roused by an impulse of faith and a sudden illumination. And this crisis often occurs after other violent emotions, especially wrath.

The impuse of faith may naturally centre on figures in the temples of deities, especially in the case of laymen. But for all who enter upon the path to enlightenment, the main object of faith is first and foremost the Lama or spiritual teacher (*guru*). For it is typical of Lamaism (as too of various Indian and other religions) that one's Lama (*guru*) is superior to all 'deities', even the most prominent of all.

'To venerate a single hair of one's teacher (*slob-dpon*) is a greater merit (*bsod-nams*) than to venerate all the Buddhas of the three times (past, present and future)', a *dakini* (a kind of fairy) tells the saint Gampopa (1079—1153). And by merit we must also understand usefulness, the resulting benefit. The *dakini* goes on to inform him that he must not entertain doubt (*the-tshom*), or have rational thoughts (*rnam-rtog*). For the latter engender doubt by keeping alive the idea of a thinking 'I', whereas unquestioning faith enables one to leave behind such thoughts and ego-attachment. The Lama's dominant position, higher even than the buddhas, is common to all orders including the Geluk-pas. No 'actualization' could be brought about without the '*guru-yoga*' (*bla ma'i rnal-' byor*) : the disciple call about the spirits of the tutelary deity (*yi-dam*) chosen for him by his Lama, with whom the deity is closely fused ; then he himself merges with the Lama, who has absorbed, as it were, the deity. From him he draws the desired state of purification.

To see whether he can hand on his last secret to Marpa, Naro-pa turns himself into Marpa's nine tutelary deities in such a way that he was be clearly visible in front of Marpa. He asks him, 'Do you bow to the *yi-dams*, or do you bow to your Lama?' Marpa, seeing only the deities, bows to them. Naro-pa then says : 'As long as there is no Lama, there is not even the word *buddha* ; even the buddhas of a thousand kalpas appear on the basis of Lamas. . . These gods are only forms of myself,' whereupon the *yi-dams* dissolve in Naro-pa's heart. On account of this particular mistake Marpa will have no descendants. 'The Lama is a buddha in person' (actually present), think Marpa's disciples when he admits Mila Repa to their number, and they are filled with a feeling of certain faith.

So a disciple's absolute submission to his Lama is a must and the previous subjects him to a series of trials to test the strength and power of his faith. The bonds between them are generally determined beforehand and indissoluble. They are characterized both by a father's love and affection for his son and a vassal's subjection to his suzerain : the terms used to denote them can be 'father' and 'son', but also 'master' (*slob-dpon)* and 'subjects, servants' (*slob-'bangs*). 'He has no disciple more affectionate (*sha-tsha-ba*) and faithful (*snying-nye-ba*, "close to the heart") than you,' Mila Repa is told by his spiritual 'mother', the wife of his teacher or guru. It will be recalled that the second expression is the same one used, in the oldest texts, for a vassal being loyal to his overlord.

The disciple's submission is total. He makes his master the total gift of his person ('body, speech and mind') and possessions. He is totally devoted to his master. Henceforth he belongs to him, and that teacher on his own can lead him to salvation. If he wishes to listen to another, his own teacher must release him from his agreement (oath, *dam-tshig*). Since Marpa has totally denied to initiate Mila Repa, his wife forges a letter from him, ordering Ngokton to do so. Mila then sets about meditating under Ngok's direction, but, 'Not having been released by Marpa's order, no mystical experience of any sort occurred,' Ngok, believing Marpa's order to be genuine, is amazed : 'Yet you came with faith in me, and in my (spiritual) lineage there is none who has not quickly gained the benefit of understanding, at least as long as no vow (*dam-tshig*) prevented it.'

The trials to which Marpa subjected his disciple Mila Repa are quite famous. Not only does he set him with all kinds of useless tasks, but he puts a check on him in a thousand ways, strikes and insults him, humiliates him and drives him to despair. He checks him mentally as well as physically. But Mila's faith rises above it all. It is spontaneous, unreasoning and emotive. When he turns up at the field in which Marpa is, without knowing that it is he, 'Scarcely had I seen him than I dwelt for a moment in a state of indescribable and immeasurable bliss where the fluctuations of this world's appearances were halted' (i.e., in a rapture leading to 'the Absolute', both emptiness-of-phenomena and bliss). Later, almost driven to the point that he gives up all hope by the harshness of the teacher, who has refused him initiation, he convinces him in answer to his querry that he has withstood any 'revolt against faith' (*dad log-lta*). And when, finally, after all his distress the master admits him and promises the teachings his heart is so set on—'At that moment I thought : "Is it a dream or is it true? If it's a dream I should like never to awake !" A joy beyond measure filled me and, dissolving in tears through my excess of joy, I made obeisance to him.'

Mel Kawachen (twelfth century) had a similar experience, when looking for the teacher Tampa Gommon. One day he sees him at the edge of a field, preaching to a monk. 'Faith was born in him, his eyes filled with tears and, wide eyed with surprise, his mind became devoid of (discursive) thought (*sems mi-rtog-par song*).' In these favourable conditions, induced by sudden shock, the master says 'Loose your mind !', and at once or concentration (*thugs-dam*) is born in him.

The highly emotional nature of saints is very much plain and clear. Marpa is a strong, violent man, much given to fits of temper, but he also often weeps in secret at his disciple's true devotion and despair. Access to 'the Absolute' does not abolish the manifold forms of the phenomenal, including feelings. In the end, Marpa explains his unkind behaviour by saying that his anger was far more different from 'the world's' and that, despite appearances, he had actually 'walked in the path of *bodhi*'. This does not just mean, apparently, that the bad temper was always invented in order to test the disciple. That comes into it as well, but Marpa undoubtedly had such nature, that he could get angry very easily.

We often find emotions of any sort whatever made use of. Sochung-wa played all manner of tricks on Tampa Gommon, such as making him carry a bag of stones up a pass and then making him throw them away. One day he went so far as to accuse him of stealing, in front of a stranger which was a peculiar act of his. Seized by a violent fit of anger, the disciple drew his sword and dashed towards his master. Defending himself behind a door, the latter told him, 'Your mind (thought) is "achieved" (*rdzogs*) in anger : look at it !' Then, 'having looked, a pure full understanding was produced in him—an understanding that consisted of seeing really and in its naked state the Real Nature of Thought. Then, brimming over with joy, he grasped the flaps of his coat and began to dance and sing.

Doubtless taking his disciple's character into account—as one always must while making use of such psychic forces—the teacher induces such anger that the disciple is as it were projected outside himself by giving way to it ; his ordinary (discursive) thought completely destroyed ; and room thus made for the pure thought of contemplation which grasps 'the Absolute' directly. Translation is powerless to render the whole flavour of the text the originality doesn't last : the word *rdzogs*, which it uses to describe the engulfing of thought by anger, is a technical term denoting the afterphase of meditation and fusion with 'the Absolute'. Although his short biography tells us nothing about this disciple's character, we know that other saints of the same group (*gcod* and *zhi-byed*) were known for their ill nature. Trubbe, the son of Lab-dronma—the patroness of *gcod* (cho) in Tibet—started out by being very irascible and violent, and a goat-stealer. His son, in turn, spent all his youth in fighting. Mel Kawachen was 'very disagreeable' when he was young. Marpa, too, had a wild and violent nature and, in youth, was fond of fights.

A teacher plays vital role in his disciple's choice. For his part, the teacher bears the disciple's character in mind when initiating him. With the usual decided taste for numeric classifications, five chief emotions were singled out (anger, stupidity, desire, pride and envy) and associated with the five primordial buddhas who represent 'the Absolute' and the five initiation families corresponding to them (*vajra*, *tathagata*, *padma*, *ratna*, *karma*). As a matter of fact they are not just linked with them, but altogether identified with figures in the pantheon, just as the phenomenal dissolves into 'the Absolute'.

The ability to proceed initially from any phenomenal aspect whatever to a corresponding aspect of 'the Absolute' results not only in the need to belong to one of the five families (*rigs*, Sanskrit *kula*) according to one's nature, but also in the various pantheons. Mandalas and their deities vary with the 'family' to which they belong. The tutelary deity his Lama chooses varies with the disciple's intellectual and influence emotionally favourably beforehand. And it is by merging with the deity and Lama combined that the disciple attains 'the Absolute'.

The act of admitting conferred by one's master is the 'power' (*dbang*) to practise a particular group of meditations together with the official transmission and the 'authority' (*lung*) to read the texts in which these are described ; to which are added the master's more precise and important instructions (*khrid*). He inherits this 'power' from his line of direct transmission (*bla-brgyud*), which no doubt generally goes back to a supreme divinity. So, the meditator does not forget to invoke that lineage in his ritual practice, to ensure the validity of what he is performing.

Meditation and Ritual

A number of rites for every sort of occasion, and with various aims, are performed by those experts, the monks and yogins. And there is no doubt that below a certain level these are merely a routine, the purely formal execution of ritual motions and recitations of texts. But when we go through the handbooks of these rites we discover that in the main they only gain their effectiveness from the meditation. So meditation has a major role.

Meditation is in fact the essential practice of this monks' religion. The monasteries always have affiliated meditation cells, in out-of-the-way mountain spots, where the monks are expected to withdraw and live in privacy (*mtshams*) for a period. The retreat may last from a few days to some months, or several years (e.g., three, or twelve) ; it may even be for life long period. It may be limited to isolation in one room, but may also go as far as complete walling-in within a very restricted space, without light (*mun-mtshams*), only a small hatch making it possible to pass a little food through or communicate by signs with the disciple waiting nearby for the monks.

What a meditation consists of and how it proceeds are not common knowledge : those who have practised it are not talkative. It is not practically open to all. But some items can be set forth as given in texts.

The basic texts of Lamaism, all Indian, like the *Hevajra-tantra* or the *Guhyasamaja-tantra*, always divide the process into two parts : *utpatti-* (or *utpanna-*) *krama* (Tibetan *skyed-* or *bskyed-rim*) and *nispatti-krama* (or *nispanna-* ; also *sampatti-*, *sampanna-* : Tibetan *rdzogs-rim*). The first part is much easier to understand. It is the steady process of mental creation that consciously and voluntarily recreates, as it were, phenomenal existence (*bhava*). It consists of making 'the Absolute', the Noumenal, or absolute knowledge (*ye-shes*, Sanskrit *jnana*) turn into the relative, the phenomenal, relative knowledge, or perception (*rnam-shes* : *vijnana*). From the 'void', through just mental generation, a deity with all its inherent qualities is made to arise. To facilitate the European reader's understanding, the process might be compared to the creation of the world by a thinking God. Only there is no God, and no unique creation or beginning. This type of meditation has two functions. One is to gain an actual experience of the illusory nature or our world, but also to be freed from it and thus win salvation by travelling in the completely opposite direction. By cancelling its 'creation', its mental production, we return from the phenomenal to the noumenal ; we thus happen to detach the bonds inherent in this phenomenal world (such as karma, etc.), and we rejoin and dissolve in 'the Absolute' which is Emptiness, Reality and of course perfect happiness.

This second part, the *nispanna-krama*, is not vividly explained. And with reason. The meditative process here includes, in Tibet at least, yogic psycho-physiological techniques which the texts only refer to indirectly. We can only, for the time being, get hold of external aspects that may give a glimpse of it. The word used for this process implies various ideas of success, completion, fulfilment, perfection. It provides the name of the Dzokchen-pa order, within the Nyingmapa school—the 'Great Fulfilment' they soul aim for if the state of buddhahood or fusion with 'the Absolute'. Of the Nine Vehicles listed previously, the process of 'production' (*bskyed-pa*) belongs to the lowest of the last three vehicles, Mahayoga ('great yoga'), while that of 'great completion' (*rdzogs-pa chen-po*) is reserved for the third and last, Atiyoga ('yoga beyond'). We should not, however, take for granted that these meditations are limited to the 'old' orders (Nyingma-pa). The chief work of Tsongkha-pa, the founder of the 'reformed' Geluk-pa order, is divided into two parts. The first and more widely known, the *Lam-rim*, takes care to differentiate men according to their faculties and to recommend the slow path of moral goodness to those of whom too much should not be asked, and in any case to everyone as a necessary preliminary foundation. But the end of the first, and all the second volume (the *sNgags-rim*) are devoted to the twin procedures of production and reabsorption.

We return, then, to the 'production' process. It just liese beneath every ritual practice ; for to have any effect a rite requires the presence of some appropriate deity, who thereby gives a offering by 'blessing' (*byin-rlabs*, Sanskrit *adhisthana*)—the power of action—on the officiant. The term denoting these rituals (*sgrub-thabs* : *sadhana*) has sometimes been translated as 'coercion', giving a false impression about practice of witchcraft and sorcery. 'Evocation' might be a better rendering. It is however true that this deity, once brought into being, may 'call' or forcibly send for demon, or the 'soul' of an enemy.

The rite of mental production or generation (also called *sgom-rim*, 'meditation process' or *dmigs-rim*, 'imagination process') is summed up in greater detail in Tibetan Buddhism than in the Indian *tantras* on which it was grounded. It comprises two, or three, stages. First comes 'production in oneself' (*bdag-skyed*) : the meditator imagines himself as a particular deity. 'Production in front of one' (*mdun-skyed*) follows, in which he projects the deity just before him self visualized the universe as his palace, making it possible to worship him. Lastly may be added 'production in the vase' (*bum-skyed*) : this time the deity is caused to enter a physical 'support', which thus acquires a power that can be made use of in future.

Before 'production in oneself' properly so-called, all rituals begin with certain preparatory steps which is absolutely necessary. Their order, number and type vary with different schools and with the purpose of the rite, but the following are usually found (often 'seven members', *yan-lag bdun*, are spoken of). The line of teachers that gives the rite its validity (*bla-ma'i brgyud*) is often stated ; refuge is taken in all the buddhas, bodhisattvas, etc. (*skyabs-su'gro-ba*) ; they resolve to reach enlightenment and use one's merits for the liberation of all beings (the bodhisattva vow) is renewed ; one is purified of one's sins (*sdig-sgrib*) by confession and mantras.

Thus fully prepared, the meditator first re-creates the 'void'. From this void comes the rite's presiding deity, usually coming out of his own 'seed' syllable (such as *om*, *ah*, *hum*, *hrih*, etc.). Then by a leap at once (*skdd-cig dkrong-skyed*) the meditator becomes identified with the deity in question. It is this state alone that enables him, for instance, to send for demons (*lhar bskyed-nas bgegs dgug-pa*), etc. He then has a mightly luminous, empty, divine body (*gsal-stong lha-sku*) ; he is indissolubly (*dbyer-med*) merged with the deity, through whom he taken part in Emptiness (*nyid zang-thal du bskyed-pa'o*). 'My pure body, in *utpanna-krama*, appears luminous like a deity's body', says Drukpa Kunlek.

With the production of a deity in oneself, or oneself as the deity, that deity passes from the noumenal state, where it is one with 'the Absolute' or absolute knowledge (*ye-shes* : *jnana*), to the phenomenal state, known as its 'vow' (*dam-tshig* : *samaya*) form—because only in this form can it become evident, so as to fulfil its vow in order to help all beings. This shift is brought about by assembling the deity bit by bit, as it were, with all its many inherent qualities and attendants (requiring a vision that is very exact in the smallest details). Externally, this piecing together is matched by recitation of the corresponding iconography (*mngon-rtogs* : *abhisamaya*), which is used as a basis both for meditation as well as depiction in painting or sculpture.

Without fully agreement one might say that now the deity becomes really present—'really' in the western sense of the word. As proof of this it is related, for instance, that after a particular meditative call up of the deities represented on the painting came out, walked round in a circle and went back in : it was then noticeable that their clothes and belongings were out of order on the picture. The master Bodhisattva's concentration (*ting-nge-' dzin* : *samadhi*) at Samye was so intense that it rendered deities 'objectively' present before every-one's eyes : their statues came out of the temple, walked round it, and returned back to their places. That, too, is why in the Cho rite, which involves carving up one's own body, while meditating, to offer it to living beings, care must be taken not to do the imaginary carving while one is in the 'production in oneself' state : that would amount to cutting up the deity one had become, and be a sin. When Mila Repa, in a state of desperation, wants to commit suicide, this is how the Lama Ngok stops him : 'The Lama grasped me and, shedding tears, he said, "Do not so, great magician ! According to the doctrine of the secret mantras (Tantrism) which is the culmination of the teachings of the buddhas, our body with all its senses is inseparable from the gods. If we perform 'transference' ('*pho-ba*, passing from one life to another or into a paradise) before the right time, we commit the crime of killing the gods. Hence there is no greater sin than suicide." 'Similarly, Marpa's dying son, on the point of 'transferring' his own mind ('*pho-ba*), attained union, and 'my body, organs and senses became luminous, and of the nature of gods and goddesses'. It was, he says, because he was in the 'production process' (*bskyed-rim*) state. For the transference, he would need to have passed into the 'completion process' (*rdzogs-rim*) state. For, 'If I made the transference (implying the death of the body) in the "creation process" state, I should commit the crime of killing the tutelary deities (*yi-dam gyi lha*),' he explains. The presence of these gods in his body was then so bright and luminous, says the hagiography, that even ordinary onlookers could see them, clearly.

One application of this principle of a deity's real presence is 'production in oneself' in a support other than the meditator's body. For example, in a fearsome rite intended to drive away all demons, sacrificial cakes (*gtor-ma*) are made and thrown at them as offensive weapons. But they are only effective if they have received 'blessing', i.e., the power of the deity concerned. A small painting of him or her (the *tsakli*) is fastened to a stalk or arrow stuck in the cake. The deity is produced, by means of meditation, in the picture. His presence furnishes that receptacle with a power which will stay there even when the actual deity has left. One must be careful not to throw the cake-weapons while the deity is still there. They are only thrown away when the stalk with its attached portrait has been completely taken out : an external operation corresponding, on the plane of meditation, to the deity's 'vanishing' (*yal*—like a rainbow fading away in space).

Having become a god oneself, a question arises as to why that is not enough and why we move on immediately to projecting the deity in front of us—an operation always accorded a much more detailed treatment than the previous one by the handbooks of ritual, in which it features as the essential part. One text supplies a reason : 'production in oneself' is done entirely *for* oneself, 'production before one' for the good of others, and 'creation in the vase' for the benefit of the gods and deities.

The meditator, therefore, has the capability to produce the deity in front of him, still piecing him together according to the iconography, along with all his inherent qualities effort and paradises, attendants and suite : an exercise of high complexity and precision, requiring extraordinary concentration to accomplish. The vision must be so strong, in fact, that the deity and his vehicle appear as though 'objectively' present, independently of the meditator, like somebody made face to face in what for us is a reality. He then makes him offerings and receives his blessings. He also pleads for the service of which is the object of the rite—to give rain, drive away demons, lengthy life, and so on. Once the rite is over and the meditation is ended, the vision slowly fades away. But a general purification and purity and godliness remain, as well as religious benefits. The whole may give the devotee the impression that the deities exist somewhere, come, and go away again.

This meditation is truly doubtless not dragged very far in most cases, where the main object is the performance of a ritual for specific ends. But if it is followed all the way in the course of a retreat devoted to that sole purpose it can provide a practical experience of the nature of the universe. If the exercise is a success in fact, the mentally created deity appears as though independent of its creator, objectively existing—not only visible but accessible to all the senses. Moreover it can act and speak to the meditator as though it were somebody other than himself. If he finally believes that, he is surely lost. But if he is aware of the fact that it is he who has created it, and reabsorbs it in his mind, will he not have experienced the very nature of our phenomenal world? It is as though someone suffering from mental disorder were aware of his condition and able to induce or end it at will.

It seems that the 'completion process' originally consisted of reabsorbing the deity, created in oneself, into 'the Absolute' and thus totally merging with the previous one. In the *Hevajra-tantra*, when the officiant had attracted all the buddhas into his 'heart' in the form of so many Herukas (the type of supreme deity, representing 'the Absolute') and when he is thus dedicated (*dbang-bskur*), he is Heruka 'completed' or fulfilled in person, and that 'completed' (*rdzogs*) state is 'the Dharma space' (*chos-dbyings*), i.e., 'the Absolute'. In Tibetan custom the 'completion process' always goes hand-in-hand with yogic practices and ends in a instance changing form. In some cases even the first phase, the 'production process', is linked up with these practices.

It is impossible to go into the principles of Tantric Buddhist Goga here, but we must review a few of its key terms. In the psycho-physiological existence that is man, it distinguishes a central channel or artery (to some extent confused with the spinal column) called *avadhuti* or *susumna* (Tibetan *dbu-ma*) flanked to left and right by two others, *ida or lalana* (*rkyang-ma*) and *pingala* or *rasana* (*ro-ma*). They are attached to six 'wheels' (*cakra*, Tibetan '*khor-lo*) or psycho-physiological centres situated in the body, from the crown of the head to the very base of the sexual organ. The two lateral arteries are associated with a series of complementary pairs : *ida* corresponds to white, the moon, vowels (*ali*), Wisdom (*prajna*), semen ; *pingala*, to red, the sun, consonants (*kali*), Means (*upaya*), blood. The two must be united in the central channel, and this union culminates in Great Bliss (*mahasukha*), 'the Absolute', the *bodhicitta*. The conjunction itself is known as *yuganaddha* (*zung-'jug*). The system is shown symbols in the form of Tibetan paintings of deities, used as a support for meditation. At the top, over the main figure, is a pair of supreme deities in deep clasp (*yab-yum*) ; to left and right, a white moon and a red sun.

The process of fusion is often purely meditative, but it is commonly accompanied by a technique that causes a 'wind' (*rlung* : *prana*) or 'droplet' (*thig-le*) to rise into the central artery, and which can be practised either alone, or with a partner. Apart from realization of 'the Absolute', the procedure (with many variations from school to school) bestows upon various powers, such as that of generating great internal heat (*gtum-mo*); fleetness of foot ; and mising of it in air and, above all, a 'rainbow-body' ('*ja*'-*lus*) which is indestructible as adamant (*vajra*), is in mortal and thus enables one to 'die' (go to a paradise) without abandoning the body. Variations, as I remarked, are numerous and techniques of different types. An eighteenth-century author outlines six 'completion process' methods attributable to six different teachers. One of them consists of the 'six teachings of Naro-pa' : heat (*gtum-mo*), light ('*od-gsal*), illusory body (*sgyu-lus*), intermediate state, e.g., between death and the next life (*bar-do*), mind-transference ('*pho-ba*) and the art of taking over someone else's newly dead body (*grong-'jug*). The sixth doctrine is usually that of dream (*rmi-lam*) and the last on the list we have just read is appended as an essential co-existence. The 'light' technique aims at sustaining a state that is conscious yet free from rational thought, viz., meditation (*sgom*), even during sleep or after death. In the case of sleep, it enables one to observe, then direct, and finally abolish dreams and to remain in the luminous meditation state just mentioned. The object of this training is to preserve such a state even at the time of death, in order to succeed in catching the instant of intense light that comes out and thus to emerge from the cycle of rebirths instead of being dragged into *bar-do.*

Trances and Dances

Such techiques are obviously only practised by an elite, but they nourish even the layman's religious life insofar as they are illustrated by countless short stories and literature dealing with the saints. These are tales of famous saints who have worked miracles for the benefit of common people to convert them and to convince them of the reality of the experience or effectiveness of the method. If it is effective it assures the believer that he is somehow linked to divinity. Remember, from the fact of its identity with the creation or existence of this world in general, mental creation in the course of meditation cannot fail to have a quas-physical effect on the world. The result is a 'blessing', i.e., a supernatural force that can be inscribed within an object or person. To the extent that a Lama has received this, he can hand it on to the faithful, e.g., by laying his hand on their heads. He can also dedicate himself to the images of deities—paintings which then bear the three monosyllabic mantras *om ah hum* (and sometimes the lama's foot and hand-prints) on the back ; or statues inside which are then placed rolls of mantras or an axis known as their 'life-tree' (*srog-shing*). These are the deities' 'bodily supports' (*sku-rten*). The believer worships them wholeheartedly. For him, that is the only outward means of seeing and worshipping the supreme deities, buddhas, bodhisattvas, etc. A distinction is drawn, indeed, between deities that have 'passed from the world' (*'jig-rten las'das-pa' i lha*), which no longer incarnate themselves in a human support or vehicle, and those that have not yet done so (*'jig-rten las ma' das-pa*) and can thus be directly manifested in a human being, dearly visible to everyone. The latter group of deities are the 'protectors of religion' (*chos-skyong*, Sanskrit *dharmapala* ; or *srung-ma*). Hence they are generally of the fearsome, rough and warlike type, even when embodied in a woman. For they become incarnate in male and female mediums, who lose consciousness and go the other side : the human ego is blotted out, and the medium's body is used as a support for the deity who fills him and speaks through his mouth. For this reason such mediums are called *sku-rten-pa* ('those who serve as support for the Body'), or else 'protectors of religion' like the deities themselves. They are monks or nuns who have been chosen by a deity and then given adequate training. Each specializes in a particular deity. The usefulness of the manifestation lies in the opportunity to gather answers of deities to any inquiry. So the State, the Dalai Lama's Government for instance, itself employs some of them—such as the celebrated Nechung medium who incarnates the god Pehar. That the trance is genuine is proved by the medium's behaviour. Not only is his face transformed—it swells and turns red, with bloodshot eyes, thick, lolling tongue, etc.—but surprisingly he displays superhuman strength, supporting extremely heavy headgear, twisting swords, etc. In that state he mumbles words which are collected and interpreted by other monks. In addition, he blesses grain which is thrown to the faithful : by gathering it up, they can carry off a portion of the sacred being that has demonstrated.

There are other mediumistic specialists who possess the bodies of minor deities and belong, in spite of their Lamaist dress, to the nameless religion of the people. These are shepherds, who have on some occasion been 'chosen' by a deity and from then on have been able to embody him. They go to the other side and sing, but the only incarnate local gods, of whom we still have to speak—gods of the sky (*lha*) and of the underworld (*klu*), gods of the soil, etc. From these they get their name : *lha-pa*, *klu-pa*. Surprisingly they also incarnate the hero of the epic ; at any rate, they did way back in the eighteenth century. Similar mediums called 'heroes' (*dpa'-bo*) compete with them and fall somewhere between them and the poets and singers of the epic. Of course, their name is of Buddhist origin. The word first denoted, as it still does, the dancers and musicians of Padmasambhava's paradise, who are specially jugglers and athletes or warriors (*dpa'-bo*, *ging*).

The real poets as well as singers also go into trances, either so as to see the epic heroes and scenes from their lives in some timeless sphere, and describe them in their songs, or so that such and such a hero may incorporate himself in them and speak through their mouths. In spite of differences what happens is, for Tibetans, essentially the same as in the Lama's meditation. In the latter, the deity moves from his 'knowledge body' (*ye-shes lus*), his Noumenal existence, to his visible phenomenal aspect ('vow' form), a process described in the words 'knowledge descends' or 'falls' (*ye-shes'bab*)—on the support represented by the meditator, understood. Of the trances of Lamaic (*chos-skyong*) or popular (*lha-pa*) mediums it is similarly said that 'the god descends/falls' (*lha'bab*), and of the bard in trance, 'the epic descends/falls' (*sgrung'bab*). Conversely, when the trance is completely over and the god has left, it is said that 'the god of the epic has dissolved' (like a rainbow : *sgrung-lha yal-tshar*), using the same verb that denotes the deity's disappearance into the void during the process of meditation. Moreover just as, in meditation, the 'creation process' necessitates the piecemeal building up of the deity, accompanied by the recitation of a corresponding iconography (*mngon-rtogs*), so too the bard, in order to put himself into a trance and evoke a hero in himself, initially purifies himself with a prayer and chants the hero's description. But the chief hero, Gesar, is never overdemonstrated in this way. Having 'become buddha' at the end of his life, he has since then been way out of the world and can no longer alight on a medium. He can only be worshipped image form.

But to return to more exclusively Lamaistic demonstrations: although rituals have to render the deities present and manifest through meditation, they are of course still invisible to profane eyes, save in tales of the lives of saints. But, partly to educate the lay-folk, partly too presumably because a mask has the capability of making it easier for a deity to manifest itself, masked dances (*'cham*) have been invented and are openly performed. Here we have what might be termed a sort of rite, in which the deities called up by meditation are at the same time presented by actors wearing all sorts of masks. Scripts are ridiculous attributed to visions of whom the best known expert is Guru Chhöwang (Chhökyi Wangchuk, 1212-1273).

Masks (*'bag*) were usually worshipped at Samye in King Trhisong Detsen's day, as well as statues. They represented only the 'protectors of religion' (*chos-skyong*), not just any deities. This was not just casual masks probably share with mediums the peculiarity of making it easier for these deities to become manifest. The 'protector of religion' Pehar is closely associated with a mask that was kept in his temple. When Sakya Pandita and Phakpa met a young monk whose face resembled the mask in the Gorum temple at Sakya, they at once thought that Kurgyi Gömpo, the Sakya 'protector of religion', had incarnated in a man. This mask, which bears the name 'Black able-to-fly' (*Nag-po'phur-shes*), was still preserved at that very temple in the nineteenth century, and was worshipped there as one of the four 'supports (*rten*) of miraculous manifestation'. The deity it represents, a special form of Mahäkäla worshipped at Sakya, is also—as we should expect—the principal figure in masked dances. The same deity appears in the form of Yeshe Gömpo. When, at the close of the fifteenth century, the Seventh Karma-pa ruler saw this Yeshe Gömpo's mask, known as the 'Black Sumbha', at Mönpathang, he also saw the Gömpo in the form of a person (*dngos-su gzigs*).

Thus, masks make us know about the presence of certain protective deities. In the masked dances Mahākāla, in one form or another, usually fills the office of presiding deity (*gtso-bo*). Referring to the celebrants in these dances, Drukpa Künlek says : 'They say that they are the body of Mahākāla.' Although the dances differ a lot from one another in their style and pantheon, they are mainly performed for the rite of driving out evil spirit. A human figurine (of dough, paper or hide)—naked, ugly, tied up and lying on its back—represents evil, the enemy, the devil, and is stabbed by the principal deity, then dismembered by an attendant (a stag). Previous rites, inside the temple, have inserted a demon or the enemy's 'soul' into it. But the word used for the execution means 'to set free, release' (*sgrol*, *bsgral*). It is an everyday term of Tibetan Tantrism denoting any ritual murder, from that practised by certain Tantric orders (the eleventh-century 'robber-monks' to the execution of demons by the hero of the epic, a deity, or a 'sorcerer'. For they basically go about billing the body and a demonic part of this 'soul' ; but at the same time they 'free' a sound part, the conscious principle (*rnam-shes*), by dispatching it to a 'paradise'. This critical act is carried out in duplicate, by a masked actor representing the principal deity on the one hand, and on the other hand and by the celebrant of the actual rite on the other. The celebrant and his assistants are the only ones not wearing masks. Indeed, it is they are the ones who call forth the deities who are present in mask form. They wear large black hats and a coat adorned with fresh human heads and dried skulls. Travellers tend to call them 'sorcerers' or even Bonpos they indulge in black magic. They are in fact the officiants ; mantra masters (*sngags-pa*, 'Tantrists') who like to frequently go to the cemeteries to perform their austerities.

The show usually lasts two days : an orchestra accompanies it and marks the dancers' steps, some slow and highly formal others quick and lively. Before and after the crucial moment of the enemy's 'liberation', the deities pass in procession just before the crowd. But strange to relate, the terror that people might easily feel in the presence of so much that is sacred is frequently relieved by the antics of buffoons, who provide a safety-valve in the laughter they arouse. Masks are worn by these jonal people too, but in this case their function is to disguise the actors, realistically, as Indian philosophers (atsara). Venerated as they are, these saints make the Tibetans laugh merely by their pretty absurd foreign appearance, with dark faces and frizzy hair. Yet while committing a crime a thousand freely improvised pranks they mimic every ritual action, even the most solemn of the Tantric officiants.

Tradition—The Nameless Religion

Just as Christian missionaries adopted and got accustomed to pagan Europe's festivals and sacred places, and figures from its pantheon, so Lamaism accepted, crowned with its authority and set its seal upon many features previously unknown to Buddhism, or as for that matter even to Indian Tantrism. In this it did no more than continue what Buddhism itself had already done in India, where it had long been absorbing deities and practices from the area's other religions, together with foreign, as well as Indian, folklore.

It would be a mistake on our part to take for granted, however, that all non-Buddhist elements absorbed by Lamaism in Tibet were not so exotic. Tibetan historians themselves have clouded the issue by constantly mixing up two separate points : the fact that Bon was there before Buddhism, and the judgment that everything preceding the latter religion was naturally 'barbarous', uncivilized and in appropriate resembling to an age of darkness. Hence the somewhat over-simplified conclusions drawn by early European students, who tended to present Bon as the primitive religion of Tibet. Further, by equating 'primitive' with 'savage', everything in Lamaism that seemed frightening, twisted, demonic or mediumistic soon came to be regarded as Bonpo and primitive. From that to describing it all as 'Shamanism' was but a mere step. The truth is somewhat more complex. It is often impossible to tell which of Lamaism's not specifically Buddhist elements is indigenous and which foreign, which one was really Bonpo and which was not. We shall have more to say about Bon, but we may remark at once that the Indian Tantrism that was introduced to Tibet, in spite of the kings' mistrust, already contained a great number of fearsome deities and rites, animal sacrifices was a common practice.

The 'Religion of Men' : Songs and Legends

Some Tibetan historians of later times, including those who particularly give stress on Bon, we come to know that before the introduction of Buddhism, during the legendary period of the kings Nyatri and Pude Kunggyel and before Songtsen Gampo, 'the kingdom was protected (i.e., ruled) by the Bonpos, the storytellers and the singers'. Of these only the Bonpos are usually remembered, because they are better known than any other specialists. The latter must have had a religious character, their functions being parallel with those of the Bonpos. Still, the first sort (*sgrung*) were storytellers and the second (*lde'u*) singers of puzzles, perhaps also of pedigrees. Between them they must have presented what is known as the 'religion of men' (*mi-chos*) as distinct from the 'religion of the gods' (*lha-chos*), a term denoting at first Bon, and later Buddhism. The few examples of 'religion of men' that have come down to us under this name are merely wise old sayings told by the old men of the sects and always uttered in a poetic style characterized by the use of metaphors, phrases and proverbial sayings. They also take account of religious beliefs, however ; though without separating them from the code of social behaviour. Part of the reason is probably that the two great organized religions, Bon and Buddhism, united the properly religious elements in their respective systems, leaving the 'religion of men' nothing but the morality that ought to act as a preparation for that religion. 'Basing oneself on the field of the religion of men, the religion of the gods (Buddhism) will grow there as a fruit', says a chronicle. In this, the Tibetan missionaries were just following the policy of Nāgārjuna, who is not widely accepted of having encouraged and even written popular stories and a collection of wise old sayings much read and quoted in Tibet. 'Custom of men well adhered to, country of gods soon arrived at. Ladder of gods and men climbed up, shore of salvation within reach'.

But the 'religion of men' was a religion (*chos*, though this word also has the meaning 'custom'). In the process of invoking to local gods of the soil, which have preserved not so exotic deities to some extent, and more notably the ancient style of the songs, we are told that a given deity bore such-and-such a name in the 'religion of men' and some other new one in the 'religion of the gods' (Buddhism). The sacred mountain Nyenchen Thanglha, for instance, was called Yashur in the 'religion of men' and Pancasikha in the 'religion of gods', one of these rituals tells us. And in fact this name (*Ya-bzhur*) can be come across the ancient manuscripts of Tun-huang, both in a mythological or legendary tale and in a manual of divination. It is important to know that Tibetans still did not ascribe it to Bon, but to the nameless religion which may be termed indigenous.

A fourteenth-century chronicle based on earlier documents gives us the information that the 'religion of men' was the sign of a king's good government. 'The nine basic forms of the religion of men belong to the pattern (or precedent) of the body of a lion. The right foot : reciting the manner in which the world came into being ; left foot : relating the fashion in which living beings appeared ; hindquarters : relating the divisions of the earth ; right "hand" : telling the genealogy of the rulers ; left "hand" : telling the genealogies of the subjects ; "middle finger" : telling the way in which the (Buddhist) doctrine was born ; neck : relating the tribes (or villages) of each ruler (?) ; head : recounting the families of father and mother ; tail : songs of joy with symbolic allusions.'

The 'tales' (*sgrung*) certainly formed part of the narrative material described here as making up the 'religion of men'. A very sound historian quotes the tale of Masang as an example. The tale in question recounts the origin of the nine Masang clans (kinds of deity) along with whom the Sakya noble family and others claim some relationships. Formerly independent, it was incorporated in a collection of Lamaistic tales based on the Indian collection of Vetala stories. But some of its themes are presently found in the epic. The Masang 'King-of-Milk', an ox-headed man born from the union of a man and a cow, comes in between in a fight between a god and a demon, on the former's side, and as a reward is granted the sending of a heavenly son to reign on earth. So no wonder that a seventeenth-century work describes the legendary account of the Tibetans' ancestry as 'religion of men'. And we learn from a quite early records of various events that, when the translation of Buddhist works had been completed under King Trhisong Detsen, 'the minister Gö said : "You have spread the religion of the gods (Buddhism). Now, what will you give men, as narrations of the religion of men?" Then they were given the pedigree of rulers, the local divisions of the people, the salutations and marks of courtesy towards the hierarchy and the Triple Gem (Triratna), tales and stories (*gtam* and *lo-rgyus*), chastity and diplomas (*dge* and *yig-tshang*).

The epic, and the genealogy of the great sect of Lang (*Rlangs po-ti bse-ru*), also cite significantly titled works on the creation of the world and its beings, as sources of their various accounts. The head of state and the protagonist in the epic, know about everything through having certain 'mother' (*ma-yig*) or 'ancestral' (*pha-'bum*) books, on which oaths are taken—because they are highly sacred—and which set forth the origin of the world and the clans, together with their whole future being predicted beforehand. One of these works was called the 'Great Opening of the Body of the World'. Perhaps this body was that of the lion with which the various traditions were associated, or that of a dismembered animal whose fragments made up the country. Another work was entitled 'Oral Tradition, or Origin of Tribes' : surprisingly it dealt with the origin of the clans from an egg. Nowadays, this work is included in the Bonpo literature. But the epic quotes it, on the subject of the clans that came out of the egg, without breathing a word about Bon, and the same story forms the opening of the Lang genealogy. It is the 'genealogy of subjects', which is linked after a brief introduction of the 'genealogy of rulers' : those, it will be remembered, were two of the nine topics of the 'religion of men'.

An egg appears, as the purest form of the five elements. From its outer shell is born the White rock of the gods on high (masculine in Tibetan), from its inner fluid is formed the White lake of marine shell (feminine), and from the sticky part in the middle come all beings. The soft part of the egg converts into eighteen eggs of which one (or six), in the middle, is as though made of marine shell. It is a shapeless man, without limbs or senses, but certainly endowed with thought. In accordance with his wish, sense organs break through and he turns into a handsome young man, king Yemon or Sangpo Bumtri. He has a son by a queen. After some generations we reach gods, one of whom, Ode Kunggyel, is elsewhere regarded as the royal dynasty's ancestor, who came down from heaven to earth. Two generations later, with Thingge, we come to the ancestors of the great nations (Tibet, Hor, China), and then to the ancient clans, one of which gave rise to that of Lang.

Bon Po Chronology

The beginning of the account is highly complex and resembles Bonpo creation myths. We can observe the strong influence of India, Iran or even China for that matter : for an informed scholar from Drigung, in the twelfth century, this Bonpo chronology starting from an egg is a belief of the ones holding unorthodox opinions (*mu-stegs*, brahmins) of India ; and in fact it is found in the *Mahabharata*. The remainder of the genealogy is as tangled and ill-preserved as most of the other genealogical legends, all constructed to the same pattern. The fact is that ancestral legends were like the armorial bearings of some noble families. They would quarrel over them, each family claiming divine origin and trying to take possession of famous ancestors. Fluctuations and variants were all the commoner because these legends were recited on the occasion of various contests at the festivals celebrated in honour of the god of the soil. The dialogues held till the present date at horse-races, evidence for which goes back at least as far as the fourteenth century, highly praised clans or families in hymns and fine speeches. In one variant of the egg legend preserved in the epic, two birds are mentioned. There are eighteen eggs in their nest : six white, six yellow and six blue (the colours of the three levels of the world and their deities). From the six middle eggs come men. Then we observe three smiths each belonging to one of the three realms—of the gods on high (*lha*, white), on earth (*gnyan*, yellow) and under the earth (*klu*, blue). To these three is added a human smith who comes from the middle realm. It is presumed that they go on to fashion the eggs in some way, but there the narrative breaks off and only returns to the subject with scraps of other versions.

When historians regard the ancient storytellers as having 'protected the Kingdom' on the same basis as the Bonpos, it is because the correct recitation of legends of origin was a religious act absolutely necessary for upholding the order of world and society. The 'singers of riddles' (*lde'u*), named as the third type of specialists, must have had similar duties. We have specimens of their style, from a well-informed historical author : they are mysterious. But the word's derivations implies question-and-answer songs dealing with the creation of the world and with human and divine genealogies. In the epic, experts in these songs (here called *le'u*) practise their art during the races that formed part of the festival of the holy place, and are generally meant to elect the winner as king of the country.

The ancestral legend of the egg provides, in the epic, the subject for alternating songs between boys from the land of Ling and girls from China. A Ling boy, 'Easy mouth' or 'Easy speech', has caught a girl and threatens not to let her go unless she can answer his all questions. The riddle contest is then matched by a whole series of competitions : trials of strength, magic, conjuring, racing, dice and archery. The existence of different versions, and their fragmentary nature, are explained by the fact that the same story is told in various ways each time by each of the contestants, to bring out this or that ancestral relationship of the singer's ; and also by poetic inspiration, inducing the singer to embroider around his subject. While the subjects of the story and a set of cliches are generally the same the free improvisation varies with the singer's gifts.

In the modern period, such alternating songs between boys and girls, turning on mythological issues or the origin of the dwelling-site, were performed chiefly at the New Year for ceremonies. But they also formed an integral part of the marriage ritual. According to the custom boys representing the bridegroom, known as 'buyers' (*nyo-pa*) in Ladakh (but *nyi'u* among the Horpas), had to visit the bride's house. A group of girls closed the door, and only opened it when their sung questions had been equally bartered for the boys' sung answers : the songs were mostly filled with metaphors and enigmatic expressions, and everything known about the world was their subject. In the course of a long exchange of songs, the bride's party challenges the opposing party in words like these :

'Since you say that you have come in accordance with the words of truth (*bden-tshigs*, a sworn oath possessing magical force), [tell us then] :

Who catches the wild yak by the horns?
Who seizes the tiger with his hand?
Who picks up water in his lassoo?
Who builds a castle out of sand?
Who strikes water with a sword and wounds it?
Which bird can give birth?
Which beast of prey can lay eggs?
Who follows the footprints of the pheasant running over the rock?
Who sews a cloak for the slaty ground?
Who accepts our challenge and recognizes us?'

And the answer :

'He who catches the wild yak by the horns,
Is Makchen Rampa.
He who seizes the tiger with his hand,
Is Saya Pechö.
He who picks up water with his lasso,
Is the *yaksa* Shongthok.
He who builds castles out of sand,
Is the bird Karakukti.
He who strikes water with a sword and wounds it,
Is none other than the water itself.
The bird that can give birth,
Is the bat.
The beast of prey that can lay eggs,
Is the weasel.
He who follows the footprints of the pheasant running over the rock,
Is no other than the grass.
He who sews a cloak for the slaty ground,

Is Byishokara (Visvakarman, artificer of the gods).
Those who accept your challenge and recognize you,
Are ourselves, and isn't the answer good?'

The bride's party continue :

'Since you came yesterday, came to the castle,
Tell us three kinds of castle,
Tell us three kinds of space,
Tell us three kinds of lake,
Tell us three kinds of land ! All right?'

And the boys reply :

'Since we came yesterday, came to the castle,
Khyunglung Ngülkar, Tromo Semakhar and Mashang Tril-bukhar, these are the three kinds of castle.
The boundless space of the sky, the unobstructed space of the Dharma, the endless space of wealth, these are the three kinds of space.
Maphang the bathing lake, La-ngak the poison lake, Gomo the conch (?) lake, these are the three kinds of lake.
Tusita land of gods, Jambudvipa land of men, Anavatāpta land of *nāgās,* these are the three kinds of land.'

These songs would be worth quoting in their completeness but we lack the room. Collected at the turn of the century, they blend naturally together the standard concepts of Lamaism, some specifically Bonpo elements, the traditions of the epic and popular ideas. They treat all the three levels of the world, each inhabited by its own deities, the different realms of nature each with its representative animal (the white lion of the glaciers, etc.), the four *lokapālas* and the four legendary kings ruling over the four points of the compass. Despite their modernized appearance, these songs may give us a glimpse of what the ancient *lde'u* were like. They did not forget the main roots.

The stories and songs, then, were supposed to 'protect the kingdom', like the rites of Bon, through the power of religion. They express the wisdom of the elders and their trustworthy nature lends its confirmation to the social and world order, the structure of the environment and that of the group inhabiting it. The marriage songs begin with an indirect reference to the 'word of truth', a Buddhist term which in everyday speech has taken on the meaning of a formula for swearing and calling to witness, charged with high magical energy (imprecation formula : 'As sure as . . . !', or 'May I be punished if what I say is not true !'). For the epic, exact recital is most important as it is for the rites and magical formulae in

Buddhism. The epic, the songs and the racecourse recitations, as also the plays performed during harvest time, gladden the god of the country (sacred mountain) and set up a relationship between him and the group taking part in the festival. In fact it is a celebration of the Lord's supper.

In order to approve the group's relationship with gods and ancestors, it is essential to go back in each recitation to the origin of such and such an institution, and the recitation must be absolutely authentic. This is the case even with Lamaist rituals which always refer to the origin, the mythical precedent, that justifies each rite. Curious this is to relate, these accounts in the ritual texts always have a dramatic nature and are remarkable for their highy polished literary expression as works of poetry. In the epic, long poetical narrations are devoted to the origin and symbolic explanation of the bard's hat, or the hero's horse and sword. Wedding songs highly praise the origin of marriage, clothing, the hat and the 'sheep of good fortune' ; racing hymns, the origin of the races and of the clans taking part in them. These accounts are frequently called *gtam-dpe*, a term whose second syllable combines the meanings of example, metaphor, maxim, tale and book. During the exchange of dialogues 'sayings' (*dep*) of the elders are cited as authority. When describing the 'religion of men', the different parts of the lion's body are used as a pattern or metaphor (*dpe*) for different types of tradition. By conforming to the patterns and precedents laid down in the times when things came into being we take our place in the order of the world and there by help to uphold it.

Take, for example, the ceremony of calling for good fortune (*g.yang-'gug*), for which a beribboned arrow, a mirror and a 'good-fortune bag' (*g.yang-khug*) are made of use : 'The material of the good-fortune bag is wool. The father was the sky sheep Reddish-white, the mother the earth sheep Reddish. These two united and had sons. Of five kinds were the lambs.' Or a ceremony (*bsangs*) in which clouds are formed of sweet-smelling smoke are produced on high places : 'Song of the *bsangs*. Ho! The origin of *bsangs*, whence comes this origin? The origin of *bsangs*?—it comes from the sky. For its father, it had the great thunder ringing in the sky. For mother, it had the great lightning running over the earth. Their son, a wild horse, is the glacier's essence ; is the ocean's water-bubble ; is the turquoise lake Mapham's foam ; is the best medicine's power.'

Those are only shreds and pieces of ancient songs which even Buddhist writers felt they must preserve. But, in the Tun-huang manuscripts, we have early texts of this type in which the accounts of origins are quite lengthy. They deal, for example, with the falling out and parting of the yak and the horse, and the horse's descent from heaven to the land of men. Unfortunately the ancient language which no longer has ordinary use of these documents makes them very hard to translate.

Oaths and Tombs

Since Tibetan chronicles teach us very little about the old religion, let us see what we can learn from the T'ang Chinese annalists. They are unfortunately not very interested in religion or only know a few of the forms it takes which is a surprising fact. What little they tell us relates to the ninth century, when Buddhism had already come into contact with the native religion. Tibetans—they say give more stress on to demons and believe in wizards and witches. They worship a god who is a male goat, in fact a wild one with large horns (*yüan-ti*, perhaps Tibetan *gnyan* which denotes both the ibex—*ovis Hodgsoni*—and a class of gods of the soil). They like the Buddha's religion, and believe in cursing.

When swearing the Sino-Tibetan peace treaty of 822, the Triple Gem (Buddha, Dharma, Samgha) and the Buddhist saints were called to witness, the sun, moon and stars. Sacrificial victims were made as offerings. The text was read by a monk of ministerial rank (the *dPal-chen-po*) who performed a rite before the Buddha after the swearing, but the others had previously smeared their lips with the blood of sacrificial animals. On the occasion of another oath, taken at the Chinese capital in 756, the Tibetans said that they were not used to infact go to the Buddhist temple for the purpose and that they anointed themselves with animals' blood. But according to a less official Chinese work the Tibetans, on two oath-taking occasions, brought a god's statue to swear by, and this statue was deposited in a Buddhist temple.

A spoken curse used to be read over water, which was then drunk ; and this custom (*mna'-chu*) was prevalent in Lamaist ceremonies, where the celebrant 'binds by oath' minor deities who thus become his vassals or subjects (*'bangs-su mchi*). We already know that the makes a claim Tibetans used to renew the bonds of loyalty between vassal and sovereign by a small annual oath and a significant great oath every three years. Those who practiced with craft and black magic then sacrificed victims (men, horses, asses, oxen, monkeys, sheep and dogs) and the curses consisted of vowing the same fate to whoever should violate the oath. Chinese annals state that the gods invoked in witness were the gods of sky and earth, or more specifically the sky, earth, mountains, rivers, sun, moon and stars. The Tibetan text of the oath of 730 also calls to witness the gods of the sky (the *lha*), of the watery subsoil (*klu*) and of the earth (*gnyan*) ; and the text of the oath of 822 names' sun, moon and stars. The custom of sacrificing victims to confirm an oath (*mna'-grib*) is said to have persisted till the present day in Kham. The formula for taking to witness has survived : 'The sky knows it.' The modern custom, reported in Kham and Sikkim, of setting up a stone at the time of oath is already mentioned on the stele of 730 (*mtho-rtsig*) and in the old Tun-huang chronicle. In the latter case, dated to the sixth century, the stone was erected on the tomb of the minister in whose favour the king pronounced the oath and accompanied by the sacrifice of a hundred horses which was necessary. This stone must presumably have borne the text of the oath of mutual loyalty. On the pillar bearing the inscription of Trhisong Detsen, at Chonggye (where the tombs of the early kings are), two discs can be seen above the text, most probably representing sun and moon. The pillar with Trhide Songtsen's inscription, at the same place, bears swastika patterns and an anthropoid face. In Ladakh and Lahul, stones—sometimes anthropomorphous—are raised in memory of the dead.

It is possible therefore that early standing stones sometimes included a human face and represented the victim-witness or the tomb guardian. Similar stones (*balbal*), representing enemies struck to death, are known on the Turkic tombs of Mongolia (*kereksür*). In Tibet, it will be recalled, five or six 'common fate' friends were sacrificed in their own lord's tomb. Where the Tibetan text says that the 'guardian of the tomb' behaved like the dead man and hence substituted for him, altogether an early Chinese text makes a claim that after a warrior's death in battle a man used to be posted beside the dead body : he would answer questions addressed to the dead man and accept food and clothes in his place. The tomb of King Drongnyen Deru contained three 'subjects' who were buried there alive with the King's statue. In modern Tibet, an image of the dead person dressed in his clothes received offerings during the intermediate period of forty-nine days between the period of death and rebirth.

In early Tibet, the tomb was square, made of piled-up stones, with a flat roof. On top of it was thrown up a mound planted with trees of various kinds for use as a temple and place of sacrifice. In addition to the stone set up for witness (*mtho* or *tho*, nowadays a kind of altar of heaped-up stones), white stones would be handed over to the beneficiary of the oath, to be built into the foundations of his future tomb. According to one T'ang historian, the tombs of men who died on the battlefield—an honoured death—were rendered in white clay all round, and usually separated from other tombs. Another tells us that a red roof built beside the tomb carried the painting of a white tiger, the symbol of warlike valour.

6

The Dalai Lamas

Dalai Lamas, always had and will have a prominent role in Tibet's political religious and many other matters. Dalai Lamas, indeed have a long history in Tibet. People worship them like gods. I shall perhaps be pardoned if I deviate from the main subject at this stage to describe from a more personal standpoint the lives of the priest-kings or god-kings, whose rule-period has formed the subject of the preceding chapter. The Dalai Lama is considered by Tibetans as a Bodhisatwa, i.e., one who has attained the right to Nirvana, but agrees to be reborn for the spiritual benefit of his fellow men. In almost every Asiatic country which has had a spiritual ruler, the latter has been the object of worship but has not been allowed to exercise power and has been quite often kept more or less as a prisoner in his palace. The actual power has been wielded by a Minister, and has frequently been hereditary in the Minister's family. Even in Bhutan, a country adjoining Tibet and inhabited by men of Tibetan race the spiritual ruler, or Shab-tung Rim-po-che, known to Europeans and Indians as the Dharma Raja, did not govern at all. The duty of government was deputed to the Desi or Deb Raja, who was a priest himself and who in latter years had himself ceased to govern. The real power lies for at least fifty or sixty years with the Penlop (Chief) of the Tongsa district, which covers the eastern half of Bhutan. The present Penlop has assumed the hereditary title of Regent of Bhutan and the Desi has retired. Thus in a country akin to Tibet in race, religion, and language, the actual power lay for many years not even with the second, but with the third man in the kingdom.

Dalais: The Virtual Ruler

But Tibet has at several times proved an exception to this almost universal rule. Since the time of the fifth Dalai Lama, i.e., from 1641, the Dalais, when they succeeded in attaining their majority, have at times ruled in fact as well as in name. A noteable example of this was the great fifth Dalai Lama, who himself conducted the administration for several years before placing it in the capable hands of his Chief Minister, Sang-gye Gyatso. But the most striking example of all is the present God-king, who for the last twenty or thirty years, while introducing salutary reforms on the religious side, has also controlled the variety of details of the secular government. How numerous and how varied the duties of Buddha's Vice-regent are, even I can in some measure realize after being in close contact with him for nearly two years in India, and even more after eleven months' close personal intercourse in Lhasa.

When a Dalai Lama himself rules—and probably when a clever Minister rules in his name—his authority is without rivals. Even though the Council and Parliament are united in opposition to his proposals, he can enforce them, and has not infrequently done so. Backed as he is worshipped by people who regard him as more than Pope, as in fact a Divinity ruling on earth, there can be no direct opposition to His Holiness's orders. The Nepalese have a characteristic proverb, which says :

There's no answer to an order ;
There's no medicine for death.

Things are not indeed as strict as this in the Lama's sphere, for the great wastes of Tibet cannot be controlled as easily as the fertile little lands of Nepal, and the Tibetan nomad wandering over his mountains is not so susceptible to discipline as the Nepalese peasant tied to his farm.

In actual practice also the Dalai's power is limited through his being kept in ignorance of events by monasteries, officials, and others. His position debass him from touring frequently and seeing things for himself. Governmental proposals and important events come to him from the Council, through the Lord Chamberlain or the Chief Secretary, both of whom thus exercise great influence. But the Dalai has his private and semi-private employees, who bring him news and enable him to sift, in some degree, the official sources of information. In districts far from Lhasa, the natural independence—one might perhaps say the democratic tendency—of the Tibetan character asserts itself, and disagreeable orders are apt to be regarded but lightly.

A few of the earlier Dalai Lamas were born in grand families. Among these was Yön-ten Gyatso, the fourth, the son of a Mongol prince. But the 'Great Fifth' was apparently the son of a peasant at Chung-gye, two days' journey south-east of Lhasa. And in the later incarnations the Dalai Lama has almost invariably been chosen from a family of humble position. If he be selected from one of the leading families of the country, several of which are descended from the brothers of previous Dalai Lamas, that family is likely to become powerful which is a disadvantage. Public appointments too are not usually given to members of his family during his lifetime. But these may hold, and usually do hold, private posts about his person, which carry great, though unacknowledged, influence.

Dalai Lamas do not indulge in drinking wine or spirits, but they may and do eat meat, a necessary article of diet in Tibet, where the climate is cold and fruit and vegetables are scarce, often indeed unobtainable. As, however, the taking of life, even for food, is to Buddhists a sin, a religious ceremony is performed on behalf of the animals so killed, and this is held to insure their rebirth in a higher state of existence. Thus the loss of their lives means a gain to them, according to their religion. Dalai Lamas do not marry, but keep altogether apart from women.

How Dalai Lama is Appointed

The method of appointing a successor is unique. For the following description of it I am indebted to His Holiness the present Dalai Lama, to the late Prime Minister, and to other high Tibetan authorities.

Some Dalai Lamas are more believed in, some less. One of the former class, before he dies, or—as the Tibetans say—before he 'retires to the heavenly fields', will usually tell those round him, where he is likely reincarnate. He may give particulars as to the house in which the small boy will be found, the stream, if any, near it, the shape of the mountains round it, &c., &c. His attendents are themselves afraid to ask for these particulars, when they see their divinity ill, for they fear that they may thereby make him more eager to go.

Three or four years after the Dalai Lama has 'departed', the Tashi Lama, if of age, and fifteen or twenty other great lamas, e.g., the abbots of Sera, Drepung, and Ganden—the three huge monasteries near Lhasa—the State Oracle at Lhasa, known as the Nechung, and the Oracle at Sam-ye, one of the most famous monasteries in Tibet, decide as to the tract of land in which the new Dalai Lama is likely to be found, the year of birth of his father, his mother, and himself, the kinds of trees growing near his house, and so on.

Inquiries in the district indicated are then set on foot, and lead usually to the tracing of three or four boys whose birth has been proclaimed by heavenly manifestations. For instance, a rainbow has appeared over his house from a clear sky when he was born, and his parents have had heavenly visions regarding him. Particulars of these miraculous births are laid before the Oracles and lamas referred to above, and these decide as to who is the new Dalai Lama. The latter, a boy of three or four, has to recognize the sacred thunderbolt, the bell and other religious implements of his predecessor—or rather, as one should say, of himself in his previous life.

The young boy will be found to carry on his person some of the marks that distinguish the incarnation of the four-handed Chenrezi from ordinary mortals. Among such signs are :

(a) Marks as of a tiger-skin on his legs.
(b) Eyes and eyebrows that curve upwards on the outside and are quite long.
(c) Pretty large ears.
(d) Two pieces of flesh near the shoulder-blades indicating the two other hands of Chenrezi.
(e) An imprint like a conch-shell on one of the palms of his hands.

The present Dalai Lama bears the last three signs. An unearthly light is believed to issue from his face when he blesses pilgrims, so that even his ministers and immediate attendants find it hard to look him in the face.

The names of the different candidates had, however, usually to be placed in the golden urn, presented in 1793 by the Chinese Emperor Chienlung. One was picked out with a pair of chopsticks, and opened by a Tibetan Grand Secretary. This generally contained the name of the new Dalai Lama. The Prime Minister asserted to me that this has always up to this time been the same as the name favoured by the Oracles. In the case of the present Pontiff the Tibetan Government represented to the Chinese Emperor that there was no doubt about the identity of the new Dalai Lama, and therefore no need for the Amban to perform the ceremony of picking out a name. The ceremony was accordingly remitted, a ceremony which appears also to indicate that the Chinese Lord paramount was then merely nominal.

By presenting the urn and arranging for the Amban to assist at the choice of each new Dalai Lama and other high Incarnations, the Chinese Government no doubt hoped to gain some hold over the personage who rather influences not only Tibet but Mongolia, and is revered by many millions in Asia, and even by some in European Russia. For the Lama, owing his position in some measure to their representative, might naturally feel bound to repay his debt by flattery to their requests. According to Chinese accounts they had good grounds for their bringing about changes, for at the time the choice of a high Incarnation was often made corruptly. A ruler of Ladakh had many relatives who were chosen among the highest of the Incarnations. A Tashi Lama chose a Dalai Lama from a prominent family in the Tsang province ; the latter in turn made his first cousin Tashi Lama when the former Tashi Lama died. But the climax was reached when the Ne-chung Oracle of Lhasa declared that the reincarnation of the Grand Lama of Urga would be the child that the wife of the reigning prince of the Tushot Mongols was expected to bring forth. For the child was born, it was a girl.

Lönchen Shatra, the late Prime Minister—whose early death was a very heavy loss to his country—told me the story of the finding of the present Dalai Lama, then a boy of two or three years old, in words somewhat as follows :

'The Ne-chung Oracle gave certain particulars, showing the names of the father and mother, the approximate whereabouts of his house, the kind of country round it, and so on. The Oracle of Sam-ye also gave some particulars, e.g., that a mountain by the house was "shaped like an elephant".

'After this, a leading lama, with a number of doctors of divinity in attendance, was instructed to go to a lake named "Mu-li-ting" in Sanskrit-Tibetan and "Chö-kor Gyal-ki Nam-tso" in popular Tibetan. Here he was to see a vague image of the Dalai Lama's house and surrounding country. The lama went accordingly, but found the lake frozen and under snow, so wondered how he could see as directed. But soon afterwards a strong wind got up and blew off the snow, making the ice clear to the lama, who was viewing at it from a neighbouring hill. Then, so the story goes, the lake rose up on end and the lama looked into it as into a glass. And in it he saw the image as foretold.

'Later on in a dream the lama saw the baby Dalai in his mother's arms. When he arrived at the house, he found the baby in the arms of his mother, and the face of the boy corresponded with the face in the dream.'

'A deputation of priests and officials waited on the boy, who picked out property of the late Dalai Lama from among a large number of articles. And in spite of his tender years he was able to indicate occurrences that had happened in the lifetimes of previous Dalai Lamas. Among other cases he indicated that of a Chief of Li-tang, to whom a former Dalai Lama had given an image of Buddha. For fear of losing this, the Chief had encased it in a golden urn, and hidden it in a beam in his house, unknown to anybody. The young Dalai Lama told people that the Chief of Li-tang had done this.

'Dalai Lamas cease identifying property and telling of such occurrences, when they grow older.

'If there is no doubt as to the true Dalai Lama, the names are not put into the golden urn. The names of the 9th Dalai Lama, Lung-tok Gyatso, and of the present one were not put into it.'

The Prime Minister, who narrated this account to me, was an intellectual and has strong common sense. As a Tibetan invested with full powers at the diplomatic Conference in 1913-14, he proved himself to be more than a match for his Chinese colleague. But in matters of religion Tibetan faith is strong and has a lot of depth.

The father of a Dalai receives the rank of Kung, the highest rank held by a layman in Tibet. He receives also the badges of the Ruby Button and the Double-Eyed Peacock Feather. There are very few Kungs ; they are descended from the fathers of recent Dalai and Tashi Lamas.

The abandonment by China of the use of the golden urn in the choice of the present Pontiff is a measure of the growing impatience felt by Tibet towards the Chinese Lord Paramount and of the steady decline of the latter. This decline is further evidenced by the attainment to his majority of the present Dalai. The four immediately coming before him all died before they could take up the reins of government. Thus for nearly a century Tibet was administered by Regents. As pointed out in Chapter V, this enabled the Chinese to enjoy much greater power in Tibet than would have been likely under the administration of the Dalai Lamas themselves.

When seven years old, or even earlier, the Dalai is brought to Lhasa, in his palace, known as the Potala. At the age of eighteen he is entitled to receive his full powers. The present Dalai Lama was taken from his mother when about three years old and brought to Lhasa. His father and mother thereafter saw him only at occasional visits. 'The Master of the Bed Chamber', so the Lord Chamberlain informed me, 'took his mother's place, fondling him in his arms, and looking after him in every way. He also gave him his early education, and it is largely owing to him that the Dalai Lama has become so learned and wise.'

The title Dalai Lama (or more properly Ta-le Lama), being of Mongolian origin, is used mostly by Chinese and Mongols. The Tibetans know him rather as *Kyam-gon Rim-po-che*, 'The Precious Protector' ; *Gye-wa Rim-po-che*, 'The Precious Sovereign' ; *Buk*, 'The Inmost One' ; *Kyam-gön Buk*, 'The Inmost Protector' ; *Lama Pön-po*, 'The Priest Officer'; sometimes also as 'The All-Knowing Presence', and often simply as 'The Presence', *Kün-dün*.

The Seals of Authority

The Dalai Lama informed me that he had five chief seals of office.

'The Golden Seal of the Rainbow and of the Earth' bears on it the name of the Emperor of China, who ruled at the time of the fifth Dalai Lama. It is a red seal, almost a inch square. It is supposed to be kept in the personal custody of the Lama himself, and is one of the major symbols of his authority. It is not stamped on documents these days but is found on some of the more ancient title-deeds of the old families of Tibet. Another seal of primary importance, known as 'The Inmost Seal', bears on it the words 'Gan-den Po-trang', 'The Blissful Palace', and 'Dalai Lama'. It is red, square, and a little larger than the first seal. It is usually applied to title-decds of large properties, and to other documents issued by the Lama personally. A large photograph of His Holiness, which I took for him, and which he presented to me, shows him seated on his throne, and adorned in the robes in which he blesses the pilgrims and others in his Palace at Lhasa. This he signed himself and sealed with the Inmost Seal. The signature runs, 'In accordance with the Precepts of the Lord Buddha the Great Dalai Lama, Unchangeable, Holder of the Thunderbolt, the Thirteenth in the line of Victory and Power.'

Chinese Control over Tibet

In foreign affairs the Dalai Lama is expected to act in conjunction with the two Councils, the Greater and the Lesser, and along with the National Assembly. Until the expulsion the Chinese Amban in 1912 and his troops from Lhasa, it was the custom, when the matter was of great importance, that their decision should be communicated to the Amban, who used to submit it to the Chinese Government. The Tibetan report was known as 'The Request for Power', and the Amban's communication as 'The Golden Ears'. After sending their report, the Tibetan authorities considered themselves at free to act according to their decision, without waiting for the Emperor's reply, which of course was not received in less than three months, even in urgent cases. By this practical method they gained their own way, while pleasing the dictates of Oriental courtesy.

It is now clear that, for many years prior to 1904, China did not have much control over Tibetan foreign policy. Nor indeed was Tibet in the habit of acknowledging her authority, except while avoiding foreign pressure. In cases related to these the Tibetan Government was able to plead the Chinese relationship, and the consequent impossibility of taking action until a report had been submitted to the Emperor and a reply obtained from him, a plea by which several months' delay could always be taken for granted. Among other instances in which the Tibetans availed themselves of the Chinese relationship may be mentioned the Dalai Lama's refusal to reply to the two letters that the Viceroy of India wrote to him in 1900 and 1901. As regards the first letter he wrote, 'The Ambans, when they first came here, made an arrangement forbidding us to correspond direct with your Government'. Lord Curzon's second letter to the Dalai Lama was returned even without being opened.

Per contra their unacceptance of the Chinese suzerainty is evidenced by their refusal to acknowledge the Anglo-Chinese Convention of 1890 as binding on Tibet, when Colonel Younghusband in 1903 pressed for its observance. Similarly by their refusal to permit the Amban to go to meet the Expedition of 1904. And once again, by their refusal to acknowledge the deposition of the Dalai Lama by the Chinese Emperor after this Expedition. The Emperor's proclamation was disfigured and bespattered with filth, and the Tibetan Government continued to submit matters for the orders of the Lama, though His Holiness was absent in Mongolia.

Internal Administration

In the internal administration also a Dalai Lama is always supreme. An appeal lies to him against any decision of the Council in cases of exceptional importance. If, for instance, the dispute is between persons of high rank, or if a large landed property is involved, the party oppressed by the decision of the Council may apply for the interference of the 'Precious Sovereign'. Such appeals are known as 'The Placing of the Names of the King and Ministers' ; and are so called from the fact that the petition is addressed in the names of the Dalai Lama and Council. In every murder case also the decision of the Court used to be submitted to the Dalai Lama for confirmation. But the present Dalai Lama gives his Prime Minister full charge in criminal cases, for it is held to be unfitting for His Holiness to touch things which are of such nature.

Although in Tibet, as elsewhere, rank and position are shown by the height of the seat above the floor of the room, yet a Dalai Lama, the Supreme Head of Tibet, will frequently sit on a lower seat than a learned Lama, when seeking knowledge from religion from the latter. This usually takes place when the Dalai Lama is a youth. But even when His Holiness was 36 years old, at the time of his flight to India, there were in Tibet two learned Lamas, who had the privilege to sit equal with the Dalai Lama himself.

Such is the respect paid to learning by the Buddhists of Tibet, where it is regarded as the highest of all moral attainments. To the

Christian, Love is the greatest virtue ; to the Tibetan Buddhist Learning. In India the man or woman who desires to please, will address you as 'Protector of the Poor' or 'Incarnation of Justice', but in Tibet as 'Learned Sir'.

The two leading officers in the Dalai Lama's household are the Lord Chamberlain and the Chief Secretary. The former is the head of all the ecclesiastical officials in Tibet. The recent rector was a clever doctor, and, as such, always attended His Holiness in addition to his ordinary duties, which include, among other charges, the control of the parks round Lhasa.

The Chief Secretary is the most important medium for communication between His Holiness and the outside world. As such, he has many enemies, but holds great power. For, when the Dalai Lama, dissatisfied by the Council's handling of some important issue, takes the direct control in his own hands—as happened once during my year in Lhasa—the Chief Secretary for the time sets aside the Prime Minister and the Council.

The Chief Secretary has ten assistants for his help who combine the duties of secretaries and aide-de-camps. One of these was attached to my Mission in Lhasa ; his alertness, political sharpness of mind and knowledge of his own national concerns, would have made him a man of mark in any country.

The Master of the Bedchamber, the Court Chaplain, and the Chief Butler wield considerable power indirectly, because they have right to reach His Holinesss, and can put in a word on this side or that. The four orderlies are men of great stature : when we were in Lhasa, all were way beyond six feet and one was just seven feet in height. They and the soldiers of the Bodyguard are patient with crowds, but are not to be lightly disregarded.

7

British Missions in Tibet: 1903–1904

The long-continued ignorance by the Tibetans to see the provisions of the Treaty of 1890, as provided by the appendant regulations signed at Darjeeling in December 1893, together with their infringement of the border-line adjusted between Tibet and North Sikkim that runs along the watershed thwart the Kongra-lamo Pass, were not in themselves matters of vital consequence. Several attempts had been made in the past to bring these laxities into order. But they have not being succeeded in following a definite steps to enforce compliance that it would have been undertaken, had not other situation arisen that suggested the advisability of convincing the Tibetans that the British Government was not the one outside Power which might be played with and defied. The detection on more than one occasion, during the years 1900 and 1901, of confidential communications passing between Russia and certain persons of position at Lhasa by way of Darjeeling convinced the Indian Government that the time for asserting ourselves had came. Moreover, the publicity afterwards flauntingly done by the Russian newspapers to these so-called "Missions" from the Dalai Lama (in singular contrast to the privacy of their passage over the Indian frontier) showed a *ballon d 'essai* possibly precedent to a Russian consulate at Lhasa. Definite action had, therefore, to be taken with the view to convince Tibet, rather than Russia, that, if any outside Power was to have influence in Tibet, it should be England and not Russia. With such crucial issues at stake, when dealing with so barbarous and childish a Government as the Tibetan (which evades the larger issues), all small rights of ours that had been openly infringed had necessarily to be seized upon and made much of, even if it were only to give an excuse to effect the larger settlement.

Contemptuous Treatment

This necessity appeared to be given more importance by the contempt with which the Tibetan authorities had treated some particulars letters written by the Viceroy personally to the Dalai Lama himself . Among these, one letter had been sent for delivered in August, 1900, from the Ladak side of Tibet. Captain Kennion, then political officer at Leh, had himself gone as far as Gartok to post the letter to the Urkhu or Garpon there for transmission to Lhasa. After six month this official had been sent back to Leh with the statement that he dared not forward it as had been said earlier. In June, 1901, a second letter was again prepared and delivered from Darjeeling, enclosed with first letter. Both of these, kept in a silken cover, were entrusted to one Urgyen Kazi, who was Bhutanese and ready to go on a complimentary mission from the Dharma Raja of Bhutan conveying presents of two elephants and a leopard to the Dalai Lama. The envoy arrived Lhasa in August, among those two elephant one has died on the way. His account of his efforts to present the letter is worth quoting : —

> I told the Chikyab Kempo that I brought a letter from His Excellency the Viceroy. He reported this to the Dalai Lama. On the fifth day after my arrival, I gave His Excellency's letter to the Dalai Lama. The Chikyab Kempo went with me, but left the room and there was only a servant present who was serving tea. On this servant leaving the room, the Dalai Lama commenced to talk, at first, about things concerning Bhutan, and then about the Government. Regarding the letter, the Dalai Lama said he could not take it without consulting the Council and the Amban, and, as he knew they would not agree, he did not wish to call them, as he said he was afraid the Chinese Amban would make a fuss and probably create a disturbance, in which case he could not be responsible for my life. He went on to say that he was precluded from writing any letter to any Foreign Government, as during the time of Tangyailing Demo Rimpoche an agreement was entered into by the Lamas, Sehaffis and Ambans that no letters should be written without first consulting the Ambans. I then pointed out that the letter was written by the greatest official under the King. To this the Dalai Lama answered that this agreement was not made by him but by his predecessor, and that he was sorry, but he could not receive a letter or send an answer. This

he repeated on two subsequent occasions when I went to visit him, and that he could not, by himself, break that agreement. "You know," he said, "that this agreement was made by Tangyailing who, in his time, did a great deal of harm ; he fought with China and Nepal, and even treated his own subjects badly." He also said that, since he had taken over the Government, he had quarrelled with no one and only wished to lead a holy life. With your Government, he said, he wished to live in amicable relations . "Your Government must not be angry with me. I have never done it any harm. I allow my subjects to trade in the products of the country, such as yaks' tails and wool ; but if any of the subjects of your big Government come in here, I am afraid disturbances will follow." I pointed out that allowing merchants in would do no harm ; to which he replied that might be, but that he doubted it ; and pointed to the manner in which the Chinese and Nepalese were always making trouble. The Dalai Lama also said that he would try to get the agreement about writing broken, but that it would take time. I asked him just to give me a line, saying that he could not accept the Viceroy's letter, but he refused again, saying that it would be an infringement of the agreement. The Dalai Lama is a clever man, and is really sorry that he was unable to accept the Viceroy's letter or send any letter. Also that the Dalai Lama and the Chinese are not on good terms, but that he fears them. This is all I can remember.

First Mission of Mr. White

Further the step taken was the delegation of Mr. Claude White, political officer in Sikkim, to proceed to the frontier of Sikkim, and destroy the boundary marks erected by the Tibetans at Gyao-gong La, by which runs the line of the old limits between North Sikkim and Tibet, to disperse the Tibetan guard there, and to arrange a new boundary 8 miles further north along a line of demarcation going through the Kongra-lamo La. This accession of territory, that was secured to Sikkim under the Custom with China and Tibet in 1890, may be styled the Gyaogong plateau and is almost a desolate mountainous tract along with lands lying north of the Dongkya Pass and surrounding the Chola mo lakes visited by Hooker. Chinese officials had been sent to meet Mr. White ; and Mr. White had been instructed to suggest that Great Britain would probably left to Tibet the disputed lands if the Tibetans would agree to open Phari as a trading centre to British subjects.

In the June of 1902, Mr. Claude White proceeded, from Gangtok to the Gyao-gong plateau to meet the Chinese Commissioners. The 150 Gurkha Soldier escorted him under two officers Captain Murray and Lieu. Coleridge. He was also accompanied by two veteran surveyors, Rinzing and Lobsang. Due to that the negotiations with Ho Kwang-hsi and Captain Parr, Chinese Commissioners, led to no particular decision ; but the Tibetan boundary erections were destroyed new ones set up on three other Passes, and the whole tract between the old and new frontier lines meticulously surveyed. At Kongra-lamo the boundary appears to have been adjusted again north than the actual Pass (such as it is), namely, at P'u-chung-pang, 3 miles or less below the Serpurbu Pass. Mr. White took so many photographs, then he was in position to fix them by triangulation of definite distant points in Tibet observable from lofty localities. His observations for altitude were so many ; but, in view of Mr. Douglas Freshfield, his fixtures as a rule give a greater height than is virtually correct.

On his expedition one curious result is given by Mr. White in a letter dated 20th October 1902 : "I have got the following information , that is interesting, as it is the first time that the Dalai Lama has acknowledged a Europen official. I understand that the Tibetans had contemplated stopping all communications with India, but that, owing to the Commissioner at Yatung, Captain Parr, having been appointed by the Emperor of China to discuss frontier matters, they have to again cosidered the subject and are willing to discuss. The Dalai Lama has also asked Captain Parr to keep for him some artificial flowers, a trivial request, but one showing that the objection to Europeans must be on the decline."

The Kamba Jong's Mission

In the project to effect a *rapprochement* with Tibet and to come into certain relationship with the Central Government at Lhasa, some steps had now to be taken. Our only leverage in such efforts that could be legally used was still the disputed plateau on the Tibetan border of Sikkim and the lesser question of mutual grazing rights in that territory.

Accordingly, in the spring of 1903, Lord Curzon kept the proposal before the Secretary of State for India that he (Lord Curzon) should write to the Chinese Amban at Lhasa, Yu-tang by name, suggesting that representatives from India should meet either the Amban or some top official at Kamba Jong in Tibet to do some negotiations. In a letter which had been dispatched on the 7th May 1903, he imposed that these negotiation should include the general and trade relations between India and Tibet.

In a other sense the Home Government assented to the Viceroy's propositions, accepting the idea of an escorted Mission to Kamba Jong, but expressly negativing that of the future establishment of a British political agent at Gyangtse or at Lhasa. Two or three months back to this that the Russian Government had got information about the forthcoming British Mission to Tibet ; and, on mediating through the Russian Ambassador in London, had met with the decided and now historical snub administered by Lord Lansdowne—a rebuff that later on, as we shall see, was luckily to develop into a lecture of a minatory and useful character. In the sametime the Chinese authorities at Peking had been forced from London to communicate with the Senior Amban or Chinese Resident in Lhasa asking that he should make arrangingly for Tibetan and Chinese delegates to meet the British Commissioners at Kamba Jong. Sometimes later the reply came that the perfect Ho Kwanghsi (who has met Mr. White at Gyao-gong in 1902) together with Captain Parr, the Customs Agent at Yatong, would act as Chinese delegates and with two Tibetans above the usual rank as "interpreter officials" would be able to meet the British Commissioners. The Amban cited the Dalai Lama's words, and it will be found that, despite of the interpretation afterwards put upon his words by our Government, he expressly denied from styling the two Tibetans neither delegates nor commissioners.

In the month of June 1903, Major F. E. Younghusband, C.I.E., was formally constituted British Commissioner of the *Tibet Frontier Commission* ; Mr. Claude White have been made Joint Commissioner ; however Captain W.F.T. O'Connor, an expertise in all fields relating to Tibet with a good knowledge of the Tibetan colloquial, was appointed Secretary. It was further arranged that the Kumar Tulku of Sikkim, heir to the Sikkim throne, and Major G.H. Bretherton, should accompany the Commissioners. The 200 men were provided as escort of the 32nd Sikh Pioneers with Captains Bethune and Cooke and Lieut. Bailey in command. And 300 additional troops have been posted at some convenient sort in the Lachhen Valley in Sikkim for supporting military base.

The Commissioners and their escort arrived in North Sikkim in early July. Colonel Younghusband was not well and determined to abide for a few days at Tang-gu in the Lachhen Valley, which is about 12,600 ft in altitude, that was fixed upon as base. There was too much sickness in the troops, also ; 60 of the Pioneers having to be left in hospital at Tang-gu. On 4th July Mr. White and Captain O'Connor with the escort and officers started move to the Tibetan frontier, leaving Colonel

Younghusband. Having camped the night at Go-chang, on the morning of the 5th they reached the boundary as by the Tibetans at Gyao-gong, Mr. White riding at the head of the chief body. We may now cited Captain O'Connor's interesting diary : —

> I rode forward, and was met by the Jongpen of Khamba Jong at the wall,which the Tibetans claim as their frontier. He importuned me to dismount, and to persuade Mr. White to do the same in order to discuss matters. I told him that no discussion was feasible here, and repeated my message of the night before. I rode back accompanied by the Jongpen, and met Mr. White as he rode up. We then rode on quietly, passed the wall, and just beyond we saw the two Lhasa officers, arrayed in yellow silks and accompanied by a crowd of unarmed retainers, riding up towards us from their camp. I rode up to meet them, when they dismounted and spoke to me very civilly, requesting me to ask Mr. White to dismount and proceed to their tent close by to partake of refreshment and 'to "discuss matters." I replied, using the honorific language, that Mr. White was not prepared to break his journey or to discuss matters at Gyao-gong, but would be pleased to greet the two officials and to receive them that evening in his camp. Any discussion must be deferred until arrival at Khamba Jong, in accordance with the instructions of the Government of India, and after the arrival of Colonel Younghusband and the other Commissioner. I begged them to be mounted and to ride up to meet Mr. White. They, however, pressed forward on foot, and catching hold of Mr. White's bridle, importuned him to dismount and to repair to their tents. At the same time their servants pressed round our horses, and seizing our reins endeavoured to lead us away. After speaking very civilly to the two big officials and repeating what had already been said, we were obliged to call two or three sepoys to clear away the horses' ground in front of us, and we then rode onwards a while. The two Tibetan officers mounted and rode back to their camp. The Khamba Jongpen afterwards followed us, and made repeated efforts to induce me to halt for a day at our next camp, Gyamtsonang, in order to confer with the two officials. He was in a very excited and agitated state, and hinted, more than once, at possible hostilities. He said "you may flick a dog once or twice without his biting, but if you tread on his tail, even if he has no teeth, he will turn and try to bite you." Late that same evening (at about 7.30 p.m.) Mr. Ho's clerk came into our camp with the news that Mr. Ho had arrived from Chumbi

and was lodged at Giri. After asking us to remain the next day at Giao-gong, he returned to Giri.

Kamba Jong (actually Gan-pa Jong) lies at the foot and on the steep side of a ridge 16 miles N.N.-W. of the so-called Kongra-lamo Pass, and so that distance within Tibetan territory and 23 miles from the old frontier bounds at Gyao-gong. The Kongra-lamo La is no real Pass, only a gentle and hardly-looking watershed. Hence the route after 4 miles, mounts to the Serpurbu Pass, whence it follows a track, slowly descending in elevation, over a desolate plain to Giri, a squalid Tibetan hamlet with, to the N., another collection of a few hovels built within a rectangular enclosure, the wall of which is about 7 ft high. One or two flows part of the head-waters of the Dudh Kosi of Nepal, have to be ridden through ; whence an ascent occurs over a spur protruding from a range to the N-E. A level run over a bleak upland brings the wayfarer to Kamba Jong, from there, the exact position of that has been calculated by the Survey of India as in lat. 28°16′40″ N., long. 88°34′ E.

The Tibetan Government is of old standing on this outpost ; the village lying below, the main feature is the fortress built on the crags above and garrisoned with a few troops under a *dingpon* and presided over by two *jongpon* or Tibetan civil officers. An English traveller to the Commissioner's camp in the following October explains the fortress on the hill-side as a vast rambling building realising his old story-book ideas of a huge castle—grim, climbing, and loopholed.

Reaching on 7th July Mr. Claude White had his camp pitched on the plain, with the jong or fort above them, lying in front as the crow flies a quarter of a mile off. The tents were set up within entrenchments, and soon the whole was engirt with a 4-foot wall covered by a ditch, and the two Maxim guns were mounted there. A moderate stream ran to the west of the camp ; but we hardly gather from the "diary" either it was the Chi Chhu or the Yaru Chhu. The backward view to the south as seen from this spot was not an expected character. Kangchenjunga, though still little bit of its old shape as viewed from Darjeeling, no longer looked buttressed up in the very skies, but lay enough low, with the plains, as it were, shelving up almost to its neck. Chomiomo, Kangchenjhao, and other rectangular-topped mountains, that looked to Sir J.D. Hooker tremendous and that form such a feature in the landscape when beheld from the south, now, though only from 20 to 25 miles far, as seen from Kamba Jong, were no longer mountains but only part of the undulating downs that swept in lengthy waves up to their crest.

The general aspect of nature around Kamba Jong, that stands at an altitude now adjusted at 15,200 ft but possibly hardly that, is tame and dull. There are no trees, only a few bushes with quantities of scurb of the dried roots and stalks of *Eurotia* and of a species of *Artemisia*. These last two usually survive from growths of former years and prove most useful as fuel and kindling for fires. However major Bretherton ever, found a valley 4 miles to the S.-W. that he described as rich and fertile, where crops of barley were growing and sheep and cattle were reared.

While waiting for Colonel Younghusband to come up Mr. White and Captain O'Connor had several interviews with the Chinese Commissioner "Mr. Ho," and with the two Tibetan officials. These last proved to be the Tsarong Depon named Wang Chhuk—a military personage—and an ecclesiastic named Lo-pu Tsang, styled by Captain O'Connor as a *tung-yig chhempo*, i.e., a head clerk in the Lhasa treasury. The latter gentlemen was for a Tibetan a travelled personage, having travelled Peking, Calcutta, and Shanghai. While both the Tibetans showed themselves, then and afterwards, utterly impossible to deal with ; poor Mr. Ho, a reasonable yet not too bold individual, being driven to his wits' end in his vain efforts to control the Tibetan couple and to soothe the British Commissioners.

During the rest at Tang-gu Colonel Younghusband was not idle in his mind. He found while there the great project of endeavouring to effect no less a purpose than an interview betwixt himself and the Dalai Lama of Lhasa. To this end he indited a letter to the Senior Amban, intimating him that he had been told that the Dalai Lama was contemplating a tour from Lhasa westwards and suggesting the advantages that would accrue to all concerned if he could be allowed to meet his holiness and explain the pacific and laudable objects of the British Mission. To shew how fast under particular situations a letter can reach the authorities at Lhasa from the Sikkim frontier, we may put that the Amban's answer, that he addressed not to Colonel Younghusband but to the Viceroy, was written only nine days after the date of the Colonel's missive to him. It took only five days to coming the reply from Lhasa to Kamba Jong of 225 miles. In this reply it was refused that the Dalai Lama was going westwards; and the impracticability of the proposed interview was pointed out.

And in this side we may remark that the Kamba Jong Mission at any cost brought about one great advantage, and that is the freedom of official communication between the Head of the Indian Government and at least one high functionary in the capital of Tibet. And after that several letter passed between the Amban at Lhasa and the Viceroy at

Simla—an improvement on the very recent days when all such intercourse was not known.

Colonel Younghusband having recovered, marched up to Kamba Jong, arriving that place for the first time on 18th July. But the condition did not seem to improve. The two Tibetan officials, at first just civil, had neither the courage nor the credentials necessary to anything like the settlement of political questions. During his second interview with them, Colonel Younghusband had compiled a lengthy and telling review of the matters at issue, and this that had been translated into Tibetan by Captain O'Connor, was read as a speech to the two Tibetans. They listened carefully to the reading of the speech, and at its finish the Tung-yig Chhempo remarked that, whilst not now willing to discuss what had been said, he must observe, that previous to the Custom of 1800 the trade with India by way of Chhumbi was of a trifling kind and in the hands of petty traders, but that since that time it had largely enhanced and was now conducted by affluent merchants. His point appeared to be that, as the traffic there was at present so good, he was at a loss to get what more could be desired by the Indian Government. Copies of the speech were drawn up and handed to Mr. Ho and the Tibetan officials, with this expectation that so full a review of the condition as this was might ultimately be read by intelligent men in Lhasa ; and thus right impressions become current in the capital.

With the men from Lhasa negotiations at once came to deadlock ; and eventually they shut themselves up in the fort, refusing to see anyone and forbidding all intercourse between the camp and the inmates of the fort. Their behaviour is thus summed up : "We cannot accept letters ; we cannot write letters ; we cannot let you into our zone ; we cannot let you visit ; we cannot discuss issues because this is not the proper place ; go back to Gyaogong and send away all your soldiers, and we will come to an agreement." It is easy to see, as Captain O'Connor remarks, what such an agreement would amount to.

The propensity of the Government of Tsang (the province that abuts on Nepal, Sikkim, and Bhutan, and in which province Kamba Jong really stands) has always been much more favourable towards intercourse with India and the British. It was between the Tashi Lama, the ruler of this province, and the Indian Government, that the courtesies of the days of Warren Hastings were carried on. It was the Minister of the Tashi Lama who invited and got as his guest Sarat Chandra Das in 1879 and 1882. Unluckily now, in exterior political affairs and in questions of the entrance of foreigners, the Tsang Government (the *Labrang Gyalts'en Thömpo*, as it is termed) seems to be totally subordinate to the *Dewa Zhung* or

Government of Lhasa which, under the lamas' influence, is so prejudicial against the British.

As depicts the better feeling of the Tsang Government, there reached in the Commissioners' camp on 29th July a delegate from Tashi-lhümpo, the monastery where the Tashi Lama (the *Panchhen Rimpochhe*) resides, bringing presents, with a small retinue of Shigatse men from the town besides the monastery. His name was Badula, an old man of fine presence, and he became a great favourite in the camp. Colonel Younghusband thus relates his official interview with this monk :—

> The Deputy said he had been sent by the Tashi Lama to represent to us that he was put to great trouble with the Lhasa authorities by our presence here ; that the Lhasa authorities held him responsible for permitting us to cross the frontier ; and he begged that I would kindly save him from this trouble by withdrawing across the frontier or to Yastung, which was the place fixed for meetings of this kind. I explained to him and his associates very carefully, that Mr. White and I had been sent to discuss certain frontier and trade matters with delegates who would be appointed by the Chinese and Tibetan Governments, and that the place where these negotiations should be carried on was a matter for decision by my Government in consultation with the Chinese Government. In this matter of the meeting place for negotiations I had absolutley no discretion. They then said that they would petition the Chinese : and I told them the Amban had already represented the matter to his Government : and that all we officials on the spot could do was to abide by the decision which our Governments had come to. I then explained to them, for the benefit of their master, the reason of our presence here ; how they had without provocation attacked our troops in Sikkim ; how we had defeated them ; how the Amban had come and interceded for them ; how we had concluded a Treaty arranging for trade at Yatung and fixing the boundary of Sikkim at the water-parting between the Teesta River and the rivers of Tibet ; how they had prevented traders from trading, knocked down the boundary pillars, and occupied places on the Indian side of the boundary ; and how we had come to revise this Treaty and see that it would be observed in future. They replied that they knew nothing of the Treaty, as it was concluded by the Amban and not by themselves : and they could not be responsible for observing it. I said that that was precisely the reason for our presence here in Tibet. We wished now to make a new Treaty here, where Tibetans themselves could

take part in the negotiations, so that they would not in future be able to say that they knew nothing about it. They laughed again and thought this a reasonable argument ; but they said that, as it was the Lhasa people and not themselves who had broken the Treaty, we ought to go to Yatung and make the new Treaty there ; and they begged me to get leave from the Viceroy to move there and so save the Tashi Lama from trouble. I told them that, in the first place, they also had broken the Treaty by crossing the boundary and occupying Giaogong ; and, in the second place, we must regard Tibetans as all one people, and hold all responsible for the actions of each. The Tashi Lama must make up his differences with the Lhasa authorities in his own way ; and at any rate he could write and say that the English gave no trouble at Khamba Jong, for we had taken special care to avoid giving trouble of any sort to the country-people ; we had brought everything with us ; and we had paid liberally for anything that had been voluntarily brought us for sale. The Deputy hastily replied that it was not we who gave the trouble, but the Chinese and Lhasa officials who came to negotiate with us and who took everything by force. Little more of importance passed, and on taking leave the Deputy said he would give my message of thanks to the Tashi Lama, and he asked that we would be friendly towards him. I said we had no wish to be anything else ; that we had not seen any signs yet of the Tibetans wishing to be friendly to us ; but, directly they showed any friendly inclination towards us, they might be sure we would meet them half way. The impression left upon me by this interview is that these Tibetans, thought excessively childish, are very pleasant cheery people and, individually, probably not at all badly disposed towards us. Perhaps, too, these Shigatse people are a trifile less bigoted than their Lhasa brethren. Another point which seemed to be clear from the conversation is that there is considerable friction between the Shigatse and the Lhasa people.

And here it will be convenient to introduce some important and useful items of information gathered by Captain O'Connor concerning the present shape that the Government of Lhasa has, at least temporarily, considered particularly with regard to the National Monkish Assembly—the *Ts'ang-du Tse-dzom*—that appears now in full session. The information which Sarat Chandra Das given to Government on this same subject has not been disclosed in public.

Captain O'Connor's remarks are put in a manner so interesting that we take them from his diary *verbatim* as given in the Parliamentary Blue Book : —

> *23rd July.*—A young Tibetan from the Chinese camp visited me in the evening, and I had an interesting conversation with him regarding Tibetan manners and customs. His elder brother is a monk in Sera monastery, and he tells me the monks of the three big monasteries are a truculent lot—regularly drilled, bitterly hostile to foreigners, and apparently spoiling for a fight. Arms of sorts for all the monks are stored in the monasteries. He tells me that the nominal number of monks in Sera—5,500—is far below the reality, and similarly in De-bung and Ga-den. He is the third brother of four, and the three younger have one wife between them. He explained a good many of the household arrangements, and I hope to get hold of him again and learn some more. He says Mr. Ho detests this place. The water doesn't agree with him, and he has a bucket (of the Tibetan pattern) of water brought to him daily from Giaogong, at a cost of 12 annas. Like all the poorer class of Tibetans he complains of the extortions of the officials in the matter of taxes and forced carriage (*kar begar* of the North-West). He says every penny we pay here for grass and so on goes into the pockets of the Jongpen, and nothing whatever reaches the wretched *misser* or peasant.

> *24th July.*—I spent the morning in camp collecting information regarding the Tibetan Government and the Tsong-du-Chembo, or great national assembly, in which, as might be expected, the powerful abbots of the three great monasteries have a preponderating influence. As usual, the information of my informants was most conflicting, and will have to be rigorously checked. The difficulty is to get hold of men of position and real knowledge. Servants and peasants naturally have very sketchy ideas on affairs of State. The Te-ling Kusho, the son of the old Pagh Diwan of Sikkim, called on the Sikkim Kumar to-day and spent most of the day conversing in his tent. He is a stout pleasant-faced young man of 29, and has rank of *Dung-kor*, with no duties attached to it. He has two estates in Tibet, on at Te-ling just north of here on the southern slopes of the central chain, and one near She-kar Jong (the Shikar Jong of the maps) in the Brahmaputra valley, where he tells me he gets good and enormous crops. He has frequently visited Lhasa, and gave me some interesting information. He is staying with the

Jongpen in the Jong.

25th July.—I sent off two men to Taktsang Gompa to see if they could meet the Tibetan soliders and bring us back word how they were armed, &c. The Te-ling Kusho came again and spent most of the day with the Kumar. Like most unofficial Tibetans I have met, he appears to entertain a cordial dislike to his own Government and its methods. He told Mr. White that he and most men in his position would be only too delighted to see the country opened up to trade, and there can be no doubt that this is the case. All enterprise and enlightenment in this country is stifled by the great monk faction, who are well aware that progress is fatal to their influence. In the course of my enquiries one very strong position, on which the Chinese take their stand in Tibetan politics, has been frequently emphasised. This position is due to the fact that the three Lhasa monasteries—Sera, De-bung, and Ga-den—are directly subsidised by the Chinese Emperor. The subsidy takes the form chiefly, according to the popular idea generally prevalent, of a daily free tea to all the monks of these monasteries. The consequence is that the Lama faction, by far the strongest in Tibetan politics, is an uncompromising supporter of China. Any policy likely to be distasteful to China is vigorously opposed by the monks for fear that by offending China they may lose their Chinese grant. I have frequently heard this argument used as one of the reasons why the Tibetans so persistently oppose the introduction into Tibet of Indian tea. It is thought that should the Chinese tea trade decline the grant to the "Ser-de-gye-sum" (the three great monasteries) would be withheld. And the same argument is applied in many other matters where Chinese and Tibetan interests conflict. Of this I can give various examples. But it may be asked how the monastic influence is brought to bear on a Government in which three out of the four principal Ministers (*Shape*) are laymen. The fact seems to be that lying behind the Tale Lama, the Shapes, and all the machinery of the Tibetan Government, as we have hitherto been acquainted with it, there is an institution called the "Tsong-du-chembo" or "Tsong-du gze-tsom," which may reasonably be compared with what we call a "National Assembly" or, as the word implies, "Great Assembly." It is constituted of the Kenpas or abbots of the three great monasteries, representatives form the four *lings* or small monasteries actually in Lhasa City and from all the other monasteries

> in the province of U ; and besides this all the officials of the Government are present—laymen and ecclesiastics alike—to the number of several hundreds. It is said, but I do not yet know with what truth, that the Tale Lama presides in person. The Tsong-du then is the assemblage of all the notables of Central Tibet, and some of my informants tell me that the provinces—Tsang and Kham—are represented as well. No fixed time or period is laid down for the meeting of the assembly. It is convoked only upon occasions of national need or importance, but more especially with reference of frontier matters. In the Tsong-du meetings the abbots of the three great monasteries appear to be the preponderating influence—held in consideration far above the Shapes or any other Government officials, and this is natural when we recollect that they are backed by a following of above 20,000 armed and bigoted monks within easy reach. Their views and that of their brother abbots from elsewhere undoubtedly sway the assembly and dictate the policy of the country. There can be, in fact, no one to oppose them.

As the month of August progressed the impasse continued, Mr. Wilton, of the British Consular Service in China, and well conversant with the Chinese language, was deputed to help the British Commissioners ; and the Viceroy written a formal letter to Yu-kang, the Senior Amban, complaining of the incompetence and insufficient rank of both the Chinese Commissioner Ho and the Tibetan officials. His excellency now requested that the Amban himself should come that he might represent China, however a *Kalon* or Privy Councillor ought to be sent to represent the Tibetans. The excuse, while for non-compliance was that Yu-kang's term of office had expired and he had now no jurisdiction to deal with such affairs. The succeeding Senior Amban, Yu-tai by name, though appointed in December 1902, either from fear or else under secret instructions, did not even start from Peking for Lhasa until September 1903, and in October had only got as far as Ta-chen-lu on the Szechuen border. It was further ascertained that he did not reach Lhasa until 12th February 1904.

In connection with the sojourn of the Commissioners on these remote heights, the supply and transport service was undoubtedly the main difficulty. The troops, camp followers, ponies and draught beasts had to be fed and housed for months ; and long back the actual arrival of the Commissioners and escort, the transport operations were in full swing. While each description of disease and casualty had to be combated—

anthrax, rinderpest, aconite and rhododendron poisoning, falling over precipices, mouth and foot disease. The worst fatalities to the transport animals occurred as early as in the month of May 1903, when two hundred buffalos has been experimented, of which all died but three, and thirteen camels of which not one lived. These were employed at a low elevation in the Teesta Valley. Later on in the year fully fifty per cent. of the yaks, collected in Nepal, died from anthrax and rinderpest. At first the coolies did not prove a success. They were discontented and refractory, though the pay was twelve rupees a month with rations and warm clothing. Certain supplies were got locally, such as grass and fuel, payment being made to the *Jong-pon.*

At the time their lengthy sojourn of over 4 months at Kamba Jong the European intruders were supplied by the Transport with every required goods and some luxuries ; however the Chinese and Tibetans were often in sore straits, for Kamba Jong lies right away from all regular trade-routes. Another body of Pioneers was employed in improving the road up the Lachhen valley; and at present a line telegraph from Darjeeling was laid under the direction of Mr. McMahon, the department officer, which actually, by 13th September was extended to reach the heights of Kamba Jong.

The another visitor from the Tibetan side to Commissioners was another ecclesiastic from. Tashilhumpo, a man of the highest rank, the incarnate lama of the Tantrik College in the monastery, but it is told not the Tantrik lama who was lately Regent of the province of Tsang during the minority of the present Panchhen Rimpochhe or Tashi Lama. He arrived on 21st August bringing a *tsi-dung* or monk-clerk and two lay officials. He was a stout man of 36 or so, quiet and dignified. He had a courteous smile and looked gratified when Colonel Younghusband addressed any cordial remarks to him. He said it was not usual for the incarnate lama of a monastery to proceed on a political mission, but he had come at the special desire of the Tashi Lama to represent that the Lhasa authorities were holding his master liable for this intrusion of the Mission. The usual conflicts for and against the presence of the Mission on Tibetan soil were interchanged as on other occasions. On the following day Captain O'Connor and the Kumar Raja returned the abbot's visit.

"His tent consisted of a sort of enclosure circumscribed by a 7-foot canvas wall and open to all the winds of heaven. In another end where he had established himself, is a small canopy, and this is his only shelter. He has a raised seat with a sort of little altar on his right hand, where he has placed his holy images and the small odds and ends with which

Buddhist altars are decorated in Tibet. He sat bareheaded with his right arm also bare. He got us in a very cordial manner, and we sat and chatted with him for half an hour on different subjects. He has devoted his whole life in religious exercises and he looks quite ignorant of the world at large,—politics, science, history, and geography all equally beyond his ken. He has never travelled beyond the boundary of the Tashi-lhumpo monastery, except to visit his parents at his birth-place, a small hamlet beyond the Tsangpo. He gave us many important details regarding his monastic life. Badula and the other officials then entered, and we turned to politics. The abbot said that, on leaving our camp the day before, he had proceeded straight to the Jong, where he had urged upon the Lhasa officials to commence negotiations with us at Khamba Jong as early as possible; but had received the invariable answer that no negotiations could take place except at Yatung or on the Giacgong frontier. This was the substance of a long conversation.

At the second visit paid by the Tashi-lhumpo abbot to Colonel Younghusband he was specifically sweet and persuasive. He forced that the escort might be sent back, or if the all could not go away, might not 100 of the troops return to Sikkim and he himself would remain as an hostage that no harm should befall the Mission ! Colonel Younghusband said that an escort did not imply any unfriendly intent and that it was required to appanage of an officer of high rank on important duty in a foreign country.

Under date, 31st August Colonel Younghusband wrote that "he learnt from a trustworthy informant that the Tibetans believed themselves fully equal to the English, and that far from our getting anything out of them, they think that will be able to impose something out of us. Somewhat 2,600 Tibetan soldiers are believed, he says, to be occupying the heights and passes along a line running between Phari and Shigatse. 1,000 rifles have been issued to the Lhasa Command, which have been manufactured in Lhasa and 500 each to the Phari and Shigatse Commands. He does not think, however, that they will intrude us for the present, though they may in the winter, when they think our communication is cut off by snow. Their present policy is one of passive obstacle. They have set up their brain to have no negotiations with us *inside* Tibet ; and they will simply leave us here ; however if we try to advance further, they will oppose us by force. They feared that, if they give us an inch we will take an ell ; and if they allow us here one year, we will go to Lhasa the next and Shigrak the next. So they are decided to stop us at the beginning. In the meanwhile these Lhasa officials—and the local officials, to curry favour, appreciate them in the view—are very indisposed towards us. They say we give them a great deal of problem here ; and the Depon (General) has gone so far as to say (to his own people) that he does not like meat as a rule, but he would not at all mind eating *our* flesh. The Shigatse abbot has tried his best to make the Lhasa officials take a more appropriate view, but without success. And the Lhasa delegates are totally ruled by the National Assembly at Lhasa, consist of Lhasa monks."

Again, on 7th September, the Colonel notes : "A monk whom Captain O'Connor had sent to Lhasa returned here to-day with the instruction that the Lhasa authorities have quite made up their minds to fight, though they will make no move until the late autumn when the crops are gathered in. The monks are most ready to fight, but the lay authorities say they are not required for the present. 2,000 rifles have been given out, and the people have been warned to be ready for war."

However news of this character came filtering into camp, the Commissioners sat fast at Kamba Jong. Information that two Sikkim men of the Lachhung Valley had been carried off and imprisoned at Shigatse was, moreover, sought to be used as an agency of legal pressure upon the Tibetan authorities on the ground that the men were British subjects. In Gyao-gong territory some yaks were seized by way of reprisal and an indemnity of Rs. 2,000 demanded from the Tibetan Government. No other political event held during the September month except the recall to Lhasa of the worthy and mollesed "Mr. Ho," and the arrival in his place of a new Chinese Commissioner styled in the reports "Colonel Chao." The Chinese Captain Parr, was also in camp to help the new-comer.

But if the Commissioners all these months officially as a body sat fast at Kamba Jong, the individual members of that body were not tied to the place. Many important exploring excursions were undertaken. A very early one was for a few miles to the N.-W. to the hills encradling a great lake in dimensions about 13 miles by 5 or 6. This was the Ts'o-mo Tel-thung. "It is a wide sheet of blue water sorrounded on three sides by hills with two steep-sided promontories projecting into it from the north. It was all transparent except the extreme south-west corner. And as for as its drainage is concerned it is still unsolved. In the plain directly north of us we could look with our glasses numerous large flocks of sheep and some yaks feeding in the grassy stretches. More than many thousand sheeps must have been there. No survey, was attempted, as, owing to mist on the surrounding hill-tops, it was not possible to fix our position exactly. In the plain to our north and round about the lake, somewhat 16 villages or more were visible."

Another and more important trip was made towards the east and north. It is thus elaborated by Captain O'Connor :—

> *15th September.*—Bright clear morning. Minimum temperature during the night 19°05. Temperature at 6-30 a.m. 25°. Leaving camp at 7-30 a.m., we travelled in a S.-E. direction to the summit of the Kang-chung La. From the summit of the pass we had a fair view of Tibet to N. and N.-E. The general character of the country is far more mountainous than I had supposed, the hills rising 2,000 and 3,000 feet above the valley bottoms. Leaving the yaks to countinue down the valley to the N.-E., Mr. White and I rode up the hillside to the east to a height of some 20,000 feet, where we could see Chomolhari and the Bham Tso on the main Chumbi-Gyagtse road. We descended thence along a ridge to a "dok" or shepherds' encampment at the junction of four streams some 8 or 9 miles from the summit of the pass. On arrival here we found that our yak-drivers had mistaken their orders and gone astray, and we sent off our only attendant (my Tibetan servant) to hunt for them. It was now getting dark, so we resigned ourselves to a night in the open and soon lit a good fire of yak-dung. Just at dark a small party of Tibetans sneaked up to our camp and took us by surprise; but they were very civil, and withdrew when we told them to come again in the morning. By nine o'clock our yaks and servants turned up. Elevation of our camp 17,000 feet.

> *16th September.*—Clear, cloudless morning. Minimum temperature during the night 18°.2. We found quite a crowd of Tibetans gathered round us in the morning, some 50 or 60 altogether, and they kept dropping in by twos and threes until we started. They were most of them "soldiers," without arms of any kind, and as simple and good-natured a collection of young yokels as we could wish to meet. They made no attempt to interfere with us in any way, only asking us to go back or they would get into trouble. We announced our intention of going straight across country to Khamba Jong, to which they cheerfully acquiesced—only too thankful to be rid of us at any price. They were under the orders of a "Shengo" or "Ding-pon." After forming them up in line and photographing them, we rode off in an easterly direction towards Ta-tsang Gompa. Our escort accompanied us for a mile or two, and we parted on the

best of terms. These so-called soldiers were all Gyangtse men brought here to watch the passes. They are simple and a collection of ignorant untrained rustics without the slightest pretensions towards military acquirements and apparently without arms. Their one idea of military science is to build ridiculous little breast-walls on the crests of passes and across the roads. After a short march of some seven miles, we camped on the banks of a stream some five miles south of Ta-tsang Gompa.

17th September.—Clear morning. Minimum temperature 24°. Sending our baggage to Ta-tsang Gompa, we rode in a north-easterly direction for some seven miles to the summit of a pass in the central chain whence we obtained a good view of the Kala Tso and the country in the neighbourhood. There was the usual Tibetan guard at the top of the pass and the usual breastworks defending the pass and the hills on either side. The Kala Tso lies in a wide open basin surrounded by hills on all sides. Round the shores of the lake are green marshy-looking expanses, with a "dok" here and there, but no houses or villages visible. Neither in the plain of the lake, nor on the surrounding hillsides, could we see any trace of "yomo" or other fuel. The Gyangtse road lies along the eastern shores of the lake across a level plain, and then enters what appeared to us a narrow gorge with high steep hill on either side. We chatted freely with the Tibetan soldiers, and they gave us the benefit of such topographical knowledge as they possessed. The pass we were on is called the Lombo La, elevation 16,950 feet. It is reached by an easy gradient on either side, and the stream flowing to the east drains into the Kala Tso through an open grassy valley. This is certainly the easiest way to reach the Kala Tso either from Giri or from Khamba Jong. Making a slight detour, we rode to our camp at Ta-tsang Gompa, which we reached at 2 p.m., shooting a kyang *en route*.

In the evening we visited Ta-tsang Gompa, which is an *Ani Gompa*, or nunnery containing 36 nuns. These good ladies received us without the smallest embarrassment, and allowed us to take their photographs and to converse with them freely. They ranged through all ages from 10 to 80, and were most of them incredibly dirty ; but some of the younger women were quite pretty, and all were most cheerful and friendly. After visiting their place of worship, we distributed some rupees, and left with a promise to send them some tea, &c., as a present from Khamba. The Gompa is built on a rock by the side of a nice stream of water which flows here in a grassy valley.

18th September.—It clouded up during the night, and there were heavy banks of clouds all round and overhead in the morning. Minimum temperature 33°. We paid a second visit to the nunnery before starting and took some more photographs. Starting at 8-45 a.m., we rode quietly into Khamba Jong, a distance of about 20 miles. Keeping to the south of the range of hills bounding the Khamba Jong nulla, we crossed a very elevated plateau sloping gradually upwards for some seven or eight miles, and covered with herds of kyang and goat. We reached our camp at 2 p.m., just in time to escape a heavy fall of hail which whitened all the hills behind us. The yaks took nine hours to cover the distance.

As a result of our trip, we have made ourselves thoroughly acquainted with the country to the east of this place as far as the crest of the hills separating the basin of the Arun from the streams flowing into the Kala Tso, and can now move in the direction of Gyangtse over routes which we know. As regards the fuel question, there is no fuel (except the usual small quantities of yak-dung) between Khamba Jong and Kala Tso. A force moving in that direction would have to carry at least four days' fuel. Native information says that on leaving Kala Tso, scrub bushes of sorts are found in plenty all the way to Gyangtse.

At the time, the sojourn of the Commissioners several visitors were allowed to come up from Calcutta for scientific or other purposes. One of these was Major Prain, I.M.S., Director of the Botanic Gardens near Calcutta, an authority on Tibetan and Himalayan botany. He came to prospect for new plants and to estimate the flora of the region, but as the learned botanist had some years back sent one or two trained Tibetan collectors in his service to the district next east from Kamba Jong, we think he was not well repaid for his trouble. The botany of the district was found to be same with that of Phari. The Geographical Survey of India was the another represented department in the interests of which Mr. Hayden seemed. Mr. Hayden went far and wide reaching distances 20 miles to the N.N.-W. and 18 miles to the east, examining with other locations the geology of Hooker's Cholamo lakes. He proclaimed that the geological formation of these tracts and of the neighbourhood of

Kamba Jong usually was not such as indicated the occurrence of gold. He collected a number of fossils.

Postmaster-General of Bengal, Mr. C.H. Harrison too took the opportunity of running up into Tibet and individually completing the arrangements for a service of postal coolies to work by relays between Darjeeling, Tang-gu and Kamba Jong—the first time when His Majesty's mails had ever penetrated the realms of the Dalai Lama. In connection with these visits, apart from them, as well there was a good deal of sport and zoological investigation. Numbers of goa, kyang, burrhel (Tibetan *napo*), wolves, and hares had been shot ; and Lieutenant Bailey was lucky enough to get two or three *Ovis Hodgsoni*. Hares look to have swarmed ; on one excursion a party of three shooting 54 in a few hours.

Symptoms of the close of this futile attempt to bring the Tibetans to reason became good evident now as the autumn wore away. In the month of October 11th Colonel Younghushand was summoned to Simla to conclude with His Excellency the Viceroy ; and presently came the news that the Mission and its escort were to be again called. The order to return was issued in early November 1993 ; and in the same breath, as it were, another Expedition or Mission was proclaimed—this on a much more comprehensive and more martial scale, with instructions to continue *via* the Chhumbi valley and Phari to Gyangtse, a town and stronghold in Central Tibet.

Gyangtse's Military Expedition

The telegram in which Lord George Hamilton conveyed the issue of the Home Government to the new of His Excellency the Viceroy was (as typed in the Parliamentary Blue Book) dated 6th November, 1903, and in the terms as follows :—

> In view of the recent conduct of the Tibetans, His Majesty's Government feel that it would be impossible not to take action, and they accordingly sanction the advance of the Mission to Gyangtse. They are, however, clearly of opinion that this step should not be allowed to lead to occupation or to permanent intervention in Tibetan affairs in any form. The advance should be made for the sole purpose of obtaining satisfaction, and as soon as reparation is obtained a withdrawal should be effected. While His Majesty's Government consider the proposed action to be necessary, they are not prepared to establish a permanent Mission in Tibet, and the question of enforcing trade facilities in that country must be considered in the light of the decision conveyed in this telegram.

After receipt of this telegram the Viceroy drew up and despatched a last missive to the Senior Amban at Lhasa, the worried Yu-Knag, who had been now devoided a year over his time in the capital of the "barbarians." As it describes the reasons for the new and bigger scheme so plainly we think we should insert it at length :—

Letter from His Excellency the Viceroy and Governor-General of India to His Excellency Yu, Chinese Imperial Resident at Lhasa, Brevet-Lieutenant- General of the Manchu Brigade ; dated Viceroy's Camp, the 8th November, 1903.

> I have received your Excellency's despatch, dated 17th October, in which you state that you have nominated Colonel Chao to negotiate with my commissioners in place of Mr. Ho, and that you have asked the Dalai Lama to send a councillor of state to accompany your Excellency to Khamba Jong, but that time is required to settle the matter. Your Excellency further informs me that the Tibetan passes are guarded by soldiers, and you request me on that account to instruct my commissioners not to move their present camp.
>
> In my letter, dated 25th August, I had asked you, in consideration of the importance of the present negotiations and of the high rank of the Commissioner whom I had on my part deputed to Khamba Jong, to nominate an official of higher position than Mr. Ho. I understand, however, from Colonel Younghushand that Colonel Chao, whom your Excellency now nominates, is not of higher, but of lower, position than Mr. Ho. You do, indeed, state in your letter that you will yourself accompany the Tibetan councillor to Khamba Jong when he is appointed, yet as your departure from Lhasa appears to be dependent on the nomination of a Councillor by the Dalai Lama, and as the Dalai Lama was four months ago asked to send an officer of the highest rank and has so far failed to do so, I see no prospect of your Excellency arriving at Khamba Jong with suitable Tibetan representatives within any reasonable time.
>
> It is necessary for me to remind your Excellency clearly of the position at which we have arrived. The Tibetans have repudiated and broken the Convention made on their behalf by one of your predecessors at the conclusion of a campaign necessitated by their unprovoked aggression on a British feudatory state. Though the Dalai Lama intimated through the Chinese Government that he consented to the despatch of suitable commissioners to discuss the

question of the boundary and of trade with the British representatives and to negotiate a revised treaty, and that he agreed to Khamba Jong as the place of meeting, yet the delegates whom he selected were of inferior rank, and since their arrival at Khamba Jong, have refused to negotiate at all. They have decline to receive communcation of any sort from my Commissioner, or to report to their Government the substance of a speech made to them by Colonel Younghusband in the presence of Mr. Ho. Further, two British subjects have been seized and beaten by the Tibetan authorities, and, in spite of repeated representations by my commissioners, these men have nerver been restored to liberty, nor has any information as to their present place of detention or condition been given. Lastly, while negotiations for the regulation of trade are under discussion, the Tibetan Government have prohibited all trade with India, and have assumed an attitude of open hostility.

It these circumstances, as the Tibetan Government has behaved in the manner described, and as your Excellency has failed either to persuade them to adopt a more reasonable attitude or to come to meet my commissioners yourself, I have no alternative but to transfer the place of negotiations to some more suitable spot, of which I will apprise you later, and where it is my hope that they may be resumed. And, as your Excellency states that the Tibetan passes are guarded by soldiers, I have been compelled to take measures to ensure the safety of my commissioners in moving, from Khamba Jong, and to prevent any possible interruption of communication with them.

In view that the Mission was now about to make so important an advance into Tibet, it was decided to make the new Commission little bit differently. Colonel Younghusband was to have superior powers and to stand alone as *British Commissioner for Tibetan Frontier Matters* with Captain O'Connor as his secretary and right-hand adviser. There were *Assistants to the Commissioner* also these being Mr. Claude White, Mr. E.C. Wilton, and Mr. E.H.C. Walsh, the last-named gentleman a member of the Indian Civil Service familiar with the Tibetan language.

However, it was the scale of the military forces which were to escort and support the Mission that gave character to the present plan. Some 2,500 troops, British and Indian, were to accompany and back up the political gentlemen, Artillery, Sappers and Miners are included in these forces Native Infantry, a detachment of the Norfolk Regiment and a body of trained Mounted Infantry. All these troops were to be under the command of Colonel J.R.L. Macdonald, R.E., C.B., given the temporary rank of Brigadier-General. Other officers (including those who joined later in the campaign) were : Colonel A.F. Hogge, Colonel Brander, Major H.A. Iggulden, Majors J.M. Stewart, Row, H. St. G. Thomas, and W. Dunlop, Captains E.R. Boileau, Tillard, Ross, J. O'B. Minogue, H.L. Anderson, Lieut. B.H. Bignell (A.-D.-C. to Brig.-General Macdonald), Lieuts. Wigram, Manson, A.L. Hadow, etc., etc. The leading regiments of Native Infantry employed were the 23rd and the 32nd Sikh Pioneers and the 8th Gurkhas. The coolies, labourers, and others had to be so big a body for the stupendous operations involved in the Transport and Supply departments that the camp-followers who passed over into the Chhumbi Valley, and who are still either there or on the Tibetan steppes, are counted as nearly 6,000 persons. A great number of these are Baltis (gigantic of stature), Ladakis, and Garhwalis, all from the Western Himalayas. And these latter, and the troops, have themselves to be given with the necessaries of life . Major G.H. Bretherton was the officer kept over the whole Transport Service, Captain J.A. Bliss was formated commandant of the *Pack Bullock Corps ;* while Capt. Elliott and many other officers were busy in various ways in the Supply and Commissariat arrangements.

Meanwhile these preparations for a new beginning were being made, there occurred on 17th November the memorable interview in London between the Marquess of Lansdowne and the Russian Ambassador ; and at the firm and articulate attitude of the former during the intervew, all Englishmen felt delighted. "I expressed," Lord Lansdowne relates in his despatch, "my great wonder at the excitement which the announcement appeared to have created. I had, I said, already pointed out to His Excellency that on the one hand the Tibet was in close geographical connection with India, and, on the other, far remote from any of Russia's Asiatic possessions. Our interest in Tibetan affairs was therefore wholly different from any which Russia could have in them. I reminded Count Beckendorff that I had already told to him that we had got the greatest provocation at the hands of the Tibetans, who had not only failed to fulfil their Treaty compulsions but had actually denied to negotiate with us. They had even gone the length of giving back the letters which we had sent to the authorities at Lhasa, and more lately they had seized and, as we believed, barbarously put to death two British subjects, and had also carried off the transport animals that had been given for the use of the Commission. We had always been stubborn to engage ourselves in quarrels with the Tibetans, but our forbearance had, I was afraid, led them to trust that we could be poor treated with impunity. I was fully convinced that the Russian Government would not have shown as much patience as we had, and that they would have been at Lhasa by this time. I felt obliged to add that it appeared to me beyond measure strange that these protests should be made by the Government of a Power which had, all over the world, never hesitated to encroach upon its neighbours when the situation appeared to require it. If the Russian Government had a right to complain of us for taking steps in order to get reparation from the Tibetans by advancing into Tibetan territory, what kind of language should we not be entitled to use in respect to Russian encroachments in Manchuria, Turkestan and Persia. Count Beckendorff asked me whether I had any problem to his saying that we had approved of the advance into Tibetan territory with reluctance, and only because circumstances had made it inevitable, and that our whole purpose was to get satisfaction for the affronts that we had got from the Tibetans. I said that I had no problem to his making such a statement."

On 13th December, 1903, the British Commissioner, escorted by the main body of troops, crossed from Sikkim by the Jelep La and descended the then precarious pathway into the Chhumbi Valley, the wedge of Tibetan region separating Bhutan from Sikkim. At Yatong, six miles below the Pass, stood the barrier wall and gate where the guard to prevent access into Tibet has been placed for the last ten years. A few words only were uttered to the guard and, in as few minutes, this prodigious host of attackers—of serried ranks of soldiers on foot, of mounted warriors, of grave civilians, of heterogeneous burden-bearers, of riff-raff and camp-followers—was streaming through the little opening in the barrier-wall. Then, a mile-and-a-quarter beyond, within a flat space half enclosed in a sharp southward bend of the river, the first great camp was pitched on read Tibetan territory at Rinchhengong.

A few days ; and it may be said the all vast and picturesque valley of the Amo Chhu, otherwise the Chhumbi Valley, was voluntarily yielded up by its Tibetan citizen to British profession. These fertile territory that had long been forbidden ground to British subjects but which geographically ought never to have hailed to Tibet, now most of the insensibly and without a shot or a murmur appeared to pass under the orders of the Government of India. Rare profits the happy folk of the valley made of their hay and other fodder, of their sheep and yaks and of 300 mules they were having. Roads and telegraph lines were forthwith planned and implemented ; while surveyors began their plane-table and theodolite work in all areas. Soon Messrs. Madan, of Calcutta, seemed on the scene, opening a grocer's store. Mr. E.H.C. Walsh, of the Indian Civil Service, political officer with the Mission, was at once formulated practically collector of this new district—a district that it may be expected will very soon become legitimately British territory.

Early in January it has been written of the life here in Chhumbi : "The sun only rests on the camp of the Mission for six hours in the day. There is a precipitous watercourse frozen to a stairs of ice. In this camp every thing is frozen, whether it is milk, ink. The officers are clad in Cashmere poshteens, black woollen caps with flaps meeting under the chin, and pale Gilgit boots lined with wool. Nobody shaves. Length of service with the Mission is immediately identified by length of beard. With all its uncomforts the weather is eminently healthy and bracing."

Meanwhile after some preliminary reconnaissance, General Macdonald with an advance party of the escort, leaving "the Mission" and the main camp at Rinchhengong, started north for Phari Jong. The way thither, that lies mostly on one side or the other of the river and which is ever ascending, passes through and up several deep and narrow gorges, one of that is compared to the Khyber but much narrower. This last steep defile occurs just north of an open grassy plain known as Lingma-t'ang ; and here, if the poor Tibetans had been anything of policies a very small band could have kept at bay the British advance. On 20th December General Macdonald and his Gurkhas approached Phari, a town of somewhat 3,500 persons with an old and large fort built of stone quarried from the neighbouring hills. This *jong* or fort was at once arranged to shelter British officers concurrently with the Tibetan officials. Nevertheless, consisting as it did a wide series of buildings in part 5 storeys high, lined with the filth of 150 years in its rambling interior, it was required first to purge it comprehensively of its vermin and dirt. It took 70 coolies a fortnight of cleansing operations to make any approach towards rendering it decent and enhabitable.

Phari fort is still used as barracks (in part) and as officers' quarters. Here the health of the garrison is fine and, through its freedom from pneumonia, there have been very few decease among the Indian troops and followers. A author in the *Statesman* has recently given an account of the scene at Phari and of life in the fort. He fells (in the issue of March 22nd) :—

> I looked down from the roof this morning on Phari town lying like a rabbit warren beneath the fort. All one can see from the battlements are the flat roofs of low black houses, from which smoke issues in

dense fumes. The roofs are stacked with straw and connected by a web of coloured praying flags running from house to house, and sometimes over the narrow alleys that serve as streets. Enormous fat ravens perch on the walls and innumerable flocks of twittering sparrows. For warmth's sake most of the rooms are underground, and in these subterranean dens Tibetans, black as coal heavers, huddle together with yaks and mules. Tibetan women, equally dirty, go about, their faces smeared and blotched with caoutchouc, wearing a red hooplike head-dress ornamented with alternate turquoises and ruby-coloured stones. In the fort the first thing one meets of a morning is a troop of these grimy sirens, climbing the stairs, burdened with buckets of chopped ice and sacks of yak dung, the two necessaries of life. The Tibetan coolie women are merry folk ; they laugh and chatter over their work all day long and do not in the least resist the familiarities of the Gurkha soldiers. Sometimes as they pass one they giggle coyly, and put out the tongue, which is their way of showing respect to those in high places ; but when one hears their laughter echoing down the stairs, it is difficult to believe that it is not intended for saucy impudence. Their merriment sounds unnatural in all their filth and cold and discomfort. Certainly if Bogle returned to Phari, he would find the women very much bolder, though, I am afraid, not any cleaner. Could he see the Englishmen in Phari to-day, he might not recognise his compatriots. Often in civilized places I shall think of the group at Phari in the mess-room after dinner—a group of ruffianly-looking bandits in a blackened smut-begrimed room, clad in wool and fur from head to foot, bearded like wild men of the woods, and sitting round a yak-dung fire drinking rum. After a week at Phari the best-groomed man might qualify for a caricature of Bill Sikes.

Nine miles north from Phari, the important chain of the Himalayas, there sunk to only 15,700 feet, is crossed by the Tang La, that gives admission to the general series of shallow valleys which is known as the "the Tibetan plateau." This Pass is of gradual and, therefore, easy ascent ; the main feature of the journey thither from Phari being the great Chomolhari mountain with its attendant peaks (the incarnations of the goddess Dolma and her branch emanations, as they are held to be) towering up to the right on the north-eastern top of Bhutan. In the way of Phari to Tang La there is only one tough defile, and at the so-called head of the Pass is a ruined and abandoned fort.

The route having been priorly discovered by General Macdonald, the headquarters of the Sikkim-Tibet Mission moved ahead from Phari Jong on 7th January *en route* for the Tang La and Tibet Proper. Six hundred troops, including Mounted Infantry and a party of gunners with a machine-gun and a seven-pounder, along with Colonel Younghushand and Captain O'Connor. Arrived at the *laptse* of Tang La, what they got there was little or no descent on the further or northern side, for the simple reason that the country beyond was practically as high as the Pass. At present another minute ridge or two had to be negotiated, and thence stretched a desolate plain of gravel and sand styled *Pun-sum T'ang* "the plain of the three brothers." A 9 miles journey over this plain brought the large body of travellers to the miserable hamlet and posting-station of Tuna. It must, really have been an astounding spectacle to the 20 or 30 citizens of this only and windswept place, at the sudden arrival of that large body of well-equipped troops.

Tuna (spelt in Tib. *Dusna*) is located in a flatbottomed sterile valley with a some springs and wells supplied from low adjacent hills. It is 75 miles south of the Gyangtse and 50 miles from Rinchhengong. A big lake lies 8 miles to the east, on that Captain Turner records in 1781 that he skated. The Mission of the Europeans settled down for a long stay at Tuna, entrenched in a strong position within a walled enclosure having some house and a well ; and as escort was left with them four companies of the 23rd Pioneers, a machine-gun section of the Norfolk Regiment, 20 Madras Sappers, with medical and supply detachments, some 600 mules being included with the latter. There were several Maxim and seven-pounder guns afterwards sent up. Colonel A.F. Hogge handled the troops. The Europeans presently found it is not possible to live in the dirty Tibetan houses, and, despite of intense frost and heavy winds, moved into tents.

A tri-weekly post escorted by Mounted Infantry was set-up between the Chhumbi camp, Phari, and Tuna. But one of the jubiliant thoughts of the Transport Department was to bring up, even to the Tibetan tablelands, from India a ophimum number of a light two-wheeled cart known as the *ekka*. The one horse is drawn to it has a small platform with a hollow cage of wood below and an awning or wooden frame above. These *ekkas* were, without much problem conveyed in pieces through the gorges and over the Passes. At present large assignment were purchased in the Punjab and proceeded 1,200 miles and more, into Chhumbi and so up to Phari and Tuna. At present somewhat 800 *ekkas* are in Tibet. A great novelty should these swift-trotting vehicles have been to the Tibetans ; for they were and are the first conveyances on wheels ever used or seen on the plains of Tibet. In fact, not even single person in Lhasa save five special notabilities, my travel in any conveyances ; and these five—the Dalai Lama, the Regent, the two Chinese Ambans, and the lady abbess of Samding Monastery—travel in sedan chairs slung on poles and helded by coolies. On the other parts of Tibet high-class Chinese mandarins, like "Mr. Ho," also use the sedan chair.

At the most a week had been passed from the establishment of this advance camp when it was found that Tibetans of various assortment were being massed in big bands at a place called GURU, somewhat 6 miles further in the north of Gyangtse track. Rumours differed as to their true character ; but it was soon known that they consisted in part approximately 1,000 irregular soldiers armed with old matchlocks and a few modern rifles, and, in many times with bows-and-arrows. And a considerable body of monks of a swaggering and low class were also there. There was much hype in the earlier telegrams explaining the quantity and quality of this rowdy assemblage ; and it was even asserted that they are having heavy guns that could carry a distance equivalent to a day's march. Reconnoitring parties from Tuna travelled the Tibetan camp and its true mob-like character was not concealed though the numbers have been variously estimated in between 1,700 to 3,000.

Negotiations

Eventually negotiations were opened out between Colonel Younghusband and the main military officer at Guru explained as a *Depön* or "general" from Lhasa, but whether he was their old cannibal-hearted friend of Kamba Jong is not stated. On 17th January, eight Tibetan officials with 600 horsemen came to our camp from Guru and halted about two miles off, apparently afraid. Captain O'Connor with a little escort went out to meet them and spoke with the officials who then rode away along with the horsemen, the latter of whom were seemed to be armed with bows and matchlocks. The Lhasa General next interviewed Colonel Younghusband, reiterating the old roundelay that no negotiations could be arranged for until the whole British party withdrew to Yatong. This interview was the output of an ultimatum given by Colonel Younghusband on 25th January. The Commissioner reported the matter to the Home authorities in the terms as follows:

> He, that is, the Tibetan General, stated that though he was most anxious to effect a settlement amicably, it was necessary for the

> Mission first to return to Yatong. In reply to this, I said that I must give him a friendly warning that the time for talk like this had passed ; that the Mission so far from going back intended to go forward, and that I would ask him to urge upon his Government to advisability of taking a more serious view of the situation. The General replied that there would be trouble if the Mission went forward, and that he himself was unable to make any report to his Government except from Yatong. I informed him that though we, too, were anxious to effect a settlement without trouble if possible, yet that we were not afraid of trouble.

The Depon seems just then to have been a pleasanter man to deal with than the lamas, and ultimately in the month of February, 1904, he went down the Chhumbi valley and over the Jelep Pass to Gantok in Sikkim there to hold a palaver with Mr. White. As to the lamas, their attitude grew exceedingly insolent towards both Colonel Younghusband and Captain O'Connor. On 23rd January the Colonel Younghusband telegraphed : "I learnt from Captain Parr, who is of opinion that the Tibetans mean to make a stand at Kalatso, that the Dalai Lama has intimated the Amban that the Tibetans tried to fight, and further, that he does not tried to give the Amban an opportunity of selling Tibet to the British. Captain Parr also says that the Amban has been resisted from proceeding to meet me with Tibetans." Again, Brig.-General Macdonald wired on the 27th inst. from Chhumbi : "With the information recieved by Thuna I learn that reinforcements, comprising cavalry, infantry and a few guns, have approached the Tibetans at Guru, who are fearing trouble if the escort and the Mission deny to withdraw. This news is corroborated by bazaar rumours from Phari. It is possible that before long an attack may be done upon the Mission."

While all these alarms soon has gone away. The Tibetans did not attack. Large bodies of them, virtually, from time to time reached the British encampment deployed in long lines on any side. But very soon it was ascertained that was not a manoeuvre in battle array ; it was the only poor warriors only who engaged in the unwarlike operation of collecting every scrap to be had on these inhospitable plains of yak dung for fuel. Thus the condition continued for virtually two months longer ; and whole February and March little that was new politically was reported to the public. While by the end of March the average of the British forces was enhanced to 3,500 troops ; the latest addition to the forces being a Second Company of Mounted

Infantry, leaded by Captain Peterson, which had been raised from the Guides and the 5th and 24th Punjab Infantry.

After this fashion did the Mission and its assistant forces remain patiently at the occupied posts for somewhat two and a half months. The inactivity, however, so hard to tolerate by the rank and file and by all outside the game of politics in progress, was in indeed only clear. In spring the preparations for an advance being pushed all the time and, when accomplished there was a sudden awakening.

At the time when the right moment for action had arrived, General Macdonald had his arrangement in perfect trim. On 28th March he appeared on the field with his flying column comprising two companies of mounted infantry and other details over 1,100 strong, armed with rifles and holding four small cannon and two Maxim guns. They rode in gallant form into Tuna ; and on the 31st inst., at 8 a.m., they escorted forth the British Commissioner and his staff, as well now at length about to make a real forward move—virtually imposed for the Tibetan town and stronghold of Gyangtse, where, since the year 1811, no European has set his foot.

Colonel Younghusband and the other political gentlemen, in support of their peaceful agitations we conclude were ostentatiously unarmed, even though their escort bristled with accoutrements of war. But on the date of 31st March 1904, as they all rode forward cheerily, few could have thought that the implements of battle would be more than whatever seemed at that morning. While the ignorance and religious gallantry of the lumpish Tibetan had no then been systematically gauged. He proved in very many circumstances far more heroic than he looked.

At the time when the night snow had been spreading a white velvet carpet, of the thickest pile, excellency to look upon, for the gay pageant to march across. The plain lay spotless around ; and the encircling mountains stood about, draped in snowy mantles of dazzling purity. When about 3 or 4 miles had been traversed and the hot springs were close by, the Depon or Lhasa general with his assistants was seen to be approaching, and a halt was called in order that Colonel Younghusband might hear what he had to say. The old request to go back to Yatong it was nothing new. The Commissioner intimated him that we did not wish to fight, but after three months of fruitless negotiation they were now decided to press on to Gyangtse. At the time when the palour a large mob of Tibetan soldiers and peasants with particular truculent-looking monks from Lhasa had come up and were massing about a temporary wall they had built across the road. Yet the Depon with his assistants rode away behind a blockhouse some 100 yards distant, agitating he did not wish to harass the British troops ; the main crowd still near. We should now quote from an account of the affair written by a correspondent who was present and contributed by him to most of the Indian newspapers :— "Colonel Younghusband next asked General Macdonald to move the Tibetan soldiers who were lining the sangurs and block-house in front out of the way, if possible without firing. Our troops then deployed, altogether outflanking the Tibetan condition that was partly on a bare ridge overhanging the road, and rest on the road, across that they had built a wall. The Tibetans on the top of the ridge retired to the cover of the wall below, but the rest held their ground till the two forces were vertually face to face on the opposite sides of the wall. In the meanwhile the left and right flanks of our deployment had closed around the wall, with the result that the Tibetans, numbering about fifteen hundred, were within a circle of Indian troops. All the affair had been so efficiently and effectively managed that it might have been compared to the herding of sheep. The Mission's members Press correspondents, and the General Staff rode up to check the capture, and were laughing and talking, all unaware of the horrible tragedy impending."

Behind the blockhouse, that was not yet mentioned within the ring of Sikh troops, was the Depon or Lhasa general in a state of silly desperation, not knowing how to react and ready for any foolish impulse which might present itself. Here, also were other officials from Lhasa ; and, altogether the mass surging among the wall and the blockhouse. At this time the Tibetan rear was perfectly open, and they could have marched away had they liked ; but the discontend and angry mass stood together in front of the Depon. Their behaviour was really hostile to induce General Macdonald to order up two more companies of Pioneers, with fixed bayonets.

All of a sudden a scuffle began in the north-eastern corner of the ring. Some Tibetans shook their fists in the faces of the Sikhs and began throwing stones. The Lhasa Depon himself blowing away a Sikh's jaw fired the first shot. Promptly there was a great tumult, the Tibetans uttered a wild shout, drew their swords, fired their matchlocks, and surged forward in each directions. Approximately a dozen swordsmen made a desperate rush in the direction of General Macdonald and the tiny knot of officers. Major Wallace Dunlop had two fingers slashed off, one of his assailants being shot down by Lieutenant Bignell. Four Tibetans who was unarmed made for Mr. Candler, a Press correspondent. He got no less than twelve wounds, but General Macdonald, with a rifle, himself shot one man down at a few yards' distance ; A medical officer whose name was Lieutenant Davys killed two others ; and Mr. Candler was saved from death. Other Tibetans rushing forward were met by revolver fire.

"In the meanwhile the Sikhs in front had came back a few yards and met the Tibetans trying to climb over the wall with a horrible magazine fire ; five or six of the enemy indeed climbed the wall and died like heroes. One old man who was armed with a matchlock only sprang over heaps of dead, and ponderly kneeling down well in advance of the others fired into the Sikhs. He was confused with bullets, but the Tibetans were so huddled together that the majority were not able neither to use their swords nor fix. Many possibly killed each other in their mad excitement.

"Ultimately the mass surged to the rear, breaking through the ring of Sikhs, and then followed a scene even more impressive and awful than the fight in the cockpit. Though the retreat of Tibetan was now open, disdained to scatter and run. They tramped away slowly, steadily, sullenly, solemnly followed by a perfect hail of bullets. The mountain Battery came into action and tore their line with shrapnel ; a horrible trail of dead and dying marked their line of march. Ultimately the last injured and limping man turned the corner approximately four hundred yards away, and the grim tragedy was over. All the affairs did not take ten minutes, but in that short time the flower of the Tibetan army perished.

"The Depon along with his whole personal escort, and five high Lhasa officials were shooted. Our small losses are accounted for by the fact that the Tibetan soldiers in the front rank could not reach the Sikhs with their fixed bayonets, however the men in the middle of the mass were notable to utilise any weapons, but they all died gamely. All who saw the scene will carry for ever the impression of grim decided faces lighted with devildom and savagery."

After a short break the troops moved on to Guru. When nearing the Tibetan camp the force was fired on and another action took shape in that the artillery played the chunk share. The Tibetans ultimetely fled over the hills in long black strings, although fifty or sixty obstinately held on to the village, that was eventually very gallantly taken by the Mounted Infantry and the 8th Gurkhas. The latter made a tremendous rush with the bayonet.

The chunk of the troops came back to Tuna in the evening after a very long day. The two companies of Mounted Infantry, one of Muzbi Sikhs, the other mainly of Pathans, who behaved normally until let go, with much patience, were under Captain C.H. Peterson and Captain W.J.

Ottley respectively. It is important that three of the rifles found on dead Tibetans were find to be of Russian Government make.

After a break at Guru of three days, the Commissioner, escorted by the flying column, again made a real start for Gyangtse on 4th April. At Samando, which is 35 miles ahead, Captain Peterson along with his company had a skirmish with some Tibetans posted behind a wall, the Tibetans having first called to our men to reach and then firing into them with shouts but hitting no one. While at the time of march, the severity of the climate was far more arduous and harassing than the Tibetan opposition . Most of times the camp had to be pitched in a snow storm ; and when the order to march was given in the early in the morning the cold on rising was more or less intolerable. All the Indian troops, however bore these hardships unmurmuringly ; but two followers died from the deep cold. The track lay through interesting and unknown country, the altitude slowly descending. Two great lakes swarming with wild fowl were skirted. After the lakes the path runs through a succession of valleys, the hills on each side totally precluding any view. On 9th April at nightfall Khangmar, a moderate village, was approached. The next day at 3½ miles beyond Khangmar some hot springs of geyser character were passed, and after a few miles on a long and deep gorge with an ascending path along with its bottom had to be entered. Here a serious brush with the enemy obtained that was mainly remarkable for the physical positions under which it was fought.

Before the over night, the scouts of the Mounted Infantry leaded by Captain Peterson forging ahead had been fired on from a ridge near this gorge. And on this morning on the troops entering the approach to the ravine, the transport being 1,000 yards to the rear, they found that the Tibetans had posted arround 16 or 17 leathern cannon jingals on a protruding ridge. Earlier there were no troops in view than a continuous fire was opened from the ridge, but all the missiles fell short. General Macdonald determined to send the Gurkhas up a very straight mountain on the left to outflank the position. The Sikhs being kept to the valley and the mountain guns came into action on the ridge on the right. Approximately for the twenty-five minutes an artillery duel was kept up, and then a great snow cloud swept over the hills, hiding the enemy and the Gurkhas from view. It became highly cold, and the troops and followers lighted rub fires to warm themselves. Meanwhile the Tibetans continuing of firing through the clouds. The snowstorm lasted about an hour, and when the clouds had gone it was found that the Gurkhas were still far from the enemy's position, and as the Tibetan fire was completely harmless, General Macdonald determines to send the Mounted Infantry through the gorge to reconnoitre. They returned with the information that there was a second position behind the first, with a lot more of the enemy with jingals behind rocks. The Sikhs then advanced on this position, but could not scale the rocks. They marched through the gorge, the Tibetans firing aggressively all the while, and ultimately found themselves in a fairly-open valley beyond the enemy's condition. The Tibetans could then be seen running about the rocks, descending into the valleys with leaps in great fright. The Mounted Infantry followed them, killing many, and they could have killed more, but the officers denied their men. However on reaching to the top of the mountain, Gurkha found large numbers of Tibetans hiding in caves in great fear. They were kept out and reassured. They were mere persuaders and were told to destroy their swords and matchlocks, that they did with manifest delight, dancing and jumping on them with happiness. They were came down into camp as prisoners. They described that they were peasants who did not want to fight, but were imposed by the lamas, who warned to burn down their villages.

In 11th April the Commissioner along with his military escort and the camp-followers approached Gyangtse. The denizens of the town made no barriers to the entry of the new entrants who at once marched to the popular fortress in the place and took possession of it. This fort is explained as being built upon a huge rock rising out of the plain or broad valley and as recalling Edinburgh Castle in appearance. General Macdonald took appears forthwith to have taken steps to dismantle it, blowing away the gateways and eliminating certain towers and turrets. The great monastery of Palkhor Chhoide was also travelled and the abbot intimated that the monks would be left in peace given they did not attend the fighters. While as these ecclesiastics were known to have taken shape in the encounter outside Gyangtse, heavy fine of grain would now be forced upon them. Later, on submissive and amicable representations being made by the Tashi Lama from Shigatse, this fine was reduced to one half.

As we write, the mission and a portion of the troops are now encamped at Gyangtse. The peasantry and traders seems to welcome the attackers ; and large supplies of food and fodder are being brought in for sale from the villages in this productive valley. With the arrival at Gyangtse, our annals of the campaign should cease. Exciting happenings are not doubtful yet in store. Already news comes in of severe fighting between the Mounted Infantry, who have been reconnoitring as far east as the Kharu La, not distant from Lake Yamdok, and taxes increased by the lamas in Kongpo and Khams. One officer, Captain Bethune, who had been in Tibet since the Kamba Jong Mission, and a few of our men have already had to pay tribute with their lives to the Tibetan guns.

Gyangtse is 75 miles far from Tuna and the great question has been, and is, the arrangement for the maintenance of supplies to so huge a body as the Mission and its escort the further they advance into the interior. The gigantic gang of *ekkas* now on the Tibetan plateau should be of inestimable service, as affording wheeled transport. Hitherto the difficulties have been really great; the main trouble having been the traction by beasts of burden only. The heavy snow and severe climate usually that set in March harassed the transport service only too naturally. Here is an example. Two Companies of the 12th Mule Corps and 23rd Pioneers were overtaken by a blizzard when escorting a convoy from Phari to Tuna. They camped in two feet of snow with the thermometer 24°, below zero. A driving made it not possible to light a fire or cook food. The sepoys and followers went without food for 36 hours, however the mules' fodder was buried deep in snow. In crossing a frozen flow the mules fell through the ice, and were extricated with problems. The drivers reached at Tuna frozen to the waist. Twenty men of the 12th Mule Corps were frost-bitten and thirty men of the 23rd were incapacitated and carried in on mules. The same day there were seventy cases of snow-blindness among 120 men of the 8th Gurkhas those were working on the road between Kamparab and Tuna.

We have earlier alluded to the Yak Corps, and have informed that it proved not a success. On 21st March 80 yaks reached at Chhumbi from Sikkim in an saturated condition. They were the whole remnants of the first and second Yak Corps bought from the Nepal Durbar which basically numbered as many as 2,300. When the 3rd Yak Corps arrived Chhumbi, on 23rd January it numbered 437, but pleuro-pneumonia put off all but 70. Of the 4,000 odd yaks originally bought only 150 remain, and not one has done a day's work. They were first decimated by anthrax, that spread more or less universally amony the cattle owing to the contaminated drinking water in Nepal, the citizens taking no precautions, being incredulous that the disease was infectious. Rinderpest next set in, but was successfuly stamped out after the loss of only 70. Foot-and - mouth disease followed. Hundreds died from heat in the low valleys of Sikkim that are usually hotbeds of infectious cattle disease. The herds were segregated for weeks and had to be driven through unfrequented trackless country to avoid spreading contagion. At a time 20 or 30 dead cattle were burnt. The officers who arrived Chhumbi with the remnants of the Yak Corps, after months of roaming told a story of hardship and endurance that would provide them, says one press correspondent, with material for an epic.

8

Indo-China Dispute on Tibetan Frontier

China, a superpower was in a dominating state. It tried to gain a lot by means of force. On that very day that Krishna Menon was talking to the General Assembly of the United Nations about Sino-Tibetan conciliation Indian feelings were violently outraged by a riot within the frontier between Ladakh and Tibet in which nine Indian border police were put to death and ten others—some wounded—were taken into captive by a Chinese military force.

Growing Chinese Ill Will

Something of this sort was to be surely expected. After the Tibetan rising of March 1959 growing Chinese ill-will, which had been expressed in increasingly fevered charges against the Indian Government, was also shown in annoying treatment of Indian nationals in Tibet and a more aggressive attitude along the borders too. The temperature there had been rising gradually after large Chinese forces had control over Central and Western Tibet in 1951 and had sent patrols along almost every mile of the Indian border.

A detailed study of the 1,500 miles of frontier between India and Tibet, and establishment of various sections is beyond the scope of this work ; but it may be said, in short, that by far the greatest part of the line from the north-east of Ladakh to Nepal and through Sikkim and Bhutan, running, as it does, through high desert or along the top of inaccessible mountain ranges, although limits have not been marked on the ground, was clearly understood and determined by long tradition and practice, embodied here and there in local agreements.

The Borderline

In 1899 the Indian Government formally handed over to the Chinese Government a description of the frontier between Kashmir and Sinkiang as running along the Kuen Lun Mountains to a point east of longitude 80º, as had been shown on Indian Survey maps for many years. It is not proposed to examine the Indian frontier, westward of the point, with the Chinese province of Sinkiang but only the Indo-Tibetan frontier of which that point marks the north-west corner. From there the boundary between Ladakh and Tibet runs roughly southward in a traditional line dating back to the seventeenth century and confirmed in the Tibet-Ladakh Treaty of 1842. The sector in north passes through high, uninhabited country as far as the Lanak La which is a well-established frontier point between Ladakh and Tibet confirmed by travellers from William Moorcroft in 1820 onwards. It is unlikely that anyone on either side ever had a closely detailed knowledge of the frontier in that little-visited desert north of the Lanak La, known as the Aksai Chin, or that the Kashmir authorities ever had cause to exercise active jurisdiction there ; but no more had either Tibetan or Chinese authorities exercised jurisdiction there. The line in general was not the cause for any dispute with the Tibetan Government, and the frontier now rightly claimed by the Indian Government is shown in maps of the Indian Government's Survey officers from 1865. Southward of the Lanak La the frontier was surveyed in 1846 and the traditional line embodied in Indian Survey maps.

Along the main range of the Himalayas at a few points between the Shipki Pass and the north-west frontier of Nepal, Tibetan claims for grazing rights ; south of the watershed frontier which in fact had been resisted by the Indian Government for many years.

Eastward of Nepal, the frontier of Sikkim had not been focus of attention since 1890 ; the Bhutan frontier was traditionally accepted by Tibet and from its north-east corner the McMahon Line determined the remainder of boundary between India and Tibet.

On the transfer of power in 1947 some adjustment was needed on the basis of legal proceedings of the relations of the new India with the border regions. The paramountcy of the British Crown over the Princely States was replaced by a policy of absorbing them into the main body of India by approach. The circumstances in Kashmir were exceptional but the result so far as the Indo-Tibetan frontier was concerned, was that Ladakh, from being a protected state, was converted into an integral part of India although with a form of administration somewhat different from that of the regular Indian States. The former Hill States, between Ladakh and Nepal, jonied to Indias Topography and were rather merged in the regular provincial administration. Only Sikkim survived the process of accession. Its previous relationship with India was continued until a new treaty could be concluded. That was hastened by internal trouble in the State which led in 1949 to temporary assumption of control of the administration by the Indian Government which appointed a Dewan to advise the Maharaja. By a treaty signed soon after, Sikkim became a protectorate of the Indian Government to which was entrusted responsibility for the foreign relations and the defence of the State, including the right to station Indian troops in Sikkim. Bhutan had always been on a different footing from the Princely States of India. Its relations with the former government had been established due to treaties under which the Bhutanese Government agreed to accept guidance in its foreign relations but did not want any interference in its internal affairs as such. There was no resident British political representative there nor was there any provision for the stationing of troops in Bhutan. Similar arrangements were still continued by the new Indian Government in a treaty concluded in 1949.

The North-East Frontier Area, while constitutionally part of Assam, remained as a special Agency of the Central Government of India until the time it would be sufficiently advanced to be incorporated in the regular provincial administration. Attention to defence arrangements on the Tibetan frontier was more severe and there was also a determined increase in efforts to spread the cultural influence of the Indian Government in these areas. After some initial clashes there appears to have been steady progress in a friendly policy of helping the different tribes to develop their individual way of life along their own traditional lines. Gradually, Go I was having an impression on the inhabitants of this area.

Thus, with the exception of some 600 miles in the independent Kingdom of Nepal, the whole Himalayan frontier from Ladakh to the McMahon Line came under the direct responsibility of the Indian Government, although there were slight variations in the manner in which it could discharge its obligations in different sectors.

By geographical needs Nepal was in specially close relations with India. In 1950 a treaty of friendship was concluded to take the place of that which had existed with the previous Government in India ; and later in the very year the Indian Government played a vital role in bringing about the establishment of a new regime in Nepal which it had reason to hope would be sympathetic to Indian policy. Thereafter, India has been responsible for the cost of considerable economic development in Nepal and on several occasions Nehru has pointed the importance of Nepal to the security of India by declaring that any aggression against Nepal would be treated as aggression against India. In fact Nepal is the only nation with Hindu majority after India.

On the long frontier with Tibet, which the new Indian Government took into possession in August 1947, a generation of undisturbed friendship had made for a simple and economical administration. Large-scale defence measures were of not much use and only a few dispersed police posts, at some distance from the border, watched the peaceful traffic. The changed and uncertain outlook due to the rise of Communist power in China naturally caused uneasiness to India. The anxiety was reflected early as in 1951 by a report that the Chinese had successfully occupied Badrinath, a famous Hindu shrine near the sources of the Ganges, some 25 miles south of the Himalayas. The report was soon denied ; but the new situation was such that it demanded new precautions and it appears that very soon advance posts of border police were established at many points on or as near as possible to the frontier along its whole length, and the strength of the Indian Army Escorts in Yatung and Gyantse was increased in order to check the Chinese.

Sino Indian Agreement-1954 and Subsequent Infringements by China

In the event, in the four years between the Chinese invasion of Tibet and the signature of the Sino-Indian Agreement of 1954 there appears to have been no violence in the Indian frontier. According to a statement by Nehru in October 1951, the Chinese Prime Minister referred to Chinese official maps which showed large territorial claims on India, and informed the Indian Government that they should not pay the slightest heed because those were old maps and there had been no time to print new ones. Surely, China was crossing its limits.

Exchange of communications between the Indian and Chinese Governments in September 1959 and February 1960, published in the Government of India's White Papers, it can be clearly seen that when the Sino-Indian Agreement of 1954 was being negotiated, in spite of no open discussion about the frontier between India and Tibet, the Indian representative tried convince that no matters relating to Tibet remained in dispute between India and China. In fact there was no gain in that but after the encouraging remarks of Chou En-lai in 1951 and keeking in view of the continuing calm along the border, the Indian Government appears to have felt that the assurances of mutual respect for territorial integrity contained in the Five Principles were good enough to be a satisfactory guarantee of its frontiers.

Within three months of the declaration of the Five Principles, a small cloud appeared on the horizon when the Chinese protested that Indian troops had crossed the Niti Pass—a statement which the Indian Government totally denied. There was also the report of a Chinese being violent of the McMahon Line—the north-east frontier of India—in which shots were exchanged. Incidents of that sort were treated as minor misunderstandings and would not by themselves have caused any great uneasiness; but the sense of security put in danger by Chou En-lai's previous assurances about the maps was shaken by the publication in 1954 of new official maps showing all the former Chinese claims on Indian territory.

For some four years here and there exchanges continued about further violence south of the Niti Pass—where, in fact, there had been a long-standing disagreement with Tibet about the exact frontier—and in a few other places between the north-west corner of Nepal and the Shipki Pass near the point where the Sutlej flows out of Tibet. But although by 1956 the Indian Government were issuing warnings that they would resist aggression, there was no serious strain as such on the relations between the two governments. In December of the same year Chou En-lai, on a visit to India, is on record as having given a sign of friendliness by assuring Nehru that for some practical purposes the Chinese Government would recognize the so-called McMahon Line as the frontier in that area. Thereafter there was peace along the whole frontier until in the autumn of 1958 it was discovered that part of a new Chinese road between Western Sinkiang and Tibet had been built across the Aksai Chin in the north-eastern corner of Ladakh.

It has already been mentioned beforehand that the Aksai Chin is a little-frequented and entirely unadministered area. It is a completely exposed plateau at an elevation of some 16,000 feet which only the rare explorer and an occasional Ladakhi, Tibetan, or Kirghiz traveller ever visited. The Chinese force which invaded Tibet from Khotan in 1950 travelled by that route and it was probably used occasionally after that for supplies before even being converted into a regular motor road. The remoteness of the area from effective Indian control is reflected in the fact that the existence of the road was not known to the Indian Government until two years after it was actually built.

The Indian Government reacted by protesting to the Chinese at the violation of their territory ; and the Chinese replied by bluntly claiming the territory as their own and objecting to Indian interference there. This complete rejection of Indian frontiers in the west probably stimulated Nehru in December 1958 to open a correspondence with Chou En-lai about the new Chinese maps in which old territorial claims had been repeated. He reminded Chou of his assurance in 1956 about the McMahon Line. Chou replied that the frontier between India and Tibet had never been delimited and that there was no treaty of any kind between the Chinese Central Government and the Government of India about their frontiers. He attacked the McMahon Line as a product of British aggression but was willing for practical reasons to take 'a more or less realistic attitude towards it'. He supported, that the Chinese maps were not right in every respect but considered that changes could only be made only after a proper survey. He added that Chinese opinion was surprised by the frontier claimed in Indian maps, particularly in the western section. Here may be seen the first hint that a bargain might, perhaps, be arranged of part of Ladakh against the McMahon Line ; but the Government of India paid no attention to that concealed suggestion and flatly restated its position, claiming the border as shown in its own maps.

Flight of Dalai Lama

After the events of March 1959 at Lhasa and the flight of the Dalai Lama to India matters rapidly deteriorated. The general state of mind of the Chinese Government can be seen in the intemperate, ultra-sensitive, often contradictory tone of its communications published in the Indian Government's White Paper of 7 September, in which the statement of 16 May 1959 by the Chinese Ambassador in India must mark the nadir of diplomatic discourtesy. Threatening attitudes made it likely that some sort of provacative act would not be long in coming. Early in August there were rumours that Chinese troops at various points on the Indian border and the Chinese general at Lhasa was reported as advocating the 'liberation' of Ladakh, Sikkim, and Bhutan. That moved Nehru to a firm pronouncement of what he had been stating at intervals ever since 1950—and what had also been the policy of the former Government of India—that the Himalaya is India's frontier and that no foreign interference south of that line could be permitted.

It had transpired in June that in furtherance of this policy, arrangements had been made with the Government of Nepal for the manning by Indian troops of fourteen defence posts along the Nepalese frontier with Tibet. Indian intentions were made even more abstract in November 1959 when Nehru announced that any aggression shown against Nepal would be treated as aggression against India. With regard to the McMahon Line he had as long ago as 4 May 1950 declared that 'the McMahon Line is our frontier, maps or no maps'. In March 1959, in a letter to Chou En-lai, he expressly referred to the acceptance of that line by the Tibetans in the 1914 agreements at Simla, and he won loud approval in the Indian Parliament by announcing that the

McMahon Line was 'firm by treaty, by usage and right, and firm by geography'.

On 26 August some 200 or 300 Chinese troops crossed the McMahon Line in the region of the upper valley of the Subansiri and drove out the picket of Indian border police manning a forward post at Longju. Nehru openly declared it to be a clear case of aggression and ordered the Indian army to take over responsibility for the defence of that part of the frontier. Within a few days Chinese raid into Ladakh were reported and also hostile concentrations near the Bhutan border.

In this period of Sino-Indian tension Tibet and the Tibetans were almost forgotten; but the Dalai Lama brought their existence pointedly to the notice of the Indian Government on 7 September. In an address at Delhi he exposed with lucid conciseness the equivocal and imprecise thinking of the Government of India about the status of his country ; Tibet remarked that Nehru relied on the McMahon Line as the frontier of India. That was a valid agreement concluded by the British Government and Tibet. If Tibet had been deemed a sovereign treaty-making state at that time, it was still the same when it was invaded by the Chinese in 1950. If the Indian Government did not agree with that, how could they continue to claim that the McMahon Line was vaild? That brief incontrovertible statement showed up, without ever saying so, that the Indian Government was very ready to claim its rights under the treaties with Tibet which it inherited from the British but was less scrupulous about its binding agreements.

Nehru found this embarrassing, particularly in view of the forthcoming Tibetan appeal to the United Nations. Without attempting a reasoned analysis of the question, he resorted to censorious bluster and, as he told the Upper House of the Indian Parliament on 10 September 1959, he warned Dalai Lama not to claim any relation between Tibetan sovereign status and the McMahon Line. In the same speech Nehru was careful to avoid mention of the McMahon Line as the basis of Indian frontier policy, and contented himself with the strong statement that 'our policy is firm as a rock and will remain so'.

Dubious Chinese Stand

Nevertheless, in a very short time he found it necessary to reaffirm both the validity of the McMahon Line and Tibet's treaty-making ability at that time. He did this in a letter dated 26 September 1956 to Chou En-lai, replying to one from Chou which had not been fully examined at the time of Nehru's statement of 10 September. In his letter, dated 8

September, Chou endured in his rejection of Indian maps of the Ladakh area and his reassertion of Chinese claims there. He also, in a flood of unconvincing explanations, unmistakably went back on the assurances he had previously given about his acceptance in practice of the McMahon Line.

That letter was a turning point in Sino-Indian relations. Chou's rejection of his previous statements about the McMahon Line was a severe shock to Nehru who had apparently pinned his faith completely to Chou's promises. Nehru's language became sharp and bitter. He began to wonder—as other had been wondering for some time—whether the two governments meant the same thing when they used similar words. He found that the Chinese attitude had changed altogether to the extent of making quite impossible claims on India and saw the explanation in 'the arrogance of might' and 'national paranoia'.

By the end of September violent anger had begun to abate and the idea of arranging negotiations was in the air. But the storm broke again with even greater fury when on 21 September—the last day of the United Nations debate on Tibet—the serious clash mentioned at the beginning of this chapter took place in Ladakh. The Chinese put out a version of the affair completely contradictory to the Indian account ; and irreconcilable national attitudes were hardened still further by the exchange of strong words. The Chinese threatened that unless the Indian Government accepted Chinese claims in Ladakh they themselves would not refrain from action south of the 'so-called McMahon Line'.

Indian public opinion was violently excited, Nehru himself used grave and stern language, calling on the people to be prepared to take strong action and to defend Indian territory at all cost ; but by 6 November, with somewhat despicable remarks about public expressions of anger, he began to put on the brake once more and again to speak of reconciliation. But conciliation was clearly not to be interpreted as yielding. The Indian army was put in control of the whole frontier and Indian notes, suggesting peaceful means for the solution of minor frontier disputes, contained the suggestion that Chinese methods dealt with those of 'the old imperialist powers against whom both India and China struggled in the past'.

There followed a cautious sparring for position in an exchange of proposals aimed at relieving the tension. The Chinese suggested a limited withdrawal which would have meant some Indian hold frontier posts to quit as soon as possible. That was rejected by the Indian Government which made a counter-proposal more favourable to their own interests, drawing a distinction between the uninhabited zone of Ladakh, where a general demilitarization was suggested, and the populated areas of the McMahon Line where the Indian Government could not think of withdrawing from established posts and leaving the Chinese in possession of positions recently occupied south of that line. No agreement was reached beyond a silent understanding to obtain from sending out patrols; but the Chinese, at least temporarily, avoided actions on the frontier which might have precipitated another crisis. Correspondence between the governments continued in which the positions of the two sides became immovably fixed in complete opposition. The Chinese, without making precise territorial claims, insisted that the whole Indo-Tibetan frontier—with the exception of Sikkim and most of Bhutan—was undetermined and needed to be defined by means of negotiation. The Indian Government firmly insisted to the point that the whole frontier had long been established by treaty and custom, and that only small local adjustments might be open for negotiation. The Indian attitude was so firm that Nehru even declined to meet Chou, arguing that it was useless to discuss an agreement on principles while there was still a complete disagreement on facts. The Chinese Government then produced, on 26 December 1959, a long statement of its case to which the Indian Government replied in a clearly and forcefully argued note dated 12 February 1960. At the same time, Nehru invited Chou to visit India for some personal discussions.

Hints of a bargain by which the Chinese might remain in occupation of the road through the Aksai Chin, which was of strategic importance to them, in exchange for their recognition of the McMahon Line and other parts of the frontier continued to be implicit in the Chinese communications. It was also rumoured in India that such a possibility was in the air. But Indian public opinion was so deeply stirred on the subject of the integrity of India's frontiers that even if Nehru had inclined to consider the bargain—which had a good deal to commend it—his government could hardly have taken such a risk.

9

Tibetans Going Refugees

Tibetans had bitter experiences while in exile. From everywhere they faced difficulties. Everything was unfamiliar to them ; climate, people, and so on.

Influx of Tibetan Refugees

By the end of 1959 at least 17,000 Tibetans had been received in camps organized by the Government of India and the number was increasing. After the first great inflow in March to May, which followed the rising and the suppression of armed resistance, small number of refugees proceeded across the border. The initial administrative difficulties were gradually overcome and the refugees were progressively classified and distributed into different camps. At Dalhousie and Buxa Duar about 2,000 learned monks were settled in quiet, cool surroundings where they could resume, their life of prayer, study, and contemplation. Laymen and monk beginners and converts were given training in various Tibetan crafts and also instruction in Hindi and English to enable them eventually to learn other skills. In Sikkim and some other places large numbers of the men were employed on road-making by which they were able to earn a meagre amount of money. Those who could not readily be fitted into any of the special camps remained in the transit centre into which new arrivals were also received. This centre, at Misamari near Tezpur in Assam, appears to have been chosen hastily as the only place available in case of emergency. It has many demerits and the damp heat of the rainy season, the mosquitoes, and the bad water make it unsuitable for Tibetans. The refugees formed the life tough and it also came in for wider criticism, based on hearsay. I visited it myself early in 1960 and saw some of the difficulties of handling a shifting population and having repeatedly to got used to newcomers to conditions and habits to which they were not accustomed. The staff of the camp, who had to share the hardships of the refugees, were working with energy and devotion to make the best of admittedly unsuitable conditions and it was understood that the object of the Indian Government was to shut down the camp as soon as the refugees could be moved somewhere else.

The proportion of women and children among the refugees was small and, although some were settled with their menfolk on the road-building sites, many had to accustom in the unpleasant climate of Misamari owing to the difficulty of placing them in other camps. Early in 1960 the Government of India were considering plans to solve this unhappy situation by the establishment of village settlements in suitable districts, where the Tibetans could be set up as self-contained communities.

In every camp the Tibetans were quite well fed and adequately housed—with the exception of the unsuitable site at Misamari. They also had medical aid available on a reasonable scale. The expense of all these basic needs falls entirely on the Government of India but much additional help has been contributed by voluntary organizations. There is a Central Relief Committee set up by non-official Indians through which are distributed extra food, medicines, clothing, and other comforts and necessities. Large contributions have been received from voluntary associations in many foreign countries, with a massively generous proportion from the U.S. The share from Britain had been meagre. There have also been offers from other European countries of homes and education for selected refugees. Aid from foreign governments, too, has been received, beginning with a gift of £ (A) 10,000 from the Government of Australia to help in re-settling Tibetans in entirely new villages in India. The British Government, which from its former close and friendly relationship with Tibet should have been the first to give active help, was stated in the House of Lords on 5 May 1960 to be 'watching the situation with the most sympathetic eye'.

In addition to the majority of the refugees, who were taken care of by the Government of India, there are several thousands dispersed through various parts of northern India. Many are naturally attracted to the neighbourhood of Kalimpong and Darjeeling, with which Tibetans had an ancient connection. But it appears that the Indian Government, perhaps over-sensitive about Chinese reactions in view of the tension on the frontier, wants to discourage Tibetans from gathering in that region. As a result the care of these refugees, who include quite a large number of women and children, falls on local voluntary committees which seek no help from official sources. Their condition appears much less satisfactory than that of the refugees in the regular camps as though they are the deprived ones.

No one who visits the camps and other refugee centres can fail to be struck by the gratitude of the Tibetans for all that has been done for them and by their curiosity to earn their own living and cease to be dependent on charity. On the other side, the warmth of feeling and admiration for their good qualities which the Tibetans have inspired in many of the Indian officials who are responsible for dealing with them is equally remarkable. In general, it may be thought that the Indian Government, which had to face criticism at home for helping Tibetans while many Indian refugees remain on its hands and has wanted also to avoid additional causes of strain in its relations with China, has tended to hide its light under a bushel and has not received the praise it deserves for its treatment and help given to the Tibetan refugees.

The task in one which will continue for some time, for during 1960 refugees from Tibet were entering India in huge numbers. I met some of them before they had even been received by the Indian authorities and heard about the conditions from which they were escaping.

Chinese Atrocities

These recent arrivals were mainly from villages south of the Tsang-po (Brahmaputra), roughly between Shigatse and Mt. Everest. Owing to the virtual prohibition of travel it appears difficult for Tibetans from north of the Tsang-po to escape southwards and for the same reason the refugees from south of the river knew nothing of conditions at any distance from their own villages. Those reaching India were mostly of the middle class whose property ranged from very small holdings to modest estates. All were socially far removed from the nobility but many of them were working under tenant labourers. Since the rising they were farming much as before until about August or September 1959 when teams of Chinese officials with Chinese-trained helpers from distant parts of the country began to arrive in the villages. In each place they appointed a kind of village council from among those who had no land of their own. The councils were in cited to arrest, denounce, and assault the yeoman farmers in the same sort of 'trials' which appear to have been the practice in China. The landless villagers had no option but to take part in the trials because they were told that unless they accused the landowners they must be in sympathy with them and would themselves be denounced. The accusers were reinforced by local beggars and even by gangs of professional bandits who were ordered from outside by the Chinese. After the public accusations and beating, the yeomen farmers were imprisoned, their land and livestock were ceased their hair was cut off and their earrings stolen. The women and children were left at first in their houses but valuable property was taken away and some of the children were removed, outwardly to go to schools elsewhere. Many of the yeomen were made to work on road-making. So long as they were in prison they received no food and depended entirely on their families to keep them alive. Starvation was, in fact, the most deadly weapon used by the Chinese. Their promises that those who cultivated the land should have the year's crop were soon dishonoured. The whole of the harvest of the yeomen was brought to public treasury and an allowance of about 28 lb. of barley per month was made to each member of the household who was allowed to remain. The condition of landless cultivators were not much better off. They were persuaded by arguments which it would not have been much careful to ignore, to contribute the greater share of the crops they had grown to 'the people'. In general, they were left with no much between a quarter and a third of their harvest, and the organization of agricultural settlement was put in hand to look after future cultivation.

These social 'reforms' were accompanied by religious cruielity such as there had been at Lhasa. In each village the Dalai Lama was publicly abused. Lamas and senior monks were denounced, assaulted, and also imprisoned. The ordinary monks were made to starve in the monasteries and were ordered to marry and settle on the land as the alternative to starvation. The temples as well as monastery buildings were stripped of the sacred images and books, which were taken away in huge numbers and destroyed on the spot. A few old monks were allowed to stay in the deserted monasteries or to seek shelter in the villages and were given a small allowance of just mere barley.

The refugees from this cruel exercise of power included farmers and monks who either fled to avoid the denunciation and assaults they saw being practised on others or who managed to escape from detention either before or after being brought to trial. Many more tried to escape than succeeded. Unfortunately those who were caught were taken back to punishment and imprisonment or forced labour. Beating and pelting with stones appear to have been a common pratice and a number of the victims died as a result ; there were many who committed suicides ; but formal executions seem to have been very rare.

So violent a change of a farming society inevitably destroyed the pattern of agriculture and was followed by something approaching famine. In an effort to restore production the Chinese postponed the idea of collective or communal farming ; but, already, many of those on whose work they were counting—the former landless labourers—had joined the flow of refugees into India. Some of them told me, at the end of 1960, that they had been driven to by broken promises, fear of being moved to another part of Tibet, and—most of all—by the meagre rations which were not enough to keep them alive.

It is in keeping with the Tibetan nature that almost all the refugees, struggling needy into India, grieved far more on the attacks of their faith and the sacrilege against their religious teachers and holy places rather than over the loss of their own small possessions.

In spite of the apparently overpowering military check active resistance has not been entirely crushed and in June 1960 there were reports of fresh outbreaks of fighting in different parts of Tibet, including the border with Nepal. By the end of 1960, Chinese retaliation against the fighters, continued to take away property of small farmers, and the desperate shortage of food combined to swell to about 60,000 the number of refugees for whom—and for those who escape in future—India and Nepal, with the help of the free world, must take responsibility.

From this story the Tibetans come out as the people deeply conscious of their separateness and resenting foreign entry into their way of life ; devoted to preserving their peculiar culture, institutions, and above all their religion ; united by sharing unquestioningly in the same ideas rather than by being fitted into any close administrative system ; not eagerly desirous or aggressively inclined towards their neighbours but seeking to maintain their own rights by intractable persistence rather than by violence ; more interested in the reality of independence than in the show of it. For 1,300 years they were successful in preserving a purely Tibetan form of government, changing and developing to meet different circumstances but always containing elements and ideas which can be traced way back to the sixth century.

Attention has been drawn to a regularly happening pattern in the relations between Tibet and China over those centuries, but it is not be appropiate to suggest that the past can provide a sure pointer to the future. The pattern repeated itself in a wide but clearly defined framework. The rival neighbours, although differing in language and customs, were limited by the same difficulties of communications, and guided by similar political concepts. The possibility of the greater seeking to change the bases of the thought and life of the less never arose.

The breaking up of that framework by the attack of the West into China in the nineteenth century ended the long-existing, hidden sympathy and the similarity of thought which had made co-existence possible.

Certain considerations of geographical remoteness, climate, altitude, and natural resources prolonged the advance of the mechanized and industrially minded age. But from being people of the same Inside world the Chinese became part of the Outside; and having acquired the techniques and taken the measure of that world they have made the Tibetans pay for humiliations imposed on China by the foreign actions.

It is, perhaps, important that the present crisis in the life of Tibet marks the first time that the Chinese properly have ever exercised authority there. The former connection had been with the Mongol and Manchu rulers of China, both people of the steppes and both having the same ideas as the Tibetans. In those two periods, but more especially under the Manchu dynasty, the significance of Tibet lay in the need to preserve the religious influence of the Tibetan church from being used against the interests of China. Such considerations had ceased to exist long before the seizure of power by the Chinese.

Tibet a Distinct Entity

Tibet with its meagre peaceful population could so easily have been allowed to live on, under remote Chinese control, and to develop on its own lines, preserving those qualities and differences which made its civilization valuable to the rest of the world, without constituting the timid threat to China. But the mania for imposing accordingly which possessed the Chinese at the same time as they possessed new ideas and overwhelming power, gave little hope that anything so obstinately 'anachronistic' as the Tibetan Government and religion could share in that Brave New World. With the removal of their natural leaders in the destruction of 1959 the Tibetan people have been hard put to it to retain their spirit under the pressure of constant public speeches and regimentation. But the conquerors were not content to dominate the spirit. By deporting much of the male population, by dispersing and resettling communities, and by pouring in floods of their excess population the Chinese, who already have been successful in spoiling other races, threaten the very existence of the people, the language, the literature, the customs, and even the name of Tibet.

Some politicians and writers, with no personal knowledge of Tibet, have expressed the opinion that what the Chinese have done is only to carry out the long overdue reform of an oppressive social system. Such armchair critics should consider whether they are not in fact giving their approval to the domination of a small people by a cruel foreign power followed by the abolition of one whole order of society, the destruction of religious institutions, and an attack on the right to private property even on the smallest scale. Two reports by the International Commission of Jurists are still available. The second, entitled *Tibet and the People's Republic of China*, published in August 1960, contains detailed statements taken from Tibetan refugees by well qualified lawyers. It concludes that the Chinese have committed exterminated the race by mass murder by force to destroy the Tibetans as religious group and that they have violated human rights in Tibet in sixteen different ways including murder, rape, torture, destruction of family life, and transporting. The Dalai Lama, who himself gave evidence to the Commission, has stated that between 1955 and 1959, 65,000 Tibetans were killed and at least 10,000 children transported to China. On the other hand, the Commission finds that there is no support for Chinese affirmations that no human rights were enjoyed by the people of Tibet before the entry of the Chinese.

Considering the international position of Tibet the jurists consider that the Agreement of 1951 between Tibet and China, whether or not it can be held to have been concluded under constraint came to an end when it was formally rejected by the Tibetans in 1959. Tibet then resumed the status of independence and, in the view of the Commission, there is no obstruction in the Charter of the United Nations to the question of Tibet being raised before and decided by organs of that body.

But the Communist occupation of Tibet, however illegal in every respect is, for the present, a hard fact and what can be the future of the Tibetans in their terrible condition is hard to see. Those now in India as refugees will have a focus for their devotion and their hopes in the person of the Dalai Lama, whose presence and religious authority will continue to inspire a feeling of unity and individuality. It is, of course, necessary and it is desired by the Tibetans themselves, that they should get used to the world in which they have to live ; but they will need to be given both help and encouragement to preserve the essence of their way of life. The key, as always, is religion and so that it may be given full right and chance to continue as a living force, it is desirable to keep the Tibetans together, as far as possible, in self-contained communities, as the Indian Government is planning to do. It is of vital importance that in each community provision be made for the practice and teaching of religion. The introduction of Tibetans to Western knowledge and ideas should be done with utmost care. It will not be enough simply to bring them, at the hands of foreign teachers, some ready-made methods of education. The Dalai Lama has himself taken the initiative by setting up a school under his own supervision where the refugees will be taught by his own people. If the

Tibetans themselves and especially the religious teachers can make a synthesis of their own beliefs and ideas with the learning of the outside world a distinctive and valuable Tibetan community may survive in the foothills of the Himalaya and may even flourish.

As for the Tibetans remaining in their own country, the odds seems not going in their favour. A few million Tibetans are faced by excess and brutal power and by a vast number of aggressive, doctrine-infatuated, rapidly increasing Chinese. It is not always easy to get a great deal of correct information. The two neutral observers at Lhasa—the Indian Consul-General and the Neaplese Officer—are restricted in their contacts and movements ; the Dalai Lama himself can receive occasional reports although the danger to informants and agents is quite obvious ; the refugees know only about their own limited areas. But none of the obstacles can prevent news finding its way out and the Chinese themselves have had to admit that resistance is continuing. The spirit of the Tibetans has not been totally crushed and those who know them will continue to believe that even in the darkest misfortune the red hot ashes of faith will be kept alive, as they were before, and that something of the Tibetan character with its patience, courage, devout simplicity, honesty, and kindliness, will survive to add its rare value to the rich diversity of the world for ever.

Dalai Lama Escape

Tibet was under turmoil. There was no Law and Order. In such a situations. The Dalai Lama ; left for India. For Eighteen long days the Dalai Lama rode down through the jungle-covered hills of Assam. Led by Gorkhas, the various groups in the surrounding camped in the midst of lush rain forest, the sight of tropical birds, insects, monkeys and great flowering trees contrasting as clearly as possible with the arid plateau of Tibet just a few miles behind. Reaching Tawang, forward headquarters for the Kameng Division of the North-East Frontier Agency (NEFA), they settled down temporarily in bungalows, where the outside world made its first contacts. On the day of their arrival, an Indian air force transport flew in low over the large meadow below the town, dropped half-filled sacks of flour, shoes and fedora hats and then circled higher to unload heavier cargo by means of parachute. Continuously for three days the planes came, while below the Tibetans watched sadly incapacitated by malaria, cholera and typhoid vaccines. Pressing on to Bomdila, a major town up to which roads had been dug and electricity laid, the Dalai Lama received a telegram from Prime Minister Nehru welcoming him and extending all "facilities" for his residence in India. Heartened by the official greeting he halted once more, restored from the last traces of his illness and prepared to meet the world press, which was gathered at nearby Tezpur, a tea-planting centre on the Brahmaputra River in Assam. The Dalai was facing a lot of hardships. He had to do whatever he could do for the good of his people.

Little more than two weeks before, Nehru had announced the Dalai Lama's safe arrival to a standing ovation from the Indian Parliament. A week earlier, however, Peking had already issued a detailed official notice presenting its view of the disturbance in Tibet. In it, the revolt was portrayed as a minor insurrection engineered by an "upper-strata reactionary clique" seeking to reestablish its rule over "the darkest feudal serfdom in the world." "The spirit of these reactionaries soared to the clouds and they were ready to take over the whole universe," stated the New China News Agency on March 28. "With the aid of the patriotic Tibetan monks and laymen," it continued, "the People's Liberation Army completely crushed the rebellion. Primarily this is because the Tibetan people are patriotic, support the Central People's Government, ardently love the People's Liberation Army and oppose the imperialists and traitors." The official notice declared that the Dalai Lama had been "blatantly abducted" and "held under duress by the rebels," who, it implied, were acting under orders not just from Taiwan and the United States but from India as well. The small Himalayan trading town of Kalimpong, populated by Tibetans who where send out of their country during the 1950s, was identified as "the command center of the rebellion" and the fact that India's Parliament had recently discussed Tibet was referred to as an "impolite and improper" interference in the "internal affairs of a friendly country."

Nehru responded mildly to Peking's indictments. Granting right in Parliament that Kalimpong was indeed the focus of "a complicated game of chess by various nationalities," he nonetheless dismissed the notion that India had played a major role in Tibet's revolt. He further sought to reassure China by citing his firm adherence to Panch Sheel, which precluded involvement by either nation in the internal affairs of the other. The Prime Minister's position, though, as he himself termed it, was "difficult, delicate and embarrassing." A popular sympathy for Tibet had swept India, compelling its government to offer some gesture of support. Nehru accomplished this by granting the Dalai Lama refuge. Yet, as he was acutely aware, such an act left India open not only being accused of violating Panch Sheel but also to the considerably more damaging charge of having fallen into the anti-Communist camp of the Cold War and thereby lost its nonaligned stance, the cornerstone of the Republic's foreign policy. To forestall such criticism, Nehru stress laid that his support of the Dalai Lama was humanitarian only, based on a "tremendous bond" growing out of centuries of spiritual and cultural exchange between India and Tibet. The Dalai Lama was not to be allowed to use India as a base for a Tibetan independence movement or to engage in politics of any kind. Above all, he was to be isolated from the press and public in an effort to soften Peking's increasingly inflammatory posture. But the latter was with great difficulty achieved.

Since the first word of fighting in Lhasa had appeared late in March, news of a revolt in remote Tibet had leaped into world headlines. Over a hundred correspondents flew in from Paris, London, New York, Africa and East Asia seeking what was already billed as the "story of the year." Choosing Kalimpong as the best spot to begin their search, they converged on the Himalayan Hotel, run by David Macdonald, a former British trade agent in Tibet and an acquaintance of the Thirteenth Dalai Lama. While "Daddy" Macdonald took to his bed from worry on hearing of the Fourteenth Dalai Lama's flight, the press wandered hastily the surrounding peaks with binoculars, addresseds the town's more prominent Tibetan citizens, drove a hundred miles a day back and forth to Gangtok in search of leads and, under increasing pressure from their editors to provide front-page news on the whereabouts of the mysterious "God-King," began issuing fabricated reports over Kalimpong's antiquated Morse-key telegraph. Competition for a scoop was so stiff and genuine news so scarce that much of the reporters' time was spent surreptitiously tailing one another for sources. With word of the Dalai Lama's crossing into the NEFA, however, they could, just by looking at the map, infer that he would eventually come out at Tezpur. Thereupon the press corps decamped en masse, first to Shillong, the capital of Assam, and then to Tezpur itself. Sleeping on the couches and billiard tables of the local Planter's Club, they were blocked by the town's tiny airstrip with single-engine planes hired to race exclusive photos of the "God-King's" arrival to Calcutta's Dum Dum Airport and the presses of the world's periodicals beyond.

In the early hours of April 18, Indian officials lifted a travel ban previously imposed on a small road camp called Foothills, thirty miles from Tezpur, where, shortly after dawn, the Dalai Lama was to arrive. Those able to acquire transport caught their first glimpse of the exiled leader as, followed by his mother, sister, Ngari Rinpoche and the seventy remaining men of the Tibetan government, he stepped from a jeep, walked down an impromptu carpet of tarpaulins laid between facing rows of Indian troops and entered an overseer's cottage for a breakfast of cornflakes, poached eggs and toast. Emerging, the Dalai Lama was met by a shiny red Plymouth, the Tibetan and Indian flags mounted on piece of bamboo above its headlights. An hour and a half later batteries of microphones and television cameras came to life before Tezpur's Circuit House as once more he walked smiling, but silent, inside. While Tenzin Gyatso looked through hundreds of letters and cables sent by leaders and wellwishers from all around the globe an Indian and a Tibetan official appeared before the press to read a statement composed by the Dalai Lama in the third person. Giving a capsule history of the key events leading up to his flight, the document revealed for the first time that the Seventeen-Point Agreement of 1951 had been signed "under pressure from the Chinese government" and that from the day of the PLA's arrival in Lhasa "the Tibetan government did not enjoy any measure of autonomy." It then totally denied Chinese claims that the Dalai Lama had been kidnapped stating that he had come to India "of his own free will and not under duress." "His country and people have passed through an extremely difficult period," the statement summed up, "and all that the Dalai Lama wishes to say at the moment is to express his sincere regret at the tragedy which has overtaken Tibet and to fervently hope that these troubles will be over soon without any more bloodshed."

Chinese Reaction

China reacted very harshly. "The so-called statement of the Dalai Lama... is a crude document, lame in reasoning, full of lies and loopholes," the New China News Agency declared two days later. "Actually, Tibet's political and religious systems were all laid down by the Central Government in Peking. . . . Not even the title, position and powers of the Dalai Lama were laid down by the Tibetans themselves. In modern history the so-called Tibetan independence has always been a scheme of the British imperialists for carrying out aggression against China and first of all against Tibet. . . . Indian expansionist elements inherited this shameful legacy. . . ." Citing as evidence of his abduction the fact that the Dalai Lama's statement had not been written in the first person and that an Indian official had passed out copies of it to reporters, the dispatch upgraded Peking's earlier accusations in what was perceived in New Delhi as an unwarranted and bellicose reversal of the facts. "The publication at the present moment of this so-called statement of the Dalai Lama, which harps on so-called Tibetan independence, will naturally cause people to ask : Is this not an attempt to place the Dalai Lama in a position of hostility to his motherland, thus blocking the road for him to return to it? What is meant by independence here," it stated, "is in fact to turn Tibet into a colony or protectorate of a foreign country."

Dalai Lama Moves to Moussories

At one o'clock in the afternoon of April 18, a few hours after his arrival in Tezpur, the Dalai Lama boarded on a special train for the three-day ride to his newly designated residence, the former British hill station of Mussoorie in the mountains north of New Delhi. Riding in a private saloon, behind the long, black barrel-nosed steam engine of Indian Railways, a pilot train clearing the tracks in advance, the Tibetans headed west across the dusty northern edge of the subcontinent, crossing Assam, Bengal, Bihar, and finally Uttar Pradesh, where, turning due north, they approached Dehra Dun, the railhead eighteen miles from Mussoorie. Tens of thousands of white-clad Indian students and labourers lined the train's route, choking the stations it passed through, chanting *Dalai Lama Ki Jai—Dalai Lama Zindabad.* ("Hail to the Dalai Lama—Long live the Dalai Lama.") Along the empty tracks between towns, farmers waited for hours on the edges of their fields, palms pressed together in reverence, for a glimpse of the holy man. At the major stops of Siliguri, Benares and Lucknow, Tenzin Gyatso left the saloon to address mass gatherings. It was not until early in the morning on April 21, as the Dalai Lama drove into the cool, pine-covered slopes of Mussoorie, the snow-capped peak of Nanda Devi visible in the distance, that his month-long, 1,500-mile journey concluded at Birla House, a summer resort owned by the powerful and wealthy Birla family.

Located on a pine-and-oak-covered headland overlooking Happy Valley on the outskirts of Mussoorie, Birla House was built in the style of an English country home : two stories marked by steep dormers above a prominent veranda and a terraced garden filled with flowers like irises, lilies and blue and white violets. Inside, it was furnished in deep-backed chairs and couches, portraits great personality like Gandhi and Nehru scattered here and there with paintings of Hindu gods and goddesses on the walls. There was a large radio in the drawing room before which the Dalai Lama and his Cabinet soon began listening to news bulletins while a chamber next to the Dalai Lama's bedroom on the second floor was converted into a sacred place for meditation. With Tenzin Gyatso and his family kept behind Birla House's new fourteen-foot-high barbed-wire fence and the Tibetan government quartered mainly at the Happy Valley Club, headquarters of the Provincial Armed Constabulary, a thick security screen of roadblocks and undercover agents effectively sealed the Tibetans from all contact with the press or any other visitors.

Nehru Meets Dalai Lama

On April 24 ; three days after the Dalai Lama's arrival at Birla House, Prime Minister Nehru drove through the streets of Mussoorie, dressed in his traditional tight white pants, black knee-length coat, buttonholed rose and Congress Party cap, to loud cheers from thousands of hill folk and vacationers. Stopping to address assembly of travel agents, his professed reason for making the trip, Nehru commented that he had come to fulfill "an old engagement," not realizing he would "meet a big traveler." In response to a reporter's question he pointed out that India's interest in Tibet was "historical, sentimental and religious and not essentially political." "Our entire policy," Nehru said, his words clearly directed to Peking, "whether it relates to cooperative farming, community development or industrial expansion, is based on cooperation." After inviting the Panchen Lama and other Chinese officials to visit the Dalai Lama and see for themselves that he was not held "under duress," Nehru drove past the police tent pitched at the gate of Birla House and posed with the Tibetan leader for a shortround of photographs on the lawn. The two men then went inside, where they discussed for nearly four hours, assisted only by an interpreter. "I explained the full situation to Nehru," recounted the Dalai Lama. "His advice was to rest and consider things well without being hasty. Like a true, old friend he showed every sign of sympathy. It gave me happiness and hope. Yet at the same time, he cautioned me in line with reality. So because of this I felt a little discouraged, somewhat helpless, in fact." The "reality," Nehru made clear, was that, although offering "sympathy," India would never considerably support the cause of Tibetan independence. "I mentioned casually to Pandit Nehru," continued the Dalai Lama, "that we had established a temporary government in southern Tibet. He became slightly agitated. 'We are not going to recognize your government,' he said immediately. You see, I think we came from Tibet with some blind, unreasonable hope that with support we could still make a stand. But after discussing these matters with the Indian government we realized that, in reality, it was not so easy. Despite their sympathy they had to follow their policy of complete nonalignment. Of course, Pandit Nehru was a very knowledgeable and a greatly experienced person. But I think because of the Tibetan crisis he must have gotten a lot of headaches."

Nehru indeed found himself in an increasingly complex and tense situation. The initial discussion of Tibet in the Indian Parliament took place in late March and early April and gave way, in May, to a lively, often sharp and bitter debate. While India's Communist Party articulated China's view of the crisis, accusing the government of entertaining designs on Tibet, virtually all of the other opposition parties labelled Nehru's stand as one being calm and quiet. The previous year, Acharya Kripalani, leader of the Praja Socialists, had blamed Panch Sheel as "born in sin to put the seal of our approval on the destruction of an ancient nation." Now India's leading politicians rebuked their Prime Minister for failing to stand up to Peking, whose successful conquest of Tibet paved the way for a direct attack on the country's northern regions, parts of which China already claimed as properly belonging to itself. "I cannot understand how it is possible to be friendly with this nation with this mentality," said Kripalani. "Yet our efforts to save it [friendship] will only result in this : They will not give us credit for good intentions. They will only give us credit for cowardice." "The tragedy of Tibet hangs heavily on our conscience," asserted K.M. Munshi. "For a young independent nation like ours, with its spiritual heritage, our handling of the Tibetan situation has been a crime in history."

While admitting shock "beyond measure" at Peking's charges. Nehru refused to alter his position emphasizing it was of "the greatest consequence" that India and China get along. Indispensable to this was the Dalai Lama's good behaviour. Given the current atmosphere a Sino-Indian war could be sparked by the slightest provocation—a battle India was utterly unprepared to fight. Recognizing that as a guest in India his position, and with it Tibet's sole hope for an independent future, hung in the balance, Tenzin Gyatso temporarily took Nehru's advice to "rest" and "consider things well" and set about adjusting to his new way of life.

Dalai Lama Starts giving and Audiences

The great changes in the Dalai Lama's circumstances soon became visible. By public demand, he commenced giving a weekly *darsban* or blessing from a silk-draped chair on a rickety wooden stage at one end of the Birla House lawn. As summer began, Tibet's exiled "God-King" turned into Mussoorie's greatest tourist attraction until, on June 3, after being showered with rose petals by an audience of five thousand wellwishers and called to reappear twice on a balcony by latecomers chanting *"Darsban ! Darsban !"* his ministers, already in a storm over many Indians attempts to shake hands with "the Presence," cancelled all future showup. Tenzin Gyatso, though, took keeness not only to shaking hands but also to abolishing almost all of the centuries-old protocol surrounding him. "In the past there was too much formality. You couldn't talk, you couldn't even breathe freely," he remarked. "I hate being formal. Now, the new circumstances made it easier for me to change things. In this way, you see, becoming a refugee was actually useful. It brought me much closer to reality. And also it deepened my understanding of religion, particularly impermanence. Although the world is always changing one never notices it. Then suddenly your home, friends and country all are gone. It showed how futile it is to hold on to such things."

While the Dalai Lama adapted, Indian officials paradoxically did their best to maintain past protocol. Three years after his arrival confusion still reigned, demonstrated by the experience of one journalist who having been instructed not to touch or to turn away from the Dalai Lama, staggered backwards toward the door at the conclusion of his audience. For a moment the Dalai Lama looked on amused. Then he walked quickly after the reporter, took him by his shoulders, turned him around and gave a slight friendly push.

Within two months the Dalai Lama's self-imposed silence ended. Since early April thousands of refugees had begun coming from Himalayan passes leading into Bhutan, Sikkim, Nepal and India. With them came news of a wholesale effort on the part of China to totally uproot Tibetan society and culture. As they had been in Kham, "democratic reforms" were about to be imposed : collectivization of property and labour class division, daily political "reeducation," dismantling of the clergy, as well as plans for an inflow of Han settlers to begin the Sinicization of Tibet. In addition, there were reports no just of mass imprisonment and execution but of repeated cruel deeds, torture, rape and dismemberment, carried out directly by the newly established Military Control Committees in each region. The full dimension of Tibet's tragedy now compelled the Dalai Lama, against Nehru's warning to launch a campaign for international support.

On June 20, Tenzin Gyatso held his first news conference. Under a large open-sided tent, pitched on the lawn of Birla House, scores of reporters listened to the Dalai Lama read a lengthy statement cataloguing the destruction in Tibet, while identifying China's ultimate aim as "the extermination of the religion and culture and even the absorption of the

Tibetan race." He called for an international commission to investigate the reports of such disorders and chaos made clear that the Seventeen-Point Agreement was cancelled and stated : "Where I am, accompanied by my government, the Tibetan people recognize us as the government of Tibet. I will return to Lhasa," he added, "when I obtain the rights and powers which Tibet enjoyed and exercised prior to 1950."

The Dalai Lama's first concern, however, was the problem of refugees. By the end of June almost 20,000 Tibetans had fled their homeland, the first of repeated waves of departure eventually totalling 100,000. While those closest to the border had been compelled to scale the world's highest and least frequented passes, others, travelling inland from Kham and Amdo, had fought their way free in running battles lasting three and four months. These saw their ranks drastically reduced ; a typical group of 125 survivors, who reached Assam in June, reported that they had set out 4,000 strong. Most of the refugees were starving or wounded, ill from the low altitude and stunned by a profound culture shock on descending to an alien world. "During the summer of 1959 my immediate task was to somehow save the refugees," said the Dalai Lama. "They came just as the hot season started, wearing heavy boots and long robes which had to be burned, as they were completely useless. It was necessary to take very close care of their health. Then, with the little knowledge we possessed, we took it as our duty to tell these 'fresh' refugees that it was not so easy to return to Tibet. 'We will have to remain in India for a longer period than expected,' we said. 'We will have to settle mentally as well as physically.' "

Two large transit camps were established to handle the inflow of refugees one called Missamari, located ten miles from Tezpur ; the other, Buxa Duar, a former British prisoner-of-war camp situated near the Bhutanese border in West Bengal. The camps represented an effort not only of the Indian government but also of the opposition parties, who, led by Acharya Kripalani, united to create a Central Relief Committee that was instrumental in obtaining food, medical supplies and international aid. Disinfected, fingerprinted, interrogated by Indian intelligence, issued blue-green trousers and brown bush shirts, the mixture of monks, guerrillas and families waited in barracks to be let out for road work to the cooler regions of northern India, a plan the Dalai Lama and New Delhi had jointly devised to check the growing number of calamities. As July began, the first group left Buxa, to be followed shortly by hundreds more, deployed over a twelve-hundred-mile arc across the Himalayas. With their own limited chances for survival lay the sole hope for Tibet's eventual self-determination.

The Great Escape of Chopel Dhaundub and Family

After almost three days of tramping over the 25,000-foot mountains separating Tibet and Bhutan, Tempa Tsering, his parents and two younger sisters faced their aim. Beneath them stretched the heavily wooded slopes of the southern Himalayas, breaking for the first time in days the uncharted wilderness of brilliant snow-capped summits, ridges and defiles that they had struggled through. Six months earlier, the revolt had been completely crushed. Tempa's father, Chopel Dhondub," together with all the able bodied men in the village of Drumpa, had been sent behind bars by the PLA. Released, he was rearrested after only a few weeks, and then set free again, just in time to see his wife beaten and denounced in *tbamzing* or public "struggle session." He then received notice that Tempa, though only ten years old, was to be sent away with thousands of other Tibetan children to get educated in China. Frightened of losing their only son. Tempa's parents decided to runaway.

In the middle of October 1959, Chopel Dhondub led his family out of Drumpa. Departing after midnight, his wife and their five-and eight-year-old daughters hurried from the village in silence. A short while later, he and Tempa followed, leaving the door of their home locked so as not to arouse any suspicion. Trailed by their dog, who refused to be turned back, the family walked east, carrying a few bags of food and clothing, before heading south, off the track, into the mountains separating Lhoka from Bhutan. Climbing all night, they ascended to 18,000 feet. The two girls clung to their parents' backs, Tempa walked between, holding their hands. With each step forward the adults sank waist deep into freshly fallen powder that rendered the ascent extremely difficult. As dawn broke, they stopped to sleep behind a boulder, huddled together on a blanket on the snow. Only then they realized that their dog had disappeared, stuck, most likely, in a drift and was helpless.

On waking at sunset, Tempa's family gazed out over a vaulted world of jagged peaks and indigo sky, the sere umber-colored hills of Tibet beginning to glow in the fading light far below. After a meal of melted snow, dried meat and roasted barley, they moved upward again, the moonlight so bright on the snow and ice that their eyes had to be covered every few steps. By dawn all were really exhausted. Tempa's youngest sister had started to vomit from the thin air and altitude ; the others had lost their appetites. Without eating, they fell asleep under an overhang in a depression between summits. The next night the long trek continued. At three in the morning a needle-thin ridge suddenly loomed ahead. One at a time, Chopel Dhondub led his children and wife carefully across an invisible cleft dropping away in the darkness to either side. Once the ridge had been safely negotiated, however, the incline gradually descended. Camping again in the snow, they awoke the following afternoon and, less fearful of capture, traversed a wide, saddleback slope until, with the sun setting and the wall of mountains they had passed through now rising behind them, the foothills of Bhutan could be viewed. The family would have been greatly relieved if it was not for the condition of their youngest child. For two days she had refused to eat and drink. Throughout the last march she had laid limply on her mother's back, unresponsive to attempts at reviving her. Listening with curiousity to her daughter's labored breathing, Tempa's mother called out toward four o'clock that the child was "not keeping well at all." The group came to a halt about an hour above the tree line. Sitting down, Tempa's mother lifted her daughter from her back and began to rock her. At that moment, while the others looked on, little girl stopped to breath. "It was a shock," recalled Tempa. "One moment she was alive and the next, just when the worst of the climb was over, she died."

As the sun sank below the last ranges, Tempa and his family wept over the dead child. Finally, Chopel Dhondub took his youngest daughter's extra clothes from one of the bags they had brought, dressed her small body in them, and scooped out a shallow grave. He then buried his child, covering her face with packed snow. Still weeping, the family set off down the mountain. Four hours later, among boulders and waist-high shrubs, they laid out their blanket, made their first hot tea in three days and were fast asleep.

Tempa and his family now lay on the edge of a world that in every respect was unknown to them. Once before Chopel Dhondub had traded in Bhutan. He, at least, had seen a forest. The others never had. As with many of the refugees coming from Tibet, their knowledge of the globe consisted image of China and India, which was not vivid beyond both of which, they thought, stretched only the great ocean. Unaware that the Dalai Lama had runaway the Chinese having kept his departure secret—the family, now that its flight was complete, had no further goal. As a result, on the following day they simply took the first path they found, which, after another nights' camping in the forest, led to a village.

To the Tibetans, the local Bhutanese, wearing knee-length checker-board robes and short, braidless hair, looked like fellow countrymen who, had lost for generations, had fallen into an odd, half-remembered mimicry of their ancestors' ways. To the Bhutanese, however, the refugees were mere strangers. Since early spring thousands had already come this way, disoriented and sick, not a few of them starving. In the immediate result of the uprising, the Bhutanese government had closed the main passes, fearful that China would attack if the refugees were permitted to enter. But with the great inflow of religious and political figures, some of whom were related to the royal family itself, they finally modified their policy. Tibetans were subsequently permitted to pass through the kingdom on condition that they proceed to India. Although some 4,000 refugees eventually remained in Bhutan, the rest were compelled to beg their way across the country, bartering the few pieces of jewellery, images and *thankas* they possessed, so that, on their going out a month later, most were needy. Following the pattern, Tempa, his parents and sister crossed Bhutan, camping in the woods by night, begging in hamlets each day.

Within a week a routine emerged. Arriving at the outskirts of a village, the family divided into two teams, mother and daughter in one, father and son in the other. Passing from house to house, they appealed for whatever leftover food, mainly rice and vegetables, the inhabitants would spare. Returning to their camp outside the town, they ate and then continued to travel. Discovering that people were more generous to the children, Chopel Dhondub instructed his son to beg alone, but this, though profitable, only increased Tempa's already perseverence of getting lost, an anxiety they all shared. Unlike Tibet's limitless perspective the abundant forest, so thick that it often blocked out the sky, created intense claustrophobia often worsened by the constant fear of separation. Dread of what lay hidden among the trees increased the Tibetans' unease. Tigers, wild boars and poisonous insects were all present. Tempa's father warned the children about snakes, describing them as creatures who resembled the black and white ropes used by Tibetan traders but who moved. Constant watch however, was sufficient to guard against the omnipresent leeches. Each day they would latch on unnoticed and gradually swell with blood up to two inches in length. Salt and fire were the sole antidotes. Preserving their few matches for campfires, Tempa and his family begged for salt for the leeches and wrapped themselves in their hot Tibetan clothing. Practically all the time, Tempa's mother wept continually over the loss of her beloved daughter. In the few words they exchanged before sleep each night, the others never mentioned the tragedy for fear of upsetting her more.

As the family's trek across Bhutan progressed, they met other refugees too, flowing like so many parts of a river down through Thimbu, the capital, and then to India. Finally, after five weeks of walking, they entered a large meadow in the woods filled with Tibetans preparing to cross the Indian border two days beyond. Among them, Tempa's father came across a family he knew. He joined their cooking fire, and the two groups exchanged accounts. Entering India together, they arrived a few days later at Buxa.

Located in an airless pocket between three jungle-covered hills, Buxa's thirty concrete barracks, enclosed by a high barbed-wire perimeter, presented a dismal setting. At the time of Tempa's admittance, thousands of refugees were encamped inside and outside the camp's gates, the majority incapacitated from the heat and low altitude. To relieve overcrowding, the Indian government had begun shipping out sizable contingents, either for road work or to the more spacious transit camp at Missamari, where, after two weeks, Tempa and his family themselves were transferred. "We left Buxa in a large group and walked about two miles to the railroad," recalled Tempa. "Everyone was discussing the train. No one had ever seen one ; we had only heard its new Tibetan name, *rili*,from the English word 'rail.' I was very excited listening to people talk about big houses that moved, but when we first arrived there was so much rushing that I had no chance to look." Herded by Indian police into a narrow passage dividing two stacks of triple-level wooden bunks, Tempa managed to get a window seat, from which vantage point he soon received a terrific shock. "It was so funny," he remembered. "When the train started I actually thought the mountains were moving out, not us. I was staring through the window and thinking, 'How do these mountains move so quickly?' I just couldn't understand it." By nightfall, though, as the train turned south and the Himalayas vanished, he had begun to adjust. Then, after a second night, they arrived at a town called Rangapari from where the refugees were sent in trucks to the new camp.

Externally, Missamari was larger and less depressing than Buxa. Built on a sandy flat by a river in the jungle, the camp comprised 150 bamboo barracks laid out in neat rows. Up to100 people lived in each. Around them grew a profusion of kitchen vegetables ; cucumber vines, which had blanketed many of the buildings' roofs in only a few months, offering a small quantity of shade against the tropical sun. Up until the arrival of Tempa's family, Missamari's almost 15,000 inhabitants had been predominantly men : Khampa fighters and monks who had fled Lhasa in the midst of the uprising. They had bitter experience of camp life. At Missamari, erected for the Tibetans in little more than two weeks, the water supply was contaminated, sanitation was inadequate and the rations of potato curry, rice and lentils, though plentiful, were detrimental to a people used solely to a diet of barley, butter and meat. The result had been an epidemic of deadly amoebic dysentery. Smoke from the cremation ground on the riverbank five hundered yards away drifted over the barracks daily. Old and young died first, unable to resist the infection, succumbing usually in a day or two. Weeping was the most noticeable sound in the campground, occasionally mixed with the rapid hum of a sutra, recited by a lone monk now dressed in government-issue clothing like all the rest.

Tempa spent almost three months in Missamari. Each day his family sat listlessly on their beds, hearing of about deaths. Their sole consolation was the hope that soon, led by the Dalai Lama, they would return back to Tibet. Constantly, illogically, they spoke of it. There seemed little doubt that their stay in India could only be temporary. By late winter of 1960, however, a Tibetan official in the camp announced that they would soon be sent north for road work. Chopel Dhondub deduced that a return to Tibet was far less likely from a road gang than from Missamari itself. With this realization the family lost their resolve. Unaffected till now, both Tempa and his remaining sister sufferd from dysentery. In spite of the small white tablets given to her at the camp's dispensary, the little girl's health deteriorated. Her periodic outdoor playing—from which she often ran inside, frightened on seeing a dark-skinned Indian—ceased. She stayed in bed all day, too weak to move or eat. A short while before the family was to leave for road work, Tempa's second sister died too.

Two days later, Tempa and his parents were put on a train, their destination not known to them. During the ride Tempa's mother refused to let go of him. Too distraught to eat, she wept continually, repeating over and over, "We escaped the Chinese only to bury our bodies in a foreign land." Tempa's father sat listlessly beside his wife, speechless from the loss. After three days on the train, the 160 refugees on board disembarked at a small town before the foothills of the western Himalayas. A Tibetan government official greeted them at the railway station, but his Indian counterpart had failed to show up. For three days more the travellers camped on the platform, during which time their first Tibetan New Year's in exile came and went without celebration. When their presence was eventually discovered, they were taken by truck to a group of old army tents, torn and patched after years of use, pitched in uneven lines on a rocky slope near an Indian village called Bawarna. A few hundred yards away down a path through pine trees, lay the head of the road construction.

Work began a week later. A whistle blew at 7:45 each morning and the refugees proceeded through the woods to the road. Standing for roll call taken by Indian overseers, they were divided into groups of ten ; men were given axes and crowbars to cut and clear trees, women were given shovels to dig the roadbed, children baskets to remove dirt and stones. With an hour's break for lunch, they laboured until 5:00 p.m., receiving little more than a rupee, or to cents, a day, just enough to purchase rice and once a week some meat and vegetables. Shopping in the village after work, the refugees had their first unofficial contact within the foreign land.

As they discovered, in common with one road group after another, contact with the local people, though necessary, was quite often dangerous. Whatever infectious diseases were present among the inhabitants—tuberculosis in particular—passed easily to the Tibetans, who, lacking the proper antibodies, most often died. Within a few months of the exiles' arrival in India it became clear that the task of transition was more threatening than that of escape, moreover it was universally destructive, affecting virtually every family, that the survival of the refugees as a busy group was itself called into question. In most of the cases, a visible illness could not even be found as the cause of death. The Tibetans themselves inherited such fatalities simply to heartbreak and the shock of exile. Tempa's mother now appeared afflicted by just such a malaise. After two weeks on the road she completely lacked the strength to work and took to the straw and blanket the family used for a bed in their tent. Compelled to labour hard for survival. Tempa and his father were unable to tend to her. In the evenings they carried her to Bawarna's small clinic, but the medical worker in charge could find no specific symptoms to treat. Still devastated by the loss of her two daughters, she hesitated alone until, one Sunday, the Tibetan official in charge of the road camp arranged for a visit to nearby Dharamsala, the Dalai Lama's new residence, to which he had shifted from Mussoorie a few months before.

After driving for two hours, the road workers were let off in a small hillside hamlet called McLeod Ganj just above the main town of Dharamsala. From there, Chopel Dhondub carried his wife on his back up the steep cobblestone path leading to the Dalai Lama's residence. At its entrance, the group had to passed through a security check and then were directed onto a narrow strip of lawn before a veranda on the south side of a large house. The Dalai Lama appeared and they all lied flat on the ground as a sign of giving respect. The young leader spoke of plans and improvements underway, after which they filed by to receive his blessing. Then the brief audience ended. Two days later, back in Bawarna, Tempa's mother looked up at her husband and son from bed and said, "Now that I have seen His Holiness I feel relieved. If I die, that is my fate. I'm satisfied." The next day Tempa's father sent him to work alone. That night his mother held his hand and remarked, "Now you must take care of your father. One day, I know, you will go back to Tibet." When Tempa returned from work the following day, his mother lay dead.

Nearly two weeks later Chopel Dhondub began vomiting. As with the children, his state quickly deteriorated. He was taken to a hospital in Palampur, an hour's drive away. Tempa, just approaching his eleventh birthday, was left alone in the tent his mother had died in. In the mornings, the Tibetan government official collected him for work, telling the Indian overseers not to demand too much labour from him. In the evenings, he walked the boy into Bawarna to buy for him sweets. Each night Tempa lay alone crying, terrified that his father would die as well he would be an orphan. Miraculously, Chopel Dhondub returned a week later weakened but alive.

Yet another separation was in store for the refugees. There were forty children in Tempa's road gang, all of whom, it was decided, were to be sent to the newly established nursery in Dharamsala, set up in the spring of 1960 to take care for the hundreds of young people left deprived on the roads. On hearing the news, Tempa refused to leave his father. Even when Chopel Dhondub assured his son that he was now out of danger, insisting that there was no future for him carrying dirt and stones on a road gang, Tempa remained headened. But the adults were not dissuaded. Distraught, Tempa was packed onto a bus and driven in tears to Dharamsala, separated, finally, from everything he had known. It was a year before he heard from his father again. In the meantime a new life, pieced together by the Dalai Lama and the Tibetan government-in-exile, began to take shape for him and the others of his generation.

Effort to Seek International Support

While refugees continued to descend throughout the summer and autumn of 1959, the Dalai Lama made an effort to obtain international support for Tibet. Responding to his call for an impartial inquiry, the International Commission of Jurists launched an investigation into the manifold accounts of Chinese wickedness as well as Tibet's international legal status. After compiling an initial document by the end of July, a full report was issued one year later. In it, the commission concluded that, despite the doubt shrouding its legal status, Tibet had, in reality, been a fully sovereign state, independent in both fact and law of Chinese dominion. Regarding violations of human rights, the commission determined that Red China was responsible for "the gravest crime of which any person or nation can be accused—the intent to destroy, in whole or in part, a national, ethnic, racial or religious group as such"—genocide.

Encouraged by the International Commission of Jurists' preliminary findings, the Dalai Lama left Mussoorie by train on September 8. Arriving at the Old Delhi station by six o'clock the next morning, he was greeted by thousands of Indian supporters, driven to Hyderabad House, the Indian State Guest House, and then on to confer with Nehru at the Prime Minister's residence Teen Murti. There, he told the reason for his trip. "It was my decision, despite strong opposition from India, to approach the United Nations," recounted the Dalai Lama. "To begin with, I personally met with the Prime Minister to explain our stand. After listening, Nehru said, 'Now that you've decided to appeal, all right, go ahead.' At that moment, I really felt how beautiful freedom is. Our right was accepted although we had been discouraged against this whole idea of approaching the UN. Because of my past experience with the Chinese it was almost unthinkable ; an extraordinary surprise within my lifetime."

United Nation's Approach

After Nehru's agreement Tenzin Gyatso cabled the United Nations Secretary-General, Dag Hammarskjold, the same day, prepared a delegation to follow and then engaged on an unprecedented round of diplomatic calls, trying to raise support for the appeal. "Compared to the Dalai Lama of today, I myself was a bit confused," said the Dalai Lama, reflecting on his visits to New Delhi's diplomatic corps. "It's always more useful to talk person to person, but sometimes it was hard to know how to start. Then, gradually, my own style grew. I had more courage to express myself and was less concerned about diplomatic formalities. During 1959, though, I lacked this confidence in myself. Therefore it was very difficult sometimes. I used to be quite anxious."

His efforts, nevertheless, proved out. As a result of them, Ireland and Malaya co-sponsored Tibet's case to the Steering Committee of the

General Assembly, where, unlike its cursory dismissal in 1950, the issue was now debated deeply. In many respects the discussion reflected that of India's Parliament. As introduced by the sponsoring nations, Tibet's unfortunate condition was depicted primarily as one involving human rights ; the underlying issue of its nationhood was denied as the Chinese Nationalists on Taiwan, though not in occupation, also claimed sovereignty. In his opening comments, Dato Ismail Kamil, Malaya's representative, cited the conclusions of the International Commission of Jurists' initial report, which maintained that "almost all the rights which together allow the full and legitimate expression of human personality appear to be denied to the Tibetans at the present time, and in most cases for some time past." "On the basis of the available evidence," the report concluded, "it would seem difficult to recall a case in which ruthless oppression of man's essential dignity has been more systematically and efficiently carried out. In his rebuttal, Vasily Kuznetsov, the Soviet Union's representative, dismissed the report's validity, accused the appeal's sponsors of attempting to "utilize the United Nations in order to intensify the Cold War," and maintained that "a nonexistent Tibetan question has been fabricated in order to worsen the international situation and the atmosphere in the Assembly." Like India's own Marxists, the entire Communist bloc, following Russia's lead, voiced Peking's view of the Tibetan issue as "wholly and completely within the domestic competence of the Chinese People's Republic," even the discussion of which "would constitute a gross and wholly unjustified interference" into China's internal affairs. Thus, Tibet's case—just as Nehru had predicted—fell immediate victim to the broader aspect of global conflict. Nonetheless, by meeting's end a large majority voted to include the issue on the agenda of the 14th General Assembly, where many of the Third World countries joined Western democracies in passing a resolution in Tibet's favour by a vote of 45 to 9 (with 26 abstentions). Though not identifying the People's Republic of China by name, it called for "respect for the fundamental human rights of the Tibetan people and for their distinctive cultural and religious life." As continued reports of at nrocities of in human nature and wholesale destruction were brought out by repeated waves of refugees from Tibet, two more resolutions were passed in 1961 and 1965. In these the United Nations considerably hardened its language. It not only registered, as in the second resolution, "grave concern" and "deep anxiety" over the "severe hardships" imposed on the Tibetans through the "suppression of their distinctive cultural and religious life," but "solemnly" renewed its call "for the cessation of practices which deprive the Tibetan people of their fundamental human rights and freedoms, including most importantly their right to self-determination."

In December 1959, with the initial UN appeal behind him and the end of his first year in exile coming near, Tenzin Gyatso went on pilgrimage. At Bodh Gaya, site of the Buddha's enlightenment, he stayed in the Tibetan monastery within sight of the great second-century Mahabodhi Temple next to the Bodhi Tree, under which the Buddha had attained nirvana. Here the Dalai Lama met with some sixty representatives of the refugees, who pledged fight for Tibet's freedom. Afterwards, for the first time in his life, he appointed a group of 162 monks. Then, travelling on to the Deer Park at Sarnath, where the Buddha's first sermon had been delivered, the Dalai Lama drove with a typically reduced attendents of sixteen through a crowd of 2,000 weeping Tibetans who were camped around tea stalls beneath the trees, selling old clothes and a few of the valuables that they had managed to hold back. Remaining for two weeks, he preached religiously in the traditional Tibetan style, seated on a high brocade-draped throne in front of the crowd. At the conclusion, Tenzin Gyatso spoke for an hour or so in the advisory manner that he would address his people with from now on, presenting a long-range plan he had formulated in which the exiles' reconstruction and their struggle for Tibet's independence would be combined. "For the moment Tibet's sun and moon have suffered an eclipse," said the Dalai Lama, "but one day we will regain our country. You should not lose heart. The great job ahead of us now," he revealed, "is to preserve our religion and culture."

10

The Reconstruction

The Dalai Lama's thought of exiled society took root in entirely new headquarters, an abandoned British hill station called Dharamsala, located a day west of New Delhi on the northern margin of the Punjab. An elevated place across the lower ridges of the Dhauladar Range, a plumb barrier of snowcapped peaks fencing in the Kangra Valley, Dharamsala had been established by the British around the early 1860s as the summer seat of the Jullundur Division. Starting with a military cantonment on the shoulder of the tallest crest, Mun Peak, they had gone on to found a small town, called McLeod Ganj, on a almost negligible ridge facing the plains below. A row of columns was erected to house shops, fronted by a elegant park of cedar trees, a birdbath and stone benches. Down the hill rose the rusticated belfry of St. John's in the Wilderness, an Anglican church, while, scattered well apart over the slopes, more than a hundred bungalows established sporting small tower on buildings and gingerbread woodwork, vaulted ceilings and multiple wings, and dubbed with a flock of romantic names such as Ivanhoe, Eagle's Nest, Chestnut Villa, Wargrave and Retreat.

MacLeod Ganj

By the turn of the century, McLeod Ganj supported one of the most vigorous societies, outside the cities, of any in the Raj. With the rail line put through to Pathankot, seven miles from the foothills, bureaucrats from both Delhi as well as Lahore flocked to the mountains. In the spring the woods were coered with primrose, mistletoe and red and mauve rhododendron, followed in June, after the onset of the monsoon, by an explosion of buttercups, violets and honeysuckle. Wildlife abounded : leopards, panthers, porcupines, foxes, jackals, hyenas, red-faced monkeys and huge white-maned langurs roamed the lower hills, joined in the colder months, when they descended to fodder by black and brown bears. Above McLeod Ganj hawks and white-bellied vultures wheeled in wide gyres on all sides. Partridges, pigeons, ravens and snow pheasants flew tamely into town. Slated to become the summer capital of the Raj, Dharamsala's future seemed secure until an earthquake struck in 1905. The British picked Simla and those local officials who remained relocated their offices 1,500 feet down the hillside to the less exposed Lower Dharamsala. On August 15, 1947—India's independence day—they departed as well.

Only one man remained to preside over the unreal life of McLeod Ganj : N.N. Nowrojee. As proprietors of a general merchandise "Oilman" or "Europe Store" as they were called, the Nowrojee family had lived in Dharamsala since its start. Parsees, they had journeyed to India themselves as refugees, fleeing religious persecution in Persia over a thousand years before. The family line had remained intact there since a long time and, with the founding of their own business in McLeod Ganj, had become, to generations of British bureaucrats, something of the hamlet's guardian spirit. Entrusted now with dozens of left over bungalows, N.N. Nowrojee, fifth proprietor of Nowrojee and Sons, did not succeed to bring the village back to life. For twelve years he offered the buildings free to charge to schools and as tourist lodges to the state government, but there was no one to take. Finally, on hearing through friends of the central government's hunt for a permanent residence for the Dalai Lama, he approached New Delhi directly. His tale of a forgotten ghost town wasting in the woods proved secret enough to warrant inspection, following which, to his surprise, Delhi deemed it ideal. First, however, the Tibetans had to agree. "Pandit Nehru personally chose Dharamsala for us, based on what he called its 'peace and tranquillity,' " recounted the Dalai Lama. "From our viewpoint, though, it had good as well as bad sides. Delhi is the nerve centre. The nearer to Delhi, the better the communication. Dharamsala's disadvantages, then, were clear. But we also saw its potential. It was open and there was more room to expand. Thus, after complaining at first that we were reluctant to move, once our officials visited and formed a good opinion, we decided to shift."

Dalai Lama Selects Dharamasala

On April 29, 1960, after a little more than a year's stay, the Dalai Lama left Mussoorie. Travelling by overnight train to Pathankot, he was met at the station the following afternoon by state and municipal authorities, as well as a few thousand Tibetan refugees en route to Dalhousie for casual road work. Stopping to console the crowd, many of whom were weeping uncontrollably at the sight of their leader in such reduced circumstances, Tenzin Gyatso adviced them not to lose courage, promising that "one day we will go back to Tibet." Then, led by an escort of police jeeps, he began the two-hour drive up the narrow, boulder-strewn valleys leading to Dharamsala, the shining white summits of the Dhauladat Range rising ahead.

"It was a very small town," recalled the Dalai Lama seeing Lower Dharamsala, "but the local people gave me a hearty welcome—all they had to offer." Driving slowly past the old British post office, police station and district headquarters, Tenzin Gyatso's motorcade entered the tumbling warren of fruit and vegetable stalls, open-air barbershops, tailors, cobblers and sweet-sellers turmoiled around the main street bisecting Katwali Bazaar. Three thousand people, hill folk in their bright embroidered mountain caps, Sikhs in scarlet and blue turbans, bureaucrats and businessmen wearing black suits, their wives clad in saris, and even Gurkhas, descended from the still-active army cantonment, lined the route showering their new neighbour with flowers one of which carried a small caterpillar, which, as the Dalai Lama recollected rather ungraciously bit him on the leg. With the sun tinting the adjacent dome of Mun Peak violet, the column drove five miles more up steep switchbacks through the cantonment to McLeod Ganj, where at 5:00 p.m. it passed beneath a freshly hewn bamboo gate dressed in fir boughs and coloured streamers, a big golden *welcome* written across its top. Behind it, 250 Tibetan refugees who had arrived a week before began performing full-length prostrations, while khaki-clad Indian police violently urged them back. N.N. Nowrojee stepped forward, introduced himself and directed the Dalai Lama to a waiting jeep for the drive up the hair-raising track leading to his new home, Swarg Ashram. "When I arrived at Swarg Ashram it had become quite late, so I didn't see much," remarked the Dalai Lama. "The next morning I woke up at my normal time of five and the first thing I heard was a bird, peculiar to this place, chirping very loudly. Karakjok. Karakjok. Like that. Later I was told that one of our senior officials had been kept awake all night by this bird. Then I didn't engage in a meditation session, but just looked out at the mountains and the view. It was the first day of May 1960. A very nice day and quite hot."

Under Nowrojee's direction four bungalows had been repaired to accommodate the Tibetans. The original seat of the District Commissioner, Highcroft House, renamed Swarg Ashram or "The Heavenly Abode," had been chosen as the Dalai Lama's residence. Roughly a quarter of a mile above McLeod Ganj, the building occupied a small flat on the western edge of the mountainside. The view was stuning the entire enclosure seemingly anchored on a prop of rock flung into space, yet the house itself was almost windowless, a thirty-two-room thing; a rather large one-storied, with cavelike chambers lit by trap-like dormers and heated in winter by only a few tiny fireplaces. On its front end—turned sideways, for lack of room, to the vista—two giant bay windows jutted into a covered porch overlooking a narrow walkway, beyond which a stone wall dropped twenty feet to a grass lawn, previously used as a tennis court but soon to become an audience ground. Behind, three outbuildings, including the kitchen, rose on progressively higher and smaller levels up the mountain. While the three villas was fully prepared to house the eighty government officials, the Dalai Lama's senior and junior tutors and New Delhi's liaison officer were even more removed, Swarg Ashram received the benefit of guard huts, barbed-wire fencing and, in time, a tall concrete gate, standing inconsistently amidst the dark green pine groves cloaking the hillside, the sole emblem of the hidden compound's prestigious occupant.

A New Routine

From day one in Dharamsala the Dalai Lama realized that he was very much alone in the woods. With the departure of the 250 refugees for road work a few weeks later, only Nowrojee remained in McLeod Ganj. Constantly on call, he supplied the Tibetans with everything from blankets, toiletries and thermoses to cooking oil and umbrellas. Life in Swarg Ashram itself was crowded. Like anything behind the Dalai Lama's monastic bedroom, prayer room and office—all at the front of house—lived his mother, his two sisters, his brother-in-law P.T. Takla, the Masters of Robes, Ceremonies and Food, the Lord Chamberlain and an assortment of secretaries and translators. Both Tibetan and Indian guards patrolled the grounds, leaving the only free space just beyond the gate. Soon after his arrival the Dalai Lama began trekking up the mountains, sometimes climbing as high as 16,000 feet to a pass below the peck of Mun Peak, from where he would descend for the night to a hikers' lodge called Triund. Only a few companions accompanied him. "We used to climb very steep hills," remembered the Dalai Lama. "It would have been very difficult for the Indian guards to follow us. Poor fellows, they wore heavy boots, which had slippery nails in their soles, and they also carried large guns. So instead we had them put their rifles down and just wait below for our return. We were all very friendly. We often drank tea and ate together in a good meadow that I found in the woods. I really enjoyed it. That was one of my new experiences in Dharamsala and it had its own special beauty."

The Dalai Lama's life in Swarg Ashram was altogether different than that in Tibet. Its rigours included two to three buckets of water a day dripping during the monsoon from an unrepairable ceiling around his bed ;

its pleasures, snowmen and snowball fights the first winter, table tennis in the main sitting room, where Tenzin Gyatso took meals along with his mother and, after office hours at five, a regular badminton game on the lawn before the covered entrance to building. A novel series of pets including a young deer and a number of independent-minded Lhasa Apsos, added to the household's informal atmosphere.

Though the Dalai Lama found more time in Swarg Ashram for spiritual matters, the bulk of his day focused on the refugees' condition. By waging a constructive fight for Tibet, through the re-creation of Tibetan culture abroad, he was assured that Peking efforts was reasonable that its rule over his homeland would fail. Moreover, such an effort not only would prevent the decline of the refugee community but would offer the chance to modernize, if in embryo, Tibetan society, fashioning a pattern of sorts for the Tibet of the future, once its freedom was regained.

Reconstruction to the Government

As the first initiative, the government had to be reconstituted. Using Mortimer Hall for a Secretariat, the Cabinet divided its ministers and workers among six portfolios : Home Affairs, Foreign Affairs, Religion and Culture, Education, Finance, and Security. A bureau was established in New Delhi to serve as the Tibetan link with the Indian government and the various international relief agencies that were coming to the refugees' aid. It was followed by four offices, in New York, Geneva, Tokyo and Katmandu, each in its way acting as an unofficial embassy for the government-in-exile. Ten civil service ranks, scaled up from the seven in Tibet, were created, while the Dalai Lama, assisted by Indian lawyers, set out drafting a democratic constitution upon which to found the first elected government in Tibet's history. Rehabilitation, however, was the immediate task of much concern. "At the beginning of our work," related the Dalai Lama, "two factions existed among the community of our responsible people. One thought we Tibetans must concentrate in northern India ; the other—including myself—felt that it didn't matter where we lived. The important thing was to find a place and settle properly so that we could preserve the Tibetan identity, culture and race." The Dalai Lama's view eventually won out, as northern India, despite its desirable nearness to Tibet's border, lacked large tracts of unused land. Once apprised of the Tibetans' wishes, Prime Minister Nehru canvassed the chief ministers of India's less populated southern states for vacant countryside. Karnataka responded affirmatively, offering an uninhabited stretch of jungle situated in gently rolling hills fifty-two miles west of

Mysore. As a joint investigating team from Dharamsala and New Delhi soon discovered, the available land was uninhabited save for a single road running down from Mysore along which lay a few primitive villages. Regardless, its potential was equivalent to that of Dharamsala ; whatever success the Tibetans managed to take for cibly from the land would be their own.

In the second week of December 1960, almost two years after their arrival in India, the first group of 666 Tibetan refugees left their camps along the northern thoroughfares to build permanent homes in the south. "No one had the slightest idea where we were going," recalled Lobsang Chonzin, a stout, aquiline-featured farmer who became leader of the settlement's first village. "A Tibetan government official told us that we had been chosen to pioneer new land. Then a few weeks later he came to put us on a special train that travelled south for three days. At the end, buses were waiting at a station in a big city. They took us straight into the countryside, further and further, until we finally saw our destination, a group of tents in a clearing in the middle of the jungle."

Efforts to Recreate New Settlement

Unlike the subtropical rain forests of Bhutan and Assam, through which most of the refugees had passed, this new jungle, at the very heart of the Indian subcontinent, was psychologically as well as physically quite remote. The few mud-and-twiq villages the refugees had glimpsed from the buses as they drove through, hung with brilliant clusters of red peppers, bananas and mangoes, sheltered a small, drak race of semi-aboriginal people who looked altogether alien. The Tibetans' sense of displacement gave way to disorientation after the buses had gone and only a few Indian police stayed on to help organize homesteading. Aware of the fact that the ancient expanse surrounding them was the natural abode of elephants, tigers, wild boars and other dangerous animals, the settlers' first act was to fashion tall bamboo posts into a protective rampart around one of the larger tents. Inside, they built a makeshift altar upon which to place a precious image of the Buddha given to them by the Dalai Lama. As night fell they dug pits, lined them with stones and cooked their first dinner. "We forced ourselves to eat," continued Chonzin, "but we all felt so frightened and forlorn that no one could speak. Many people sat helplessly on the ground crying to themselves. We could hear the calls of wild animals in the jungle and, unlike in Tibet, you couldn't see a thing. Wherever you looked there was nothing but trees."

In the following morning, a group of monks, seated before the sacred image in the tent, began praying for success. They continued for a week, after which the work of felling and burning the forest began. An axe, a saw and a machete were given to each family of five, and two rupees or twenty cents a day were paid out as salary by the Indian government. With new groups of 500 sent down from the north at six-month intervals the settlement, known as Byllakuppe, struggled into existence. "The heat was the worst," said Chonzin, shaking his head. "For two years, day and night, smoke and fire covered everything—even during the monsoon. Then we would work all day in the pouring rain and come home at night to find our tents blown down. Under these conditions many people died. They would recall Tibet, look at where they were and just give up." As fresh ground was broken a new danger appeared. Workers felling trees farthest from the tent camps repeatedly met and were often trampled to death by elephants filled with rage. A chain of guard huts had to be built around each clearing ; these were manned day and night by sentries equipped with tin cans, gongs and firecrackers both to sound the alarm and to scare off unwanted interference of the intruders. The fight against the elephants took on almost mythic dimensions ; settlers, armed with slingshots and other homemade weapons, walked warily through newly cut roads in the jungle, while those caught alone by an elephant not infrequently returned to their tents a day or two later, having spent the short time up on a tree. In the midst of the besieged colony's panes of childbirth, the Dalai Lama arrived on a tour of inspection. "During my first visit to Byllakuppe," he recalled, "the people made a special tent for me of bamboo walls and a canvas roof. Still, it could not keep out the tremendous dust produced by clearing the forest. Because of such circumstances, the Tibetans were quite low-spirited. The death rate was high and due to the heat of the sun and burning trees all of them had become quite dark and thin." Opposed by a pervasive sense of hopelessness, the Dalai Lama offered the only encouragement he could—assurance of eventual prosperity. "Whenever I visited our larger settlements I always promised that we would prevail," he observed. "I pushed and pushed and pushed and finally, year by year, the picture completely changed. Then, when things got better I teased the people about their once dark, thin faces, which now had become quite healthy and smiling. I told them that in the past I was only making empty promises, because I myself, poor things, could offer them nothing. But those Tibetans always followed my word without the slightest doubt. As a result, we succeeded. It was just like watering an old flower about to wilt. If you water it with some hope it will immediately become fresh and enthusiastic."

New Settlements

Early in 1962, the first group of settlers moved into more than a hundred brick-walled, tile-roofed homes, taking their prized butter lamps, offering bowls and scarf-draped photos of the Dalai Lama with them. The first of Byllakuppe's eventual twenty villages, housing 10,000 people on 5,500 acres, camp No. 1 served as the original model for virtually every refugee settlement developed for the next two decades. Little more than a year after its establishment, the inhabitants watched, along with those of camp No. 2, as their names were randomly pulled from a container and they were allotted an acre of land apiece. Thereafter, the attempt to transform Byllakuppe into a full-fledged farming community was in advance.

Despite the fertile soil, it was not easy. A crop of lentils, cotton, tobacco and corriander sown on twenty-eight acres in 1961 had not done well. Then almost fifty times as much cotton and tobacco was sown, all of which failed completely. Farming in southern India was so different from Tibet's unique high-altitude agronomy that it seemed the settlement would founder, until an agricultural adviser from a relief organization called Swiss Technical Co-operation arrived to offer guidance. Conducting soil tests, he determined that maize should be planted, sustained by fertilizer and farmed by tractors rather than the bullock plows the Tibetans were practising. The new methods and crop worked. Maize proved so successful that by 1966, six years after its founding, the settlement was self-supporting. Three years after that, with 77,000 fruit trees planted, a dairy and poultry farm and a second crop of ragi (a cereal grass) raised to diversify the harvest, Byllakuppe was making a substantial profit on its produce.

By then 38 settlements harboring almost 60,000 people were scattered throughout India, Nepal and Bhutan, all starting out on land too remote or inhospitable for local people to care for. After houses were built, farming quite often proved so refractory that many settlements had to basically rely on traditional Tibetan handicrafts, such as carpet weaving, for their income. Yet by the early 1980s only 3,000 refugees remained on road gangs, while some 44 settlements, linked by commercial, political and religious ties, looking to Dharamsala as their capital, housed almost 100,000 refugees, the remaining having emigrated to twenty-four countries around the world.

The refugees' rehabilitation was further increased by what many international relief agencies working closely with the Tibetans came to consider an economic miracle. While a number of industrial efforts, including a woollen mill, lime plant, limestone quarry and fiberglass factory, all failed, the exiles found that collective marketing and purchasing, carried out through agricultural cooperatives, had an immense potential in India's disorderly economy. Once more Byllakuppe led the way. In 1964, the settlement's first six camps inaugurated a co-op, Luksum Samdup Ling ("Preserving Tradition-Fulfilling Wishes"). Sixteen years later, Byllakuppe's fourteen "new" camps founded a second co-op, Dickey Larso ("Revival of Happiness"). With funds from the Swiss Technical Co-operation and, later, from the Mysore Rehabilitation and Agriculture Development Agency, the co-ops transformed the settlement. Restaurants and stores were attached to its villages ; seed, fertilizer, trucks, a flour mill and dehusking machine purchased to boost production ; and a large workshop built to fashion furniture, carts, knives, axes, and farming tools in the quest for self-sufficiency. Young men were sent to Norway, Denmark and Iran to be trained as tractor mechanics. On their return they expanded the settlement's variegated fleet of Escorts, Soviet Zetors and Ford tractors, creating in the process a repair and machine shop that soon took over all the business for fifty miles around.

While the co-ops marketed the settlement's produce, as far away as Bombay and Calcutta, individual settlers continued to continuosly a trade that came to account for the livelihood of almost a quarter of the refugee population : selling sweaters. Capitalizing on the success of a Tibetan hand-knit sweater business in Kalimpong, thousands of refugees began to sell gaudy green, purple, yellow and red machine-made products purchased from previously unpatronized Punjabi factories. Each winter they set up shop out of tin trunks on the sidewalks of bazaars and marketplaces all across India. Their success was such that by the latter half of the sixties a Tibetan sweater fad was sweeping the subcontinent. The sudden popularity of "Tibetan" sweaters enabled an average worker to earn up to 5,000 rupees or $ 626—seven times more than his or her wages on the road. The nomadic business of sweater-selling brought about a lot of change and not only improved their diets, but also fulfilled the traditional Tibetan's love of trade and travel. Introduced through it to their host country, they used the opportunity to promote their cause, every sweater, stocking-cap, or scarf sold contained a small card that explained how the refugees had been forced down "from the roof of the world" to the "hot plains of the subcontinent."

Dalai Lamas Treasure

A further resource came from the Dalai Lama's personal funds too. Over a thousand pack animals had followed the Tibetan ruler's 1950 flight from Lhasa to Yatung, each laden with 120 pounds of treasure. Sent to Sikkim as a precaution in case Tenzin Gyatso would be forced to flee Tibet, forty mules bore gold, six hundred carried silver and the remaining animals, sacks of centuries-old coins. Though the Dalai Lama returned to the Potala, this relatively small share of his *labrang* or household treasure did not. Guarded by a single unknowing Lepcha sentry, it remained hidden for nine years in the Choegyal of Sikkim's abandoned stables located on the hillside below the place in Gangtok, the capital of Sikkim. When before dawn one morning in 1960 a long convoy of trucks departed the capital for Calcutta, half the population of Sikkim awoke to what most imagined was the sight of their king fleeing his own country. Only after the treasure was safely deposited in the underground arched roof of a Calcutta bank did the truth emerge, spawning unchecked speculation in India's press over the "God-King's fabulous fortune." In fact, after its conversion into currency and subsequent investment, only $ 987,500 materialized to form His Holiness the Dalai Lama's Charitable Trust, the resource from which virtually every exile project found seed money.

Preservation of Culture

With economic security, the refugees' cultural reconstruction was convinced. The Dalai Lama had begun the work of preservation from his first days in Swarg Ashram. "We divided our culture into two types," he explained. "In the first category we placed that which, we determined, needed to be retained only in books as past history. The second category included whatever could bring actual benefit in the present. These things, we resolved, must be kept alive. Therefore, many of our old ceremonial traditions I discarded—no matter, I decided, let them go. However, our performing arts, our literature, science and religion as well as those crafts from which we could earn a livelihood—painting, metalcraft, architecture, woodworking and carpetmaking—these, we took special pains to safeguard. To achieve this we employed modern methods although they were altogether new to us and posed many difficulties."

As the wellspring of Tibetan civilization, religion was the first priority. Unlike other Asian nations to which Buddhism had spread, Tibet alone contained the entire collection of the Buddhist Dharma ; the full scope of sutras, tantras, their accompanying book of common prayer and most critically the guru-disciple lineages, founded on oral transmission, which served as unbroken links to the origin of the oldest of the three world faiths. Only 7,000 of Tibet's more than 600,000 monks and a few hundred or so of its 4,000 incarnate lamas had fled. Those left behind had been defrocked, while new refugees brought word of the country's 6,524 monasteries being gutted by Chinese teams specially assigned to ship their valuable artifacts to the homeland, either to be melted into uncoinedgold or silver or sold via Hong Kong on the international antiques market. For each scholar who died on a road gang, centuries of learning were lost, causing the Dalai Lama to take emergency steps to remove them from the deadly labour, even before their lay follow country-men.

By August of 1959, as its last inmates were shipped out to road camps, Buxa Duar began receiving groups of refugee monks, assembled to salvage the Dharma. By the following year, almost 1,500 monks were living in the barracks of the newly named Buxa Lama Ashram, rising at 5:00 a.m. for group prayers in its central courtyard, then breaking into their monastic colleges to conduct memorization, debate and tutorials with senior scholars and incarnate lamas. Scouring road camps, the monks collected as many scriptures as possible from which they began lithographing with stone and ink over 200 volumes of major works—only a small fraction, however, of Tibet's 1,200 years of philosophic writing. With members of the Gelugpa sect predominating (those of the other three orders more often finding refuge at monasteries in Sikkim, Bhutan and Nepal), examinations for the Geshe degree continued after only a year's break and it seemed as though the religion would rapidly mend. Then monks began to die. With their occupants sleeping sixty-six to a barracks and the bamboo beds only six inches apart, tuberculosis ran unchecked. Each morning following prayers, 200 to 300 men would queue up behind the twenty-foot barb'ed-wire fence, waiting for hours in the scroching sun to be checked by the camp's single medical worker. "We were eager to save our religion," recalled Khentrul Rinpoche, a lama from Sera Monastery, who lived in the camp from its start. "But after just a few years the number of monks dying increased to the point that the rest couldn't help wondering whether or not we'd ever escape from that place alive. Watching our friends become dark and thin and their teeth turn black, we constantly had depressed, suffocated feelings. We could only endure this hardship because we knew that the religious tradition of Tibet depended on us alone."

By 1968, the large settlements of Byllakuppe and Mundgod were finally ready to begin receiving survivors. Once moved south, the monks clinged to farming and started to gradually build over 150 new monasteries, filling them with young converts and creating the most clear emblems of Tibetan life in exile. The monasteries in turn complemented a series of cultural institutes, primarily based in Dharamsala.

The first institute founded, three months after the Dalai Lama's arrival in Swarg Ashram, was the Tibetan Dance and Drama Society. Its seventy-four members—only twenty of whom had been performing artists in Tibet—managed to conserve in the play performing ground four abridged Lhamo operas (the often week-long spectacles performed in Tibet's larger cities), two historical plays, numerous *cbam* or monastic dances and even a reconstituted marching band which often played for the annual March 10 rally in Dharamsala, summoned to commemorate the Lhasa uprising.

Unique Medical Science

But a year later, in October of 1961, the Tibetan Medical Center was founded under Dr. Yeshi Dhonden, one of only three Lhasa-trained physicians to escape. Tibet's unique medical science, developed natively over 2,100 years, was salvaged in a small hospital, pharmacy, astrology department and school, which by the late 1970s had graduated enough Tibetan doctors to staff the larger settlements. The third major institute to be opened was the Library of Tibetan Works and Archives, started in November 1971, in an imposing Tibetan-style building situated in the middle of the government's new Secretariat compound, Gangchen Kyishong. Located halfway between Lower Dharamsala and McLeod Ganj it soon became a magnet for hundreds of Asian as well as Western scholars who previously had scant access to Tibetan culture. By 1984, the library's numerous teaching and collection projects had accumulated over 50,000 volumes, an estimated 40 per cent of Tibet's literature—the remainder having been destroyed both before and during the Cultural Revolution in Tibet. In New Delhi, Tibet House, founded in 1965, supplemented much of the library's work, while the Tibetan section of All India Radio was made larger and a number of refugee publications appeared. But by far the most extensive and crucial of the cultural projects lay in the school system. Created by the Dalai Lama in order to preserve the Tibetan identity while introducing the "exile generation" to the modern world, it was looked on by all the refugees, monks and laymen alike, as the most essential hope for the future of their cause.

The bus on which Tempa Tsering left the road camp in Bawarna for the Nursery in Dharamsala arrived in McLeod Ganj around afternoon.

Discharged into the hands of Mrs. Tsering Dolma, the Dalai Lama's elder sister, and the Nursery's principal a monk named Thubten Nyingee, the children were led up a crooked dirt road through the woods in Conium House, a barnlike building of whitewashed stone walls and zinc roofing inhabited for five months now by almost 200 orphaned and semi-orphaned youngsters.

The Nursery for the Tibetan Refugee Children

The Nursery for Tibetan Refugee Children, as Conium House was formally known, had been founded by the Dalai Lama less than three weeks after his own arrival in Dharamsala. Its immediate catalyst was a report of children dying among a refugee group delayed by heavy snows en route from Missamari to different work sites in Ladakh. Fifty-one children were taken from the group and housed with Tibetan government workers in their bungalows until, under the direction of the Dalai Lama's sister, the Nursery opened on May 17, 1960. Removed from road work, few of the children died, though the majority were harassed by a wide range of ailments from tuberculosis to dysentery, influenza, scabies and severe malnutrition.

Tempa's own dysentery had long gone, but he remained withdrawn and uncommunicative. Deloused and with a newly shaved head, he was given his first Western clothes, a pair of shorts and two shirts, and seated in a long line of children for a dinner of rice and boiled lentils dished into beaten-tin bowls. Afterward, he and thirty others unrolled their blankets on the floor of a room in Conium House and prepared to sleep, the sick mixed in with the healthy, as there were too many to be isolated. The next morning the day began with prayers, exercise and a class in the Tibetan and English alphabets, followed by an afternoon of unsupervised play. Throughout, Tempa did not want to participate. A month later, however, with his room packed each night with 120 children, so crowded that no one could move, he finally began to focus on the present. One day a ball was kicked toward him during a game of soccer in the courtyard. Returning it, he joined the other boys, from then his incapacitating depression slowly began to lift.

Tempa's interest in life was restimulated most by three encounters he now had with the Dalai Lama. One morning, the older children were taken through the forest to witness a prayer session at Swarg Ashram. It was actually Tempa's first religious ceremony. As he sat on the steps of the Heavenly Abode's porch, gazing at the Dalai Lama on a throne circled by monks performing the graceful *mudras* or hand gestures of tantric ritual while they recited scripture, he experienced an unusual feeling of reverence that, far more than the small quantity of physical well-being afforded by the Nursery, gave him a sense of security.

On a second less formal occasion he made contact with the Dalai Lama himself. At that time Tenzin Gyatso walked from Swarg Ashram to Conium House to share a traditional Tibetan dinner of *tbukpa* or noodle soup with the children. Before his arrival, the Nursery was very much excited few of its adult teachers having had such close contact with their leader in Tibet. Marshalled like a regiment on a parade ground, the children greeted the Dalai Lama, who immediately asked as to what were they studying. Tempa was told before the gathering to write the letters *A*, *B* and *C* on a slate. The Dalai Lama watched carefully and, giving him a warm pat on the shoulder, said, "Very good." "Of course," recalled Tempa laughing, "I liked him from that moment on."

A third meeting with the Dalai Lama marked Tempa's departure from the Nursery. One hundred sixty of the oldest children had been chosen to attend the Mussoorie School, the first were educational institute to be created in exile, founded one year before. In their company, Tempa hiked to Swarg Ashram, where the Dalai Lama, seated on the porch with the children gathered around, advised them to study hard so that in future they could help those who would not have the same opportunity. At the conclusion of his remarks, Tempa led the group in reciting the eleven-verse Long Life Prayer of the Fourteenth Dalai Lama. "My friends said I was so nervous that I was shivering and forgot whole parts," he recalled. "But I think I got the chorus right, at least where it says, 'Bless Tenzin Gyatso, Protector of the Land of Snows. May his life not fail, but last a hundred eons, and may his will be effortlessly accomplished.' "

"In Tibet I had a great desire to establish a modern school," said the Dalai Lama. "From the early fifties on, I felt the need very strongly. Without any knowledge of how such a school functions I just thought over and over, 'We must have a modern school. We must have a school.' But I didn't even know how many classes to have." Returning to Mussoorie after his 1959 pilgrimage, the Dalai Lama went about the town for a suitable building that to begin his project. Eventually he found an old home called Kildare House, belonging to an Indian army officer who, convinced the building was haunted by the ghosts of Moslems killed there during the riots at India's partition, was glad to sell at a low price. Located in a rocky clearing not far from Birla House, eight of its decaying rooms were opened on March 3, 1960, to fifty young men—monks, Khampa guerrillas and government officials—aged eighteen to twenty-five. Although the Dalai Lama was not well versed in modern education, two recent exiled were : Mary and Jigme Taring, among the first Tibetans to have been educated in India, under whose guidance the Mussoorie School was fully entrusted.

The Tarings were a pioneering couple. Jigme Taring was a prince, the nephew of the Choegyal of Sikkim ; while Mary was the daughter of Wangchuk Gyalpo Tsarong, a senior Cabinet minister under the Thirteenth Dalai Lama and a descendant of Tibet's famous eighth-century physician, Yuthok Yonten Gonpo, With their background as surety against criticism from Tibet's dislike of foreigners the Tarings were the foremost proponents of modernization in their generation. In exile, they represented an invaluable asset to the fledgling governmemt.

After arriving at the new school Tempa found in their guidance the first substantial explanation of his situation. "All of us children called them Mother and Father and they really acted like that," he recalled. "After a while there were three or four hundred kids, but the Tarings took an interest in each and every one. They explained over and over, in classes, in meetings and alone, what had happened to us. Above all they said that we were Tibetans. We had been driven out by the Chinese, and somehow we had to get back, to regain our country. This was the responsibility children like us had. We had to work for all the Tibetan people, not just ourselves. From hearing this again and again I stopped being completely absorbed in my own tragedy. I began to see that I had a greater duty. The Tarings made sense of it all to us. They gave that to the children."

Tibetan Schools Society

Following the Tarings' lead, two more residential schools, one in Simla, the other in Darjeeling, started. The Dalai Lama then approached the Indian government to propose a long-range plan. Consulting with Nehru at a private luncheon in New Delhi in May 1961, he received the Prime Minister's support for the founding of an autonomous body within the Indian Ministry of Education, called the Tibetan Schools Society ; its sole purpose would be to run a network of residential and day schools staffed jointly by Indian as well as Tibetan teachers. Education being one area in which Nehru could freely aid the Tibetans without political consequences, his support was so generous that by 1964 the system included well over seven residential schools housing, in the main, over

500 children each, four day schools in the settlements, three transit schools at road-construction sites and a number of grant-in-aid schools indirectly supported by the Society. Nevertheless, there had to be obstacles. In organizing the large residential schools, the dearth of such basic necessities as flat land caused immense difficulty. Situated in mountainous regions that offered few buildings with surrounding grounds, the schools were forced to adopt whatever facility was available, while the children themselves, for the most part, coverted it : in Darjeeling, an old barracks of the North Bengal Mounted Rifles ; at Mount Abu, the abondoned place of the Maharaja of Bikaner ; in Panchmari, the defunct Royal Hotel ; at Kalimpong, a woollen warehouse unused since the heyday of Tibetan trade. By 1966, almost 7,000 youngsters had been saved from road gangs. Half, however, were overage, and many of those who would have failed to complete high school by the age of 20 were forced to withdraw. There were also problems with the faculty. Because the TSS was not a full-fledged component of India's school system, teachers were concerned over tenure, reluctant to work in remote settlements and as only university-level faculty could instruct in English—the medium chosen by the Dalai Lama—hard to find to begin with. Those finally hired could not even talk to their Tibetan counterparts until a vocabulary list of 500 Hindi and Tibetan words was circulated from New Delhi.

The children, though, were learning, and surprisingly they were the first generation in Tibet's history to see maps of the world and hear of other nations. As Tempa reflected, "When we were first taught geography, it was almost unbelievable. The teacher showed us a globe and pictures of different peoples, but until it was thoroughly explained, I found it hard to accept that the world was really so large. I just couldn't comprehend it. In Tibet, India had always been the end of the earth for us." The young Tibetans' enthusiasim was particulary stimulated by the bizarre objects represented by the Western aid workers, who, as the first Caucasians they had seen, were jokingly nicknamed "yellow heads" for their blond hair. Meanwhile, their own Tibetan instructors were now being systematically prepared in a Teachers Training School established in Dharamsala, and a textbook committee and a printing press were soon issuing a syllabus covering Tibetan language, history, literature and religion from first grade through the end of high school. By the time the Tibetan Schools Society changed its name to the Central Tibetan Schools Administration in the early seventies, 9,000 children were attending its thirty-two institutions ; ten years later 15,000 studied in fifty-two schools, the majority of whom chose to continue on to a university. Advanced studies in Tibet's own academic tradition were managed by the Institute of Higher Tibetan Studies, founded in January 1968 in Benares as well as the Buddhist School of Dialectics, began Dharamsala nearly five years later. In order to continue care for orphaned children, a system of Tibetan foster homes was created, beginning in 1962 with the Mussoorie Homes run by Mary Taring. By the end of the decade, with 600 children in twenty-five Tibetan-style households staffed by live-in parents, Mussoorie was outdone only by the Nursery in Dharamsala, which changed its name to the Tibetan Children's Village. Placed under the direction of the Dalai Lama's younger sister, Pema Gyalpo, it relocated to Egerton Hall above the military cantonment and began rapidly expanding over the hillside. Towards the close of the seventies its city-like campus housing over 1,000 needy children six months to eighteen years old was regarded by UN agencies and others as a example for rehabilitating refugee children and was indisputably the most successful enterprise in exile.

At the age of fourteen, after two years in Mussoorie, Tempa was accepted at St. Gabriel's Academy, a secondary school outside Dehra Dun. In company with many of the older refugee children, whose age made them unfit for the Tibetans' budding institutions, he was forced to spend the next decade in the alien environment of Indian schools. "After arriving at St. Gabriel's," he recounted, "even though there were six Tibetans, the sense of being an outsider just grew deeper and deeper. The more contact we had, the more we felt removed. Only a handful of people had heard of Tibet. The rest kept asking, 'Where is your father? What does he do? Who are your brothers and sisters?' Each time they asked, you couldn't help but recall your past—that you are a refugee and you have no country—but still these people remained very ignorant of what we were. Overall it inculcated in me a further awareness of being Tibetan. My desire to have Tibet back, to regain my own country, just increased."

He was then transferred to Dr. Graham's Homes, a missionary school in Kalimpong, Tempa's anger at what he perceived to be a popular disregard for Tibetans, the idea that they were "backward and uncivilized," clearly showed itself in competitive drive. Excelling in academic work, he became, during his five and a half years at Dr. Graham's, head of virtually every sports team, earning the titles of proctor, vice-captain and finally captain of the school, under whom the entire student body was administered. With his name inscribed on the school's commemorative plaque listing outstanding students, Tempa's success was such that a special assembly of graduates the first in Dr. Graham's history—was convened after graduation to honour him. "I had to be independent," he commented, valuing the reversal in his character following the shock of his sisters' and mother's deaths. "Deep down I realized that I didn't have anything unless I created it for myself. And I think that kept pushing me ; the loss of Tibet, of my parents, the breakdown of a family—all of it. For my own good as well as the Tibetan people's—there was so much personal as well as national loss—I just had to succeed in building it back up."

Madras Christian College

When he arrived at Madras Christian College, however, one of India's most esteemed schools, Tempa found himself, as the first Tibetan in the city, the object of constant racial harassment. Within a week the taunts became so frequent that he thought of withdrawing. Instead, he walked into the principal's office and requested permission to address the college. "I just told him that I was so disappointed and embarrassed," stated Tempa. "Not only the students but even the teachers hardly knew the first thing about Tibet. 'I can't continue explaining to people where I come from,' I said, 'so I'd like to address the whole school at once.' " A few days later, Tempa walked alone onto an empty stage, a packed auditorium of excited undergraduates seated before him. Nervously he read a speech oulining Tibet's recent history until, reaching the uprising in Lhasa and the subsequent flight of the refugees, he suddenly found himself not going with the text from the text and relating the events of his own life. Save for a brief account he had given to a close teacher two years before, it was the first time that Tempa had spoken publicly of his personal tragedy. He was overwhelmed by a standing ovation at the talk's conclusion, Tempa went on to duplicate his success at Dr. Graham's, studying now to become a doctor, there being at that time only three or four Western-trained Tibetan physicians. Despite three years of applying to aid organizations, though he was not capable to locate a sponsor for medical school. As a result of which irrespective of his long record of outstanding academic work, Tempa Tsering faced the world with no expectation. It seemed a great defeat. The only choice remaining was to join his father, now living in Byllakuppe, and become a farmer.

Tempa travelled inland by train, journeying from India's eastern seaboard to Mysore. Boarding a battered country bus, he rode fifty miles south to the Cauvery Valley. On either side the country turned increasingly wild, until even the roadside fields were given permanently to jungle. At the small town of Cauvery, he landed and set out on foot for the settlement.

Crossing the Cauvery River, he saw men and women from Byllakuppe spreading their washing to dry on wide boulders painted in bright, primary colours with the national mantra of Tibet, *Om Mani Padme Hum*. Turning off the main road by the settlement workshop, he entered an entirely Tibetan atmosphere. Lush, fields in wavy pattern stretched to the horizon, crisscrossed by neat rows of haystacks crowned by prayer flags. At high points rose in brownish red colour and white walls of Byllakuppe's six monasteries, including the rebuilt Sera and Tashilhunpo, scattered by villages, schools, the old settlement office and a hospital. On the long roads uniting the camps, fringed in brilliant purple dye and yellow flowering bushes, a company of monks, farm workers and women with babies tied to their backs, rosaries in hand, passed by. Only the heat and the jungle-covered hills circling the settlement's perimeter remained as evidence of Byllakuppe's un-Tibetan locale.

Tempa had visited Byllakuppe frequently since taking up his studies in Madras. Before, he had met his father on only three occasions in the eight years subsequent to departing the road camp at Bawarna. Now it was for the first time since leaving Tibet father and son both lived together. The changes in both were instantly visible. Chopel Dhondub, like most of the elder refugees, had clung to all the old Tibetan views. Physically, he had altered by turning smaller and darker ; emotionally, due to the strain of work, by becoming more moody—a trait usually suppressed in Tibetan society. Tempa, on the other hand, was now a hybrid, the product of circumstances and learning beyond his father's understanding. Their differences reflected a threshold in the refugee experience : the maturation of the first generation in exile, and with it, a change in the Tibetan character. "As soon as I started living with my father again he immediately pressed for an arranged marriage," said Tempa. "In Tibet this was normal, but I told my father that it was none of his business. It wasn't his marriage but mine." Though Chopel Dhondub couldn't prevail, other families continued to arrange marriages for their children, life in the settlements far more so than that of Dharamsala or other urban centres, fixing of to conservative ideals even, on occasion, to the point of violence. As Tempa related, "When long hair and bell-bottoms came to India all the young Tibetans naturally took them up. The elders couldn't understand it. They thought it looked disrespectful. In Byllakuppe, when we danced to the Beatles, our parents actually came out and threw stones at us. But we never reacted. We never said even a word to them. We just took it. Then, when things cooled down, we explained, 'You have to change. We're living in the world now. This is the way things are.' Gradually, after lots of patient discussion, they began to accept it."

A more fundamental shift concerned religion. Under the demands of exile life Buddhism's all-pervasive influence was naturally reduced. Though they had studied the Dharma in their TSS syllabus, the younger generation found few occasion for its practice and they grew critical of Buddhism's social function in a heretofore unimaginable manner. As a monk from Byllakuppe observed, "Many of these young Tibetans won return my smile on the street. They see that I am a fellow Tibetan but these robes are just like a prison suit. The monks, they think, are the reason we lost Tibet." "Too much religion, too little politics," remark of Tempa, describing the widespread belief among his equals that religion, carried to the extreme it was in Tibet, had undermined the organization of the state. "Basically the younger generation is more political than religious. For my father, religion came first, politics second. But I think this generation, for the first time in centuries, feels the opposite."

Young and old never differed in values and ideas though, in their commitment to Tibet's cause. "When I first began to visit my father in Byllakuppe," said Tempa, "every time we met he would say, 'I was born and bred in Tibet and I want to die in Tibet. I want my body buried there— not in India.' I learned a lot from this. After my mother saw His Holiness she said, 'That's good enough for me. Now let me die peacefully.' Then she gave up. But not my father. He's never stopped fighting. All those that lived—the survivors—they're all like that."

Tibetan Youth Congress

Tempa remained in Byllakuppe for a year or so. In search of a more stimulating occupation than farming, he volunteered to work part-time at the settlement office, while joining the local branch of the Tibetan Youth Congress. Founded in 1970 by a small group of young Tibetans, the Congress had quickly grown as the largest political party in the exile community. At its week-long inaugural conference in Dharamsala, Tempa disclosed for the first time his long-held thoughts on Tibet's political struggle. Now, given the chance to work for the Congress, he interest-ingly took over its local adult education programme, lecturing in the evenings on health care, still a major problem among the refugees. He obtained a film projector to show documentaries on Gandhi's nonviolent fight for national liberation, the Satyagraha movement. Next, he requested for books from the schools he had attended, assembling, a parcel at a time, the settlement's only library. Within a few months his disappointment at failing to become a doctor passed as he was elected general secretary of the

Byllakuppe chapter, the largest of the Youth Congress's forty branches, comprising about 10,000 members.

Not long after Tempa's election, the Dalai Lama came to Byllakuppe to offer the Kalachakra Initiation, a religious event attended by Tibetans. At an audience with the Youth Congress, Tempa once more met face to face with the Tibetan leader : the first time he had met him in person since his childhood days at the Nursery in Dharamsala. "The example of His Holiness had the strongest effect on me," said Tempa. "As the leader of his people he was so uplifting and farsighted. We all know how simply he lives and how hard he works and cares for the Tibetans, but when I actually saw this in practice, I felt personally inspired to do something more for my country."

A few months later, the entire government-in-exile appeared in Byllakuppe to hold its annual report meeting in the settlers' presence. Attending the event as a Youth Congress observer, Tempa was fascinated by the proceedings, conducted according to the democratic constitution promulgated by the Dalai Lama in 1963. During a break one day he was approached by Mr. Kundeling, a Cabinet Minister whom he had known to some extent in the past. On hearing that Tempa had graduated from college only to be some a farmer, Mr. Kundeling persisted him to leave Byllakuppe and join the government in Dharamsala. He then instructed the secretary of the Information and Publicity Office to give him a job. A few weeks later, a letter arrived from the office offering him a position as an assistant secretary. "After receiving the letter I discussed it with my father," Tempa related. "I had just finished school and I felt a responsibility to look after him. I told him this. I also told him that the Byllakuppe settlement office would not be happy if left. Then I said, 'This time you make the decision. So far, I've made almost every decision in my life without your knowledge. Now this is up to you.' He replied immediately, 'From our point of view Dharamsala is the central government, whereas here it's just one office, looking after three thousand people in the old camps. So obviously, if you go to Dharamsala, you'll be of more service to all the Tibetan people. For myself, if I know you are sincerely working for His Holiness, then, even if I have to die alone, with no one to pour cold water in my mouth in the last days, I won't have a single regret.' When he said that, everything was clear. I said, 'O.K.', and I went to Dharamsala."

A few weeks after, still, after fourteen years in India, with few more possessions than his own clothing, Tempa said farewell to his father for what would be another six years. Taking a bus from Cauvery to Mysore, he boarded a northbound train to Pathankot in the Punjab, from where another bus took him on the border of Katwali Bazaar, Lower Dharamsala. There, he caught the local bus for the half-hour ride five miles farther up the hill to McLeod Ganj. On the way he watched eagerly through the barred windows as the road zigzagged up the pine-covered slopes leading to the military cantonment and the Tibetan Children's Village above. After driving through Forsythe Ganj, another small village in the hills, the spindle-like ridge on which McLeod Ganj sat drew into view. In a few minutes more, St. John's in the Wilderness passed, alone in the woods, and then the galvanized canopy of Nowrojee's front porch have in sight, a characteristic press of Tibetan monks, gaddis, or hill folk, and a few local tourists from lower in the valley beneath it, idly watching the agitation at the head of town. As the bus halted, Tempa jumped off, fetched back again his bag from its roof and entered the energetic press of "Little Lhasa," as Upper Dharamsala had rather thoughtfully come to be known.

Since the first days of the Dalai Lama's tenure, McLeod Ganj had tremored through an onslaught of development. Its permanent population now approached 4,000, with hundreds of pilgrims, traders government officials and foreign visitors in periodic residence. The clear and calm colonial park at its centre had been destroyed without a thought by the Tibetans. Three rows of buildings housing shops, restaurants and hotels had already replaced it. At their centre rose a tall gold-crowned *cborten*, dedicated, as its plaque explained, to the memory of all those suffering under Chinese occupation in Tibet. Day and night it was circled by a stream of faithful, spinning two lines of prayer wheels and reciting mantras. Outside of town stood their homes : an off hand jumble of tin and stone shanties, ascending floor over roof like a ziggurat up the hill, graced by marigolds in the windows and hundreds of faded prayer flags strung between the trees just overhead. The people of Little Lhasa were mainly sweater sellers who left their unheated huts in the cold winter months to ride the rails between Indian cities in search of commerce. When in Dharamsala, they made full use of their closeness to the "Precious Protector" by each day making around ; a reconstituted Lingkhor or Holy Walk, similar to the one in Lhasa, surrounding his new residence, Thekchen Choling. It was toward this that Tempa proceeded, walking out of the far side of town and turning down a narrow road to the knoll-like crest capping the farthest of the ridges surrounding McLeod Ganj.

Island of Mahayana Teaching

Built in 1968, Thekchen Chöling or "Island of the Mahayana

Teaching" encircled a great expanse of forest and hillside through which the Dalai Lama could stroll, tend his flower gardens, look after wild birds and meditate. The green wavy iron sheel roofing of his modest private cottage dominated a kitchen complex, office building, security and secretarial quarters all located at progressively lower levels leading to the front gate.

Across a flagstone *cböra* or debating courtyard, used by the young monks of the Dialectical School and flanked along its southern end by the cells of Namgyal Dratsang, the Dalai Lama's personal monastery, stood the new Central Cathedral, a three-story lemon-yellow hall topped by gold pinnacles and designed by the Dalai Lama himself in a modern language of people. Turning the battery of prayer wheels that lined its outer walls, Tempa entered the bright interior to offer prayers before its giant images of the Buddha and Tibet's patron saints. Then, continuing down the hill via a rocky shortcut through the trees, he approached the new Secretariat compound of the government-in-exile, Gangchen Kyishong or "Abode of Snow-Happy Valley." Halfway to Lower Dharamsala, Gangchen Kyishong had been built out of the same necessity as Thekchen Choling : to replace the cramped, perennially leaking quarters of the old British bungalows. On the white pillars that framed its front gate the government's emblem—two turquoise-maned snow lions holding the eight-spoked wheel of the Dharma before snow-capped peaks, the sun and moon—proclaimed its identity. To maintain congenial relations with New Delhi, no Tibetan flag was flown. Within, on a long flat, surrounded by the more temperate foliage of the lesser slopes, rose the monumental edifices of the Library of Tibetan Works and Archives and the Cabinet building, its ground floor an assembly hall for government meetings. The library was flanked by an amphitheater of dormitories for its hundred resident scholars and the Cabinet, by tiers of buildings lodging the government departments, on the uppermost of which, setback in typically Tibetan style with a wide roofscape before it, were the two rooms of the Information Office. Tempa's quarters, which he was shown after reporting to his new superior, lay in a chalet-like log building facing the secretarial mess, not far away. With the knowledge that he had arrived at the very heart of the political struggle for Tibet, he settled in his first night, eager to begin work the following day as an active member of his government.

11

The Fight of Tibet: 1959–1984

The people of Tibet, struggled for acquiring free Tibet. India played a vital supportive role by allowing Tibetan refugees to settle in India.

The Government in Exile

The Government-in-Exile that Tempa founded in the summer of 1974 was an odd mix of introduction of novelties bureaucracy and the hierarchic evidences of the Ganden Phodrang of Tibet, the religious rule formed under the Fifth Dalai Lama in 1642. Recognized by no one save its own people—all of whom refused to accept Indian citizenship—Dharamsala's powers were circumscribed, its resources very little yet the government's poverty surprised even Tempa. Its offices operated in a clutter of semi-audible phone lines, second hand typewriters and formal portraits of the Dalai Lama, and the living quarters for the then 141 Secretariat workers, cramped together on the hillside around Gangchen Kyishong, were barely functional. The building in which Tempa lived had no heat or running water ; his room, which he shared with another young man, was in a bad state. Each day a shower of old Indian newspapers, mud patches and beaten-tin cans fell from the rotting walls onto his narrow cot, so worn that it could not even resist Tempa's weight and sank beneath his weight to touch the concrete floor. Meals were taken in the spartan Secretariat mess and came out of Tempa's salary which, remained undecided around fifty dollars a month, provided for only the barest essentials.

The Information Office was the most political of Dharamsala's departments. To promote Tibet's cause it consulted closely with the four offices established abroad as well as the large bureau in New Delhi. It maintained a listening room to monitor Radio Lhasa's daily broadcasts and screened recently escaped refugees for the latest information on China's occupation—a job to which Tempa was assigned. At the same time, he was put in charge of answering the querries addressed to Gangchen Kyishong from around the world. He also cut clippings on political, scientific and cultural developments for translation in *Sbe Ja* or *Knowledge*, a current affairs magazine published to keep the refugees well informed of global events. Meanwhile, as his first weeks passed, Tempa himself made familiar with the structure of the exile government.

The Structures of the Government

At the head of government stood the Dalai Lama and his Cabinet, the Kashag. Below them, six major departments and two subdepartments (to which those to Health and General Audit were added in the early eighties) were divided among the ministers. Here the resemblance to Tibet's former government collapsed. Just up the hill, behind Tempa's own quarters, were the homes and office of the seventeen-member Commission of Tibetan People's Deputies, the body of elected representatives who, in exile, acted as a parliament. Unlike the Tsongdu, Tibet's old National Assembly, the deputies were popularly elected to three-year terms—three men and one woman from each province, a clergyman from each of the four religious sects, including one for Bon, Tibet's indigenous religion, and an additional final member appointed by the Dalai Lama for distinguished service in art, science or literature. Their most important task was shared with the Cabinet ; together they comprised the Tibetan National Working Committee, the highest policy-making organ of the government. They also conducted the Annual General Meeting, in which each department head was questioned in public on his section's performance during the past year. Although the deputies' ability to redress Tibet's unfortunale condition directly was limited by the constraints of refugee life, the Dalai Lama believed that engaging in a democratic experiment in itself constituted an essential ingredient in his nation's struggle. "Just to criticize China was not sufficient," he explained. "We had to have a definite alternative of our own. So for this reason we created a representative government and to do this, we discussed and prepared a draft constitution."

In framing the constitution, the Dalai Lama took up a blend of socialist guidelines, to ensure the equal distribution of wealth, and democratic procedures for conducting representative government. He also drew heavily on his own personal beliefs. "From a very young age I always felt how all-important the people are," he related. "Therefore, any ideology that stands for the benefit of the poor, the downtrodden, the lowest people, I feel is sacred. The very thought of democracy, though I couldn't put it in words, was with me in Tibet. Now, theoretically, Marxism also stands for the majority—the working class. This touches me, yet there is something wrong with its implementation in the present Communist states. Their excessively rigid atmosphere actually spoils the value of human life. On the other hand, while freedom is necessary, one must have an equal economic opportunity with which to exercise it. So it seems portions of both systems are needed."

On March 10, 1963, the fourth anniversary of the Lhasa uprising, the constitution was published carefully labelled as a "draft" pending approval by the six million majority in Tibet. In exile, save for a few noble families and Khampa chieftains, who thought that their power would wear away the majority of the refugees greeted the document as a momentous, if puzzling, step into the modern world. Among its seventy-seven articles, provisions were made to balance the immense powers of the executive branch, in the person of the Dalai Lama, with a strong legislature and supreme court. Renouncing war "as an instrument of offensive policy," it declared the fundamental rights of all Tibetans to include those of universal suffrage, equality before the law, life, liberty and property, as well as freedom of religion, speech and assembly. Fulfilling socialist ideals, state ownership of the land was provided for as well as a prohibition against the accumulating of wealth and the means of production "to the common detriment." Once passed by popular referrendum, the exile government set about supplying the constitution, as best it could, with a representative framework, one, however, which had already been in place for three years.

Impatient to begin Tibet's experiment in democracy, the Dalai Lama pushed through the refugees' first elections as early as the summer of 1960—only months after his arrival in Dharamsala and more than a year before the constitution's outline was even announced in the autumn of 1961. The election had been an extremely casual affair. Most Tibetans had never thought of participating in government, much less heard of voting ; politics had been the business of monks and noblemen for centuries. As a result, there were no candidates. Assembled in their various road camps, people simply wrote on slips of paper the names of those they respected most. The sole requirement was to vote for a representative from one's own region or, in the case of the clergy, one's sect. Naturally, all of the thirteen men whose names appeared most frequently were either important lamas, nobles or tribal chieftains from Kham and Amdo. By September 1960, they had joined that Dalai Lama in Dharamsala to begin an undertaking as peculiar in its way as their election.

Unfamiliar with administrative procedure, the first group of people's deputies decided that, rather than oversee policy, they should gain experience by working in the various government departments as deputy directors. The second assembly of representatives, elected in 1963, continued in the same capacity. Those who failed to be reelected easily found new jobs with the understaffed administration. It was not until the third group of deputies was sent to Dharamsala in May 1966 that the government's legislature and administration were finally separated, it having developed that, once trained, the deputies' participation in the bureaucracy necessarily compromised their ability to regulate it.

In spite of the improvement, the electoral process itself continued to be run by the administration. In 1963, the second elections saw the introduction of election committees, ballot boxes and female representatives (to comply with the constitutional article ensuring equality of the sexes). In 1966, the third elections included actual candidates, mounted by the election committee at Dharamsala and not by political parties as campaigning, in exile, was considered a potentially making unstable activity. It was not until 1975 that the fifth Commission of People's Deputies finally instituted a two-tier vote whereby candidates could be popularly chosen in primary elections. However, even after fifteen years of clarifying the electoral process, many people—particularly older Tibetans—still found the concept of a popular vote obscure. As Lodi Gyari, chairman of the seventh assembly of deputies, noted, "A lot of people go into the election tent and just pray to His Holiness. 'I don't know any of these candidates, but please let me choose the right one to help the Dalai Lama and the people.' Then they close their eyes, put their finger down and ask the election officer, 'Would you see whose name is here.' When they hear it they reply, 'Oh, it's so-and-so. I'll vote for him.' "

Resistance, not to representative government, but to its main prerequisite, that of individuals declaring themselves as candidates, also put an obstruction on the acceptance of democratic procedure. "If I go and ask someone to vote for me," continued Lodi Gyari, "it would be considered an act of great shamelessness. It's very funny, you find this in many Oriental cultures, but we are raised to always say, 'I am very unable and uneducated.' If someone does not behave like this, it's considered a clear indication that he has personal motives and is not out for the common good." As a result, of which some deputies found themselves elected against their will, unaware even that the committee in Dharamsala had nominated them as candidates until they were called to be sworn in. On the opposite end of the spectrum, even those who were willingly elected were disqualified by either the Dalai Lama or the National Working Committee, who could judge them unfit to hold office.

Dalai Lama's Position

The issue of how much authority the Dalai Lama should impart lay at the very heart of the struggle to create a true democracy. The Dalai Lama had used the constitution to weaken his position, ironically against the wishes of his own people. In its final draft, Article 36, section (e), provided, "in the highest interests of the state," for the Dalai Lama was accused by a two-thirds majority of the National Assembly inconsultation with the Supreme Court. Resistance was such that over 150 representatives had assembled in Dharamsala to refuse to approve the constitution unless the clause was deleted. "Of course this was my idea," the Dalai Lama related. "If we were to have a true democracy there had to be provisions whereby the Dalai Lama's powers could also be changed. But at the time people complained, mainly, I think, out of an emotional feeling and also because it was something new and difficult to understand. I had to convince them that it was absolutely necessary not just for the present but for the future of all the Tibetan people. This point was one of the most important issues of the early sixties."

"After working in the government for some time, I could see that just holding elections does not create a democracy," observed Tempa Tsering. "Even in office, many of the deputies were very apathetic. They were more comfortable with the idea of an all-powerful executive than they were with a free legislature. So for this reason, I believe, democracy has yet to take hold. It's only among the younger generation that people have a real understanding of the democratic spirit." In the Tibetan Youth Congress, Tempa found a truly political climate of the same time. Becoming helped with its leaders, who, though they still lacked an office, all lived in Dharamsala, he realized that they, not the government, represented the Dalai Lama's aspirations for a politically open society.

Youth Congress

From its beginning the Youth Congress had captured the commanding role in the Tibetans' political life. Dedicated to struggling for the independence of Tibet, it had been created by four young men, all from upper-class backgrounds and educated in the best British-based schools in India.

"In 1970 things were still pretty bleak in Dharamsala," recalled Jamyang Norbu, a Youth Congress convener, describing the organization's birth. "There were no Westerners, only the Peace Corps people who came around at Christmastime to sing carols. Among the Tibetans there were a lot of idealistic youth. It was very bohemian, not intentionally, but just because the life was so hard. Each night five or six people would crush into your room to sleep. No one had any money, so nobody gave a damn. Whatever you got, you would just spend in a few days. A group of us used to get together and drink barley beer and, if we could afford it, rum. Then we'd always start talking about Tibet. It was a bit sentimental, I suppose. We'd say, 'So what are we going to do? What is our dream?' Then someone would declare, 'One of these days I'm going to get across that pass with my tank and see the Potala.' That sort of talk. After as while we'd make tea on a kerosene stove, but we never had enough glasses or spoons, so we'd always have to stir it with a toothbrush."

Enough late-night talks produced a common agreement. Young Tibetans in exile were in touch with one another ; many felt that the refugee government had continued, despite its efforts at reform, in the lesser traditions of its predecessor in Lhasa. "There was too much mediocrity. It had become the fashion to play it safe," continued Norbu. "It's always the same old story. The people with conviction and talent stayed behind and fought in Tibet to the last, and a lot of second-level people, bureaucrats, made it out. In India, the whole establishment always kept quiet. It was not particularly the Indian government who clamped down on them, but their own selves. No one was pushing."

To unite exile youth in a more hostile and forceful struggle for Tibetan freedom, the group decided to hold a small conference. Once informed, the Dalai Lama offered to cover the meeting's cost on the condition that it be expanded to include representatives of the younger generations as well. "His Holiness didn't impose any terms on us. He just took a very sympathetic, laissez-faire attitude of 'Let it grow and let's see what these kids can do.' Everyone was thrilled," said Norbu.

A month later, on October 7, 1970, 300 young Tibetans sat before a pennant-lined table outside Conium House, a large green map of Tibet lay covered behind them. At the conclusion of the national anthem, the Dalai Lama, flanked by his two tutors and the Cabinet, stood up to give the opening address. There followed a week-long debate, unlike anything that had taken place before, either in exile or in Tibet. "No one had anticipated how outspoken the proceedings would be," related Norbu. "People asked the Cabinet point-blank about the past. How could the Chinese get into our country just like that? Why didn't the army put up a good fight? What really happened at Chamdo when it fell? Then there were very probing questions about favouritism in the present administration and misuse of funds. One of the ministers was really shivering. The tablecloth wasn't long enough, and you could see the folds in his Tibetan *cbuba* trembling. So because of all this our relationship with the government started right off on a little note of tension."

With the Tibetan Youth Congress officially inaugurated midway through the conference, the role of loyal opposition was effectively filled in the exile community. Yet it was an awkward situation. Heavily dependent on the younger, better-educated English-speaking refugees, the government counted almost 40 per cent of its employees among the Congress, a figure which grew to 75 per cent by 1984. An awkward combination of the establishment and its chief fault finders was thus created. When Youth Congress members in the government criticized bureaucratic errors and corruption the Cabinet saw disloyalty in its ranks and reacted by attempting to undermine the TYC Central Executive Committee, or Centrex. "Centrex repeatedly made clear to the Kashag that we always considered them the rightful government of Tibet," said Jamyang Norbu. "Our loyalty was beyond question. But just because of this, we maintained, the Congress was not obliged to behave in a servile way or agree with all their decisions. When we challenged the Cabinet we felt that we were acting out of idealism, but they only saw us as a threat to their power."

Structure for the Restoration of Tibet's Rightful Independence

Two years after the founding of the Youth Congress, in July 1972, a second popular organization called Struggle for the Restoration of Tibet's Rightful Independence was inaugurated in Dharamsala. Its leadership was given over to the Commission of Tibetan People's Deputies, who primarily employed it to collect the refugees' voluntary tax, consisting of up to 2 per cent of their monthly wages, and accounting for almost a third to the exile government's revenue. Simultaneously, trouble between the Cabinet and the Youth Congress continued to grow, resulting in the Tibetans' first real test of democracy, produced by a dramatic comparison during the spring of 1977.

The engagement evolved from a chain of events beginning on March 10, 1977, the eighteenth anniversary of the Lhasa uprising, celebrated that year, among other gatherings, by a TYC-organized demonstration at the Chinese embassy in New Delhi. There had been many Tibetan demonstrations at the embassy previously, some of them violent turning. This time, plans were drawn up to break into the compound and disrupt it. The Intelligence Bureau or IB, India's internal secret service, however, got word of the arrangements. Early on the morning of the 10th as hundreds of demonstrators gathered near Majnu-ka-Tilla, the Tibetan refugee camp on the banks of the Jumna River in Old Delhi, police circled the area. The few hundred Tibetans who managed to get through were all subsequently arrested after a pitched battle at the embassy. They were released without being charged, but not before the protest had been joined by a thousand more refugees. The gathering set for new purpose, the demonstrators decided to hold a hunger strike calling for the implementation of the United Nations' three resolutions on Tibet. A Coordinating Committee for the newly formed Tibetan People's Freedom Movement was created and a large tent, equipped with beds for the strikers to rest on and a medical unit to monitor their condition, erected across from the UN Information Office near the Lodi Gardens. From eighty-three volunteers three teams were selected, their members to fill in one at a time as each person died. The strike, it was decided, would only be called off only if the United Nations agreed to take up the matter of Tibet. "We put the fear of God into them," recalled Norbu. "We called in the volunteers one at a time and said, 'This is for keeps. We are going to live, but you will die. It's going to be very difficult. You'll be lying there starving to death and we won't be paying any attention to you. We'll be laughing and talking. So you better pull out now.' That reduced the numbers right away. Finally, we came up with three guerrillas, a woman and three other men for the first group. Then we put them all under the charge of a real tough character, an ex-guerrilla who didn't give a damn about death. This was our insurance to guarantee that no one would weaken their will with false sympathies."

The strike started at 10:00 a.m. on March 20, 1977. Within a few days the Tibetans received more press and television coverage than even at any other time since the Dalai Lama's arrival eighteen years before. There could not have been a more opportune moment. India was in the midst of elections following Indira Gandhi's twenty-month-long emergency. Within a week, the Janata Party was voted into power on a dramatic wave of popular libertarian sentiment. The coincidence was surprising. The Janata leaders, who had been banished to the opposition for decades, were the same men who had championed in Tibet's cause most noisely. Now, given power, they were finally in a position to recognize the exile government, and at the very time when the Tibetans, encouraged by widespread support for the strikers throughout the diaspora, had gathered their most unified political effort to date.

Recognizing the moment's potential, Lodi Gyari (then president of the Youth Congress) decided to speak directly to the Janata Party leaders, many of whom were known to him. With the dual pressure of their past commitments to Tibet and the hunger strike—whose massive publicity was clearly harmful on the eve of their inauguration—he hoped to obtaın formal pledges of support for Tibetan independence. Without notifying the Cabinet in Dharamsala, who undoubtedly would have put down the plan, Gyari, joined by Jamyang Norbu and a heavy monk nicknamed Gosey or the "Blond Lama" (from his skin being slightly yellow), went immediately to Janata Party headquarters. " 'How the hell are we going to get in?' I asked Lodi," recalled Norbu. "They were choosing the Prime Minister and the building was packed with people and press. Besides, we looked a mess. I had come down from Dharamsala in a hurry with just a toothbrush. I was wearing shorts, a blue jean shirt and flip-flop sandals. Lodi was in his white Indian pajamas with his briefcase and then we had this portly monk. But the three of us just got a taxi and drove over anyway."

Meeting with J.P.

When they arrived, the young men pushed ahead of the journalists and somehow managed to catch the attention of the secretary of J.P. Narayan, the Janata Party's most respected elder statesman and kingmaker. The secretary, however, did not allow them permission for a meeting. " 'Just tell J.P. we're Tibetans. He's never refused a Tibetan.' That was Lodi's line," said Norbu. "I told him, 'Lodi, all your bullshit is not going to get us anywhere this time.' But the next minute the secretary came out and said, 'Gentlemen, please come this way.' Then all the reporters started to make noise. "How come these low characters are getting in?' and we just walked through."

Offering Narayan a white scarf, Lodi Gyari congratulated him on the Janata Party's victory and requested for support for the hunger strike. Narayan at once agreed. Furthermore, he promised to secure the backing of Morarji Desai, the Prime Minister-to-be. Somewhat taken aback by their success, the three left a few minutes later. Over the next days an unprecedented series of letters and politicians about to be appointed to the new cabinet arrived at the tent. One and all pledged to back Tibet's cause : the first time that the refugees' struggle had been publicly overlooked by their host country. In exchange for its unique gesture, the Janata Party secured the pause of the hunger strike and the fast was broken on its tenth day as Acharya Kripalani offered orange juice to the seven Tibetans. Puffed up Gyari and Norbu returned to Dharamsala, in the wake of the strikers' violent welcome, bringing with them the Janata Party letters to present to the Cabinet.

The result was total chaos. Acquired by the youth in contacting the new Indian government, the Kashag condemned the entire affair. It blamed the strikers of recklessly endangering all the refugees' efforts, there being no way of knowing what, once in office, the government's final stand on the Tibetan issue would be. To repair the damage, the Cabinet demanded the resignation of the leaders of the Tibetan People's Freedom Movement, whose key members also headed the Youth Congress. For days Dharamsala was filled with angry crowds accusing the government. Both the Cabinet ministers and the people's deputies (who, it was assumed, were in collusion with the Kashag) were addressed in public, few of the refugees comprehending why they had turned against the victory. Finally, to defuse the crisis, the Coordinating Committee of the Tibetan People's Freedom Movement disbanded and, as an act of protest, the four founding members of the Youth Congress resigned from its Central Executive Committee. Not long after its inauguration, the Janata Party renounced on all of its promises, preferring, like its predecessor governments, to keep the Tibetans from impeding a still-hoped-for peaceful coexistence with China.

The limits of political freedom in exile had been clearly drawn by the confrontation. Yet, as evidence of democracy's strength, within a few years all of the youth leaders were not only back to politics but working in that very posts they had previously attacked—as a Cabinet minister, as directors of the Information Office and of the Drama Society, and, in Lodi Gyari's case, Chairman of the Commission of Tibetan People's Deputies. Meanwhile, the Youth Congress received Tempa Tsering as their new leader. Not long after his arrival in Dharamsala, Tempa had found his name put up among thirty other candidates for election to Centrex. On the basis of his reputation as general secretary of the Byllakuppe branch, he was voted in 1974 to be the Congress's treasurer. Four years later, he was elected to be an adviser to Centrex, among the highest posts in the Congress and one of the most powerful positions in exile society. Under Tempa the Congress took up a new militant course of action. Its leaders decided, in strict secrecy, that the time had come to employ terrorism in the fight for Tibet. Though the idea had been discussed for years, its adoption now seemed unavoidable made so not just by the failed attempt to win public backing from India's new government, but by the outcome of a clandestine martial struggle already underway since 1959.

The Secret Mission

Early in 1961, the leader of Gendun Thargay's 500-men road gang called him aside for a private talk. "You've been chosen to go for training," said the foreman. "You'll need an X-ray and a photograph of yourself." Obtaining the two items in Tezpur, Gendun returned to the camp a few days later and was introduced to another young man, who, like himself, was also from Kham, tall and roughly built. "Tell your friends that you are going to work in Darjeeling," said the foreman. "From now on, whatever happens you are sworn to secrecy." Vowing to neither ask questions nor to disclose what had already happened the two men received packets of money, an address in Darjeeling and a six-digit number which, presented at their destination, would gain them access. Not such as to what type of training they were to receive, they departed, all the while fearful of capture by IB agents who, searching for Chinese spies among the refugees, had banned unappproved travel by Tibetans. On the train the next day, though, Gendun noticed two other men, like him and his partner strikingly robust and undoubtedly from eastern Tibet. When they got down one stop before Darjeeling, Gendun hurriedly followed and on a conjecture sought their aid. Inquiring whether they knew of a good restuarant in the neighbourhood he received a subdued assent and was guided to a small cafe. There, after a brief meal, a truck arrived. Without a word concerning the seeming shared mission, the men told their companions to lie on the truck's floor. When it eventually stopped, Gendun looked out at the exact address he had sought in Darjeeling. Presenting his number at the door, he was ushered in, and henceforth permitted to leave only for short walks or an occasional meal. Though the people who ran the house never so much as mentioned their work, in the interim, Gendun clearly felt that he had come under the protection of Chushi Gangdruk, Tibet's still-active guerrilla resistance.

After three weeks in Darjeeling, Gendun Thargay was told to store away his few belongings. Given money, he was then allowed to the nearby market to purchase for himself a single pair of sneakers. Returning to the house, he waited through the day with four other men—all from Kham and Amdo—his only belonging a *tung-wa* or cloth bundle worn around the neck, containing red protection cords and barley grains blessed by the State Oracle. At five o'clock, Lhamo Tsering, a high-ranking officer in Chushi Gangdruk, arrived with a document in hand. He told the men either to leave or to sing the paper, which, as a recruitment form for the National Volunteer Defense Army, fixes a limit for them to obey to the death any order given by a superior. All five signed and at six o'clock sharp under cover of darkness, a canvas-roofed jeep picked them up at the bottom of the hillside street on which the house stood. At a second stop, six more men got into the jeep, compelling Gendun to hang out the back as it drove south from Darjeeling, heading for the border of East Pakistan.

Inside Pakistan Captivity

"You don't have to think about what's under you—mud, water or shit," said the man in charge three hours later. "When we arrive in a minute, do only what I say, just like in war." Pulling onto the shoulder of the road, the jeep stopped and the men were ordered to run as fast as they could in silence across an open field. They started running, but a pair of headlights appeared, followed by the leader's sudden command to drop. The car passed and they ran again. The bank of a wide river appeared great in the darkness. Arriving, they regrouped and for the next few hours wandered back and forth along the shoreline until, plainly lost, their leader asked a member of the company who spoke Hindi to enter a nearby village and cautiously inquire whether or not it lay in Pakistan. Half an hour later the man returned surrounded by a mob of angry villagers carrying sticks and rifles. Outnumbered, the unfortunate Tibetans were promptly hustled to a nearby police station where, they were convinced, a jail cell would be waiting. On entering, however, they were surprised to witness the commanding officer dismiss the villagers and once they had gone offer a cordial reception. He then explained that not only were they in Pakistan but that the special agent whose presence they had fruitlessly sought on the riverbank had already alerted authorities throughout the region to look for their group. A short while later the contact showed up in a Pakistani army truck. The Tibetans were put inside, driven to a small house and left there for the night.

Early the next morning, at the first hint of dawn, Gendun was awaken from sleep and ordered to run to an adjacent building. From here he watched the rest of his group race over, one at a time, followed by the agent, who was clearly concerned that there be no further sighting by local people. Given food and blankets to sit on, the Tibetans spent the day indoors waiting for nightfall when the army truck once more picked them up. They are taken to a forest, and were placed in groups of threes and told to sprint again. Across a clearing lay a railroad track. On it stood a car. As he ran, Gendun glimpsed a station farther down the line. Reaching the car, he paused to have a clear vision but was quickly pulled inside by a squad of Pakistani soldiers armed with submachine guns. Escorted to a locked compartment, the metal blinds of its windows firmly shut, he soon heard a train arrive, couple with the car and begin pulling it in what he judged to be in southern directon. One day later, the sounds of a large terminal became hearable. Unhooked, the car jolted loose from the train and was drawn some distance away. The door of Gendun's compartment then flew back and a Pakistani armed man gestured for him to follow. Outside the train, the Tibetans were rushed into a waiting troop truck, which, led by a military jeep, exited the station and drove swiftly through a large city —Dacca, as Gendun learned years later. On the outskirts of the city, the truck halted before a building standing at the far end of an airstrip. Within a few minutes, a gray unmarked two-propeller craft landed and taxied directly over. Though some of the Khampas had seen Chinese planes from below as they flew bombing missions over Kham, none had seen a *namdu* or "skyboat" at close quarters. An even greater surprise followed, however, when a small door near the tail of the plane opened, a ladder descended and came out a tall, sharp-featured white man smoking a pipe.

A single row of seats ran down the right side of the plane's interior. On the left, a small photo of the Dalai Lama was attached to the fuselage. Gendun watched closely while three Caucasian men showed them how to fasten a seat belt. As the plane's propellers revived, they drew the curtains. Then, returning from the front cabin after takeoff, they opened them and passed out paper cups containing a cold brown drink. "What is this, rum?" Gendun asked the Tibetan interpreter in the group. The interpreter spoke to one of the white men in an unfamiliar language. "This is a foreign drink," he momentarily announced to his fellow country men. "It is called Coca-Cola." After sipping Coca-Cola, the passengers now were each given a tray of food. Grappling with roast beef sandwiches, pickles, sale and pepper shakers, a few of the Tibetans, wondering if it too was some kind of strange new food, unwrapped the small bars of soap beside their plates and ate them as well. Following dinner, they loosened themselves for the first time since their journey had begun two days before. In typical Khampa style, they left the odd chairs and, indifferent to their surroundings, sat cross-legged on the floor. A pair of ivory dice materialized and a brisk session of *sbo*, Tibet's most popular game of chance, was shortly underway, each player shouting at the top of his lungs as his turn came to hurl the dice down. After a brief fuel stop late in the night the men eventually went for a sleep, waking the next morning to behold a brilliant expanse of sunlit water shimmering below—they for the first time saw an ocean.

After a day in the air, the small plane landed. An army transport backed directly up to the steps in its rear and drove the Tibetans off. The climate was cool and a heavy rain beat repeatedly at the roof. Finding a small hole in the canvas, Gendun pried it larger and bending down, was able to look outside. Natives holding umbrellas against the downpour, walked past stores with Chinese characters on their signs. Gendun assumed that he was in Taiwan. The truck passed through a checkpoint in a wire fence and then stopped by two small buildings hidden behind a thick stand of trees. Inside, the Tibetans were shown to a row of cots in a barren room in which they were to spend the next twenty-eight days, prohibited when outside, to go beyond the immediate surroundings.

The men soon realized that they were aboded in a remote corner of a vast military base—not in Taiwan, but on Okinawa, as was subsequently came to be known. One day the man with the pipe spoke to them through their interpreter. He said that they had been waiting for a second group of Tibetans. It now appeared that the entire contingent had been afraid of India's IB while crossing the Pakistan border. As a result, they were to proceed alone. "Each of your backgrounds has been closely checked to ensure that you are not a Chinese spy," he stated. "You are going to receive new names in my language and from now on you must respond only to them." To the Tibetans' great amusement, they were forthwith dubbed Doug, Bob, Willy, Jack, Rocky, Martin and Lee, confirming what many to them had already guessed to wit, that the Communists' worst enemy had finally seen fit to become the Tibetans' best friend—a distant country called America.

Once more the gray airplane, its curtains, fastened, rose noisily into the sky. An odd companionship between the white men and their charges had developed. While the Tibetans gambled on the floor, drank Coca-Cola, shouted and laughed, the Westerners, clearly taken by their unrestrained spirits, walked up and down the wide aisle, time to time placing their hands in prayer before the Dalai Lama's photo and smiling broadly. Though they repeatedly order their passengers to go to sleep—going so far as to push them into their seats and turn the overhead lights out—the Khampas, accustomed to taking orders only from their own tribal chieftains, insisted to returning to the floor to gamble in the dark. In the morning a large island appeared in the sea below. After they landed, the men rested for a day, in the course of which the American with the pipe insisted on having his picture taken with Gendun. They got back on board and the aircraft took off, flying through a second night until, looking out toward sunset the following day, Gendun noticed a long coastline below, with a large city spread irregularly across low-lying hills in its midst. As they crossed a range of dun-coloured mountains, he saw the lights of another great city, among which the plane soon landed. Once more army trucks were waiting. This time, though, the temperature was extremely cold. After driving upward for three hours, a rest stop was taken by the side of the road. Stepping from the trucks, the Tibetans were surprised to see towering, snow-covered peaks under a brilliant starry sky. The mountains looked so familiar that for a moment some thought that they were in Tibet. Others, after five weeks in tight quarters, ran wildly through the freshfallen snow oblivious of their wet sneakers and were only boarded once more with a good deal of effort by their escorts. Three hours farther into the mountains, they passed a checkpoint in a barbed-wire fence and drove up a long valley. At its end stood a cluster of single-storey buildings. Inside one each man was given a bed, beside which stood a small table neatly stacked with pencil, pad and towels. The barracks was bare and spotless but Gendun found a single telltale item which had eluded the keepers, an old pencil, its eraser end covered by toothmarks. In Tibet, when writing, it was the normal procedure to hold one's pen between the teeth while using both hands to fold the paper into lines. The toothmarks convinced Gendun that Tibetans had been there before. From then onwards he was sure that he was in America.

The second island in the sea had been Hawaii ; the city on the coastline, San Francisco ; the one landed at, Denver ; the mountain base the Tibetans had been taken to, Camp Hale, eighteen miles north of Leadville, Colorado. Used during the World War II for high-altitude combat training, Camp Hale had been redesigned for the creation of a secret Tibetan army under the direct administration of the CIA.

National Volunteers Defence Army

The decision to train Tibetans in the United States was made little more than a month after the March uprising. On April 21, 1959, three weeks after the Dalai Lama's escape, General Gompo Tashi Andrugtsang, field commander of the National Volunteer Defense Army, confronted with overwhelming Chinese forces, gave orders for his Lhoka-based headquarters to be given up. While guerrillas continued to function in separate units throughout Lhoka, the NVDA's chief officers sought refuge in the NEFA, Gompo Tashi himself suffering from debilitating wounds. Setting off for Darjeeling, he met with the organization's leader, the Dalai Lama's elder brother, Gyalo Thondup, and together along with their advisers, the two men laid plans for the next stage of the NVDA's fight, which, now that China stood in outright possession of Tibet, was to be based on a real closer involvement with the CIA.

To date, the CIA's training of Khampas had been very limited. On Guam and Okinawa (the agency's forward station for monitoring its Tibetan operation), recruits had received four months of instruction, after which, armed with a tommy gun, a radio and poison, to be self-administered in the event of any capture, they were flown from Bangkok and dropped by parachute into Tibet to organize cells. While only *pons* or tribal chieftains and their sons had been used, the new project, begun in May 1959, called for the instruction of five groups totaling almost 500 men, selected both for their physical stature and to represent each district in Tibet's three provinces. As in the past, once training was complete, they were to be dropped into their native regions to organize a resistance that eventually would be linked to the broad body of NVDA troops, who hoped to reestablish to a new base somewhere on Tibet's frontiers.

The operation was a secret mission. The Tibetans were never told that they were in the United States. Thus, if any man was captured, American involvement could not be proved. Meanwhile, training a covert army of Asians in the middle of the Rocky Mountains warranted the greatest care. By mid-July 1959, the CIA had planted a front page story in the Denver *Post* reporting that atomic testing—though not bomb detonation—was to be conducted at Camp Hale. The vast area of 14,000-foot peaks and valleys covered by the camp was henceforth strictly closed for the civilian population. People who were near Peterson Air Force Base, outside of Colorado Springs, when a subsequent group of Tibetans was flown out, found themselves detained. Up to forty-seven at a time were held at gunpoint behind army roadblocks until mysterious buses, their windows painted black, had passed by. When news of unidentified Orientals in Colorado reached the *New York Times*, Secretary of Defense Robert McNamara personally had the story concealed. As a final resort, soldiers guarding the most sensitive areas of the base—as well as the Tibetans themselves—were given plain instructions to shoot to kill strangers found within the perimeters.

Gendun's group was the fourth to arrive at Camp Hale. On their first day the men were issued black combat boots and green army toils. After breakfast, they were taken on a tour of the camp's immediate area, which consisted of ten buildings near the bank of a small river. All around, heavily forested mountains screened off the outside world, but even within the camp restrictions were imposed. Their barracks, the dining hall, the classrooms and a large room with odd-looking tables called "pool" and

"Ping-Pong" were the only areas Tibetans were allowed. They were told as much at their first lecture given by a large instructor in combat fatigues. Informing the group that training would last for six months, the American concluded by asking two questions : "Will you jump from an airplane? If so, raise your hands." Pleased with the response, he smiled and said, "Who wants to fight the Chinese?"

Intensive Training

Camp Hale's curriculum covered a wide variety of topics. Addressed by their English names, stamped on plastic panels pinned to visored caps, the Tibetans were taught weaponry, survival techniques, radio operations, coding, how to organize an underground network, make letter drops and chart contact points. Morning classes began with a twenty-six-letter, ten-number code used in wireless transmission, map reading, and compass work. One-of-a kind equipment had been manufactured by the CIA specially for the Tibetans' use, including radios no larger than a hand yet powerful enough to transmit clearly over long distances. M-I rifles, mortars, bazookas and silencers were among the weapons employed. The men were taught parachuting, rock climbing and river crossing and went through exercises in which deer had to be killed and butchered on the run, the meat eaten raw for a week, while instructors (often pursuing with live ammunition) hunted their pupils. They were also introduced to the more refined arts of spying. Gendun was told that on being sent into Tibet, he must spend days in hiding, observing the daily patterns of his parents and relatives to be certain, before making contact, that they were not working with, or being observed by the Chinese. He was then taught to establish resistance cells which would report regularly to him on Chinese troop movements. They were to be ready at all times for the signal to rise up in revolt as part of a coordinated effort across the whole country. He learned how to move by night through hostile territory, how to pass, disguised, through checkposts if forced to move by day, and if captured, how to resist inquiries. Holding to a fixed story for as long as possible, he was gradually to lead the Chinese to believe that he was breaking, choosing the most credible moment to stage a collapse, after which he would present them with the supposedly true account of his identity, itself also a fabrication, prepared long before.

After a few months at Camp Hale, 125 more Tibetans arrived. A short while later Gendun completed his training and was chosen, among eighty of the most skilled men, to be dropped into Tibet. Though each man's assignment was kept secret from the others, the Tibetans learned, through a bit of their own spying, that their group was only the latest strand in a web already woven around the entire countryside. One day, while sweeping a normally guarded staff building, a Tibetan trainee found himself alone. Looking behind the large white sheets that covered a wall in the main room, he discovered a detailed map of Tibet. All across it red pins marked the location of agents. After searching thoroughly about further, he found prepacked parachute bags, with the names of his own group stenciled on them. Their contents included radios, lightweight pistols and silencers. A short while later Gendun was taken under cover of darkness out of Camp Hale to board on the plane for the long journey home. In the course of his stay, however, much had changed, altering not only the CIA-Tibetan link but the entire balance of power in Central Asia.

Chinese Attack on India

At 5:00 a.m. on the morning of October 20, 1962, Chinese artillery opened fire on a small Indian border garrison guarding the Kameng Division of the NEFA. An hour later, 20,000 Chinese troops poured over the Thagla Ridge while 1,500 miles away a simultaneously attacked Ladakh. The PLA pushed all the way to Bomdila in the east and captured 14,500 square miles of the Aksai Chin in the west before, on November 21, withdrawing to the original McMahon line separating India and Tibet in the NEFA. Only four months after the expiration of Panch Sheel, Nehru's decade-long effort at friendly relations with the People's Republic had suddenly collapsed, the victim of Chinese border claims and a plainly expansionist policy. New Delhi's humiliating defeat forced him to admit that : "We have been living in a fool's paradise of our own making" ; whereafter he turned directly to the United States for support against future aggression.

New Strategy

At the core of India's belated effort to arm its northern border lay the formation, under CIA guardianship of a new secret commando group, known as the Special Frontier Force and code-named Establishment 22, after its chief base. Raised on November 13, 1962, under the command of the Research and Analysis Wing of Indian Intelligence (RAW), the SFF was to be an entirely Tibetan force charged with the mission of guarding the world's highest border. Though its existence was firmly denied by the Tibetan government-in-exile, Indian sources portrayed its critical role in easing the difficult CIA-Khampa connection through Pakistan with a new, direct channel via New Delhi. According to the same sources, much of the NVDA's activities were henceforth administered under 22's protection directly from the Indian capital. A special communications base was set up south of Calcutta in Orissa, from which, in an area free of dense radio traffic, weekly communication with the operatives in Tibet could easily be maintained.

Returning to Asia, Gendun was taken off combat status and assigned, instead, to the staff of the Orissa centre. Here, two large receivers attached to special antennas able to pick up the most remote signals coming out from north of the Himalayas provided a steady stream of information. Recorded by Gendun and ten co-workers, the data were transmitted in numerical code by teletype to the NVDA's headquarters in New Delhi. After a time, Gendun was sent back to work in New Delhi itself. There he decoded messages in the company of three other wireless men and two file clerks in an inoffensive looking one-story building, travelling to and from work each day, for eleven years, hidden under blankets in a station wagon. Each Monday night a joint meeting of senior officers in the NVDA, RAW and CIA representatives was convened, at which cyclostyled copies of the week's transcripts from Tibet were examined and directives given. Concurrently the most visible of all efforts to fight for Tibet freedom took shape in the NVDA's new forward base.

Mustang New Base

In the middle of 1960, with CIA training well underway, leaders of Tibet's resistance chose the 750-square-mile kingdom of Mustang as the best seat for re-forming their operations. Jutting at 15,000 feet, like an elevated wedge, into western Tibet, Mustang had been appended to Nepal as a feudal state since the early nineteenth century. Over a month's trek from Katmandu, however, it was so isolated as to have no contact with the govenment of Nepal beyond paying an annual tax of little more than $100. The kingdom's principal approach from the south lay through the needle-thin Kali Gandaki Gorge, the deepest gorge in the world (by virtue of its lying between two of the planet's highest peaks, Annapurna and Dhaulagiri), and virtually impassable if defended. But Mustang's chief value lay in its strategic nearness to the Xinjiang-Lhasa road. As one of Tibet's two main arteries, the highway originated in Kham and ran along the entire northern scarp of the Himalayas through to the Aksai Chin region of Ladakh, from where it looped northwest into Xinjiang and the Sino-Soviet front beyond. Its dirt and dusty roadbed and single telegraph line united Chinese garrisons over 1,500 miles of sensitive border. Mustang also had the advantage of being one of the few remaining small pockets of indigenous Tibetan culture. As such, it was home ground for the Khampas : both a shelter from which to raid Chinese columns and nearby camps with impunity and a vital rear base for guerrillas still very much active in southern and eastern Tibet.

Late in 1960, NVDA troops began to arrive in Mustang. Though subsequently joined by guerrilla bands coming directly from Tibet, the project was spearheaded by men who had retreated from Lhoka with General Gompo Tashi. Collected from road gangs, they went to Darjeeling and Gangtok, from where, organized in groups of forty, they proceeded westward, crossed secretly into the thick jungle of southern Nepal and trekking up through the alpine terrain of the Kali Gandaki Gorge, emerged finally onto the arid, windswept Tibetan Plateau, at Mustang's border. Welcomed by the kingdom's twenty-third monarch—whose fear of the nearby PLA exceeded only that of an independent army on his won ground—they established a network of interlocking bases. Some were forward tent camps manned by only a hundred to two hundred troops ; other were supply depots built around preexistent towns and monasteries. Headquarters was placed to the rear, on Mustang's southern rim, an hour and a half north of Jomosom, the last Nepalese town. In time, twenty-five buildings housing five departments—supply, transport, ammunition, intelligence and internal discipline—rose between a deep gorge and the foot of the heavily wooded Nilgiri Mountain. At their centre stood the office of General Baba Yeshi—Mustang's commander—a three-storied building surrounded by a wall with a parapet ; a huge Tibetan powerful dog was chained to the main gate, the flag of Tibet flew in its courtyard. Besides the locale, Tibetan ponies tethered hitching posts and Khumpa troops clad in captured PLA jackets and shoulder belt with pockets for cartridges all gave, as one veteran recalled, a "Wild West flavor" to the place. But it was precisely the dry, rocky environment that made creating the Mustang base extremely difficult in the beginning. Before sufficient supplies could be parachuted in, most of the initial 4,000 men were reduced to boiling their boots and saddles for food, with some, according to one account, carrying out raids across the border into Tibet, not to attack the Chinese, but to steal livestock for their own survival.

With the airdrops came almost forty graduates of Camp Hale. From them, the National Volunteer Defense Army received a badly needed education in modern combat. They brought M-I's and Springfields, heavy 80-millimeter recoilless guns and 2-inch mortars as well as solar batteries to run hidden radio hookups, scramblers for coding messages machinegun silencers, "death pills" and miniature cameras for spying. Under their instruction, khaki uniforms were adopted and daily life became more regimented with a 5:00 a.m. rising followed by exercises for strength singing of the Tibetan national anthem, farming, survival training and tails in the hills. Their presence gave Tibet its first substantial military hope since the height of the revolt in 1958.

After revival the NVDA struck out east, north and west from Mustang's high plateau. An average raid consisted of a few dozen men penetrating Tibet for up to a month, ambushing a PLA convoy and then retreating. The country was so wild that, given a reasonable troop parity, the guerrillas were guaranteed success whenever they attacked. Some forays, though, were luckier than others. In 1966 a small party sent to disrupt transport along the Xinjiang-Lhasa road destroyed totally a Chinese convoy. It was not until the battle was over that the guerrillas discovered the head of the PLA's western command in Tibet and his entire staff among the corpses. The party had been traveling with all of their records, which now proved a treasure trove, not just for the Tibetans but for the CIA as well. Through these, invaluable information on the recently begun Cultural Revolution was obtained as well as a remarkable document revealing that by China's own count some 87,000 Tibetans had been killed in the 1959 revolt, an event which Peking had continued to portray as only a minor disturbance.

Mustang's Eopiong

Mustang's greatest achievement lay in its espionage network. Within a short time the NVDA had succeeded in establishing underground links throughout Tibet, not only the scope but the quality of information retrieved making the operation immensely profitable. Though the Chinese were suspicious of all Tibetans, the regional CCP was compelled to employ a number of minority cadres for administrative tasks. Among these were many "sleepers," Tibetans who appeared to be collaborators but in reality were, as they slowly ascended the local hierarchy, supplying the NVDA with information. NVDA couriers, travelling from place to place by night collected information from agents and were responsible for documenting not only, China's massive military buildup along the Himalayas but also the critical shifting of the PRC's principal nuclear base from Lop Nor in Xinjiang to Nagchuka, 165 miles north of Lhasa.

For all of its advantages Mustang proved to have one critical defect. It was too remote from the main theater of Chinese operations—"an isolated army in an isolated territory," as one guerrilla described the second stage of Tibetan resistance. In addition, Khampa fighters, raised for millennia as cavalry, were now denied the use of their mounts. Due to the difficulty of retreating up the unreliable passes which enclosed the plateau, only sixty Tibetan ponies were kept for the entire corps. Retreat itself inflicted the highest number of casualties. The wounded were generally left to die, Mustang's headquarters, much less its front-line camps, had little medicine and no surgical equipment. Nevertheless, in time, age, not battle, caused the greatest loss of life. "It was pathetic," recalled one of the younger guerrillas, a TYC recruit who was sent to Mustang to replace men entering their forties and fifties. "People didn't die from bullets, but just by walking to a fight and back. Once they knew a raid was on, the Chinese would send patrols to cut off its retreat. The PLA were fresh and our men had been literally jogging night after night. So the old-timers would give out. They'd take a whole tin of coffee, mix it together with water and soup in their bowls and drink it. That kept them going. But after doing this kind of thing two or three times, their hearts would just pop."

U.S. Chinese Reapproachment

As the 1970s began, a combination of external and internal pressures placed Mustang's continued existence in danger. Following Henry Kissinger's secret flight to Peking, paving the way, in July of 1971, for a U.S.-Chinese rapprochement, the CIA suddenly cut off support to the Tibetan guerrillas. With the Special Frontier Force grown into a mature unit, India had no need to maintain on its own the previous level of aid. Even worse, Nepal, no longer fearful, as it had been in the early 1960s, of a Chinese attack, now wished to counter New Delhi's influence in the region by furthering ties with Peking. Hence, in 1972 Katmandu, which had pretended the ignorance of the Khampas' presence for twelve years, took the first step toward expelling them by launching a propaganda attack accusing the Tibetans of robbery, rape, and murder.

International Rift and Disorder

Internal disorder as well plagued the National Volunteer Defense Army. In 1969 Gyalo Thondup, acting on long-standing complaints of younger CIA-educated officers, had withdrawn General Baba Yeshi as commander, replacing him with a nephew of the late Gompo Tashi Andrugtsang, the sole survivor of the first group of Tibetans to be trained by the United States, General Gyato Wangdu. Baba Yeshi went peacefully at first, journeying to Dharamsala where he was offered as reparation the prestigious post of Chief of Security, holding a rank equivalent to that of deputy Cabinet minister. He declined the position, however, and within a short time was back in Mustang. Rallying almost two hundred of his tribesmen, Baba Yeshi broke from the NVDA, publicly accused Gyalo Thondup of misappropriating funds and occupied a guerrilla camp called Mamang east of Mustang from which he openly attacked the main body of soldiers, now, in effect, a rival faction. In return, General Wangdu laid siege to the splinter group's holdout, until Katmandu, informed of the mutual destruction compelled Baba Yeshi to present himself at the capital. Three months of personal negotiations, led by Nepal's Home Secretary, followed. At their climax Baba Yeshi, according to one witness, burst into tears, pleaded for protection and then, in exchange for a grant of political refuge gave the Nepalese a detailed account of the NVDA's troop strength, supplies, weaponry and positions.

By then, the trouble had already spread to the Tibetan communities in India. Prominent leaders in thirteen settlements, populated mainly by refugees from Kham and Amdo, sided with Baba Yeshi in the dispute, believing that his rejection by Gyalo Thondup had been the result of a concerted effort on the part of the primarily Central Tibetan government in Dharamsala to disenfranchise them.

In large part the opening of a regional fault line—always Tibet's greatest internal threat—resulted from Kuomintang agitation. From the Tibetans' earliest days in exile, KMT agents had made an effort to win a faction of the refugees to their own cause. Their greatest success had been with some of the easterners in the so-called 13 camps, who, though they had no pro-Taiwanese sympathies, were happy to accept large financial contributions as an alternative to Dharamsala's support. Exploiting the NVDA split, the KMT now sought to draw the 13 group further from Dharamsala and closer to itself by successfully fueling separatist sentiment. After a failed attempt at redress in Dharamsala, the 13 group's relations with the exile administration soured and some of its members put a stop to submit the one rupee a month contribution given by most refugees to their government.

Nepalese Offensive Against NVDA

Early in 1974 the various pressures combined to destory Mustang. In a November 1973 meeting in Peking, Mao Zedong personally threatened King Birendra of Nepal with direct action unless he shut down the Tibetan guerrilla base. Agreeing on this Birendra declared all of northwestern Nepal a restricted zone and began flooding the area with 10,000 troops of the Royal Army, police and Gurkhas, summoned from duty abroad with UN peacekeeping forces. Given the single narrow track, carved into the sheer western face of the Kali Gandaki Gorge, leading north from Pokhara to Jomosom, it was a phenomenal exercise just to reach Mustang. Yet even though they outnumbered the Khampas two to one, the Nepalese, once in place, still had only a small hope of victory. After a decade and a half the Tibetans' knowledge of the terrain was unsurpassable, their stores capable of supporting them for up to two years. Accordingly, Nepal secretly coordinated plans with China for a PLA drive on the Khampas' northern flank should they attempt a retreat into Tibet.

While the military geared up for a fight, the Nepalese government took its first political step in March 1974. Sending men for secret mission to General Wangdu, Katmandu offered a trade-off : almost half a million dollars in "rehabilitation" aid and the rights to land and buildings already developed in exchange for a full surrender and dispersing the various camps. When the Khampas refused, Nepal attempted to force their hand. On April 19, Lhamo Tsering, the NVDA's chief officer in New Delhi, was arrested in Pokhara while en route to Mustang. He was then held hostage to force a surrender. It was, however, a tentative move. Because the Nepalese were frightened that any greater show of force would provoke the Khampas (who were a week's trek away) to descend and, as one observer put it, "massacre everyone," Lhamo Tsering was only placed under house arrest. In addition, he was able to smuggle a message north, ordering that under no condition should the Mustang base yield to Nepalese demands. Nepal reluctantly completed positioning its troops and called for the Tibetans to agree to five-point surrender terms by July 30 or face expulsion.

Dalai Lama's Intervention

As the situation rapidly intensified to a confrontation, the Dalai Lama himself interfered. Tape-recording a twenty-minute message in which he recuested the NVDA to disarm peacefully, he dispatched the Minister of Dharamsala's Security Department, P. T. Takla, to Katmandu. Once there, Takla requested Nepal to free Lhamo Tsering and permit both him and the guerrilla leader to bring the tape to General Wangdu and his officers. Acceding in part to the proposal, the Nepalese allowed Takla to pick up Lhamo Tsering in Pokhara. From there the two flew in a helicopter to the Stol airstrip in Jomosom. Across from the strip stood a one-story Nepalese army post, around which thousands of troops were now gathered While Lhamo Tsering was held in a nearby building, Takla rode an hour and a half north to the NVDA command, where, apprised of his mission, a large select circle of Khampa officers was waiting.

The scene that followed was sad incident P.T. Takla began his appeal for surrender by saying that the Nepalese had Lhamo Tsering in Jomosom ; if the guerrillas wished him released they would have to disarm. After two decades of waging a pitiable guerrilla war against the largest nation on earth, the Khampa commanders greeted this line of reasoning as laughable. They joked that Takla had brought good, not bad news, as that very night they would raid the post and free their comrade. Only then did Takla play the Dalai Lama's tape. There was immediate and anguished disorder. Pachen, head of the internal discipline department and one of the most respected and excited leaders, rose to speak, "How can I surrender to the Nepalese when I have never surrendered to the Chinese?" he said. "I'll never give them my weapon. But at the same time I cannot disobey my lama's orders. We should all return to Tibet this minute and die there fighting rather than live in shame." Wangdu, though, in concert with other senior officers, decided to obey the Dalai Lama's orders and surrender. A few days later Pachen cut his own throat. Two other officers followed his lead, preferring to take their own lives rather than agree to the contradictory terms of their failure.

As the Dalai Lama's message travelled from camp to camp, played over loudspeakers, columns of pack animals fully laden with weapons began heading south. Nonetheless, once informed of the Khampas' decision, Nepal changed its mind on its promise of a trade-off. Entering Mustang, it launched a "search and seizure" operation. All those guerrillas who had voluntarily disarmed were arrested and marched into Jomosom while their land and property were given to public treasury. Word of the duplicity swiftly passed to General Wangdu.

Wangdus Fateful Escape and Collapse of Fight for Tibet

With an escort of forty select troops and the guerrillas' documents, Wangdu fled. Riding west, he leapfrogged back and forth between Nepal and Tibet, attempting an end run for the Indian border 200 miles away. The PLA was already waiting for him. Over the course of fifteen days Chinese attacks twice pushed the Khampas into Nepal, while a Nepalese attack sent them back to Tibet. And then, once more, treachery undermined the guerrillas. Early in the flight, during a night march, a mule carrying food was lost. General Wangdu sent two men to retrieve it, one of whom failed to return. Instead he went to Jomosom, and in an exchange for a reprieve reported the Tibetans' escape route. Forty men of Baba Yeshi's rival faction, already recruited by Nepal to guide its army into Mustang, were hurriedly put on Wangdu's rear, while the

Nepalese themselves set up a massive ambush twenty miles from the Indian border, at the guerrilla leader's goal, a 17,800-foot pass in the Jumla District called Tinker.

Arriving at Tinker toward the end of August, Wangdu called a halt. Exhausted, his men dismounted and sat on a hillside within sight of a nearby PLA camp. When none volunteered to seek out forage and water for the horses, Wangdu personally led a party of five to survey the position of the enemy track. In a short while, the general and his patrol disappeared into a small draw before the pass. A moment later those left behind heard a storm of rapid fire erupt from all directions. As they ran to their mounts, they beheld the advance group's five ponies galloping, riderless, back toward them. Racing up to join the fight, they arrived just in time to see Wangdu gunned down while single-handedly charging Nepalese positions on an adjacent slope, the other men, save one, already dead. A fire fight then broke out, lasting the entire day and, according to one account, taking the lives of hundreds of Nepalese troops. Outrnumbered, the Tibetans finally left their horses and using ropes scaled the surrounding cliffs, outflanked the pass and escaped a few hours later over the border into the waiting arms of the Indian army.

A day after the fight at Tinker Pass, Baba Yeshi flew by helicopter from Katmandu to identify Wangdu's body. Following the confirmation, an official ceremony was held in the Royal Palace. King Birendra himself distributed prizes, promotions and cash rewards to scores of Nepalese soldiers who destroyed the Mustang. Under a large tent in the Thundikhel field, at the city's centre, Wangdu's amulet, wristwatch, rings, rifle and tea bowl were displayed to crowds of curious Nepalese who queued up for days to see the guerrilla leader's remains. Beside them were exhibited a vast arrangement of binoculars, radios and light arms from Mustang's various camps. At the south side of the field, just beyond the central post office, Lhamo Tsering and the six Khampa leaders who had heeded the Dalai Lama's order to surrender sat in Katmandu's central jail, where they languished for seven years until, in a 1981 amnesty granted by the King, they were finally set free. While the NVDA's New Delhi office survived the guerrilla's rout, its clandestine network in Tibet, painstakingly built up since the late 1950s, was now blown by the Nepalese, who forwarded Baba Yeshi's disclosures to the Chinese. A quarter century after China's invasion, the fight for Tibet seemed to have collapsed overnight in a sudden and great disaster.

Special Frontier Force

But the Special Frontier Force remained. Informed that a secret regiment, independent of the guerrillas, was being created to fight for Tibetan independence, male refugees had flocked from road gangs to assembly points at train stations throughout the early sixties. Taken to Dehra Dun, the groups were ferried by army trucks to Establishment 22, 100 kms away at the Chakrata military base. Here they were inducted and put through six months of basic training. At first Americans conducted operations ; then, after a disagreement over procedure, Indian officers took full charge. Regardless, below the highest ranks, an entirely Tibetan officer corps was developed, thus making 22—with a troop strength of 10,500—to all practical purposes a fully Tibetan army—the embryo, it was hoped, of the future army of a free Tibet.

The first—and standing—objective of the Special Frontier Force was to scout the inhospitable terrain on "the Roof of the World." Not only could Tibetans survive in the cold with far greater facility than the Indian Jawan ; they proved immune to altitude sickness no matter how many years they had lived on the subcontinent. With them India was able to develop a network of bases spanning its Himalayan territories from Ladakh to Assam. The Frontier Force's second motive was less submissive than guard duty. Having determined that an independent Tibet, serving along the lines of an Asian Switzerland, as a neutral buffer state, would afford the best protection against China, New Delhi secretly decided that, in the event of war, an attempt to wrest Tibet's liberty could be made, 22 taking the lead. As such, the Frontier Force was trained not just to scout but also as high-altitude paratroops—commandos versed in the arts of attack demolition, survival and deliberate damage. Given the existence of numerous underground groups in Tibet, supported by a virtually universal hatred of the Chinese, the men and women of 22 (two companies of female medics and communications specialists were enlisted to demonstrate Tibetan women's willingness to fight for their country) were designated to be dropped behind Chinese lines. While India's regular army would engage the Chinese head-on, the Tibetans would link up with the underground, raise pockets of resistance and split the PLA's flanks and rear.

Frontier Force New Role

War with China, though, was not forthcoming. Impatient for contact, entire companies of Tibetan commandos periodically disobeyed Indian orders and crossed the border in secret to attack PLA outposts.

Keeping under control 22 became such a problem that all of its bases had to be relocated twenty miles behind the front, and Indian troops posted between the Tibetans and their homeland. Not until a decade after its founding did the SFF have a chance to prove itself in sanctioned action—as the spearhead of India's assault, late in October 1971, in the Bangladesh war.

Wishing to assist East Pakistan in a bid for secession from its western twin, New Delhi settled on 22 as the perfect unit for the job. It was not a part of the regular army, and its shadowy existence and unique racial makeup provided perfect cover for a covert attack. Roughly 5,000 troops—half the force—were committed to the operation, an elite corps which opened the Bangladesh war with a surprise attack on a key Pakistani base. Labelled by the Indian press Mukti Bahini or Freedom Fighters, 22 went on to capture the city of Chittagong, Pakistan's main forward position, earning a reputation in the upper echelons of India's defense establishment as being among the country's best troops. Thereafter, 22 returned to its bases. During the 1977 election that ended the Republic's state of emergency, it received a new notoriety as Indira Gandhi's "own force." As was later revealed, the Congress Party leader planned to rely on its troops to suppress opposition party riots if they developed. She also kept an AN 12 aircraft on constant alert at the SFF paratrooper base, Sarsawa, with instructions to fly her to Mauritius if her life was threatened. Following the Janata Party victory, 22's prize anti-terrorist squad was posted to duty at Palam Airport in New Delhi. The rest of the Special Frontier Force, however, remained on its high-altitude bases helpless as before, unable to fulfill its ultimate mission.

The Guerillas Dreams

The Guerrillas' Demise, combined with 22's ineffectuality, reinforced the exile youths' conviction that the fight for Tibet had devolved on them. "We realized that independence wouldn't come on a plate," said Tempa Tsering, describing the youth Congress's projected turn to terrorism. "It had to be fought for and won. In a fight, whether we would succeed or not was a different question. But at lest we had to be prepared. If you aren't ready, even if an opportunity arises, you can't seize it.' In a series of meetings Tempa and the other members of Centrex discussed two potential scenarios, either of which, they believed, could serve as a suitable platform for regaining Tibet : war between China and India or the Soviet Union, or an internal collapse on the mainland itself, such as had occurred in 1911. The potential for the first existed almost daily, there having been numerous volatile incidents on both the Sino-Soviet and Sino-Indian borders. With Moscow tied to New Delhi against Peking and Islamabad in the current Central Asian power configuration, there was a direct link between the struggle of the two Communist giants, that of India and Pakistan and the question of Tibetan independence. The PRC's collapse from internal division was equally plausible as China's Communists were apparently helplessly bound to a cycle of devastating power struggles such as those that had erupted following the Hundred Flowers Movement, the Great Leap Forward and during the 10-year long Cutural Revolution.

Late in 1977, the Youth Congress laid plans to develop a freedom-fighting wing. While encouraging all graduates of the Tibetan schools to enlist for a tour of duty in the Special Frontier Force, it resolved that an elite group of Congress militants should engage directly in terrorist activities against Chinese embassies and personnel abroad. Arrangements for their training, to be conducted under the guise of a mountaineering institute, were explored. "From the moment Yasir Arafat was invited to the UN and given a standing ovation, we had begun debating the use of terrorism," said Tempa. "It was clear the world had come to this : you kill and commit destruction and you are listened to. You appeal for justice for your people and you are ignored. When we finally went ahead with the plans, though, it was only on a very selective basis. This type of action is contrary to the Tibetan character. So to begin with, we carefully sought to determine whether or not even the training itself would produce negative results among our young people."

TYC instruction in guerrilla warfare, using wooden guns manufactured in settlement workshops, got underway by early 1978. Morning exercise programmes were organized, bringing young men and women alike into the fields, wearing "Fight for Tibet" T-shirts. Carefully screened groups were given more sophisticated instruction for extended periods in the jungles surrounding the larger settlements. The Youth Congress also expanded its existing ties with the underground groups in Tibet, while publicly, at least, welcoming the possibility of non-binding support from Moscow, whose overtures to Tibetan exiles had increased since the midsixties. But the question of violence, outside the setting of an actual war, remained a delicate point for most Tibetans, putting a stop on the Congress's efforts. As the Dalai Lama, whose leadership the Youth Congress charter swore to uphold, stated : "In theory violence and religious views can be combined, but only if a person's motivation, as well as the result of his actions, are solely for the benefit of the majority of the people. Under these circumstances and if there is no other alternative, then it is permissible. Now, regarding Tibet, I believe that a militant attitude is helpful for maintaining morale among our youth, but a military movement itself is not feasible. It would be suicidal."

By the late 1970s the Dalai Lama's own plans for Tibetan independence had in many respects already ripened. Refugee society was thriving. Economically, culturally and politically—it had matured into a united whole, precisely the situation he had hoped to create two decades earlier. No longer able to count on the exiles' disintegration, Peking, he was confident, would soon be forced to terms. Convincd that success was near, the Dalai Lama set about reawakening international interest in Tibet through a series of trips across Asia and the West. Undertaken for religious purposes (hundreds of Tibetan Buddhist centre having cropped up around the world during the 1970s), the trips were also guaranteed to affect China which, since the early 1960s had been demonstrably sensitive to international opinion on the reality of its occupation. And as the liberalization following Mao Zedong's death took root and developed novel Chinese initiatives in foreign affairs, Dharamsala became—if as yet for no concrete reason—newly optimistic.

Tempars Rise and His Vision

Tempa's beliefs also underwent change. In 1978, after four years in the Information Office, he was promoted to the post of deputy secretary. Three years later, in the spring of 1981, he suddenly received word to report for duty at Thekchen Choling, the Dalai Lama's residence. The chief secretary of the foreign wing of the Dalai Lama's private office had to leave his post temporarily and Tempa had been chosen to fill it. "When I first heard this news I was worried that I was too inexperienced to work in such a high position. I didn't have the confidence," said Tempa. "But then I considered carefully. For my whole life my only hope has been to one day go back to an independent Tibet. This is the one thing for which I've struggled. Naturally, the closer you are to His Holiness, the better you'd feel. But whatever I'm doing I know I am serving him and my people. So in this respect I decided it doesn't make very much difference, and I could take the change in a normal way. But about my inexperience, I was quite concerned."

Within the year Tempa was wholly absorbed in being one of the Dalai Lama's closest assistants. Placed in charge of all correspondence between the private office and non-Tibetan world, he also translated each afternoon at the Dalai Lama's regular round of audiences with foreigners, while overseeing numerous projects with the government's Foreign Offices. At the age of 32 he looked back from his new position on his time in India. Recalling the death of his younger sister in the mountains above Bhutan, his second sister's death from dysentery at Missamari and his mother's death in the tent by the road camp at Bawarna, he recognized how much his own survival, as well as that of the nation, had been the product of the Dalai Lama's peaceful efforts at reconstruction. Travelling with the Tibetan leader through Asia, Europe, the Soviet Union, Mongolia and the United States, Tempa, and through him many of his colleagues in the Youth Congress, became convinced that Tibet's unique hope lay not where the guerrillas had failed, but in the strength of the traditional society, now rebuilt and entering the world at large.

12

Tibet Under China

There are 54 ethnic groups which have been recognised as minorities in the People's Republic of China. Their number in terms of population is very less just about 45 million. But, they are strong in their strategic and economic value. These people reside on the sensitive borders of China and spill into the Soviet Union, Mongolian Peoples Republic, South East Asia and South Asia. Economically they are important constituents as they enjoy vast land territory, nears, 50 per cent of the total land mass which consists of mass which mineral deposits and agriculture produce. Consequently to put control over these minorities the Chinese have been using assimilative policies towards them. In this effect at integration, ethnicity has emerged as a powerful and potent force.

Ethnicity

Ethnicity has been defined in several ways as its grasp ranges from sociology, anthropology, politics to international relations. Simply it can be defined as a study of individual or group behaviour based on the attributes of their geography, history, religion, race, language and culture. It is a study of the common origins of a group and their shared values developed in due course time. These groups can have common goal of achieving political aspirations. They then come out with various demands on the state structure, and also put their combined strength to fight the assimilative policies of the state. Groups when come under threat thus they resort to their historical identity to affirm their distinctiveness. This process manifests itself in the form of political ethnicity.

Ethnic distinctions have attained massive gain since the 1960's when ethno-nationalism became a potent force in world political development. It has since rapidly forwarded to the centre stage of global politics as well as literature. As new states joined the international community, differences among them were also inevitable. The states which had a majority dominated ethnic group, followed assimilative policies. The others had structures, that is of pluralist nature, where all minorities were provided equal status. They have been allowed to retain their special identity without imposition of any sort. In China the former method was adopted. The Chinese have taken both violent and other means to assimilate Tibet, an important minority into the PRC. In turn the Tibetans are increasingly using their ethnicity to counter Chinese assimilitative policies.

A number of patterns has already been described for the study of political ethnicity in various situations. Further we presumed some generalizations, hypothetically one can assume that : (1) Synthesization of ethnicity takes place over time. (2) Dissatisfaction with a changing environment which is beyond undercontrold results in group mobilization based on ethnicity. (3) Ethnicity is applied as a protective barrier by communities. (4) Deprivation increases ethnic demands and in turn takes violent and non-violent measures against this behaviour. (5) Despite mobilization, cleavages exist in ethnicity-based group society. (6) Assimilation can alter the character of ethnicity but cannot eradicate it.

Particularly for the case of Tibetans it comes to mean that : (1) Tibetan ethnicity synthesized over time that comprises of basic constituents like history, geography, race, administrative structures, religion and language. These have in some way or the other contributed towards the foundation of a particular Tibetan ethnic characteristic. (2) The Tibetans have used their ethnicity to protect themselves against Chinese attempts at assimilating them into a Chinese nation and due to discriminatory policies by the Chinese state. (3) A sense of deprivation gives way to Tibetan ethnic demands. (4) Dissatisfaction with the environment resulted in group mobilization based on ethnic grounds. (5) As the group succeeded to raise their confidence level starts mobilizing its resources, deprivation then made it take up retaliatory steps against unjust behaviour. (6) Tibetan failure in using political ethnicity to attain maximum benefits possible is because (i) there is always a cleavage in the ethnic society, that divides it into groups and the Chinese have used this factor very well as some groups are allied to the major ethnic group and are thus recipients of power and economic benefits, (ii) then there are those who support protest but even here there are (a) those who are economically sound and so advocate patience and (b) the youth and radical groups who do not agree to it and advocate violence and separatism, primarily because of their poor economic status.

Tibetan Ethnic Synthesis

The ethnic constituents of the Tibetans synthesized over time. Factors that contributed most towards the foundation of ethnic growth has been the geographical one. The foremost organized settlement recorded in the region was around 127 BC when some small tribal groups integrated under the King Nya-Tri-Tsenpo to form a single Tibetan nation. The insularity of the region produced Tibetan's image as a Shangri-la or a remote, hidden, beautiful and idyllic land. The Tibetans were look like a mystical people living in an isolated land, surrounded by the world's highest mountains (a total of five major ranges). It is obvious to some extent that the world has clothed the region in myths. For the Tibetans themselves reaching out to the world was not so difficult as they were aware of the mountain passes. Their isolation was thus illusive in character. But it did give them a special identity in the eyes of the world.

Tibetan ethnicity developed primarily on its geographical terms. Within a larger Tibetan ethnic character exist three different variations according to the national topography. The northern bleak Chang Tang region generated a nomadic class, the middle region of Kham and Amdo a pastoral and agricultural tract produced the class of the well known Tibetan warriors. In the hospitable southern Tibet a commercial and trading class exists. Thus to consider Tibetan ethnic character as singular would be a wrong presumption. Even if one looks at the Tibetans in terms of their racial or phenotypical features such as pigmentation, stature or hair, it can easily be considered as in the Mongolian race. This is primarily in the U-Tsang region where people are short statured, round headed and high-cheek-boned. But in Kham and Amdo the population is generally consists of tall, long headed and long limbed.

Early History

Historically Tibet's past is shrouded in Darwinian myths. Its modern history can be traced to the seventh century AD, which could be considered as the beginning of the movement of Tibetan population as did the building of their particular ethnic and cultural traits. It is in these early times Tibet demonstrated a military genius and extended its borders geographically as well as ethnographically. In spite of its geopolitical restraints, of being surrounded by the major nations of Asia (China, Soviet Union and India), its rapid march to grab the surrounding areas continued smoothly, which in turn helped them in building up the image of a brave warrior class.

The Tibetan occupation came in contact with the arts and sciences of the Tang empire at the time of their eastward move. In the northern territories of Sinkiang with an Indo-European race and language. In the west they came in contacts with the Turks. Striding the trading routes between the east and west Tibetan's interacted closely with all the main religions of the times— Zorastrianism, Buddhism, Islam and Christianity. As being a neighbour of India it must have also felt the influence of the Roman-Byzantine empire. Thus impact on Tibet of its neighbourhood was multidimensional. By the eighth century Tibet had not only succeeded to expand its territory but also established administrative control over it. At the royal seat of Yarlung its present day flag that features two lions facing each other began to be flown. From India as early as the seventh century, was borrowed the Brahmi and Gupta scripts which were used to devise a Tibetan one.

Changes in the regional environment especially those in China and India had an obvious effect on Tibet. Tantric Buddhism wiped out from India by Muslim invasion found root in Tibet. It was this introduction of a new variable that had brought change in the historical trends of Tibet. Tibet lead by Buddhist philosophy, like the Magadha Empire under Emperor Ashok of India, gave up the model of conquest by arms for the model of conquest by philosophy. The Tibetans enraptured the Mongol court by their philosophical religion which gave birth to the establishment of a new spiritual leadership known as the Dalai Lama. Leaving only to a few pockets such as Kham where the martial character of the race was maintained, Tibet gave itself up to Buddhism, and its basic philosophy of non-violence. Meanwhile the Mongolian's of China led by Chengiz Khan altered the set up of regional influences and domination. The Mongols (Yuan) were on the rise and the Tibetan empire were all set to decline. The Mongols united Tibet and China under one administrative unit. They appointed the Sakya Pandita and Chogyal Phagpa (a Tibetan Monk) and given full authority over three provinces of Tibet as the first priest-king. Thus was established the first legacy of history. Subsequently, finding a power vacuum, the Chinese moved in and established control by stationing in Lhasa their political officers known as the ambans who role was to become a historical dispute between the two countries. The Chinese was to prove that political control over Tibet was confirmed by their presence while the Tibetans pointing out that it only meant that political relations existed. The Mongol decline and the rise of an ecclesiastical Tibet increased Chinese intervention and consolidation of power. The reduction of the army to mere ceremonial status helped them further.

Chinese Influence

Despite political influence there is no indication that the Chinese influenced Tibetan ethnic consolidation in any way. The Chinese political influence was not long lasting. As the Manchu empire lost its control on the country as the result of which the Tibetans reasserted their independence. Chinese influence in Tibet, unlike Indian, was still minimal. The Chinese did not attempt to assimilate them with the great Han majority. This policy was also prevailed in Kham and Amdo where they were able to maintained direct rule. Under the last monastic dynasty though the Chinese viewed them as a suzerainty they were also seen at the same time to possess a different ethnic identity. In fact Chinese xenophobia accelerated by western interference and loss of territory kept all other nations out of Tibet in the forthcoming years. This passing phase of history unjustly led to Tibet being named the 'forbidden land'. A friendly outgoing people came to be seen as mysterious and unfriendly.

British Entry in China

The policy of Chinese were to keep foreigners out of Tibet did not last long. The British reached Tibet through India in 1904. Inspite of the lack of Chinese influence the British recognized Chinese suzerainty throughout the country, and did not attempt to make any socio-cultural changes in the country. The Britishers did not want to antagonisa China because they had greates trade interests in China and only minimal trade interests in Tibet. Tibet remained as it was. It was in 1911 that the revolution in China brought in a new government and a new policy. The policy under Sun Yat-sen's Republic changed drastically. The aim became the formation of a multinational state by the assimiiation of all non-Chinese nationalities like the Manchurians, Mongols, Turks and Tibetans with the Han Chinese. His government noticed that modern nations, unlike the early empires could only be held together through a policy of nationalism. Nationalism presupposes a unification under a central authority. As a result of unification the state are to be overwhelmingly powerful, combining different cultures and languages into one stream. The result has usually been the rise of sub-nationalism by various dissatisfied groups within that whole. Sinification, through language and Tibet's incorporation into the main administrative system were tried out, but resulted in failure due to the distance of far flung areas where national minorities lived and over whom the KMT could not have proper control. Tibet refused to be swayed by the power of a government with which it had neither political, social nor cultural affinity but remained nominally within the Chinese boundary. Though China under the national government tried to promote assimilation it did not interfere with Tibetan authority. As a result of which a chink in the Chinese armour the Dalai Lama forced his power and assumed personal control over the government. After that like the medieval Pope he also took care of both spiritual and political matters by his own. Which proved to be the single most important factor one in the protection of Tibetan ethnicity. Day after day the onslaught by the Dalai Lama as their spiritual leader as well as political head kept their policy of Aggravdixual of Peoples Republic of China identity intact.

In 1949, before coming of the PRC into the power it had already declared its policies towards national minorities. Tibet was mentioned as early as the CCP's Second National Congress held in 1922, where the right to the country's self-determination was accepted but within a Free Federation or a Free Republic. But by 1949 the new policy condemned non-Chinese nationalism and secessionism. The reason for this adoption was that the central government increasingly faced revolts from different ethnic minorities. Which resulted in the adoption of new policy measures. Both liberation of these areas and class struggle became equal important. Both the twin policy of horizontal class struggle and the vertical policy of national assimilation were followed by the Chinese party which was carried out in the newly created autonomous regions in minority areas. The Chinese used force to bring about assimilation. Consequently "Liberation" came to mean occupation. The Dalai Lama, tried to adhere to a Seventeen-point Agreement, put forward by China granting National Regional Autonomy but the Chinese authorities did not stopped to interfere. By 1959 the Dalai Lama and large numbers of his supporters fled to India to seek asylum in the neighbouring country. The popular revolt against the Chinese was suppressed and the facade of autonomy was not continued. By 1959, they were the winner by having complete control over the country. The issue since then is not one of suppression of human rights alone, but much more. A nation has ceased to exist, and ethnic power was the only weapon in the hands of the Tibetans.

Both history and geography played important roles in the formation of Tibetan ethnicity, religion changed it all and provided a different value system. Buddhism of the Mahayana school came into Tibet around the fifth century A.D. This period depended on magic forms, miracles and mysticism. It was akin to Tibet's earlier religions form known as the Bon. Even today most of the people practices this pre-historic religion which depends on nature worship, sacrifice and magic. It took a century to bring about a mass propagation of Buddhism where it became an all pervading philosophy. All such things attracted the attention and devotion of ordinary people to much that it came to dominate the whole range of Tibetan society. Slowly became a way of life. Promoted by the rulers of Tíbet, conversion of the majority was possible due to its Tantric content which made it akin to Bon in certain regards. Due to the religious domination it became possible to bring changes in socio-political and cultural systems in Tibet which gave birth to an ecclesiastical state. The monasteries became the linch pin of Tibetan society, according to the Dalai Lama only ten per cent of the population were monks and nuns.

Buddhism in Tibet was totally dependent on Indian philosophical thought and propagation it did not take anything from China. In China Buddhism was at second place in the religious hierarchy, and it has not much importance. Indian influence also began to decline as the Tibetans firmly grasped the nuances of the religion. The changes were inevitable and far reaching. Tibetans began to slowly evolve a religion suited to their culture and social order. Unlike in India it did not commit itself to a caste hierarchy where the Brahmins (priests) are always on top. In Tibet the priestly class could come from the Kshatriyas (the second in Hindu hierarchy) as the Buddha had belonged to it. Later the caste barriers were not last long at least among those wanting to join the religious order, producing an egalitarianism equal to one promoted by Marxist philosophy.

Buddhism was the only thing which kept Tibet in regional prominence even though its military power had declined. The most important patron-priest relationship which the Tibetans had with Mongolia and China would keep Tibet above power politics till the coming of a revolutionary China.

The core of a Tibetan ethnic identity was formed only because of all religious beliefs. The Tibetans borrowed Buddhism, and made it very different from other religions. It encompassed all their different facets of life and became the most important constituent in forming their present identity absolutely different from that of their neighbours. Thus despite its borrowings from countries around it, the Tibetans came to declare their identity which is totally distinct and separate from others. The cultural thread that strengthened the Tibetans and gave them the impetus for increasing their ethnic boundary was also Buddhism. Though Buddhism as a religion has a universalistic character the Tibetans used it to Tibetanize their neighbours. Tibetan ethnographic boundary is larger than its political geographical boundary. In the south-east the Tibeto-Burmese language extended the ethnic boundaries. In the south the mix of Caucasian Indians with Mongoloid Tibetans created a particular culture on the move, as tribes were not stationery at one place. But it also had its great effect on

Tibet to the extent that at one time it became a cultural extension of India. Later as Buddhism died out in India but continued to grow in Tibet due to the cultural deviation Tibetan ethnic identity was more strong. Mongolia is another country where Tibetan interaction had been very strong. Though closer to China their adoption of Tibetan Buddhism was one of the most important factors which kept Tibet a free independent nation even though China was conquered. Unlike in Korea, Japan and Vietnam which had strong links and adopted the Chinese language, in Tibet, Chinese influence was very less.

The Tibetans have included themselves into an ethnic group which shares a common culture, religion, language, race, history and values. Though the ethnic origins of the T'ang-hsiang, Yangtung, Sum-Pa, and others are not known or confirmed those of A Zha, Dru Gu, Hor, and Sog Po came to be traced back to Turanian, Mongolian, Turkic and Uiguric sources. The remnant population has a strong ethnic identity which also affected the neighbouring countries. Today the estimated population of Chol-Kha-Sum or the three ethnic regions of Tibet is supposed to be about six million.

Inspite to the Changes in historical and social milieu, Tibetan civilization prospered and brought forward differently, to the well known characteristics. Even in Kham which has had direct Chinese rule imposed on it, their different ethnic character stands out. The people of Kham which were totally different than those in other parts of Tibet still have closer links and developed Tibetan identity and no similarities with the Han Chinese can be discerned.

Chinese Effort at Assimilation and Resultant Discriminatory Policies

The Tibetan ethnic differentiation from the Chinese has created a plethora of problems which was not solved between the two countries. It is not a common phenomenon as globally ethnic differences more than even ideological differences, have become the hallmark of the century. Today all over the world in developed as well as developing countries, ethnic crisis are faced by the governments in power. Secessionism and militancy are the order of the day whether in the Basque provinces or in Sri Lanka. These rebellions have increased national governments attempts at assimilation. Even today the pluralist societies especially countries like United States and India which are multinational in character and provide constitutional equality to their minorities also face ethnic related problems. Assimilation is not an easy task and changes its dimensions with each every phase of history.

The PRC a majority Han populated country, when taking over territory with very different ethnic groups laid the foundation of severe discord. Used to a political class consciousness and attempting to eradicate it, which has itself not last long in the post-Mao years, they are now being increasingly drawn into a vortex of ethic power which is most powerful and difficult problem to solve. But ideologically they have no problem as the nationality-oriented states are ridiculed by Marxist philosophy, which makes the policy of assimilation much more easier. Ethnonationalism can only be the object of CPT's critique. But, the Chinese have depended on nationalism "a bourgeous" ideology for this process of assimilation. The main aim is to merge the nationalities into the larger single socialist culture. It is not a global socialist revolution which is of primary importance to the Chinese but the consolidation of its frontiers where the minorities reside. Only because of the occupation of Tibet the PRC were able to enforce its policies on national minorities. As the result of this the non-Chinese areas have become Chinese minorities. This complicates the problem for the PRC as the mere existence of minorities implies problems for the state. Besides, they lose a valid-ideological ground by using nationalism as the ultimate aim.

In order to substantiate their claims and overcome their ideological weakness the Chinese have used the cleavages and weaknesses found in Tibetan society to cut across ethnic barriers and formulate a single Chinese dominated nation. The Dalai Lama has admitted, "that the social and governmental system of the past in Tibet was neither faultless nor suited to the changing times." But then, no government is without its faults, Governing itself, follows different ways to change circumstances, an attempt to function smoothly. The Chinese took advantage of the existing shortcomings and moved into Tibet. When political attempts did not succeeded the army moved into Tibet and as a Chinese dissident mentions it was the army that arrived to Tibet first with guns and swords, and it was only later that the doctrine also came. The Chinese found in Tibet that the whole society was divided into two distinct parts, the small nobility mostly religious based and the large number of serfs constituting the majority, with no middle class. This vast differentiation in the class structure provided the basic foundation of China's assimilationist policies.

The feudal structure perpetuated by this two class system had greatly affected the economic system. As the Dalai Lama feels the most urgent single reform which the social system needed was in the large private estates. In these estates the aristocracy exercised all rights over their workers including justice. As a result such vast powers in their hands would lead to injustice. Then there was an outdated land tenure system where the farmers had not only, in return for lease of land, to give part of their produce to the state for distribution to monasteries, army and officials, but also pay for its transport.

The Dalai Lama recognizing this had before his flight to India brought in some reforms such as in the case of taxes. Even of this change, the system remained feudal and the difference between rich and poor too large for simple reforms to change the situation. The Chinese thus found it easy to carry out their assimilationist policies and the task was made easier because no local police force or army.

To assimilate the country into its fold, the PRC in its 17 point agreement with Tibet had promised the country "national regional autonomy". According to the constitution and the law on Regional National Autonomy the term meant that, "the minority nationalities, under unified state leadership, practise regional autonomy in areas where they live in compact communities, and establish organs of self-government for the exercise of autonomy." As a result of which all national autonomous areas were taken as being integral parts of the People's Republic of China, which made assimilative policies essential.

When assimilation was being carried out by a socialist government it meant following the tenets of its basic philosophy. In the first instance and of immense importance it implied economic reforms. If Tibet was to assimilate with the majority, the class structure would have to be totally changed and ultimately eradicated. Social reforms included, religious and cultural changes and a new education policy. Besides the basic tenets of its socialist philosophy, assimilation meant as in the Soviet Union, sinification, rewriting of facts and major population transfers. This could be continued by the means of local cadre formation and indoctrination. The planning was well organised and thus when implemented ultimately came to mean suppression of human rights and discrimination.

Economic Reforms

In any socialist society economic reforms are very important. Economic reforms and changes in Tibet, came as part of an overall Chinese policy. Tibet was to be liberated as part of the local global class struggle. This could be made possible only by the adaptation of economic institutions and social policies developed for the PRC to the Tibetan situation. Bringing in a series of "Democratic Reforms" the PCART divided the farming population of Tibet into a new class structure of manorial lords, manorial which represents the rich, middle class, poor and reactionaries. This made it administratively more easier to rule and to carrying out remove those people who had stood up against Chinese help would only go to the middle class and the poor. As a result of this policy, property of these state enemies was seized and distributed to the serfs. Some power remained with the traditional minority leaders.

The rural farming community is one of the important sector of a country's economy, and more so in any developing country. The Chinese had already recognized this factor and included it in its ideological interpretation of Marxism. As a result they paid greater attention to it in Tibet's takeover, though it did not pay the required dividends. Initially they distributed seed grain free of charge. But, despite the rise in production (except near famine conditions in 1968-69) there were incessant lack of food because of the newly introduced system of taxes. But, the Tibetans had always paid taxes, even if they were in kind. But the real reason was the increase in population. The Tibetan economy could not provide enough food for its own population as well as that of the Han Chinese. Subsequently as part of its general policy, in 1962 communes were set up at various centres.

Another important topic for the Chinese which disrupted their policies of assimilation was the life style of the nomads. Tibet has a large nomadic population and the only way to control them was economic. Initially they were divided into three classes, herd owners, middle nomads and poor nomads. The first class suffered the loss of their herds which were confiscated and given over to the very poor. Control and assimilation could not be achieved with this policy. Later on the system of communes was extended to this group while restrictions on their movements were also placed. But despite the strictness the nomads could not be controlled.

The Tibetans had also been well versed in trading systems. Even in exile in India their entrepreneurship in this field has been remarkable. Under Chinese occupation commerce was greatly declined as the normal trading routes to India were closed. In industry it was the Chinese entrepreneurs who have been registering business in Lhasa. Last year at least 10,000 registered their names. In this area discriminatory policies have been clearly seen.

Religious and Cultural Changes

Since the advent of Buddhism, Tibetan life has moved around religion. It was religion which changed their national aim from empire building to self-enlightenment. Buddhism permeated every part of their life. Today Buddhism is considered as an important element in the demonstration of Tibetan nationalism. It has thus become the major point of contention between the occupying forces and the Tibetans. Turning into a clash of titans, with the PRC a firm non-believer on the one hand and the Tibetans for whom life moved around the monasteries and the Dalai Lama on the other hand in a socialist China there could be no place for religion. Thus, the Chinese made it a primary target in the suggested reforms, which meant suppression of religious belief in all forms. The International Commission of Jurists who conducted a study on the subject clears the fact that even acts of genocide were committed in order "In order to eradicate this religious belief in Tibet."

Extensive destruction of monasteries took place during the Cultural Revolution. From constituting at least ten per cent of the population, monks and nuns have cut down to a handful in the monasteries which are functioning. The Chinese have marked out the religious community as the problem group. Going by the number of monks involved in the rebellion, it is obvious that this factor has contributed to a large extent to Tibetan ethnocentrity. This factor prompted the Chinese after 1979 to increase religious freedom. But, this freedom is subjected to numerous restrictions. While earlier, one son of a family usually became a monk, now permission is required from the parent, monastery, and the Religious Affairs Commission which is a part of the National Minorities Commission. In this way religious freedom has been curtailed.

Education and Rewriting of Facts

Education plays a very initial role in changing character patterns, a fact which the Chinese have taken full advantage of. They concentrate on each phase of education. In Tibet, education is imparted in Chinese while many children are taken to China for schooling. The policy was designed so, to make more Chinese and increase governmental control over them. As the Dalai Lama contends "there is danger that eventually these children will forget their way of thinking and living." In the Minority Nationalities Institutes of higher education has been provided. It is only since 1985 that a Tibetan University has been set up in Lhasa. Here also Chinese has been adopted as the medium of instruction.

Literature reflects society as it is at a particular point of time. The socialist countries have made use of this weapon to represent facts as they want them to be seen. The Soviet Encyclopaedia is proof of this. The Chinese publication reproducing two architectural panels date them to the Tang period, when expert opinion rules out any Chinese influence and considers it as being Nepalese.

Sinification of Territorial and Personal Names

The well known writer Han Suyin who usually firmly stands for Chinese official policy has announced that there are ethnic problems but counters the fact that there is any imposition as these groups are allowed to keep their own culture. Here facts do not prove her right. Besides other discriminations mentioned, outward manifestations of depriving the Tibetans of their own identity include, sinification of not only territorial but also personal names. "Eastern Turkestan" is "Xinjiang", Manchuria is "Hailungjiang" Tibet itself has become "Xizang". Even the famous cities of "Mukden" has become "Shen-Yang", "Kirin" has been renamed "Yungchi", "Shigatse" became "Xigaze" and "Chushul" is "Qiuxu". The well known German writer Harrier on his second trip to Tibet found that even the name of his friends changed "Sholkhang Tsetrung" or "Wangdu" had become "Thubten Nyima".

Population Transfer

The Chinese discovered earlier in Manchuria that one of the best ways to assimilate is by transferring their population towards the occupied territory. But this Chinese policy of migration is not new. Historical evidence of government sponsored migration goes back to the Western Chou (1077-771 BC) period. The PRC policy of transfer of Han Chinese into Tibet started as soon as the occupation of Kham and Amdo provinces. These two provinces had been receiving Chinese settlers even before 1959. This colonization of the region by Han Chinese was an effort to wipe out Tibetan ethnic character. According to Tibetan sources, the 7.5 million Chinese now outnumber the 6.0 million Tibetans in Tibet. The regionwise distribution is as follows :

Region	*Tibetans*	*Chinese*
Central Tibet ("Tibet Autonomous Region")	1.9	Over 2
Amdo (Renamed Qinghai)	0.8	2.5
Kham (Incorporated into Szechuan, Yunnan, Gansu)	3.3	3.0

(In millions)

The Chinese dispute the fact. According to them, in Lhasa only 10 per cent of the population is Chinese. On being pointed out the large number of Chinese seen are nearly 50 per cent. As these are the mobile population and the PLA. The Chinese blame the imbalance to the decline of Tibetan population before they took over the Tibet. The reasons put forward by the Chinese do not conform either with the reality of the visibly growing Chinese population nor with their own published and other sources. Since 1975, broadcasts from Radio Lhasa have been claiming news of large Chinese settlers in Tibet.

This effort at demographic assimilation is a replica of the earlier trends seen in Manchuria and Mongolia where the two countries have been over-run completely by Han Chinese population and homogeneized by this factor. The social consequences have already been manifested in Amdo having a large Han population, where there is definite sinification of Tibetan culture.

Local Cadre Formation and Indoctrination

The local population has been controlled by dividing the people into occupational divisions. These occupations being, farmers, nomads, townsfolk, traders, cadres primary school students and middle school students. Of these seven occupations, the cadres are considered to be the most important tool to exercise control. Mao had pointed out that "without a large number of communist cadres of minority nationalities, it would be impossible to solve the national problem thoroughly and to isolate the minority nationality reactionaries completely." It was clear to the CCP that ethnic control could only be achieved if a national minority group chosen and indoctrinated could be used efficiently.

The Position of Human Rights and Ethnic Discrimination as a Result of Assimilation

As ever, assimilation results in some sort of individual loss of independence. Tibet has not only been forced to give into the Chinese policy of communism and its adaptation to the Middle Kingdom but also the victim of Chinese colonialism. As such, it is the recipient of discriminations in all forms racial, economic and political. Racial discrimination is thought to have become a part of life. It has meant better education and jobs and easier self-employment opportunities for the Chinese.

The key decision-making posts are held by the Hans. Though the Chinese on the whole dispute this fact yet, when questioned directly on specific appointments, they do not contradict it by acknowledging that the very highest posts such as the post of the First Secretary of the Tibetan Communist Party are not held by Tibetans. The concentration of political power among party leaders is dominated by the Han group. This power is highly centralized. It is obviously the building up of an elite class having a complete knowledge of Tibetan society. This first generation Han Chinese of Tibet will find it easier to control the country, than it was being done from Beijing. External suppression will no longer be imposed but be used from within.

Separation has been dealt with brutally and according to Tibetan sources about 1-2 million Tibetans have been killed as a result of the Chinese occupation. One can only guess about the number held in prison. These numbers may be inflated, but it is obvious that the PRC resorted to force as a means of control the country as apologies have been made for the excesses of the Cultural Revolution. National Regional Autonomy taken together with the PRC's three magic weapons' used for defeating the enemy in the Chinese revolution ("the united front, armed struggle and party building") and which have been promoted for use in an intransigent Tibet has resulted in far reaching suppression of human rights.

In Tibet under a military rule akin to martial law it has been noticed by a recent visitor that the Chinese act as "first order colonialists". He used to say that there is no doubt that the Chinese officials would like the Tibetans to abandon their "primitive culture" and receive the "Chinese culture". They are also usually alleged that they want to remain 'aloof' from the local population. Consequently the Tibetans see themselves as second class citizens. This is very clearly visible in a traveller's account of an incident in Tibet where a Chinese guide who was taking photographs, on being reminded by him that photography in the particular place was forbidden, remarked : "But I am Chinese". Added to the economic, political and religious assimilative policies have been this indignity of social discrimination. This has been an important factor in increasing Tibetan ethnocentricity and thus cause of rebellion.

Revolt and Group Mobilization

Assimilative and its related discriminatory policies followed by the Chinese in Tibet made the local population dissatisfied and angry against them. This dissatisfaction even if initially individual, ultimately as seen in Tibet's case manifested itself in group mobilization. The Tibetan groups revolting against Chinese authority ranged from the warriors of Kham and the nomads on the move to the Tibetan students in China. The major cause of revolt against the Chinese has been the economic reforms introduced by them. These reforms have brought very little benefits to the Tibetans. Under these reforms the Chineses population has received a larger share. As a result of this, the Tibetan standard of living remained very below that of their Chinese counterpart. This became a major cause of failure in limiting the importance of Tibetan ethnicity. The condition of rural population deteriorated alarmingly, and it has been noticed that the young Buddhist monks and nuns revolting against Chinese authorities belong mostly to the rural areas. A badly managed economy affects the rural and urban areas. The introduction of communes has made the situation worst. It meant not only common dining halls but also confiscation of grain resulting in starvation. Violent attacks against the Chinese then became more frequent.

The system of political indoctrination and self-criticism (thamzig) influenced adversely Tibetan's thinking and the retaliations against the Chinese policies increased. Group mobilization and formation if given enough time ultimately grew confidence among its members. In Tibet thirty years of Chinese discriminatory and assimilative policies have resulted in ethnicity building and created the confidence required to take retaliatory steps against the superior strength of the Chinese State.

The rebellion of Tibetans against the Chinese has been handled firmly. The Chinese government while suppressing revolt to points out Article 4 of the Constitution which says that any acts which undermine the unity of the country's nationalities or may cause of secession are prohibited.

Revolt has been frequent and beside religious and cultural suppression and economic and political disparity continued between the Tibetans and Chinese is the fact that Tibet in its territory since 1959 stationed large contingents of the PLA. It has been easy to use these forces as today Tibet. An estimated 300,000-500,000 troops, of which 200,000 (15 divisions) are permanently stationed in the Tibet Autonomous Region. The presence of such large numbers of military personnel always influences the situation. As a study on the interaction of military forces and ethnic societies says that the police and military are the "exacerbators", not the "resolvers" of conflict in multi-ethnic societies. During the chaotic years of the Cultural Revolution it was the PLA which controlled the situation. Tibet, a land of monasteries has today become one of China's largest bases. This reversal of an existing situation is bound to influence the Tibetan character. If Buddhist ended their military ventures, and promoted an ecclesiastical outlook, the presence of large amounts of forces besides increasing their ethnocentricity definitely can contribute to militarize their character.

The PRC has also handled the revolts against their authority by saying that these are the violations of Art. 92 of the criminal law which says that "Whoever plots to subvert or dismember the state, commits counter-revolutionary crimes." The indication of such Tibetan character as criminal can become cause of revolt.

Ethnic Control by Soft Measures

Despite the adverse circumstances the Tibetans managed to keep their separate identity intact. This had led to the new post Mao government to accept the mistakes of the former government and reconsider their Tibet policy. Since 1980 the new policies have been the result of the Communist Party's Central Committee's deliberations which produced a document entitled a "summary of Tibet work formula. It formulated "eight great formulas and six principal plans". This eight point work formula promoted the idea that local decisions should be taken with the consent and support of Tibetan cadres and people. All the decisions are taken by local authorities except in matters of vital importance. Private enterprise and religion, it was agreed, should be liberalized. The six plans consists of economic freedom, development of local culture, renovation of monasteries and transfer of Han cadres below the District level.

As part of this policy, initially it was decided, that 80 per cent of Chinese cadres in Tibet would be withdrawn. To their promise of lifting restrictions in Tibet, it was opened to tourists. Around 1980 an average 1500 foreign tourists visited the country which increased to 15,000 in 1985 and 30,000 in 1986. Tourism in Tibet was not only important from commercial point of view but an attempt to "give the monks a stake in the status quo." This would promote assimilation while maintaining the continuity in the erosion of a separate Tibetan identity, by means other than force.

It was also decided that 24 million yuan population would be allowed to rebuild or renovate the monasteries. As part of this policy 200 monasteries and 700 sutra reciting halls were rebuilt and Monlam a traditional Tibetan religious festival was allowed to be celebrated in the presence of Panchem Lama in attendance. The Chinese came to recognize that and included it in their constitution. At 1982, besides, evidence of their superficial belief in religion had to be proved as 'State's stability and national unity depended on it." They thus even went to the extent of arranging the funeral and reincarnation ceremonies of the Panchem Lama according to traditional rites.

The softer option adopted by the PRC did not achieve the expected results. The reason was that in spite of the declaration of liberal policies emphasis was being given on non-practice of religion and propagation of atheism. The Chinese recognized of religion and propagation of atheism. The Chinese recognized religion as an important factor in the maintenance of Tibet's separate identity. Thus only the superficial and harmless aspects of religion were allowed. The subconscious pressures already existed, for practice of religion, as "every school child knows (that to do so) is evidence of one's reactionary superstition."

But, the soft measures adopted by the Chinese were not a complete failure and brought in certain changes. The general public, not political, when they have found suppressive measure removed, have come to accept the Chinese presence in Tibet. Pilgrims on return from Lhasa admit that the situation has improved. They even found the people "generally cheerful and optimistic." The young Tibetan on visit to India today prefer to go back to Tibet.

Sporadic violence continues and the Chinese twin policy is running concurrently in Tibet. Besides the exercise of a mild policy as late as 1987, Zhao Ziyang was reporting to the NPC that it was of "great importance to continuously strengthen the great unity of all nationalities throughout the country. We must carry out further profound education among the cadres and masses of the Marxist concept of nationalities to promote continuously the development of a new-type of socialist relations among the various nationalities." The policy became not only spreadly education but the use of state violence to suppress any sort of rebellion against the PRC.

The divisions in Tibetan society have thus widened divisions into those who are softening towards Chinese rule and assimilating into the majority group. Here the ethnic constituent is not of very great importance. At the same time there is a marked increase in the concept of ethnocentricity among the radical group of youth and monks defying the Chinese. Thus the division of Tibet consists of (1) those who support Chinese rule and policies and are allied to the major ethnic groups ; (2) those who are not allied but advocate wait and see policy and compromise; and (3) the youth and other radical groups.

The first group consists of not only the indoctrinated Chinese supported cadres but also the member of the Kudraks (aristocracy) who have a stake in the state. The rehabilitation of this class did not surprise the Tibetans for they believe that it was they who handed over Tibet to the Chinese.

Among the second class include the small group of leaders spread all over the country. They advocate patience, and have full faith in the Dalai Lama to bring of things back to normal. The Dalai Lama has come to their expectation them. He has come up with new proposals to solve the impasse. He put his proposal before the European Parliament at Strasbourgon on 15 June 1988. They fall short of the longstanding Tibetan demand for independence. According to the Dalai Lama this is the "Middle Way." This means, according to him, a method by which Tibet's identity can be established, and fundamental rights could be restored, and China's interests can also be accommodated. The Dalai Lama sees it as a simple problem and says that, "it is not my purpose to enter into a political or legal discussion reacted to Tibet's status. I just wish to emphasize the clear and undisputed fact that we Tibetans are a distinct people with our own culture, language, religion and history." His demand was that the real issue is the welfare of the six million Tibetans still living in Tibet.

Excessive control and use of force by the state always results in increased violence, though till now the Tibetans have not used the violence at large scale. The violence in Tibet has been used by the third group as mentioned earlier. These are of two types. The first are the youth "educated by the Chinese themselves." But, increasingly today the young monks are also defying the governmental authority. The latter have come to play a critical role in Tibetan rebellion against the PRC. The new reforms in Tibet also received a jolt when riots started by monks and the Chinese leadership realised the fact that assimilationist policies had not succeeded. Religion in Tibet had survived socialist pressures as it has done in Poland, perhaps in a much stronger form. While in Poland, the political movement is headed by Solidarity, in Tibet the monks have led the revolts against Chinese authority.

The monks taking to the streets believed Deng's statement that China's policy in Tibet was based on the principle of the equality of nationalities. The demonstrations have been turning larger and more violent. The demonstrations in 1987 have been compared with the revolt of 1959. It has also been seen as the biggest outbreak of political violence in China since the Cultural Revolution in the 1960's. The Central Government in China has been compelled to put up posters in Tibet warning that "all cadres, workers and officers must respect ethnic customs, respect the religious freedom of the masses, refrain from casual entering to the sites of religious activities and even more certainly, must not interfere with normal religious activities.

The violence being need by the monks could be due to the fact that religious teachings of non-violence are no longer being taught as they were under the older regimes. This in itself is an example of eroding values. The new monks though they consider Dalai Lama as their spiritual leader and have full faith in him have been brought up under Chinese rule and are bound to follow the new principles and new approach of thinking. In the Tibet region open to outside influence the increased use of violence will continue even if the Chinese kept a close watch over arms smuggling. Unlike neighbouring India where ethnic and cultural heterogeneity is present, Tibet has near homogeneized ethnicity and culture, which can easily manifest itself into a violent movement. There are two indicators of the fact. One is the existence of an underground movement and its call for arms, such as the one made by the Xinjiang based Committee for the Formation of a Federation of Asian Republics. The other who have shown their interest in this method are Tibetan exile in India. Despite the Dalai Lama's plea for a non-violent struggle, the Tibetan Youth Congress is showing an increasing interest in the use of violence. The formation of a number of new organizations has opened demonstrations against the Chinese. The wind of Perestroika has also affected the environment.

After the expression of peaceful policies the monks have not been as openly violent as other ethnic groups in the region, like the Sikhs in the Punjab and Tamils in Sri Lanka. But the "Chinese reportedly are walking city streets at night for fear of Knife-wielding Tibetans." The violence is not sustained but erupts on politically recognised date such as the anniversary of the founding of the PRC or the PLA's entry into Tibet. The largest of these revolts coincided with the Dalai Lama's visit to the US to present a new peace plan. The international exposure to the Tibetan issue gave the rebelled Tibetans the opportunity to demand their independence.

The revolt against authority in occupied Tibet can thus be seen as a national revolt and not racial. Though this does not mean that racial ethnicity has ended, but it has obviously experienced a decline, and this vacuum has been filled by a rising national political ethnicity. This proves the fact the ethnicity under suppressive conditions can be eroded and its character could be changed but cannot be extinguished. It also gives rise to new ethnic dimensions and formation of a small core group much more committed and revolutionary than before. The difference between violence ridden ethnic communities such as the Basque, Welsh, Tamils, Sikhs and Tibetans is that while the former are communities which have been part of a nation state and shore up their ethnicity with socio-political and economic grievances, which makes them entitled to demand for separate statehood or more power, the latter has been an independent country incorporated into a powerful neighbour. While to retain their already developed ethnicity they are revolting against this incorporation and assimilation, by a colonial power. The two situations are different and the Tibetans have a strong basis to help them use their ethnicity in gaining an independent state.

Tibet's Separate Entity—A Reality

If the aim of the Chinese was to make China a multinational state of harmonious ethnic group they have not been able to do as events have "heightened the ethnocentricity of the Tibetans." The reasons for the failure of Chinese can be highlighted here :

(a) Integration based on a false promise of historical facts which have not stood up to close inspection.

(b) Geographical continuity with neighbouring countries like Mongolia, India and Nepal which despite the number of roads constructed between Tibet and China do not make Tibet a natural part of China.

(c) Unnatural division of the country between Inner Tibet and the Autonomous Region of Tibet. The separation of Amdo and Kham the two units of Tibet which have traditionally been a part of Tibet exercised very less independence. They do so but even now have not provided the PRC the opportunity to divide and rule. This is because like other units they acknowledge the spiritual leadership of the Dalai Lama.

(d) The Chinese have not only faced a nationalist crisis in Tibet, but also an economic one. Tibet continues to be the poorest even in the undeveloped Western region. The transfer of Han populations into the region has also not helped to solve the issue, nor has its distance from the economic centres of mainland China.

(e) The Chinese have failed to assess Tibetan character. They expected the poverty stricken Tibetans especially the serfs to accept them as liberators but this class of Tibetans like the rest is submissive, gentle and deeply religious. They have found it hard to break out of the system even after a generation. The strict governance and heavy handedness of the local Chinese government has also been responsible to a large extent for their non-acceptance.

(f) Chinese recognition of Han racial superiority has clashed with a community which bases merely exist on its different ethnic identity and is willing to even forego its independence, so that its identity could be protected. The Tibetans continue to see themselves as a possessor of a special cultural identity.

The Soviets have been facing this problem with growing intensity not only in socialist countries such as Poland, but also among its ethnic minorities. The result of revolt here is always increased repression and use of force for example in Lhasa, even when the revolt is mild. Scapegoats are then always looked for and in this case it has been the Dalai Lama. Besides, freedom in neighbouring Soviet Union will have its impact on ethnic communities in the PRC. Ethnicity related problems for the Chinese will increase in the near future. Even if the mass of the people are not politically aware, a growing hard core group can rapidly change the situation. Political use of ethnicity then becomes a very important factor in resolving the issue.

The motivating factor behind the minority policy in most multinational States seems to be to achieve integration and assimilation with majority community. The activities carried out in minority areas in the name of development and social upliftment are aimed at achieving cultural and structural assimilation. The realisation of the intriguing motivating factor gives rise to local nationalism which creates tensions in relations between nation's minorities and the majority. It had been a universal phenomenon in the twentieth century. Most of the multinational States are preoccupied with the dilemma as to how much freedom minority groups should have to use their own languages, customs and faiths how to bring about socio-economic and educational developments to bring them at par with the majority, what positions they should be allowed to occupy in social and administrative hierarchies, how to deal with minority protest movements and, above all, how to bring about the assimilation of their people without much social upheaval.

China has a difficult task as its national minorities policy has been guided by a desire to integrate the culture and institutions of these groups of great diversities with those of Han majority.

Evolution of China's National Minorities Policy

Precisely around this time, the Tibetans were creating barriers all around themselves to prevent fresh winds from blowing into the Tibetan plateau in order to preserve its own distinct culture and religion and also dictated buy its status of neutrality in the Great Power rivalry. They could quite successfully, sustain their isolation. Thus, Tibet had lagged behind in the process of modernization and nation building.

When the PLA entered Tibet in 1950, the international community remained a mute witness because to them status of Tibet was not explicit. Besides the lack of sophisticated diplomacy on the part of Tibetans, the Chinese had already been 'educating' world opinion about their claim over Tibet. Instead of occupying the whole of Tibet after defeating its ill-prepared army, the Chinese Government suggested negotiation with Tibetans in their anxiety to avoid making Tibet an international issue. The negotiation led to the signing of the so-called seventeen-point agreement which was signed under dubious circumstances.

Concisely, the agreement proclaimed Tibet to be integral part of China and pledged to grant 'national regional autonomy' and assured the continuation of the prevalent political system, as would the established status, functions and powers of the Dalai Lama. It also assured the freedom of religion and social practice and stated that the Chinese Government would not use coercion to implement reform. In accordance with one of the points of the agreement, the PLA troops entered Tibet in large numbers for not only consolidating the national defence, as they claimed, but also to play significant role in the integration of these areas into the national framework.

For consolidating their hold on Tibet, the Chinese decided to proceed cautiously and patiently in their dealing with Tibetans. Initially, the Chinese used the old form of government in Tibet as their instrument and mouthpiece to control every aspect of Tibetan affairs. They enlisted the cooperation of 'patriotic upper strata' as they only could smoothen the relations between the people and the Communist Party. This arrangement served China's objective of maintaining traditional symbols of power while gradually changing the content that they symbolized. Apart from a few persons of exceptional courage such as, Tibetan officialdom, both of monks and nobles did acquiesce in the arrangements. High priority was given to the construction of road, telegraphic and postal communication. The Chinese also followed the policy of 'doing good and making friends' to gain the trust of Tibetan people. However, the Chinese activities, aimed towards the gradually weakening of the indigenous elements and institutions, aroused the resentment of the Tibetans. Further, the mass resistance of reforms introduced in Eastern Tibet made China's hold over Tibet very precarious. The Chinese tried to placate the Tibetan apprehension by withdrawing a number of Han cadres and the adoption of a policy of no democratic reforms in Tibet for at least six years in 1956. However, March 1959 revolt of Tibet paved the way for Chinese effective contol over Tibet. The revolt was suppressed ruthlessly and Military Central Commissions were set up in major cities. The Chinese made it amply clear that they considered the 1951 treaty abrogated, as well as Mao's commitment of no reforms in Tibet for at least six years land reform and socialization of the economy were carried out eventually.

As the aftermath of the suppression of 1959 revolt, the Chinese imprisoned most of the aristocrats, Government employees, monasteries as 'counter-revolutionary rebels'. They forcefully carried out the so called 'socialist transformation' of Tibet. Firstly, they introduced 'democratic reforms' in two stages to win over the common people.

To begin with the Chinese announced 'the harvest to the tiller policy to encourage peasants to cultivate the maximum areas of lands, especially those belonging to the so-called 'counter-revolutionaries.' Similar policy was announced for the nomads as well. However, when the grain was harvested, a special team of Chinese and so-called native progressives (supporters of Chinese policy) took away all the produce as 'surplus' grain. They put aside some grain as seeds and allocated ration for the year, as average of 22 pounds per person per month.

In the second stage of the so-called democratic reform, the Chinese announced the names of those remaining persons who had worked for the Tibetan government, members of aristocratic families, military and religious personnel, landowners, and businessmen as 'reactionary elements'. The properties of such persons were confiscated and distributed among the people. However, they distributed only the 'wealth of production' and the 'wealth of livelihood'. The wealth of production included the cattle, sheep, goats, donkeys and farming tools and implements. The wealth of livelihood included clothes, houses, utensils of clay and aluminium. All other kinds of wealth like gold, silver, precious stones and antiques which the Tibetans inherited for centuries, were kept by the Chinese.

Regarding nomadic areas, the Chinese found it difficult to get a firm grip over them. They registered every yak, sheep and goat owned by the Tibetans in 1959. No herdsman was allowed to slaughter more than a fixed number of sheep every year. They were taxed heavily both in livestock and dairy products. Besides confiscation and plunder of properties, the Chinese tortured the so-called 'counter-revolutionary' and 'reactionary' elements both mentally and physically through artificially created 'struggle session'. The accused were brought before the 'struggle session' and so-called local progressives were instigated to level all sorts of charges and flog them. This method of torture and public humiliation created nervous disorder and led many to commit suicide. The family members and children of this category were labelled as 'black hat' and they were ostracized from the other members of society.

Till 1961, the Chinese had declared to have completed so-called democratic reforms and stated that by these measures, "Tibet was carried to the threshold of socialism in less than three years." It was followed by systematic organization of groups of peasant households into mutual-aid teams. Later these teams were merged into agricultural producers' cooperatives which pooled their resources to reach the production targets set by the Chinese. This was a prelude to the formation of commune system which begain 1964 onwards. The process of communication was regarded as so-called. 'socialist transformation'. By August 1975, commune system had been established whole of the so-called Tibet Autonomous Region.

In the commune system, the regimentation of living conditions reached its peak. Not only were the means of production collectivized but every phase of life came under regular control of Chinese or Tibetan cadres. It facilitated vigilance, detection of sabotage activities and drilling of every aspect of people's life through regular indoctrination and creating fear psychosis. The indoctrination had been done during public meeting which were held every night after hard labour. The meetings were conducted to discuss the work of the commune; to study Mao's Thoughts and discuss ways of putting it into practice; to oppose capitalism and capitalistic tendencies; self criticism and mutual criticism. It was aimed to create mistrust among the people and to induce them to spy on each other. It, in fact, enabled the Chinese to follows of policy divide and rule.

Since all the products belonged to commune, members could get ration as per the rates fixed by the government. The masses were divided into three classes of income group, i.e., those who earn 26, 28 and 30 gyamas of grains in a month (2 gyamas = 1 kg). Since the majority of the Tibetans were manual labourers, they get 26 gyamas of grains per month. Even that much of grain could be procured on the basis of work-point earned by them. If they earned less than the required work-point, their ration would be deducted. Butter and meat, which formed essential ingredients of the staple food, were not available for the Tibetan people. In most communes, children and the aged persons were not entitled to get any ration. Therefore, the working members of the family had to share their meagre ration to feed the whole family.

Indeed, the commune system brought more land under cultivation, better irrigation facilities and effective utilization of water resources were introduced. The production also doubled or trebled. However, these were achieved at the cost of forced labour at semi-starvation ration of the Tibetan people. The actual tillers of land had no right to enjoy the fruit of their labour.

After the harvest, different forms of taxes were levied on the production of communes. The taxes such as love-the-nation tax, war preparation tax, the commune development tax, grain for famine pretention tax and so on were collected. Of the remaining grain they kept aside grain for ration and for seeds. The rest were taken as surplus grain sale, the earnings of which were supposed to have been deposited in bank but of which the commune members could make no use. Usually the highest authority of a country would fix a high amount of produce to be given to the government from each commune under it. The officials at commune level used to force the people to work more and keep them at starvation diet in a bid to contribute more than the fixed amount. Thus, they tried to gain promotion and other favours from the higher authorities.

The collected grain was stored in various granaries from where it was taken for distribution among the Chinese military and civilian personnel in towns and cities. It was also stated that "every year, it is observed that the majority of grains collected from different chues and hsiens (villages and counties) are taken away to China via Cormo in military vehicle . . .

Such exploitation can be proved from the Chinese policy of forcing Tibetans to cultivate winter wheat rather than traditional barley as the Chinese prefer former. This dictatorial agricultural policy was acknowledged by Hu Yaoband and Wan Li when they visited Tibet in May 1980. They specifically pointed out that crops in Tibet "should be grown that suit the local needs and natural conditions."

Even in pastoral areas, the Chinese had established the commune system to strengthen their control. They introduced a policy of 'fixed abode and nomadic herding' with fixed ranches and grazing grounds and access to pasture and water resources. If the animals were in ninety per cent were to remain alive, else, the nomads' work-point would be reduced. No dead animal could be disposed without prior permission of the authority. Just as farmers were levied different kinds of taxes, nomads also had to pay taxes in the form of butter, cheese, wool and livestock. Further, so-called 'surplus sale' was also imposed on nomadic communes.

The people, whom the Chinese labelled as 'black hats', were not allowed to become members of communes. They were required to do their daily work but were kept isolated under constant surveillance and were not allowed to socialize with other people.

The training of Tibetan Militia was another important integrative function undertaken by the Chinese. After the organization of the

People's communes, the PLA took up the responsibility for training the militia. As more Tibetan between the age 16 to 40 were regularly inducted in the militia, their susceptibility to one more form of state-oriented and managed socialization were increased.

Tibet as Autonomous Region

The Chinese Government decided in 1965 that Tibet was ready for the inauguration of the Autonomous Region. The first session of the Tibetan People's Congress of the Tibet Autonomous Region (TAR) opened on September 1 and creation of the Autonomous Region was declared. With this status, Tibet was to have more freedom in regard to local matters. However, the autonomy was greatly circumscribed as Tibetans have to do everything with beginning the guidance and approval of the Central Government. Both the Chinese and the Tibetan officials have only the power to endorse and implement the policy directives issued from Beijing. They justify this process of governing on the basis of democratic centralism. Further, so-called TAR consisted of only the Western and Central part of Tibet. The large chunks of northern and eastern parts of Tibet are inducted in various Chinese provinces of Yunnan, Szechuan, Gansu and Quinghai. As in the other minority areas, here too the Chinese adopted a deliberate policy of fragmentation of land and dispersal of the people to achieve integration.

Besides, social and economic transformation, various other developmental activities were started. The development of roads and communication network, apart from strategic consideration, ensures the stability of China's hold over Tibet. They also facilitate the conversion of Tibetan manpowers and natural resources as subservient to China's economic and industrial developments. Inspite of rich mineral resources available in Tibet, not even a single mineral refining industry has been set up in Tibet. All the extracted minerals are transported to the nearest Chinese province from where they are taken to various destination by trucks, rail and other means. A large section of export oriented developmental activities has been carried out such as setting up of woollen factories, carpet factories and leather factories. All the products are brought to China from where they are exported under the label of 'Made in China'. These developments did not bring about any benefit for the Tibetans as the prices of the commodities are too high for the people, nor did they get any share of export earning as they had to work to earn the required work-point to get the already fixed ration. The development of modern amenities like hospitals, school, housings and electricity facilities were restricted to major towns and cities in the year 1978.

The most destructive policy in the name of development is their attempt to destroy the distinct Tibetan culture and identity. Increasing numbers of Chinese words which have been incorporated in both vernacular as well as the written language of Tibetans. In the name of promoting traditional arts of dance and drama, they have introduced changes in dress, style, theme and music. Thus, local language and culture seems to have been diluted deliberately in the guise of development.

The beginning of Cultural Revolution put an end to the consideration of minorities' special characteristics and hastened transition to socialism and assimilation in the Han Revolutionary youth mobilized into the Red Guards and they were accused of destroying the Four Olds (old ideas, culture, customs and habits) and encouraged to travel to 'exchange revolutionary experiences'. In October, Zhou-Enlai explicitly forbade Han students to exchange revolutionary experience in Tibet but nevertheless they had entered Tibet. The Red Guards primarily aimed to destory distinct Tibetan identity, culture and religion and to achieve total assimilation of Tibetans in Chinese national framework.

Since monasteries were the centres of Tibetan culture and tradition, they were severely attacked. Most of them were completely razed to the ground. Barely a dozen or so were existing out of total of 2,000 monasteries. The invaluable works of art, literature, religious relics and monuments were subjected to wanton destruction. Images and other religious objects made of gold, silver, brass, precious stones and metals were taken to China, many of which found their way to the markets of Hong Kong, Shanghai, Tokyo and Nepal where antique collectors purchased them at exorbitant prices. Rest of them were taken to factories and warehouses from where many of them were rescued and reinstated in various monasteries in recent years.

Latest Phase of the Policy

Probably, as early as 1969 and undoubtely by 1971 and the death of Line Biao, the harshest policies of Cultural Revolution period began to be moderated. Once again, emphasis on 'special characteristics' of the ethnic minority and the need to take them into account while formulating policy towards them were gaining ground. It was argued that the minority areas should now be 'nationalist in form, socialist in content'.

The party undertook to repair the monasteries and other historic buildings and started easing restrictions on religious practices and cultural activities. They also re-emphasized the training and recruitment of local cadres as "being familiar with local conditions were better at forming ties with the masses" and that this helped 'rally' the minorities for the socialist revolution and the consolidation of the dictatorship of the proletariat.

The new leadership under Deng Xioaping, Hu Yaobang and ZhaoZiyang pledged to implement policies that were remarkably similar to those of the early 1960s. The policies of Lin Biao and the 'gang of four' were termed 'feudal' and 'fascist'. There was to be a united front again with minority elites both lay and clerical. In Tibet, nobility imprisoned since the 1959 revolt were released. The open practice of religion was once again allowed. During the official visit of Hu Yaobang, General Secretary of the Chinese Communist Party and Wan Li, Vice Premier of the State Council, they admitted the failure of China's policy in Tibet and blamed the 'gang of four' for their leftist diversion from the party policy. After the visit the reforms were listed as six prerequisites. The six prerequisites were as follows:

1. Under the Central Government's policy of equal treatment to all the national minorities of China, the autonomous region should be given more power.
2. Taking into account the great difficulties in Tibet today, the policy of granting more leisure time and food subsidies should be implemented immediately to lighten the very heavy burdens so far imposed on the Tibetan people.
3. Economic policy should be implemented in keeping with the special conditions existing in Tibet and with cooperation of theTibetan people.
4. More funds should be allocated to Tibet.
5. Tibetan culture, education and science should be revived.
6. More Tibetan cadres were to be promoted.

The CCP Central Committee stated to have instructed to pay attention to the eight principles while dealing with Tibet. Some of the principles are that all Central Departments pay attention to acquainting themselves with and studying Tibet's actual conditions. All decisions and measures must first have the wholehearted approval and support of cadres and people of Tibetan nationality. They must avoid at all costs the style of leadership and work methods characterized by subjectivity, one-sideness, generalities and demand for uniformity in everything. Cadres should be transferred from the interior to Tibet according to the actual needs and principle of cadres being few in number but efficient. The CCP Centre Committee further instructed the Tibet Autonomous Regional Party Committee to re-examine and revise the regional plan for economic construction.

Since then there is great deal of relaxation at economic front and the commune system has been dismantled. Freedom of movement within Tibet and religious freedom have been restored to a great degree. The process of withdrawing Han cadres have been started and more Tibetans have been recruited to run the administration. However this process of indigenization seems to be superficial as real authority still remains with Han cadres who hold lower position in the hierarchical structure of the administration. Further, motivation of the latest policy seems to display the foreign tourists in Tibet that they have liberalized their control over Tibet.

One of the most damaging aspects of the new policy is the unprecedented population transfer of Chinese to Tibet in early 1980s. There is evidence that the Chinese have sent as many as 6.2 million civilians into Tibet in addition to the 500,000 or more troops stationed in the country. There are no more Chinese in the north-eastern province of Amdo than Tibetans, outnumbering them by three to one. The number of Chinese in Kham is also increasing. Although, there are fewer Chinese settled in the so-called Tibet Autonomous Region than in areas of Tibet under Chinese provincial administrations, the Chinese population is growing rapidly in the Autonomous Region's cities and well over half the population of Lhasa is Chinese. If the population transfer succeeds Tibetans will soon be reduced to a small and insignificant minority in their own land.

After initial illusion of relief, it soon dawned upon the people the futility and damaging aspect of the new policy. It propelled the Tibetan people to restart their political activities to demonstrate their nationalism in full glare of the foreign tourists which enabled them to get wide international coverage of the Tibetan discontentment and demand for independence from the Chinese control.

From the above analysis one can deduce that there is no fundamental difference in aim towards Tibet between radical and moderate groups in Beijing. Both groups appear firmly convinced of the inevitability as well as the desirability of eventual assimilation. The shift in policy since Lin Biao's downfall may be seen to represent differences in tactics rather than strategy. The theoretical journal, *Hongqui*, reminded in 1981 that " the total integration of minority nationalities is something for the distant future ; its realization will be a prolonged historical process, only being attained after the extinction of classes and the state." So for the time being "the socialist period is the phrase to equalize all nationalities and build mutual confidence and to ensure the prosperous development of all nationalities." This idea seems to be the guiding principle of China's national minorities policy at present.

The Chinese attempt to assimilate the Tibetans invariably strengthened the Tibetan nationalism. Although the Chinese could remove the physical barriers between China and Tibet with the network of communication links, the mental and emotional barriers have been ever on increase. It is obvious from the frequent revolts and resistance to Chinese policies, the latest of which has been the event of March 1989 which led to imposition of marshal law in Tibet.

The study indicates that even in the tightly controlled state system, it is not possible to impose homogeneity and assimilation on the minorities. The realization seems to have widely dawned upon the world over the objective of interaction and assimilation of various ethnic groups with the majority ethnic group within a territory of nation-state system may not be even a desirable goal considering the general acceptance in modern age of the equality and dignity of all people. The unambiguous manifestation of the thinking in this direction can be noticed in recent developments in relations between ethnic Republics and Federal Government of the Soviet Union. It may not be possible for China to shut itself off for long from the developments all around and the general accepted principles of social relations world wide.

13

The Future of Tibet

In the previous chapters of this book, the changes in the life style of Tibetans have been discussed. In keeping with the main approach of this book, we have seen those changes at the grassroot level. Such observations indicate some truth in Deng Xiao-ping's new economic policy as operative since the early 1980's. Therefore I shall dish out some official Chinese statistics that might give little ideas about the observed changes in different spheres of Tibetan life, including economic, cultural and to a less extent in the political sphere. These changes, it may be noted, are not only because of overall liberalization trends discernable in China since the fall of the radical Maoist leadership, but also due to the Dalai Lama's contact with Beijing since 1979.

Invitation to Return Home

The Chinese invitation to Tibetan exiles to return home began much sooner than 1979. It seems that soon after the Sino-Indian War of 1962, China realized that the Dalai Lama and the 80,000 Tibetans who followed him into exile might be used for antichinese purposes. So in 1963 China started a special broadcast series in Lhasa Radio asking the Tibetan exiles to comeback home. The early 1960s also marked the founding of a Tibetan guerrilla base in Nepal's Mostang aided by the CIA, which must have confirmed Chinese fears.

The Dalai Lama's demand in the 1960s when the international support for the Tibetan cause was at its height—put the Chinese on the defense side. He repeatedly demanded right to national self-determination for the Tibetan's people. But as the international climate changed the western support to Tibet also declined. The Dalai Lama too changed his demand. He repeatedly called for an internationally supervised plebiscite in Tibet to determine whether the Tibetan people wished to be under the Chinese rule or become independent. The term "internationally supervised" need not exclusively refer to an UN supervision which

Beijing's chair in the UN Security Council makes difficult if not impossible. It could, for example, refer to a respected world body like the International Commission of Jurists which did an authoritative work on Tibet's historical status in the early 1960s.

By late 1970s the Dalai Lama had changed his political demand into conciliatory gesture to China. On several occasions and at international forums, Dalai Lama made the same demand : if the six million Tibetans are really happy he would be ready to return and accept whatever status the majority of them are prepared to grant to him. At the same time he made it clear that as far as he was concerned, his return to Tibet would not mean the restoration of the old order. He would not only abide by the majority wishes but also by progressive modern trends. This is what annoyed China most, which considers revolution as its monopoly.

Till May 1980, Beijing believed, that the conditions in Tibet had definitely improved and that the Dalai Lama's challenge could be met. But after Hu Yaobang's visit to Central Tibet in that year, China admitted that its deputies in Tibet had made blunders with severe consequences to the Tibetan people. The acceptance of failure became clear after the return of the Dalai Lama's first fact-finding delegation to Tibet. However, Deng Xiaoping allowed more delegations to visit various parts of Tibet, and the Sino-Tibetan dialogue continued till 1986. It is clear that the Tibetan question would have been stalemated beyond the 1980s had it not been for the convergence of two pragmatic factors : the triumph of Deng's group in China and the equally pragmatic nature of the Dalai Lama. The result is the on-going dialogue between Beijing and Dharmsala.

According to Tibetan sources, the Chinese were the first to make the first move. In 1979 Communist agents in Hong Kong contacted the Dalai Lama's controversial brother Gyalo Thondup. The message : the new leadership in Beijing would like to work for the possible return of the Dalai Lama to the "motherland".

It is highly controversial that who made the move first. When the CIA decided to discontinue the support to Tibetan guerrilla base in Mustang in the autumn of 1969, Gyalo Thondup was in dilemma. Whom to turn for help? He tried to establish a contact with the Russians in Delhi but with his past American connections they refused to meet him. Then in the early 1970s he moved to Hong Kong, hoping that the Chinese might listen to him. George Patterson told me that Mr. Thondup was trying to contact the Chinese as early as 1973.

As it has been mentioned earlier, the Dalai Lama's recent statements left the question that who should investigate the conditions in Tibet is ambiguous : That if the majority of the Tibetan people were happy, the Dalai Lama may consider for returning. The door to his fact-finding missions were to be official or not. A group of young Tibetans were anxious to break the ice. In July 1979 they discussed the possibility to visit Tibet. Though a private initiative, the visit was approved by the Dalai Lama. He felt that "it would be good if the Tibetans themselves got an opportunity to see the conditions of Tibetans in Tibet". In other words, he was prepared for any kind of contact with Tibet even under Chinese terms.

The first batch of Tibetans faced a visa problem which indicated the Chinese precondition for the proposed visit to Tibet. The Chinese Embassy in Delhi refused to give the Tibetans travel permits issued by the Government of India which described the applicants as either "Tibetan refugee" or "Tibetan national". The Chinese insisted that they must carry overseas Chinese passports. The implicit demand was that Tibetans must recognize Tibet as part of China and therefore themselves as Chinese, not Tibetans. This condition would be imposed as we shall see, whenever the Chinese toughen their position on the on-going dialogue between Beijing and Dharmsala. Thus, the fifth fact-finding delegation had to be cancelled in 1986 because the Chinese imposed this condition. However, between 1979 and 1985 during which the Dalai Lama sent five such delegations to Tibet, China introduced a special visa form in which the applicants is need not mention their nationality. In retrospect it appears that Chinese would not have made this concession had it not been for the Dalai Lama's pending visit to the Soviet Union in 1979. The Soviet Union continues to be a bargaining factor for the Tibetans who are otherwise quite helpless.

First Delegation

The Dalai Lama's first delegation left India on August 5, 1979. Its aim was to "try to understand the new leaders of China, greet the six million Tibetans in Tibet." They stopped over in Hong Kong and were briefed over by Gyalo Thondup. Although the delegation spent more than three months in Tibet, they did not publish their findings. They brought back miles of film footage, some of which was shown by the BBC TV. In Dharmsala they showed films for ten hours and gave reports for nearly eighteen hours. Those interested in Tibet in the West must have seen the most emotional scenes of the long film shot by the first delegation in the BBC TV network. One has to indeed see the lengthy film with a view to believe the message it unfolds. Judging by the sad faces and patched dresses in the crowd, it becomes clear that economic conditions must have been bad, but more than economics, it appears, people have been more starved of religion during the last two decades. This means that like in medieval Europe religion continues to be the most important thing in Tibetan life. The Red Guards (1966-68) succeeded in destroying about 95 per cent of the material manifestations of Tibetan religious life but they have failed to kill the Tibetan people's innate religiosity.

The first delegation submitted its following report to the Dalai Lama : That the people belief in Buddhism is very strong that the vast majority still cherish the Dalai Lama and dream to see an independent Tibet under him; that their economic conditions are incredibly poor ; that among the Chinese leaders the delegates met Li Xian-nian who told them that China was "willing to sort out the Tibetan problem through talks and to discuss any possibilities for the future".

Second Delegation

In second delegation there were five modern educated young Tibetans. They travelled through various parts of Tibet for more than three months. Their brief report said that the "ordinary Tibetans still lead an indescribably poor life and that they all desire the restoration of Tibet's independence." What is most important about their report is the strong proof of strong religious faith in Tibet. The delegates who with their three-piece suits were looking far from Lamaistic were received and treated like some high Lamas everywhere they went. The only fact that they represented the Dalai Lama seemed to have transformed them into holy objects. Once some members of the delegation were having their hair cut in Kham. When their hair was thrown out, people struggled to get strands as if they were some precious holy relics.

The delegates also said in their reports that 99 per cent of all monasteries and temples in Tibet were destroyed. In towns there are more new houses than old ones, "yet no ordinary Tibetan lives in those house." Tibetans are the head of all district headquarters, "although decisions are made by Chinese supposedly working in other capacities." The delegates did not meet "one single individual who was happy, who said something pleasant about the conditions, or who did not have a story of oppression and suffering to tell." Nor did they see a single Tibetan who had received a university education over the last thirty-one years. In Kham and Amdo no Tibetan language is taught in any school. However, it is taught in primary school is central Tibet for three years. Finally the delegates could not fail to observe an insidious process of sinofication which poses direct threat to the future of Tibetan civilization. Those who understand Chinese are recognised as very progressive whereas Tibetan language, dress, behaviour, culture—are considered a sign of backwardness.

The second delegation's long journey into various parts of Tibet ended with the so-called "Lhasa incident" on July 25, 1980. A massive crowd had gathered in front of the guest house where the delegates were staying. Perhaps being inspired by the crowd, one of the delegates shouted "Tibet is independent" and the crowd responded emotionally. This was not the first incident of its kind. During the first delegation's visit to Lhasa, an old woman made a similar declaration, and she was accused of undermining national unity, and was arrested.

The Lhasa incident was witnessed by many foreign reporters who were visiting Lhasa at the time.

Third Delegation

In third delegation there were seven members headed by the Dalai Lama's sister, Pema Gyalpo. They also travelled in the summer of 1982 for three months. But unlike the previous delegations this one faced some structured obstacles, which did not allow them to visit where they wanted to visit. This tended to confirm the earlier reports that the Chinese achievement in the field of education fell far below expectation. The spread of education is so uneven that the delegates demand to see various parts upset Beijing's plan of showpieces. What therefore the third delegation brought back was a bag of official statistics given by the Chinese. The delegates were briefed that there were 430 primary schools and 6,000 schools run by parents with 200,000 students who now receive Government grants, 22 high schools with 2,000 students and four colleges with more than 560 students. But, the delegation was allowed to visit only 85 schools with 39,844 students. Of these only 17,660 were Tibetans constituting 44 per cent. Similarly, out of 2979 teachers only 1024 or 30 per cent were Tibetans. None of the schools visited was "comparable in standard to schools run by Tibetans in exile".

The contacts between China and Dharmsala had been suspended since July 1980 when a huge crowd demonstrated in support of the Dalai Lama and Tibet's independence. This incident was widely published in the international press because a large group of foreign correspondents based in Beijing were visiting Lhasa at the time and they witnessed the uprecedented event. China took such a serious view of the mass demonstration that the second and third delegations were asked to cut short their visits. This provided an appropriate opportunity for the Dalai Lama to ask the Chinese leadership have a dialogue. Chinese agreed. A high ranking, three members delegation from Dharmsala left for Beijing on April 24, 1982.

Fourth Delegation

The fourth delegation spent about a month in the Chinese capital exploring and sounding various prospects for the future of Tibet. As we have seen, the Dalai Lama has always tried to link up the conditions for his return with the future status of Tibet. It is in this context that we should view the Dalai Lama's demands. If China does not meet his minimal demands, the possibililty of his returning to China is ruled out. The delegation was instructed by the Dalai Lama personally before its departure and its main purpose was to sound the various options already discussed in Dharmsala.

The Dalai Lama put the following demands : That China should change its political system into a federal one in which Tibet would become an equal and to a large extent independent member holding UN membership like Ukraine and Byellorussia in the Soviet Union ; that such an autonomous Tibetan republic should not only include Outer Tibet but also Inner Tibet which is under the present set-up absorbed by the neighbouring Chinese provinces like Yunnan, Sichuan, Qinghai, and Gansu ; that the PLA troops should be withdrawn from Tibet.

When the Chinese leaders rejected this offer the Tibetan delegates offered the new package ; that China should grant Tibet a status promised to Taiwan under the nine-point reunification programme ; that Kham and Amdo (Inner Tibet) must be united with the present day Tibet Autonomous Region ; that the PLA troops must be withdrawn and the whole of Tibet must be declared a demilitarized zone of peace.

Unification of Tibetan People

Chinese answered to this package deal in Yes and No. It should be noted that the Tibetans have been most insistent upon the unification of Tibetan-speaking people living in the neighbouring Chinese provinces with what is today called Tibet Autonomous Region (TAR). The Tibetan-speaking people are racially, culturally and linguistically the same but their territories were gradually annexed by China during the Ch'ing dynasty and early in the Republican period. Now why this demand has been most insistent from the Tibetan side is largely a reflection of the composition of the Tibetan power elite in exile. For example, all the three members of the fourth delegation are from Kham and Amdo just as the Dalai Lama is from the same region. This power group wishes that whatever benefits may flow from the present negotiations should also be extended to their homeland Kham and Amdo. It should be noted that the 17th point Agreement was not applied to Kham and Amdo.

At the same time there is a historical explanation for the present Dalai Lama's desire to unify all the Tibetan-speaking people living on the Tibetan plateau under Lhasa. His predecessor, the 13th Dalai Lama dreamt of a similar ambition. The dream is not without some historical basis. The Simla Convention (1913-14), about which so much has been written by Indian and British authors, *was* nothing but a tripartite agreement about the Sino-Tibetan frontier (Eastern Tibet) signed under the British auspices. The Tibetan government persuaded the British authorities in India to bring diplomatic pressure upon China so as to settle the Sino-Tibetan boundary dispute in Kham and Amdo. In keeping with the Tibetan tradition of offering (*skyabs-brtan*) the much disputed piece of territory called Tawang area in present-day Arunachal Pradesh (India) was presented (*skyabs-brtan*) to British India, with the hope that the British would bring about the necessary diplomatic pressure on China.

Background of Shimla Convention

Much more pertinent point seems to be this : During the Simla convention the Tibetan plenipotentiary Lönchen Shatra "produced a large number of original archives from Lhasa, tonnes of delicate manuscripts bound in richly embroidered covers" (British archives) to support his claim over disputed Khampa territory. "For some days", the same archival sources continued, "Mr. Ivan Chen (the Chinese plenipotentiary) showed evident signs of panic ; he protested that his Government would never consent to the production of evidence in regard to the country east of Batang or the discussion of Kokonor."

It is not necessary to go into details of the issue. However, suffice to say that the Simla Conference broke down because it will China refused to ratify it because of the Sino-Tibetan failure to reach an agreement on the China-Eastern Tibetan frontier. China pressed for a common boundary through Gyam-da, only about 125 miles from Lhasa. This episode shows that the early Chinese Republican government more or less recognized the British division of Tibet into two spheres of influence, namely that of the Chinese (Inner Tibet) and that of the British (Outer Tibet).

We have digressed this far to indicate that the present Dalai Lama's desire and demand for the unification of all Tibetan-speaking people in Inner Asia is not without some historical basis.

It is not only history that binds Kham and Amdo with the rest of Tibet ; Khampas living even on the far-flung Sino-Tibetan regions still continue to feel the psychological and cultural pull of the epicentre of the Lamaist world, Lhasa, I shall give an example to illustrate this point. When I was in New York in 1982, a high school friend (Tibetan) of mine, Kesang Tashi told me how his uncle living in Gyalthang, now part of Yunnan Province, tried to get a permit from the local authorities to visit his relatives living abroad. When he was not permitted he went not to the capital of Yunnan Province but to Lhasa to try to get it. Of course, he failed to get the permit ; it was a wrong administrative procedure, but a perfect example of what I mean by the psychological and cultural pull of Lhasa.

Retrospect

It should also be noted that the 1959 Tibetan Rebellion started in Inner Tibet which the British used to regard as the Chinese sphere of influence. The reason is not difficult to find out. Accepting the British division of Tibet into Inner and Outer Tibet, the Chinese Communists pursued since 1951 Sino-Tibetan agreement two different lines of policy. Inner Tibet (Kham and Amdo) was regarded as constituting part of China proper, and a radical policy was applied there like the rest of China. Hence, the rebellion began there by early 1950s. But Outer Tibet (U, Tsang and Chamdo) was regarded as Tibet proper, and a much more lenient policy operated up to March, 1959. This shows how the Chinese Communist conceptions of what constituted Tibet were influenced by the British imperialist thinking on the subject. Similarly India faces a dilemma with regard to the boundary dispute. India insists upon border demarcations marked and agreed by British India and the 13th Dalai Lama's Tibet. But New Delhi refuses to recognize the autonomous/ independent status of Tibet as the British did.

Chinese Condemnation

Although both sides became agreed to keep secret their talks, Chinese have openly condemned the Dalai Lama's demand for the unification of Tibetan speaking people in China under a single Tibetan administration. The demand, they said, ignores facts of geography and history. It is administratively impossible to rule such a vast territory. But the real reason may be something else. China views any such unification as showing the necessary seeds for Tibet's independence. It has always adopted a "divide and rule" policy since the Ch'ing days, which the Communists with greater coercive power and organizational ability have only further re-enforced. As regards the withdrawal of PLA troops, the Chinese replied that what should be withdrawn from Tibet are Han working personnel and not the armed forces. The PLA units are required to guard and defend the border. In fact in 1982 Chinese introduced a new slogan in Tibet : Decrease Han working personnel but increase military preparedness."

The Tibetan delegate's demands were also rejected by the Chinese leaders for a special autonomous status similar to the one offered to Taiwan. If it is granted, this status would largely mean the restoration of the political situation in pre-1959 Outer Tibet as guaranteed by the 17th Point Agreement. Therefore, when the fourth delegation returned to Dharmsala, the member who made this particular demand was vehemently criticized. Tibetans have bitter memories of the 17th Point Agreement (1951) and its implementation in Tibet in the 1950s. But the fact that the Chinese declined even this moderate and limited proposal indicates their fundamental unwillingness to make even minor political concessions to the Dalai Lama. They privately told the Tibetans that Taiwan has a big army and from that position of relative strength is negotiating with Beijing whereas the Dalai Lama has no other option.

Fresh Delegation

Perhaps there is still scope of hope. In the summer of 1985 six members delegation was sent to investigate the conditions in north-eastern Tibet or Amdo. This is the birth place of the existing Dalai Lama. The report they brought back is very frightening. As one of the delegates (Sample) writes "I don't know what the dinosaur felt when it knew that it was getting extinct but to me there can be nothing more frightening that the prospect that one's people, language and culture within a few generations will be mere exhibited in the museum, just as the dinosaur is today."

The fact is that the Tibetans in north-eastern Tibet have been already engulfed by Chinese. According to official Chinese statistics the total population of Qinghai (Amdo) is 3,895,706, out of which 2,359,979 are Chinese and 754,254 Tibetan. Before 1949 there were only a few Chinese businessmen at Labrang Tashi Kyil in present day Gansu province. Now approximately 75 per cent of the population of this traditional bastion of Tibetan culture is Chinese. The Dalai Lama's birth place Taktser consists of forty families out of which only eight are Tibetan, and the rest Chinese. The delegates found a distant relative of the Dalai Lama, a young man in the age of his mid thirties. He, his wife and children spoke no Tibetan. Sinofication has taken its toll. In Lhasa the Chinese outnumber the Tibetans by 70,000 to 50,000

The fifth delegation report puts this question : Will the Tibetans face the same fate that the Manchus and Mongols have already faced? In the early of this century, the Manchus were a distinct race with their language and culture ; today only two or three million Manuchurians are left in Manchuria, where 75 million Chinese have settled. In Inner part of Mongolia, Chinese outnumber the Mongols by 8.5 million to 2.5 million. It is true that Manchuria and Mongolia are more climatically suitable for Chinese settlers. But we must remember the fact that the Chinese mass media announced in early 1976 the first arrival of permanent Chinese settlers. By the end of that year some 780 Chinese arrived in Tibet. Most of them were to become farmers. A CIA report (*Tibetan Review*, November, 1979) remarks that "the key to the future settlement of Tibet by large numbers of Han Chinese is the completion possibly in the late 1980s of the Qinghai Tibet railroad. Until then settlement will have to proceed slowly and the number of Chinese settlers entering Tibet annually probably will be no more than 10,000 or so."

The Backdown

The fifth delegation was the last, because there is hardening of the Chinese position in the seven-year-old Sino-Tibetan dialogue. In 1986 the Dalai Lama decided to send the sixth delegation but it was cancelled because of the Chinese demand that they must carry overseas Chinese passport. It must be remembered that earlier delegates were not allowed to carry such documents. What is at issue is the basic Chinese condition for the continuance of the Sino-Tibetan dialogue : the Dalai Lama and his followers must recognize that Tibet is part of China, and therefore they must consider themselves as Chinese. This is quite impossible to accept for the Dalai Lama and the Tibetan exiles. It hardly leaves any scope for negotiations. As for the Dalai Lama's possible return to Tibet the Chinese have told the third delegation that he would have to remain in Beijing, not Lhasa. The Chinese have recognized the undeniable fact that the Dalai Lama in Tibet would prove a major destabilizing force. He may be responsible for another rebellion. Unless virtually house arrested in Beijing, the Dalai Lama, whether in or outside Tibet, continues to pose a dilemma to China.

If this is so, then it is time to summarize the successive delegations findings before we discuss the Chinese new measures in response to the Tibetan reports since 1959, despite the drastic changes in Tibetan economy. Tibetans continue to face tremendous economic hardships. Phuntsok Wangyal, a member of the second delegation, reports that the Chinese official figures claim the annual ration per person to be 550 lbs. but in actual fact it is 350 lbs. Others report even less : 90 to 120 kgs. of barley per year, per person. None of the delegates failed to report the destruction of monasteries carried out during the Cultural Revolution. One of the difficulties is that there is no proper idea about the number of monasteries and temples in Tibet before 1959. The Dalai Lama estimates 6,200 monasteries and temples. His sister estimates 4000 of the monasteries and temples. The number of monasteries is known in certain well-known localities. For example, in Lithang Valley, there used to be 118 monasteries and temples of which only one remains. In Sakya there used to be 108 monasteries and temples out of which only one remains. In other words the Chinese sought to destroy religion as a way of life but left some ten historically connected monasteries intact. These are Jorkhang, Potala, Sera, Drepung, Derge Gonchen, Sakya Lhakhang Chenmo, Tashi Khil, Tashi Lhunpo, Gyantse Pargo Choten and Kumbum. These ten famous monasteries have received central funds for repair work.

China started to act immediately after the first delegation's return from Tibet. It took two measures. In February 1980, Chou Enlai's 1957 article on nationalities policy was published. It was widely publicized in the Chinese mass media. This article revealed the Party's basic line on nationalities policy. It remains a mystery why Chen Boda rejected it for publication in *Hongqi*. The article was based on the party line in all the way. The article answered "No" to any of the Tibetan exile's political demands : federation or greater degree of autonomy in all Tibetan-speaking areas.

Chinese Fact Finding Mission

Secondly, the fifth Plenum of the 11th CCP Central Committee (February 1980) ordered its secretariat to work out the details of some economic concessions. In May Party General Secretary Hu Yaobang led China's own fact-finding mission to Central Tibet. After nine days of tour, the Hu Commission issued a six-point directive on the new work in Tibet. The first point reiterated the definition of regional autonomy, the only departure being its stress on a more flexible policy. "Anything that is no suited to Tibet's conditions should be rejected or modified as well as anything that is not beneficial to national unity or development of production." The second point made some major economic concessions to the Tibetan people. It exempted them from paying taxes and meeting state purchase quotas for the next few years. Products of the peasants and herdsmen may be purchased at negotiated prices. The third-point advocated a more realistic economic policy based on ecological realities in Tibet and producers wishes. The fourth point promised more Central funds which will be used for economic development to improve people's living standards in general.

The fifth point is important in the sense that for the first time a Chinese Communist document paid tribute to Tibetan Buddhist culture. "The Tibetan people", it stated, "have a long history and a rich culture. The renowned ancient Tibetan culture containing fine Buddhism, graceful music and dance as well as medicine and opera, all of which are worthy of serious study and development. All ideas that ignore and weaken Tibetan culture are wrong." In so doing the Communists identified the areas of Tibetan culture that might be preserved and studied. While pointing out the need to "make vigorous efforts to revive and develop Tibetan culture, education and science", the document stipulates that all such endeavours must be based on "socialist orientation". It maintained that education has not developed well in Tibet, and urged for the setting up of universities, middle and primary schools. It further acknowledges that some cultural relics and Buddhist scriptures have been damaged, and that "conscious efforts should be made to protect, sort out and study them."

Finally, the sixth point promised greater Tibetan participation in the administration : "Full-time cadres of Tibetan nationality should account for more than two-thirds of all government functionaries in Tibet within the next 2 or 3 years."

Economic and Administrative Reforms

On 24 June, 1980 after seventeen days the Central authorities announced their directives, the Tibet Regional People's government issued an eight-point directive. It affirmed, specified and elaborated Hu's six-point directive. It dealt primarily with economic and administrative matters : it did not touch the political issues such as the quantum of autonomy, degree of Tibetan participation in the local administration, etc. It declared that for 1980 and 1981 (later extended upto 1988) agricultural and livestock taxes were exempt. For the same period industrial and commercial taxes were waived. With effect from 1 July, 1980 the state would pay private (people-run) primary teacher's salaries. Communes and brigades would be encouraged and aided to develop national handicrafts and other side-line products. They may sell or exchange such products either locally or establish direct external clients. Towards this end, it was announced, rural trade fairs will be re-opened, border trade with border people of Nepal, India, Bhutan and Burma will be opened. Private plots of production team will account for 5 to 7 per cent of the team's total irrigated land.

By far the most drastic reforms were introduced in the spheres of labour management. From now on, declares the document government at all levels may not issue orders for production output and crop plans. Production teams, work-groups or households "shall decide their work system as they see fit". That is, they can start either year-round fixed work-groups or assign farm work to individual groups on adhoc or seasonal basis. The rigid commune system that controlled everybodys's life was broken. This self-management system marks a clear departure from the tightly structured and centrally imposed labour organization operative since 1959. Apart from economic benefits, the new labour measures will give considerable freedom to the Tibetan people who had bitter experiences against the commune system.

After the announcement of six-point directives a series of meetings were held. They had two objectives in common. They were all attended by the so-called "patriotic personages from the upper strata" (i.e., former ruling class, both Lamas and lay). At each such meeting the same call was made : "Build a united, prosperous and culturally developed new Tibet." It was Yang Jingren, Vice-chairman of the CPPCC National Committee and minister in charge of state Nationalities Affairs Commission who uttered the formula first. He was probably the author of the Chinese reply to the Dalai Lama's demand that Tibetan Buddhist civilization be preserved. The formula was repeated by Yin Fatang, Tibet Party Secretary, Hu Yaobang, the Panchen Lama, Song Ziyuan, deputy secretary of the Party Committee, PLA, leaders, etc. It is interesting to note that Ngapoi Ngawang Jigmi did not utter the formula. At the meeting of the upper strata from all circles in Lhasa Municipality Ngapo on June 3, 1980, expressed the hope that the new policy would "transform Tibet into a flourishing and prosperous area as soon as possible".

Mobilisation of Upper Strata

The mobilization of the upper strata was the result of the Chinese policy in 1950s when they tried to woo the aristocrats and high Lamas. It implies that the Chinese policy might have the support of upper strata of Tibetan society but not the masses which stubbornly continue to cling to Tibetan ways. Hence greater attention to the upper strata. The CCP

Central Committee's United Front Work Department and State Nationality Affairs Commission held a reception in Lhasa on July 9, for the 300 upper strata patriots in Tibetan religious circles; on August 23, a memorial meeting was held for a leading Tibetan aristocrat, Langdun Kunga Wangchuk. CPPCC Committee visited a group of aristocrats and Lamas. First, China released 376 Tibetan prisoners and removed all "labels" from more than 6,000 others who took part in the 1959 rebellion. It was reported that about 80 per cent of the Tibetans arrested in 1959 had now been rehabilitated. A notice was also issued to restore the original status of those in Tibet, who were wrongly designated as capitalists in 1975. In May 1981 government allocated 3,146,500 yuan to repay to those former manorial lords, herdowners and monasteries who did not participate in the 1959 rebellion for their confiscated livestock and property. In June, 1980 it was reported that 52 "patriotic Tibetan figures, who are former feudal lords, serf owners or agents of feudal lords" were commended for their patriotism, anti-imperialism and socialism.

It was the same upper strata members who are made to declare that Tibet is part of China, and to call the Tibetan refugees to return home.

Through these actions the Chinese made their intentions clear : the new measures have the support of the upper strata, common masses are not consulted. This is an indirect rejection of the Dalai Lama's demand that the Tibetan people's wishes be determined whether they are contented with their lot. The Chinese wanted that masses will not be consulted. However, the Chinese new economic policy has the support of the Tibetan upper strata. Tibet is a strange case in which the old "feudal" leader can still win a popular mandate but in which revolutionaries can lose such a popular mandate, given the chance.

The cryptic slogans like "unity, prosperity and new civilization" use the Chinese response to the Tibetan demand that Tibet be allowed to retain its own culture. The slogan was first raised on 3 June, 1980, but it was not until a year later that the slogan was explained. What we mean by unity", declared Yin Fatang in a speech, "is to be united under the great community of our motherland. Secondly, we must rally around the Party Central Committee. Third, we must do better job in uniting all the fraternal nationalities in Tibet." That then is what is meant by unity. In defining "new culture" or "highly civilized Tibet" Yin Fatang said it would be necessary to stress on spiritual civilization. "Besides science and culture, spiritual civilization also includes the communist ideology, beliefs, ideals, morality and discipline, revolutionary viewpoints and principles and relationship between people." To make that spiritual civilization does not mean the resurrection of the old Buddhist civilization, Yin stated that the purpose of literature and art was to propagate among the people ideas of "patriotism the superiority of socialism over the feudal and serf systems".

Thus, the Chinese rejected all the basic Tibetan demands, like autonomy ; the creation of a new socialist civilization. The only demand they accepted was economic development. Of this the important measures included economic assistance and exemption from taxes, to remove poverty. The other measures include participation of Tibetan on large scale in the local administration, limited religious freedom and revival of non-religious Tibetan culture.

How to Make Tibet Rich

Hu Yaobang in his six-point directive stated that the Party's central concern is "How to make a poor Tibet rich". It should be noted that China published most of the progress report during the three-member Tibetan delegation's one month stay in Beijing. Whatever the Chinese leaders might have told the Tibetan delegates, their message was clear. As far as Beijing was concerned its main concern and therefore basic concession to the Dalai Lama's various demands was economic. The general aim of the six-point programme is that Tibet will initially try its utmost to improve its poor and backward economy in two or three years, surpass the best level for the past 30 years in five or six years, and achieve affluence to a greater extent in 10 years.

We shall discuss the Central assistance allocated for the various sectors of the economy. Such a discussion will have to be based on official figures which are usually inflated. But there is no other source to verify them. In August 1980 China allocated 550 million yuan constituting 96 per cent of the region's budget. The major expenditure earmarked for various sectors are as follows : 65.9 million yuan for agriculture and animal husbandry ; 80 million for education, public health, scientific research and culture ; 4.2 million for handicrafts. Figures for Central Assistance for 1980 increased by 10 per cent and that for 1982 also by 10 per cent. This is another problem with Chinese statistics that they seldom give the base line. Increases are indicated merely by percentages.

In January, 1982 it was reported that the Central subsidy to Tibet for the year would exceed 600 million yuan. Between 1952 and 1982, the Central Government gave Tibet 5,648 million yuan. *Tibet Daily* of May 12, 1983 reported that since 1980 the Central government gave a total of 557.57 million yuan for economic development from 1979 to 1981 the Central government subsidized Tibet's finances by 1.494 billion yuan. Such subsidies increased by 10 per cent annually, beginning 1980.

Chinese reports also claim that standard of living of urban dwellers have improved in the wake of reduction and exemptions of household electricity charges, rent, remission of industrial and commercial taxes and remissions of road tolls on vehicles used by collective business, etc. They have also allowed city dwellers to engage in independent trades as well as given greater independence for factories. The average monthly wages of the workers in ten handicraft cooperatives increased from 55 yuan to 85 yuan in the second half of 1980.

In 25 February, 1981 in *People's Daily* it published that grain output has topped 1979 figures by more than 10 per cent the total number of domestic animals has increased by 13.4 per cent and collective income from sideline production has risen by 43.7 per cent since 1979 the area of private plots has increased from 169,000 *mu* to 355,000 *mu*, constituting 10.3 per cent of the arable land. The number of privately owned livestock has increased from 1.21 million to 3.48 million head comprising 15 per cent of Tibet's total. Grain output for 1980 was 1.01 billion jin, 163 million jin more than in the previous year. Rapeseed output rose by 5.6 million more in 1979, over 35.6 per cent increase.

It was reported that lives of peasants and herdsmen have also improved. All loans to peasants, herdsmen and handicraftsmen were given interest-free with effect from October 1, 1980. They received 23.7 million yuan in profits as a result of tax exemption and an increase in prices of agriculture, animal husbandry and sideline products. The latter item alone resulted in an average increase in income of 15 yuan per capita. By January, 1982 animal products to increase by 13.8 per cent and nomads income per capita by 200 yuan. The total output value of handicrafts increased in 1980 by more than six million yuan, which is 21 per cent above the previous year. Plots for private use increased to 24,000 hectares accounting for 10.3 per cent of the total arable land. Average per capita income from family sideline occupations reached 32 yuan. Some families have earned more than 1,000 yuan from such products.

In 1979, average procurement price of wheat was 17.42 yuan per 100 jin. It was raised to 20 yuan in the first half of 1980 and to 26 yuan in 1981. In 1979 procurement price of highland barley was 13.63 yuan per 100 jin. It was raised to 20 yuan in the latter half of 1980 and 32 yuan in 1981. In 1979 procurement price of a yak was 109.24 yuan. It was raised to 139.19 yuan in the latter half of 1980 and to 293.7 yuan in 1981. Thus the income of peasants and herdsmen during the period 1980-82 increased by 19.5 million yuan.

Over the past three years, 23,836 tons of diesel oil were supplied to peasants, financial subsidy for each ton being 352 yuan. During the same period 67,466 tons of chemical fertilizers were supplied, financial subsidy for each ton being 250 yuan. Total subsidies from these two commodities were 25.27 million yuan. About 16.65 million yuan has been used to control plant diseases and insects, pests. Since the latter half of 1980, state subsidies for primary school teachers wages that previously parents had paid, reduced local expenses by three million yuan. Some 32.59 million yuan were used during the past three years in helping poor communes, brigades and households. The total grand of central assistance for the period 1980-82 was 171.89 million yuan given to improve local economy, increase productivity and improve people's livelihood.

Liberal economic reforms also extended to reduction of import duties and price control. "All articles for use by national minorities" were exempted from import taxes. Such commodities constituted about 90 per cent of all imported goods into Tibet. Price of beef was reduced by 9.6 per cent, that of mutton by 8.6 per cent and that of frozen pork by 16.7 per cent. On December 7, 1980 a report in *Tibet Daily* published that "there will be plenty of meat supplies on the market to meet the needs of the broad masses for the Tibetan New Year (March 1981) celebrations." Beijing ducks, chickens, eggs, wine, fresh vegetables and fruit were flown in from Beijing and Chengdu.

As we can see, China's new economic policy is not geared towards any long-term economic development in Tibet ; it is intended to render some immediate emergency relief in the nature of some consumer goods to a poverty-stricken people as listed above. The main emphasis is to "resolutely make a sufficient retreat in capital construction", and shift the industrial focus to the construction of light, handicraft and hydroelectric power industries suited to the needs of the Tibetan people. In 1981, Tibet built 53 hydroelectric stations with total generating capacity of 47,000 KW. It was only in the first half of 1982 that China started to make capital investment to the tune of 50.063 million yuan which constituted 40 per cent of the 1982 budget. It therefore becomes clear that whether China would do some genuine economic development in Tibet based on the locally available resources and geared towards Tibetan needs.

Share to Tibetan in Local Government

In December, 1980 it was reported that the proportion of Tibetans in the local administration at prefectural, city and county levels rose from 47 to 76 per cent. Seventy-one of the 75 county governments in the region were headed by Tibetans. The 86 newly promoted Tibetan officials have average age of 30 years. Ngapoi stated that 80 per cent of the county-level cadres "should be Tibetans". At a meeting of cadres at and above section level in government organs, it was decided that "Tibetan cadres must gradually form 80 per cent of the total cadres force, barring teachers, doctors and specialized technicians." In June, 1982 *Xinbua* reported that Tibet now assumes authority in matters of appointment of leaders, passage and amendment of laws, economic development policies, taxation, cultural affairs and language instruction. It was said 54.5 per cent of administrative officials are Tibetans. Chinese authorities complain that there "is a very less presence of Tibetan candidates in the examinations." Their quality is rather poor and few can be selected. However, since 1980 some 15,000 party members of intellectual background were recruited ; 5900 people were given technical titles ; 500 intellectuals were promoted to leadership posts and 90 intellectuals previously unemployed were employed. More than 5000 Tibetan cadres at various levels were undergoing training in educational and managerial skills. More than 7,000 Tibetan cadres underwent such training between the second half of 1980 and 1981.

Now what about the Han functionaries who constitute 56 per cent of the local administration? A *Guardian* (16.10.80) correspondent found "almost all senior officials are Han Chinese ; most of them do not speak a word of Tibetan, as they are living in Tibet for many years." In June 1980, China decided to pull out 10,000 Chinese functionaries and experts from Tibet. A further, 10,000 were to be withdrawn between 1981 and 1982. These are supposed to constitute 85 per cent of non-military Chinese officials in Tibet. But as for the PLA personnel, China has shown no interest to withdraw. Regional Party Secretary Yin Fatang declared at a working meeting to the Tibet Military District that the army must show" interest to be stationed in Tibet for a protracted period to help build Tibet, of regarding the autonomous region as their home and of making even greater contribution in constructing Tibet."

Inflated Statistics and Exaggerated Claims

One of the basic problems with Chinese official statistics lies in the fact that they are highly inflated. Let us take the example of production figures. China, being a vast territory, has to depend on its numerous units for hardcore data, especially statistics. The process by which distortion and inflation of figures takes place is as follows : The local units, be they mutual aid teams, communes or factories are organized and structured in such a way as to be conducive to profitless competition. Since there is so much pressure from above for greater and greater production, the local units naturally tend to inflate their production figures in order to impress the higher-ups as well as their unit-competitors. This is the reason we have to swallow Chinese statistics with a pinch of salt. Given such limitations, I believe that there may still be some truth in the post-1980 Chinese claims because I have tried to check if such benefits are trickling down to the grass-root level. And this seems to be the case as far as Sakya is concerned which has been *my* yardstick to measure the grass-root level reaction in Tibet as a whole.

Tibet Future

The question of Tibet's future seems to be still in the air, not quite dead nor as lively as in the 1960s. At first the Beijing-Dalai Lama meeting in 1986 gave birth to some prospects for a peaceful political settlement but that also proved in vain. What the brief dialogue indicated was its unequal nature. The Chinese are in a position to dictate terms to the Dalai Lama. They have occupied the country for last twenty-eight years and are militarily in control of their subjects. Not only this : China since the Sino-American *detente* has emerged as a great Asian power to be feared, if not respected. All these big changes in favour of China have tended to put the Tibetan question, purely in rational terms, in a hopeless position.

Yet Tibet's future seems not without a ray of hope. The fact that the current Chinese leadership has shown its interest in having talks with the Dalai Lama's representatives. It means that there are still problems in Tibet beyond Chinese control. These problems, it appears cannot be wished away by continued military occupation or increasing diplomatic manoeuvres. As the foreign visitors and the Dalai Lama's fact-finding delegations have shown, one of the fundamental problems still facing China in Tibet continues to be the obstinate but silent resentment of the Tibetan people against Chinese dominance. This is clear to any careful observer of the Tibetan scene. The clear indicators of this popular resentment began to emerge with the opening of Tibet to select foreign visitors since late 1970s.

The Question of Dalai Lamas Return to Tibet

It is clear that the pragmatic Chinese leadership initially believed that to invite Dalai Lama back home will be the effective, means of resolving this non-antagonistic contradiction. But as the Tibetans began to reveal and demonstrate their fundamental religiosity and veneration to the exiled Dalai Lama during his delegations successive visits to various parts of Tibet, Beijing did not fail to visualize the possible consequences of its own initiative. The religious factor that triggered the 1959 Rebellion is far from dead—after twenty-eight years. What guarantee is there that the Dalai Lama might again prove to be a powerful rallying point for another rebellion? The current situation in Tibet seems to warrant such a speculation. The Dalai Lama has also expressed to me on several occasions his desire to be with his people and serve them rather than waste his time in exile.

However, by the time of the fourth delegation China had changed its mind. Beijing told the delegation that on the event of His Holiness return to the "motherland", the Dalai Lama would have to reside in Beijing, not in Lhasa. Thus, the solution to the popular non-antagonistic contradiction in Tibet is not the Dalai Lama's return to Lhasa which would further aggravate it but a craftily controlled quarantine of the Dalai Lama in Beijing. There he could perhaps be put to some diplomatic use such as a colourful instrument of Chinese Buddhist diplomacy. At any rate he would not be allowed to infect his people with germs of nationalism.

The Dalai Lama then, whether in or outside Tibet, continues to be a pain in the neck to China. In exile he has proved himself to be a leader of no mean stature and his cultural activity abroad must be a constant source of embarrassment to China. He has ably projected himself as the moving spirit of Tibetan civilization and the critical conscience of a subjugated people. Hence, wherever possible, China has tried its utmost to stop his activity abroad. However, since His Holiness wears a religious cloak, he manages to visit and speak to interested people in most democratic societies where such freedoms as he explicitly uses are inherent in constitutions. Through all these multi-faceted activities the personality of the existing Dalai Lama has largely substantiated the key Tibetan religious symbol, the institution of Dalai Lamas, and made it irreplaceable.

United States Policy on Tibet

Nor does it appear that the United States which had been one of the main supporters of the Tibetan cause has completely given up Tibet. Two recent US Congress documents continue to list China and

Tibet as separate countries. This may not be a prınting error. The Dalai Lama has visited the United States on several occasions despite stiff Chinese opposition. His representative at the Office of Tibet in New York continues to function again despite persistent Chinese protest.

The cause of US involvement in the Tibetan cause has a history behind it. Its involvement can be traced back to the late 1950s but its active involvement began only around 1961-62 period with the establishment of a Tibetan guerrilla base in Nepal's Mustang region. By the autumn of 1969 CIA began to lose interest in the base because of the growing US-China *detente*. Kathmandu disarmed the guerrillas in 1974-75 under evident pressure from China and with the green signal from Washington. With the Sino-American rapprochement the US Government had stopped its anti-communist offensive. The Tibetan guerrilla base dried up. But as stated before American political interest in Tibet continues.

The Soviet Union has shown considerable interest in stepping into the American shoes in terms of Tibetan question. We might mention here how a Soviet "cultural" delegation in 1979 expressed its willingness to consider any Tibetan request for aid; it explained that the Soviet Union supports the national liberation movement of any oppressed people. This occurred just before the first fact-finding delegation's visit to Tibet. Soviet cultural delegations continue to trickle to Dharmsala where the Dalai Lama resides and the Tibetan Youth Congress routinely presses for Soviet support. There are also Tibetan students, some even studying in the Soviet Union and the Mongolian People's Republic under official scholarships. The Dalai Lama has visited the two countries three times so far.

So far there appears to be no evidence of direct Soviet military involvement. But strategically the Soviet Union has greater stake in the future of Central Asia than the United States. As the transnational Marxian idealogy recedes into the background, strategic and national interests are likely to become more pronounced. For what the Chinese most feared is a possibility of Indo-Soviet nexus that may pose a serious threat to the Chinese occupation of Tibet. China saw some evidence of this during the Bangladesh war when India and Soviet Union acted concertedly. And the Dalai Lama's continued residence in India seems to lend some substance for Chinese suspicions.

Peaceful Settlement of Tibet

Yet one hopes for a peaceful political settlement in Tibet. The future of Tibet concerns not only the Tibetans themselves ; it touches the nerve centre of strategic interests of several neighbouring countries. Although China objects as a matter of principle to any third party mediation in Sino-Tibetan negotiations, yet the Chinese leaders must realize how complicated and inter-connected the Tibetan question is. For example, the Dalai Lama has insistently demanded the withdrawal of People's Liberation Army troops from Tibet, and China is quite correct in that there cannot be any unilateral withdrawal of Chinese troops without corresponding withdrawal of Indian troops from the Indian Himalayas.

It is a fact that with the fall of Tibet there has been a silent arms race between India and China. From both sides there has been a progressive diversion of scarce resources, which could be used to feed the poor peasants, to arms building. Now neither the withdrawal of Chinese troops from Tibet nor for that matter any progress in the Sino-Tibetan dialogue can be expected without an overall improvement in Sino-Indian relations. Once the Sino-Indian relations got improved, one can hope that India will not short-sightedly and selfishly capitalise on a *Hindu-Chini bhai-bhai* trip, as it did in the 1950s ; but that it will try to work towards a peaceful political settlement in Tibet. Events since 1962 have shown that the moral selling of Tibet to China cannot solve India's security problems, which are a function of geo-politics closely inter-connected with Tibet. One cannot wish away geography, it is there.

Simultaneously, China must keep in view the India's legitimate interest in Tibet as it directly affects Indian national security, just like China. And it is of no importance to pretend that it is otherwise as independent India did in the early 1950s. When the People's Liberation Army troops started moving into Eastern Tibet in 1950, New Delhi tried to persuade China that Chinese military action in Tibet would be detrimental to Nehruvian Indian's attempt to get PRC the UN seat. Such an argument may be clever in the sense it appeals to Chinese self-interest. But it seems to be useless to hide one's national security interest where it is inextricably involved and it must be stated in brutally frank manner, as British India did. When Tsarist Russia's "intrigue" in Tibet was suspected at the end of the century, the British government at once pointed to the Russians that the latter had no immediate or direct boundary with Tibet and as such their interest in Tibet was not a matter of special or serious concern as it was with British India. Hands off for no other reason than the fact it impinged on India's national security. Similarly when Chao Er-feng's troops started entering Eastern Tibet in 1908-9 British India immediately protested and warned of dire consequences should the Chinese troops cross the Tibetan frontier. When the nascent Chinese

Republic declared in 1911 Tibet to be one of the Chinese provinces, again British India promptly protested : no change in the political *status quo* in Tibet would be tolerated because such a change would affect the Indian Empire's national security directly. I mention all these incidences to show how the British did not try to hide their legitimate and real interest in relation to Tibet and how instead they tried to *convince* the other party of that legitimate interest. One hopes that China too will not be over-sensitive about "external interference in internal affairs". As has been shown Tibet is an issue in which non-interference is practically inconceivable. As long as each other's intentions are made abundantly clear, there is no reason why they should not touch the issue that virtually affects their relations : Tibet.

Future of Tibet Linked with Sino-Indian Relations

Thus, the future of Tibet looks inextricably bound up with the state of Sino-Indian relations and in particular with the silent arms race between India and China. The British saw these intricate connections, and tried to resolve the Tibetan question by a tripartite conference at Simla. Since then, of course the situation in South and East Asia has radically changed ; the balance of power has also significantly changed. Consequently a resurrection of a tripartite conference along the British lines might not be possible any longer. However, it is in the very interest of every concerned party to reveal its legitimate interest in relation to Tibet, and try to convince China of the geopolitical necessity of a peaceful political solution that would not only minimally satisfy the political aspirations of the Tibetan people but also conciliate the contending security interests of several neighbouring countries including India and the Soviet Union. In this regard, I see the role of diplomatic pressure being exerted upon China, especially by the superpowers. The Tibetan question must not be used for cold war purposes, either old or new variant. It is not in the long-term interest of any party concerned. For Tibetan people, the African proverb says it well : When the elephants fight, it is only the grass that gets trampled upon.

In the end, the author would like to appeal to Chinese leaders or CCP to consider one social fact which appears to be fully borne out by the history of Tibetan civilization. The renowned French Tibetologist R.A. Stein, in his classic study, 'Tibetan Civilization' concludes that the Tibetan case is comparable only with that of Japan. What he means is that what the Tibetans did with Buddhism within a span of seven or eight hundred years (8th-16th century A.D.) is its essence, comparable with only what Japan has done since the 19th century with modern science and technology adopted from the West. Both processes involved, though entirely different fields, enormous degreess of rationalizations of means to given ends. They involve essentially some thinking and its translation into concrete products : monasteries or machines, meditation techniques or medicine, philosophical treatise or technology, *thanka* paintings or photography, merit-saving activity (*dgewa*) or economic investment and so on.

The author happened to reflect during the last decade upon the cultural conditions for modernization/industrialization. As far as the Tibetan case goes, the undeniable cultural achievement of the Tibetan people as indicated by their history, whether in war or peace, shows that they are an efficient people. They have demonstrated in particular throughout their recorded history that they are efficient enough to rule themselves, though to be sure the Lamaist regimes depended upon either Mongol or Chinese military support. Secondly, the story of the rehabilitation of Tibetan refugees in South Asia indicates that the Tibetans are capable of entering the modern world. The Dalai Lama's settlement at Dharmsala is fully manned by bi-lingually educated young Tibetans. The masses of common Tibetan refugees' sweater-selling business in whole of India during winter is another clear indication of Tibetan people's sense of enterprise and initiative.

The cultural achievement of Tibet shows that Tibetans are an efficient people, and their history testifies to long periods of self-government and self-rule. It is hoped Beijing will consider these points in its dialogue with the Dalai Lama.

14

Various Treaties and Agreements

The treaties that were concluded among various power in more than a millennium's time make the course of events much clearer. Following are given various treaties and agreements which were concluded among various powers concerning Tibet.

1. *Treaty between Tibet and China A.D. 821—822* (*Translation from the Main Tibetan Text*)

The Great King of Tibet, the Miraculous Divine Lord, and the Great King of China, the Chinese Ruler Hwang-ti, being in the relationship of nephew and uncle, have conferred together for the alliance of their kingdoms. They have made and ratified a great agreement. Gods and men all know it and bear witness so that it may never be changed ; and an account of the agreement has been engraved on this stone pillar to inform future ages and generations.

The Miraculous Divine Lord Thri-tsug De-tsen and the Chinese King Wen Wu Hsiao-te Wang-ti, nephew and uncle, seeking in their far-reaching wisdom to prevent all causes of harm to the welfare of their countries now or in the future, have extended their benevolence impartially over all. With the single desire of acting for the peace and benefit of all their subjects they have agreed on the high purpose of ensuring lasting good ; and they have made this great treaty in order to fulfil their decision to restore the former ancient friendship and mutual regard and the old relationship of friendly neighbourliness.

Tibet and China shall abide by the frontiers of which they are now in occupation. All to the east is the country of Great China ; and all to the west is, without question, the country of Great Tibet. Henceforth on neither side shall there be waging of war nor seizing of territory. If any person incurs suspicion he shall be arrested ; his business shall be inquired into and he shall be escorted back.

Now that the two kingdoms have been allied by this great treaty it is necessary that messengers should once again be sent by old route to maintain communications and carry the exchange of friendly messages regarding the harmonious relations between the Nephew and Uncle. According to the old custom, horses shall be changed at the foot of the Chiang Chun pass, the frontier between Tibet and China. At the Suiyung barrier the Chinese shall meet Tibetan envoys and provide them with all facilities from there onwards. At Ch'ing-shui the Tibetans shall meet Chinese envoys and provide all facilities. On both sides they shall be treated with customary honour and respect in conformity with the friendly relations between Nephew and Uncle.

Between the two countries no smoke nor dust shall be seen. There shall be no sudden alarms and the very word 'enemy' shall not be spoken. Even the frontier guards shall have no anxiety nor fear and shall enjoy land and bed at their case. All shall live in peace and share the blessing of happiness for ten thousand years. The fame of this shall extend to all places reached by the sun and the moon.

This solemn agreement has established a great epoch when Tibetans shall be happy in the land of Tibet, and Chinese in the land of China. So that it may never be changed, the Three Precious Jewels of Religion, the Assembly of Saints, the Sun and Moon, Planets and Stars have been invoked as witnesses. An oath has been taken with solemn words and with the sacrifice of animals ; and the agreement has been ratified.

If the parties do not act in accordance with this agreement or if they violate it, whichever it be, Tibet or China, nothing that the other party may do by way of retaliation shall be considered a breach of the treaty on their part.

The Kings and Ministers of Tibet and China have taken the prescribed oath to this effect and the agreement has been written in detail. The two kings have affixed their seals. The Ministers specially empowered to execute the agreement have inscribed their signatures and copies have been deposited in the royal records of each party.

The treaty have been carved in Tibetan and Chinese on one side of a stone pillar near the Jo-Khang, the Cathedral of Lhasa. On another side often stone is a historical introduction in Tibetan only ; and on the other two sides are given the bilingual lists of the names of the ministers who witnessed it.

The King of Tibet mentioned in the treaty is better known as Ralpachen (815-841) ; and his Chinese counterpart is Mu Tsung off the T'ang dynasty (821-825). The frontier seems to have been not far to the west of the Kansu—Shensi border.

2. *Treaty between Tibet and Bashahr, 1681*

Professor L. Petech gives the best available information about this treaty in his valuable article. 'The Tibetan-Ladakhi-Moghul War of 1681-1683' in the *Indian Historical Quarterly*, Vol. XXIII, September 1947. At the time of that war, there was an alliance and a brief general agreement concerning the friendly relations and the exchange of envoys between Raja Kehari Singh of Bashahr and the Government of the Vth Dalai Lama.

3. *Treaty between Tibet and Ladakh, 1683*

This treaty terminated the war of 1681-83. Its conditions are summarized by Professor Petch (op. cit.) and included the cession to Tibet of the Province of Ngari, commercial stipulations connected mainly with the important trade in wool, and the dispatch to Lhasa every second year of a sort of tribute mission. This liability was taken over by Kashmir when that State annexed Ladakh in 1842, and continued to be discharged down to 1950. That mission was called the Lopchak. The frontier between Ladakh and Tibet was settled at 'the Lhari stream at Demchok'.

4. *Treaty between Tibet and Ladakh, 1842* (*Translation*)

As on this auspicious day, the 2nd of Assuj, Sambhat 1899 [16th or 17th September A.D. 1842], we the officers of the Lhasa Government Kalon of Sokan and Bakshi Shajpuh, Commander of the Forces, and two officers on behalf of the most resplendent Sri Khalsaji Sahib, the asylum of the world, King Sher Singhji, and Sri Maharaj Sahib Raja-i Rajagan Raja Sahib Bahadur Raja Gulab Singhji, i.e., the Mukhtar-ud-Daula Diwan Hari Chand and the asylum of vizirs, Vizir Ratnun, in a meeting called together for the promotion of peace and unity, and by professions and vows of friendship, unity and sincerity of heart and by taking oaths like those of Kunjak Sahib, have arranged and agreed that relations of peace, friendship and unity between Sri Khalsaji and Sri Maharaj Sahib Bahadur Raja Gulab Singhji and the Emperor of China and the Lama Guru of Lhasa will henceforward remain firmly established forever ; and we declare in the presence of the Kunjak Sahib that on no account whatsoever will there be any deviation, difference or departure [from this agreement].

We shall neither at present nor in future have anything to do or interfere at all with the boundaries of Ladakh and its surroundings as fixed from ancient times and will allow the annual export of wool, shawls and tea by way of Ladakh according to old established custom.

Should any of the opponents of Sri Khalasji and Sri Raja Sahib Bahadur at any time enter our territories, we shall not pay any heed to his words or allow him to remain in our country.

We shall offer no hindrance to traders of Ladakh who visit our territories. We shall not, even to the extent of a hair's breadth, act in contravention of the terms that we have agreed to above regarding firm friendship, unity and fixed boundaries of Ladakh and the keeping open of the route for wool, shawls and tea. We call Kunjak Sahib, Kairi, Lassi, Zhoh Mahan, and Khushal Chand witnesses to this treaty.

The agreement has been quoted in Aitchison's *Treaties*, Vol. XIV, p.15. The Tibetan signatories had been taken prisoner and it is not clear that any reference was made to Lhasa before the conclusion of the agreement. Not only the Dogra Raja of Jammoo, who had annexed Ladkh, but also his nominal overlord the Sikh ruler are cited as parties to the treaty. In fact, since the death of Ranjit Singh in 1839, the Maharaja of Jammoo had been virtually independent and proof of his position was seen in his refusal to support the Sikhs in their war with the British. Similarly, on the other side, the Chinese Emperor is cited as a party as well as the Dalai Lama.

Neither Sikhs nor Chinese took any part in the campaign in Ladakh and Tibet.

5. *Treaty betweeen Tibet and Nepal, 1856* (*Translation*)

Treaty of Peace, consisting of ten Articles, between the States of Gurkha and Tibet (Bhote), settled and concluded by us, the Chief Sardars, Bharadars, and Lamas of both Governments, whose signatures and seals are attached below. May God bear witness to it. We further agree that both States pay respect as always before to the Emperor of China and that the two States are to treat each other like brothers, for so long as their actions correspond with the spirit of this Treaty. May God not allow that State to prosper which may make war upon the other, unless the other's acts are contrary to this Treaty, in which case the State that declares war upon the other shall be exempt from all blame.

1. The Tibetan Government agrees to pay the sum of ten thousand Rupees annually in cash to the Gurkha Government.

2. The states of Gurkha and of Tibet have both respected the Emperor of China up to the present time. The country of Tibet is merely the shrine or place of worship of the Lama, for which reason the Gurkha Government will in future give all the assistance that may be in its power to the Government of Tibet, if the troops of any other 'Raja' invade that country.

3. The Government of Tibet agrees to discontinue the collection of all duties that have hitherto been levied upon subjects of the Gurkha State, merchants and others trading with its country.

4. The Government of Tibet agrees to give up to the Gurkha Government all the Sikh prisoners now in captivity within its territories, and all the Gurkha Sipahis, and officers, and women who were captured in the war, also all the guns that were taken ; and the Gurkha Government agrees to give up to the Government of Tibet all the Sipahis, also the ryots of Kerong, Kuti, Junga, Tagla Khar and Chewur Gumba, and all the arms and Yaks [chowrie cows] belonging to that country now in its possession, and on the final completion of this Treaty it will restore Tagla Khar, Chewur Gumba, Kerong, Junga, Kuti and Dhakling and will withdraw all the troops that may be on this side of the Bhairab Langar range.

5. A Bharadar on the part of the Gurkha Government (not merely a Naikia) will for the future reside at Lhasa.

6. The Gurkha Government, with the free consent of the Government of Tibet, will establish a trading factory at Lhasa, for the sale of all kinds of merchandise, from jewellery etc. etc. to articles of clothing and of food.

7. The Gurkha Bharadar residing at Lhasa will not interfere in the disputes of the subjects, merchants, traders, etc. etc. of the Government of Tibet, neither will the Tibetan Government interfere in any disputes between subjects of the Gurkha Government, Kashmiris of Nepal etc. etc., who may be residing within the jurisdiction of Lhasa, but whenever quarrels may occur between Gurkha and Tibetan subjects, the authorities of the two States will sit together and jointly adjudicate them ; and all Amdani [fines etc.] will, if paid by subjects of Tibet, be taken by that Government, and if paid by Gurkha subjects, Kashmiris of Nepal etc., will be appropriated by the Gurkha Government.

8. Should any Gurkha subject commit a murder within the jurisdiction of that Government and take refuge in Tibet, he shall be surrendered by that country, and if any Tibetan subject who may have

committed a murder there take refuge in the Gurkha country, he shall in like manner be given up to the Government of Tibet.

9. If the property of any Gurkha subjects and merchants be plundered by any subject of the Tibetan Government, the party who has stolen it shall be compelled by the Tibetan Government to restore it ; should he not be able to do so at once, he shall be obliged by the Tibetan Bharadar to make some arrangement, and will be allowed a reasonable time to make it good. In like manner, if the property of any Tibetan subjects or merchants be plundered by any subject of the Gurkha Government, the party who has stolen it shall be compelled by the Gurkha authorities to restore it ; should be not be able to do so at once, he shall be obliged by the Gurkha Government to make some arrangement and will be allowed a reasonable time to make it good.

10. All subjects to Tibet who may have joined the Gurkha cause during the war, and all subjects of the Gurkha Government who may have taken part with the Tibetan Government, shall, after the completion of this Treaty be respected both in person and property, and shall not be injured by either Government.

Dated Sambhat 1912 Chaitra Badi 3rd (2nd day) Sombar ; corresponding with 24th March 1856.

The treaty, translated from the Nepalese text, has been given in Aitchison's *Treaties*, Vol. XIV, pp. 49-50.

6. *The Convention of Chefoo (between the British Government and the Government of China), 1876*

Extract :

Her Majesty's Government having it in contemplation to send a mission of exploration next year, by way of Peking, through Kansuh and Kokonor, or by way of Szechuen to Thibet, and thence to India, the Tsungli Yamen, having due regard to the circumstances, will, when the time arrives, issue the necessary passports, and will address letters to the High Provincial Authorities and the Residents in Thibet. If the Mission should not be sent by these routes but should be proceeding across the Indian frontier to Thibet, the Tsungli Yamen, on receipt of a communication to that effect from the British Minister, will write to the Chinese Resident in Thibet, and the Resident, with due regard to the circumstances, will send officers to take care of the Mission, and passports for the Mission will be issued by the Tsungli Yamen, that its passage be not obstructed.

The above is only a separate article. The main body of the Convention did not concern Tibet at all.

7. *Convention Relating to Burma and Tibet, July 24th 1886* (*between the British Government and the Government of China*)

Extract :

Inasmuch as inquiry into the circumstances, by the Chinese Government, has shown the existence of many obstacles to the Mission to Thibet provided for in the separate article of the Chefoo Agreement, England consents to countermand the Mission forthwith. With regard to the desire of the British Government to consider arrangements for frontier trade between India and Thibet, it will be the duty of the Chinese Government, after careful inquiry into the circumstances, to adopt measures to exhort and encourage the people with a view to the promotion and development of trade. Should it be practicable, the Chinese Government shall then proceed carefully to consider trade regulations ; but if insuperable obstacles should be found to exist, the British Government will not press the matter unduly.

The rest of the Convention was concerned with the recognition of British supremacy in Burma and the clause given above about Tibet seems to be in the nature of a concession to achieve the principal object of the Convention.

8. *Convention of March 17th 1890 between Great Britain and China Relating to Sikkim and Tibet* (*Ratifications Exchanged in London, August 27th, 1890*)

[English Text]

WHEREAS Her Majesty the Queen of the United Kingdom of Great Britain and Ireland, Empress of India, and His Majesty the Emperor of China, are sincerely desirous to maintain and perpetuate the relations of friendship and good understanding which now exist between their respective Empires ; and whereas recent occurrences have tended towards a disturbance of the said relations, and it is desirable to clearly define and permanently settle certain matters connected with the boundary between Sikkim and Tibet, Her Britannic Majesty and His Majesty the Emperor of China have resolved to conclude a Convention on this subject, and have, for this purpose, named Plenipotentiaries, that is to say :

Her Majesty the Queen of Great Britain and Ireland, his Excellency the Most Honourable Henry Charles Keith Petty Fitzmaurice, G.M.S.I.,

G.C.M.G., G.M.I.E., Marquess of Lansdowne, Viceroy and Governor-General of India ;

And His Majesty the Emperor of China, his Excellency Sheng Tai, Imperial Associate Resident in Tibet, Military Deputy Lieutenant-Governor;

Who, having met and communicated to each other their full powers, and finding these to be in proper form, have agreed upon the following Convention in eight Articles :—

I. The boundary of Sikkim and Tibet shall be the crest of the mountain-range separating the waters flowing into the Sikkim Teesta and its affluents from the waters flowing into the Tibetan Mochu and northwards into other rivers of Tibet. The line commences at Mount Gipmochi on the Bhutan frontier, and follows the above-mentioned water-parting to the point where it meets Nipal territory.

II. It is admitted that the British Government, whose Protectorate over the Sikkim State is hereby recognized, has direct and exclusive control over the internal administration and foreign relations of that State, and except through and with the permission of the British Government neither the Ruler of the State nor any of its officers shall have official relations of any kind, formal or informal, with any other country.

III. The Government of Great Britain and Ireland and the Government of China engage reciprocally to respect the boundary as defined in Article I, and to prevent acts of aggression from their respective sides of the frontier.

IV. The question of providing increased facilities for trade across the Sikkim—Tibet frontier will hereafter be discussed with a view to a mutually satisfactory arrangement by the High Contracting Powers.

V. The question of pasturage on the Sikkim side of the frontier is reserved for further examination and future adjustment.

VI. The High Contracting Powers reserve for discussion and arrangement the method in which official communications between the British authorities in India and the authorities in Tibet shall be conducted.

VII. Two joint Commissioners shall, within six months from the ratification of this Convention, be appointed, one by the British Government in India, the other by the Chinese Resident in Tibet. The said Commissioners shall meet and discuss the questions which, by the last three preceding Articles, have been reserved.

VIII. The present Convention shall be ratified, and the ratifications shall be exchanged in London as soon as possible after the date of the signature thereof.

In witness whereof the respective negotiators have signed the same, and affixed thereunto the seals of their arms.

Done in quadruplicate at Calcutta, this 17th day of March, in the year of our Lord 1890, corresponding with the Chinese date, the 27th day of the second moon of the 16th year of Kuang Hsü.

LANDSDOWNE.
Signature of the Chinese Plenipotentiary

The above Convention was signed at Calcutta. Not a single Tibetan representative was present or took part in the negotiations.

9. *Regulations Regarding Trade, Communication, and Pasturage, to be Appended to the Convention between Great Britain and China of March 17, 1890, Relative to Sikkim and Tibet. Signed at Darjeeling, December 5, 1893*

1. A TRADE mart shall be established at Yatung on the Tibetan side of the frontier, and shall be open to all British subjects for purposes to trade from the 1st day of May, 1894. The Government of India shall be free to send officers to reside at Yatung to watch the conditions of British trade at that mart.

2. British subjects trading at Yatung shall be at liberty to travel freely to and fro between the frontier and Yatung, to reside at Yatung, and to rent houses and godowns for their own accommodation, and the coverage of their goods. The Chinese Government undertake that suitable building for the above purposes shall be provided for British subjects, and also that a special and fitting residence shall be provided for the officer or officers appointed by the Government of India under Regulation 1 to reside at Yatung. British subjects shall be at liberty to sell their goods to whomsoever they please, to purchase native commodities in kind or in money, to hire transport of any kind, and in general to conduct their business transactions in conformity with local usage, and without any vexatious restrictions. Such British subjects shall receive efficient protection for their persons and property. At Lang-jo and Ta-chun, between the frontier and Yatung, where rest-houses have been built by the Tibetan authorities, British subjects can break their journey in consideration of a daily rent.

3. Import and export trade in the following articles :—arms, ammunition, military stores, salt, liquors, and intoxicating or narcotic drugs, may, at the option of either Government, be entirely prohibited, or

permitted only on such conditions as either Government, on their own side, may think fit to impose.

4. Goods, other than goods of the descriptions enumerated in Regulation 3, entering Tibet from British India, across the Sikkim-Tibet frontier, or *vice versa*, whatever their origin, shall be exempt from duty for a period of five years, commencing from the date of the opening of Yatung to trade ; but after the expiration of this term, if found desirable, a tariff may be mutually agreed upon and enforced. Indian tea may be imported into Tibet at a rate of duty not exceeding that at which Chinese tea is imported into England, but trade in Indian tea shall not be engaged in during the five years for which other commodities are exempt.

5. All goods on arrival at Yatung, whether from British India or from Tibet, must be reported at the Custom Station there for examination, and the report must give full particulars of the description, quantity, and value of the goods.

6. In the event of trade disputes arising between British and Chinese or Tibetan subjects in Tibet, they shall be inquired into and settled in personal conference by the Political Officer for Sikkim and the Chinese Frontier Officer. The object of personal conference being to ascertain facts and do justice, where there is a divergence of views, the law of the country to which the defendant belongs shall guide.

7. Despatches from the Government of India to the Chinese Imperial Resident in Tibet shall be handed over by the Political Officer for Sikkim to the Chinese Frontier Officer, who will forward them by special courier.

Despatches from the Chinese Imperial Resident in Tibet to the Government of India will be handed over by the Chinese Frontier Officer to the Political Officer for Sikkim, who will forward them as quickly as possible.

8. Despatches between the Chinese and Indian officials must be treated with due respect, and couriers will be assisted in passing to and fro by the officers of each Government.

9. After the expiration of one year from the date of the opening of Yatung, such Tibetans as continue to graze their cattle in Sikkim will be subject to such Regulations as the British Government may from time to time enact for the general conduct of grazing in Sikkim. Due notice will be given of such Regulations.

General Articles

1. In the event of disagreement between the Political Officer for Sikkim and the Chinese Frontier Officer, each official shall report the

matter to his immediate superior, who in turn, if a settlement is not arrived at between them, shall refer such matter to their respective Governments for disposal.

2. After the lapse of five years from the date on which these Regulations shall come into force, and on six months' notice given by either party, these Regulations shall be subject to revision by Commissioners appointed on both sides for this purpose, who shall be empowered to decide on and adopt such amendments and extensions as experience shall prove to be desirable.

3. It having been stipulated that Joint Commissioners should be appointed by the British and Chinese Governments under Article VII of the Sikkim—Tibet Convention to meet and discuss, with a view to the final settlement of the questions reserved under Articles IV, V, and VI of the said Convention ; and the Commissioners thus appointed having met and discussed the questions referred to, namely, trade, communication, and pasturage, have been further appointed to sign the Agreement in nine Regulations and three General Articles now arrived at, and to declare that the said nine Regulations and the three General Articles form part of the Convention itself.

In witness whereof the respective Commissioners have hereto subscribed their names.

Done in quadruplicate at Darjeeling, this 5th day of December, in the year 1893, corresponding with the Chinese date, the 28th day of the 10th moon of the 19th year of Kuang Hsu.

A.W. PAUL, British Commissioner.
Ho CHANG-JUNG,
JAMES H. HART, Chinese commissioners.

One of the Tibetan Ministers was present at the negotiations in Darjeeling but he took no active part and did not sign the Regulations as well.

10. *Convention between Great Britain and Tibet. Signed at Lhasa, September 7th 1904*

WHEREAS doubts and difficulties have arisen as to the meaning and validity of the Anglo-Chinese Convention of 1890, and the Trade Regulations of 1893, and as to the liabilities of the Thibetan Government under these Agreements ; and whereas recent occurrences have tended towards a disturbance of the relations of friendship and good understanding which have existed between the British Government and the Government of Thibet ; and whereas it is desirable to restore peace and amicable relations, and to resolve and determine the doubts and difficulties as aforesaid, the said Governments have resolved to conclude a Convention with these objects, and the following Articles have been agreed upon by Colonel F.E. Younghusband, C.I.E., in virtue of full powers vested in him by His Britannic Majesty's Government, and on behalf of that said Government, and Lo-Sang Gyal-Tsen, the Ga-den Ti-Rimpoche, and the representatives of the Council, of the three monasteries Se-ra, Drepung, and Ga-den, and of the ecclesiastical and lay officials of the National Assembly on behalf of the Government of Thibet :—

(I) The Government of Thibet engages to respect the Anglo-Chinese Convention of 1890, and to recognize the frontier between Sikkim and Thibet, as defined in Article I of the said Convention, and to erect boundary pillars accordingly.

(II) The Thibetan Government undertakes to open forthwith trade marts to which all British and Thibetan subjects shall have free right of access at Gyangtse and Gartok, as well as at Yatung.

The Regulations applicable to the trade mart at Yatung, under the Anglo-Chinese Agreement of 1883, shall, subject to such amendments as may hereafter be agreed upon by common consent between the British and Thibetan Governments, apply to the marts above mentioned.

In addition to establishing trade marts at the places mentioned, the Thibetan Government undertakes to place no restrictions on the trade by existing routes, and to consider the question of establishing fresh trade marts under similar conditions if development of trade requires it.

(III) The question of the amendment of the Regulations of 1893 is reserved for separate consideration, and the Thibetan Government undertakes to appoint fully authorized delegates to negotiate with representatives of the British Government as to the details of the amendments required.

(IV) The Thibetan Government undertakes to levy no dues of any kind other than those provided for in the tariff to be mutually agreed upon.

(V) The Thibetan Government undertakes to keep the roads to Gyangtse and Gartok from the frontier clear of all obstruction and in a state of repair suited to the needs of the trade, and to establish at Yatung, Gyangtse, and Gartok, and at each of the other trade marts that may hereafter be established, a Thibetan Agent who shall receive from the British Agent appointed to watch over British trade at the marts in question any letter which the latter may desire to send to the Thibetan or to the Chinese authorities. The Thibetan Agent shall also be responsible for the due delivery of such communications and for the transmission of replies.

(VI) As an indemnity to the British Government for the expense incurred in the dispatch of armed troops to Lhasa, to exact reparation for breaches of Treaty obligations, and for the insults offered to and attacks upon the British Commissioner and his following and escort, the Thibetan Government engages to pay a sum of 500,000 l.—equivalent to 75 lakhs of rupees—to the British Government.

The indemnity shall be payable at such place as the British Government may from time to time, after due notice, indicate, whether in Thibet or in the British districts of Darjeeling or Jalpaiguri, in seventy-five annual instalments of one lakh of rupees each on the 1st January in each year, beginning from the 1st January, 1906.

(VII) As security for the payment of the above-mentioned indemnity and for the fulfilment of the provisions relative to trade marts specified in Articles II, III, IV, and V, the British Government shall continue to occupy the Chumbi Valley until the indemnity has been paid, and until the trade marts have been effectively opened for three years, whichever date may be the later.

(VIII) The Thibetan Government agrees to raze all forts and fortifications and remove all armaments which might impede the course of free communication between the British frontier and the towns of Gyangtse and Lhasa.

(IX) The Government of Thibet engages that, without the previous consent of the British Government—

(a) No portion of Thibetan territory shall be ceded, sold, leased, managed or otherwise given for occupation, to any Foreign Power ;

(b) No such Power shall be permitted to intervene in Thibetan affairs ;

(c) No Representatives or Agents of any Foreign Power shall be admitted to Thibet ;

(d) No concessions for railways, roads, telegraphs, mining or other rights, shall be granted to any Foreign Power, or the subject of any Foreign Power. In the event of consent to such Concessions being granted, similar or equivalent Concessions shall be granted to the British Government ;

(e) No Thibetan revenues, whether in kind or in cash, shall be pledged or assigned to any Foreign Power, or to the subject of any Foreign Power.

(X) In witness whereof the negotiators have signed the same, and affixed thereunto the seals of their arms.

Done in quintuplicate at Lhasa, this 7th day of September, in the year of our Lord, 1904, corresponding with the Thibetan date, the 27th of the seventh month of the Wood Dragon year.

(Thibet Frontier Commission.) (Seal of British Commissioner.)	F. E. YOUNGHUSBAND Colonel, British Commissioner.	(Seal of the Dalai Lama affixed by the Ga-den Ti-Rimpoche.)

(Seal of Council.)	(Seal of Dre-pung Monastery.)	(Seal of Sera Monastery.)	(Seal of Ga-den Monastery.)	(Seal of National Assembly.)

In proceeding to the signature of the Convention, dated this day, the representatives of Great Britain and Thibet declare that the English text shall be binding.

(Thibet Frontier Commission.)	F. E. YOUNGHUSBAND Colonel, British Commissioner.	(Seal of the Dalai Lama affixed by the Ga-den Ti-Rimpoche.)

(Seal of Council.)	(Seal of Dre-pung Monastery.)	(Seal of Sera Monastery.)	(Seal of Ga-den Monastery.)	(Seal of National Assembly.)

AMPTHILL,
Viceroy and Governor-General of India.

The Convention was ratified by the Viceroy and Governor-General of India in Council at Simla on the 11th day of November, 1904, subject to reduction of the indemnity to Rs. 25,00,000 and a declaration that British occupation of the Chumbi valley would cease after payment of three annual instalments of the indemnity, provided that the Tibetans had complied with the terms of the Convention in all other respects.

This was the first direct treaty between Great Britain and Tibet. The Chinese Amban at Lhasa was present at the negotiations and signing, but he did not sign.

11. *Convention between Great Britain and China respecting Tibet. Signed at Peking, April 27, 1906 (Ratifications exchanged at London July 23, 1906)*

[*Signed also in Chinese*]

WHEREAS His Majesty the king of Great Britain and Ireland and of the British Dominions beyond the Seas, Emperor of India, and His Majesty the Emperor of China are sincerely desirous to maintain and perpetuate the relations of friendship and good understanding which now exist between their respective Empires ;

And whereas the refusal of Tibet to recognise the validity of or to carry into full effect the provisions of the Anglo-Chinese Convention of March 17, 1890, and Regulations of December 5, 1893, placed the British Government under the necessity of taking steps to secure their rights and interests under the said Convention and Regulations ;

And whereas a Convention of ten articles was signed at Lhasa on September 7, 1904, on behalf of Great Britain and Tibet, and was ratified by the Viceroy and Governor-General of India on behalf of Great Britain on November 11, 1904, a declaration on behalf of Great Britain modifying its terms under certain conditions being appended thereto ;

His Britannic Majesty and His Majesty the Emperor of China have resolved to conclude a Convention on this subject and have for this purpose named Plenipotentiaries, that is to say :—

His Majesty the King of Great Britain and Ireland :

Sir Ernest Mason Satow, Knight Grand Cross of the Most Distinguished Order of Saint Michael and Saint George, His said Majesty's Envoy Extraordinary and Minister Plenipotentiary to His Majesty the Emperor of China ;

And His Majesty the Emperor of China :

His Excellency Tong Shoa-yi, His said Majesty's High Commissioner Plenipotentiary and a Vice-President of the Board of Foreign Affairs ; who having communicated to each other their respective full powers and finding them to be in good and true form have agreed upon and concluded the following Convention in Six articles :—

(I) The Convention concluded on September 7, 1904, by Great Britain and Tibet, the texts of which in English and Chinese are attached to the present Convention as an annexe, is hereby confirmed, subject to the modification stated in the declaration appended thereto, and both of the High Contracting Parties engage to take at all times such steps as may be necessary to secure the due fulfilment of the terms specified therein.

(II) The Government of Great Britain engages not to annex Tibetan territory or to interfere in the administration of Tibet. The Government of China also undertakes not to permit any other foreign state to interfere with the territory or internal administration of Tibet.

(III) The Concessions which are mentioned in Article IX (*d)* of the Convention concluded on September 7th, 1904 by Great Britain and Tibet are denied to any state or to the subject of any state other than China, but it has been arranged with China that at the trade marts specified in Article II of the aforesaid Convention Great Britain shall be entitled to lay down telegraph lines connecting with India.

(IV) The provisions of the Anglo-Chinese Convention of 1890 and Regulations of 1893 shall, subject to the terms of this present Convention and annexe thereto, remain in full force.

(V) The English and Chinese texts of the present Convention have been carefully compared and found to correspond, but in the event of there being any difference of meaning between them the English text shall be authoritative.

(VI) This Convention shall be ratified by the Sovereigns of both countries and ratifications shall be exchanged at London within three months after the date of signature by the Plenipotentiaries of both Powers.

In token whereof the respective Plenipotentiaries have signed and scaled this Convention, four copies in English and four in Chinese.

Done at Peking this twenty-seventh day of April, one thousand nine hundred and six, being the fourth day of the fourth month of the thirty second year of the reign of Kuang-hsu.

ERNEST SHOW.

(Signature and seal of the Chinese Plenipotentiary.)

Also exchanged were the notes by which the Chinese undertook not to employ any foreigners in Tibet.

The Tibetans took no part in this Convention and its terms were never communicated to them formally.

12. *Convention between Great Britain and Russia relating to Persia, Afghanistan and Tibet. Signed at St. Petersburg, August 31st 1907*

His Majesty the king of the United Kingdom of Great Britain and Ireland and of the British Dominions beyond the Seas, Emperor of India, and His Majesty the Emperor of All the Russias, animated by the sincere desire to settle by mutual agreement different questions concerning the interests of their States on the Continent of Asia, have determined to conclude Agreements destined to prevent all cause of misunderstanding between Great Britain and Russia in regard to the questions referred to, and have nominated for this purpose their respective Plenipotentiaries, to wit :

His Majesty the King of the United Kingdom of Great Britain and Ireland and of the British Dominions beyond the Seas, Emperor of India, the Right Honourable Sir Arthur Nicolson, his Majesty's Ambassador Extraordinary and Plenipotentiary to His Majesty the Emperor of All the Russias ;

His Majesty the Emperor of All the Russias, the Master of his Court Alexander Iswolsky, Minister for Foreign Affairs ;

Who, having communicated to each other their full powers, found in good and due form, have agreed on the following :—

Arrangement concerning Thibet

The Governments of Great Britain and Russia recognising the suzerain rights of China in Thibet, and considering the fact that Great Britain, by reason of her geographical position, has a special interest in the maintenance of the *status quo* in the external relations of Thibet, have made the following arrangement :—

ARTICLE I

The two High Contracting Parties engage to respect the territorial integrity of Thibet and to abstain from all interference in the internal administration.

ARTICLE II

In conformity with the admitted principle of the suzerainty of China over Thibet, Great Britain and Russia engage not to enter into negotiations with Thibet except through the intermediary of the Chinese Government. This engagement does not exclude the direct relations between British Commercial Agents and the Thibetan authorities provided for in Article V of the Convention between Great Britain and Thibet of the 7th September 1904, and confirmed by the Convention between Great Britain and China of the 27th April 1906 ; nor does it modify the engagements entered into by Great Britain and China in Article I of the said Convention of 1906.

It is clearly understood that Buddhists, subjects of Great Britain or the Russia, may enter into direct relations on strictly religious matters with the Dalai Lama and the other representatives of Buddhism in Thibet ; the Governments of Great Britain and Russia engage, as far as they are concerned, not to allow those relations to infringe the stipulations of the present arrangement.

ARTICLE III

The British and Russian Governments respectively engage not to send Representatives to Lhasa.

ARTICLE IV

The two High Contracting Parties engage neither to seek nor to obtain, whether for themselves or their subjects, any Concessions for railways, roads, telegraphs, and mines, or other rights in Thibet.

ARTICLE V

The two Governments agree that no part of the revenues of Thibet, whether in kind or in cash, shall be pledged or assigned to Great Britain or Russia or to any of their subjects.

Annexe to the arrangement between Great Britain and Russia concerning Thibet.

Great Britain reaffirms the declaration, signed by His Excellency the Viceroy and Governor-General of India and appended to the ratification of the Convention of the 7th September 1904, to the effect that the occupation of the Chumbi Valley by British forces shall cease after the payment of three annual instalments of the indemnity of 25,00,000 rupees, provided that the trade marts mentioned in Article II of that Convention have been effectively opened for three years, and that in the meantime the Thibetan authorities have faithfully complied in all respects with the terms of the said Convention of 1904. It is clearly understood that if the occupation of the Chumbi Valley by the British forces has, for any reason, not been terminated at the time anticipated in the above Declaration, the British and Russian Governments will enter upon a friendly exchange of views on this subject.

The present Convention shall be ratified, and the ratification exchanged at St. Petersburgh as soon as possible.

In witness whereof the respective Plenipotentiaries have signed the present Convention and affixed thereto their seals.

Done in duplicate at St. Petersburgh, the 18th (31st) August 1907.

The Tibetans were never informed about the provisions of this treaty.

13. *Agreement between Great Britain, China and Tibet amending Trade Regulations in Tibet, of December 5, 1893. Signed at Calcutta, April 20, 1908 (Ratifications exchanged in Peking, October 14, 1908)*

TIBET TRADE REGULATIONS
Preamble

Whereas by Article I of the Convention between Great Britain and China on the 27th April, 1906, that is the 4th day of the 4th moon of the 32nd year of Kwang Hsu, it was provided that both the High Contracting Parties should engage to take at all times such steps as might be necessary to secure the due fulfilment of the terms specified in the Lhasa Convention of the 7th September, 1904, between Great Britain and Tibet, the text of which in English and Chinese was attached as an Annexe to the above-named Convention ;

And whereas it was stipulated in Article III of the said Lhasa Convention that the question of the amendment of the Tibet Trade Regulations which were signed by the British and Chinese Commissioners on the 5th day of December, 1893 should be reserved for separate consideration, and whereas the amendment of these Regulations is now necessary ;

His Majesty the King of the United Kingdom of Great Britain and Ireland and of the British Dominions beyond the Seas, Emperor of India, and His Majesty the Emperor of the Chinese Empire have for this purpose named as their Plenipotentiaries, that is to say :

His Majesty the King of Great Britain and Ireland and of the British Dominions beyond the Seas, Emperor of India : Mr. E.C. Wilton, C.M.G.;

His Majesty the Emperor of the Chinese Empire : His Majesty's Special Commissioner Chang Yin Tang ;

And the High Authorities of Tibet have named as their fully authorized representative to act under the directions of Chang Tachen and take part in the negotiations, the Tsarong Shape, Wang Chuk Gyalpo.

And whereas Mr. E.C. Wilton and Chang Tachen have communicated to each other since their respective full powers and have found them to be in good and true form and have found the authorization of the Tibetan Delegate to be also in good and true form, the following amended Regulations have been agreed upon :—

1. The Trade Regulations of 1893 shall remain in force in so far as they are not inconsistent with these Regulations.

2. The following places shall form, and be included within, the boundaries of the Gyantse mart :—

(a) The line begins at the Chumig Dangsang (Chhu-Mig-Dangs-Sangs) north-east of the Gyantse Fort, and thence it runs in a curved line, passing behind the Pekor Chode (Dpal-Hkhor-Choos-Sde), down to Chag-

Pong Gang (Phyag-Gdong-Sgang) ; thence passing straight over the Nyan Chu, it reaches the Zamsa (Zam-Srag).

(b) From the Zamsa the line continues to run, in a south-eastern direction, round to Lachi-To (Gla-Dkyuii-Stod), embracing all the farms on its way, viz., the Lahong, the Hogtso (Hog-Mtsho), the Tong-Chung-Shi (Grong-Chhung-Gshis), and the Rabgang (Rab-Sgang), &c.

(c) From Lachi-To the line runs to the Yutog (Gyu-Thog), and thence runs straight, passing through the whole area of Gamkar-Shi (Ragal-Mkha-Gshis), to Chumig Dangsang.

As difficulty is experienced in obtaining suitable houses and godowns at some of the marts, it is agreed that British subjects may also lease lands for the building of house and godowns at the marts, the locality for such building sites to be marked out specially at each mart by the Chinese and Tibetan authorities in consultation with the British Trade Agent. The British Trade Agents and British subjects shall not build houses and godowns except in such localities, and this arrangement shall not be held to prejudice in any way the administration of the Chinese and Tibetan local authorities over such localities, or the right of British subjects to rent houses and godowns outside such localities for their own accommodation and the storage of their goods.

British subjects desiring to lease building sites shall apply through the British Trade Agent to the Municipal Office at the mart for a permit to lease. The amount of rent, or the period or conditions of the lease, shall then be settled in a friendly way by the lessee and the owner themselves. In the event of a disagreement between the owner and lessee as to the amount of rent or the period or condition of the lease, the case will be settled by the Chinese and Tibetan Authorities, in consultation with the British Trade Agent. After the lease is settled, the sites shall be verified by the Chinese and Tibetan Officers of the Municipal Office conjointly with the British Trade Agent. No building is to be commenced by the lessee on a site before the municipal office has issued him a permit to build, but it is agreed that there shall be no vexatious delays in the issue of such permit.

3. The administration of the trade marts shall remain with the Tibetan Officers, under the Chinese Officers' supervision and directions.

The Trade Agents at the marts and Frontier Officers shall be of suitable rank, and shall hold personal intercourse and correspondence one with another on terms of mutual respect and friendly treatment.

Questions which cannot be decided by agreement between the Trade

Agents and the Local Authorities shall be referred for settlement to the Government of India and the Tibetan High Authorities at Lhasa. The purport of a reference by the Government of India will be communicated to the Chinese Imperial Resident at Lhasa. Questions which cannot be decided by agreement between the Government of India and the Tibetan High Authorities at Lhasa shall, in accordance with the terms of Article I of the Peking Convention of 1906, be referred for settlement to the Governments of Great Britain and China.

4. In the event of disputes arising at the marts between British subjects and persons of Chinese and Tibetan nationalities, they shall be inquired into and settled in personal conferences between the British Trade Agent at the nearest mart and the Chinese and Tibetan Authorities of the Judicial Court at the mart, the object of personal conference being to ascertain facts and to do justice. Where there is a divergence of view the law of the country to which the defendant belongs shall guide. In any of such mixed cases, the Officer or Officers of the defendant's nationality shall preside at the trial, the Officer or Officers of the plaintiff's country merely attending to watch the course of the trial.

All questions in regard to rights, whether of property or person, arising between British subjects, shall be subject to the jurisdiction of the British Authorities.

British subjects who may commit any crime at the marts or on the routes to the marts shall be handed over by the local authorities to the British Trade Agent at the mart nearest to the scene of offence, to be tried and punished according to the laws of India, but such British subjects shall not be subjected by the local authorities to any ill-usage in excess of necessary restraint.

Chinese and Tibetan subjects, who may be guilty of any criminal act towards British subjects at the marts or on the routes thereto, shall be arrested and punished by the Chinese and Tibetan Authorities according to law.

Justice shall be equitably and impartially administered on both sides.

Should it happen that Chinese or Tibetan subjects bring a criminal complaint against a British subject before the British Trade Agent, the Chinese or Tibetan Authorities shall have the right to send a representative, or representatives, to watch the course of trial in the British Trade Agent's Court. Similarly, in cases in which a British subject has reason to complain of a Chinese or Tibetan subject in the

Judicial Court at the mart, the British Trade Agent shall have the right to send a representative to the Judicial Court to watch the course of trial.

5. The Tibetan Authorities, in obedience to the instructions of the Peking Government, having a strong desire to reform the judicial system of Tibet, and to bring it into accord with that of Western nations, Great Britain agrees to relinquish her rights of extra-territoriality in Tibet, whenever such rights are relinquished in China, and when she is satisfied that the state of the Tibetan laws and the arrangements for their administration and other considerations warrant her in so doing.

6. After the withdrawal of the British troops, all the rest-houses, eleven in number, built by Great Britain upon the routes leading from the Indian frontier to Gyantse, shall be taken over at original cost by China and rented to the Government of India at a fair rate. One-half of each rest-house will be reserved for the use of the British officials employed on the inspection and maintenance of the telegraph lines from the marts to the Indian frontier and for the storage of their materials, but the rest-houses shall otherwise be available for occupation by British, Chinese, and Tibetan officers of respectability who may proceed to and from the marts.

Great Britain is prepared to consider the transfer to China of the telegraph lines from the Indian frontier to Gyantse when the telegraph lines from China reach that mart, and in the meantime Chinese and Tibetan messages will be duly received and transmitted by the line constructed by the Government of India.

In the meantime China shall be responsible for the due protection of the telegraph lines from the marts to the Indian frontier, and it is agreed that all persons damaging the lines or interfering in any way with them or with the officials engaged in the inspection or maintenance thereof shall at once be severely punished by the local authorities.

7. In law suits involving cases of debt on account of loans, commercial failure, and bankruptcy, the authorities concerned shall grant a hearing and take steps necessary to enforce payment ; but, if the debtor plead poverty and be without means, the authorities concerned shall not be held responsible for the said debts, nor shall any public or official property be distrained upon in order to satisfy these debts.

8. The British Trade Agents at the various trade marts now or hereafter to be established in Tibet may make arrangements for the carriage and transmission of their posts to and from the frontier of

India. The couriers employed in conveying these posts shall receive all possible assistance from the local authorities whose districts they traverse and shall be accorded the same protection as the persons employed in carrying the despatches of the Tibetan Authorities. When efficient arrangements have been made by China in Tibet for a postal service, the question of the abolition of the Trade Agents' couriers will be taken into consideration by Great Britain and China. No restrictions whatever shall be placed on the employment by British officers and traders of Chinese and Tibetan subjects in any lawful capacity. The persons so employed shall not be exposed to any kind of molestation or suffer any loss of civil rights to which they may be entitled as Tibetan subjects, but they shall not be exempted from all lawful taxation. If they be guilty of any criminal act, they shall be dealt with by the local authorities according to law without any attempt on the part of their employer to screen or conceal them.

9. British officers and subjects, as well as goods, proceeding to the trade marts, must adhere to the trade routes from the frontier of India. They shall not, without permission, proceed beyond the mart, or to Gartok from Yatung and Gyantse, or from Gartok to Yatung and Gyantse, by any route through the interior of Tibet, but natives of the Indian frontier, who have already by usage traded and resided in Tibet, elsewhere than at the marts shall be at liberty to continue their trade, in accordance with the existing practice, but when so trading or residing they shall remain, as heretofore, amenable to the local jurisdiction.

10. In cases where officials or traders, *en route* to and from India or Tibet, are robbed of treasure or merchandise, public or private, they shall forthwith report to the Police officers, who shall take immediate measures to arrest the robbers and hand them to the Local Authorities. The Local Authorities shall bring them to instant trial, and shall also recover and restore the stolen property. But if the robbers flee to places out of the jurisdiction and influence of Tibet, and cannot be arrested, the Police and the Local Authorities shall not he held responsible for such losses.

11. For public safety, tanks or stores of kerosene oil or any other combustible or dangerous articles in bulk must be placed for away from inhabited places at the marts.

British or Indian merchants wishing to build such tanks or stores may not do so until, as provided in Regulation 2, they have made application for a suitable site.

12. British subjects shall be at liberty to deal in kind or in money, to sell their goods to whomsoever they please, to purchase native commodities from whomsoever they please, to hire transport of any kind, and to conduct in general their business transactions in conformity with local usage and without any vexatious restrictions or oppressive exactions whatever.

It being the duty of the Police and Local Authorities to afford efficient protection at all times to the persons and property of the British subjects at the marts, and along the routes to the marts, China engages to arrange effective police measures at the marts and along the routes to the marts. On due fulfilment of these arrangements, Great Britain undertakes to withdraw the Trade Agents' guards at the marts and to station no troops in Tibet, so as to remove all cause for suspicion and disturbance among the inhabitants. The Chinese Authorities will not prevent the British Trade Agents holding personal intercourse and correspondence with the Tibetan officers and people.

Tibetan subjects trading, travelling, or residing in India shall receive equal advantages to those accorded by this Regulation to British subjects in Tibet.

13. The present Regulations shall be in force for a period of ten years reckoned from the date of signature by the two Plenipotentiaries as well as by the Tibetan Delegate ; but if no demand for revision be made by either side within six months after the end of the first ten years, then the Regulations shall remain in force for another ten years from the end of the first ten years ; and so it shall be at the end of each successive ten years.

14. The English, Chinese, and Tibetan texts of the present Regulations have been carefully compared, and, in the event of any question arising as to the interpretation of these Regulations, the sense as expressed in the English text shall be held to be the correct sense.

15. The ratifications of the present Regulations under the hand of His Majesty the King of Great Britain and Ireland, and of His Majesty the Emperor of the Chinese Empire, respectively, shall be exchanged at London and Peking within six months from the date of signature.

In witness whereof the two Plenipotentiaries and the Tibetan Delegate have signed and sealed the present Regulations.

Done in quadruplicate at Calcutta this 20th day of April, in the year of our Lord 1908, corresponding with the Chinese date, the 20th day of the 3rd moon of the 34th year of Kuang-hsu.

E.C. WILTON,
British Commissioner.

Signature of
CHANG YIN TANG,
Chines sepecial
Commissioner.

Signature of
WANG CHUK GYALPO,
Tibetan Delegate.

Despite the intention indicated in Article II of the 1904 Convention, the new Regulations were, in fact, negotiated by the Chinese Commissioner. The Tibetan representative took no active part. He merely signed the regulations.

14. *Treaty between Tibet and Mongolia. January 1913*
[*Said to have been signed at Urga in January 1913*]

Whereas Mongolia and Tibet, having freed themselves from the Manchu dynasty and separated themselves from China, have become independent States, and whereas the two States have always professed one and the same religion, and to the end that their ancient mutual friendships may be strengthened : on the part of the Government of the Sovereign of the Mongolian people—Nikta Biliktu Da Lama Rabdan, acting Minister of Foreign Affairs and Assistant Minister-General and Manlai Caatyr Bei Tzu Damdinsurun ; on the part of the Dalai Lama, Ruler of Tibet—Gujir Tsanshib Kanchen Lubsan-Agwan, Donir Agwan Choinzin Tschichamtso, manager of the bank, and Gendun-Galsan, secretary, have agreed on the folowing :

ARTICLE 1

The Dalai Lama, Sovereign of Tibet, approves of and acknowledges the formation of an independent Mongolian State, and the proclamation on the 9th day of the 11th month of the year of the Pig, of the master of the Yellow Faith Je-tsun Dampa Lama as the Sovereign of the land.

ARTICLE 2

The Sovereign of the Mongolian people Je-tsum Dampa Lama

approves and acknowledges the formation of an independent State and the proclamation of the Dalai Lama as Sovereign of Tibet.

ARTICLE 3

Both States shall take measures, after mutual consideration, for the prosperity of the Buddhist faith.

ARTICLE 4

Both States, the Mongolian and the Tibetan, shall henceforth, for all time, efford each other aid against dangers from without and from within.

ARTICLE 5

Both States, each on its own territory, shall afford mutual aid to their subjects, travelling officially and privately on religious or on State business.

ARTICLE 6

Both States, the Mongolian and the Tibetan, shall, as formerly, carry on mutual trade in the produce of their lands—in goods, cattle &c., and likewise open industrial institutions.

ARTICLE 7

Henceforth transactions on credit shall be allowed only with the knowledge and permission of official institutions ; without such permission no claims shall be examined by Government Institutions.

Should such agreements have been entered into before the conclusion of the present treaty, and should the parties thereto be unable to settle matters amicably, while the loss suffered is great, the payment of such debts may be enforced by the said institutions, but in no case shall the debts concern the *Shabinars* and *Hoshuns*.

ARTICLE 8

Should it be necessary to supplement the articles of this treaty, the Mongolian and Tibetan Governments shall appoint special Plenipotentiaries, who shall come to an Agreement according to the circumstances then existing.

ARTICLE 9

The present treaty shall come into force on the date of the signature thereof.

Plenipotentiaries of the Mongolian Government : Acting Ministers of Foreign Affairs Biliktu Da Lama Rabdan and Assistant Minister-General and Manlai Caatyr Bei Tzu Damdinsurun.

Plenipotentiaries of the Dalai Lama, Sovereign of Tibet : Gujir

Tsanshib Kanchen Lubsan Agwan, Donir Agwan Choinzid Tschienamtso, manager of the Bank of Tibet, and Gendun-Galsan, secretary.

According to the Mongolian chronology, on the 4th day of the 12th month of the second year of 'Him who is exalted by all'.

According to the chronology of Tibet, in the year of the Water-Mouse, on the same month and day.

The validity of the agreement mentioned above was never clearly established.

15. *India-Tibet Frontier 1914. Exchange of notes between the British and Tibetan Plenipotentiaries*

To

Lönchen Shatra, Tibetan Plenipotentiary.

In February last you accepted the India-Tibet frontier from the Isu Razi Pass to the Bhutan frontier, as given in the map (two sheets), of which two copies are herewith attached, subject to the confirmation of your government and the following conditions :—

(a) The Tibetan ownership in private estates on the British side of the frontier will not be disturbed.

(b) If the sacred places of Tso Karpo and Tsari Sarpa fall within a days march of the British side of the frontier, they will be included in Tibetan territory and the frontier modified accordingly.

I understand that your Government have now agreed to this frontier subject to the above two conditions. I shall be glad to learn definitely from you that this is the case.

You wished to know whether certain dues now collected by the Tibetan Government at Tsona Jong and in Kongbu and Kham from the Monpas and Lopas for articles sold may still be collected. Mr. Bell has informed you that such details will be settled in a friendly spirit, when you have furnished him the further information, which you have promised.

The final settlement of this India-Tibet frontier will help to prevent causes of future dispute and thus cannot fail to be of great advantage to both Governments.

A.H. McMAHON,
British Plenipotentiary

Delhi 24th March 1914

The map referred to in this and the succeeding note was published for the first time in *An Atlas of the Northern Frontier of India*, issued on

January 15, 1960 by the Ministry of External Affairs of the Government of India.

[Translation]

To

Sir Henry McMahon,

British Plenipotentiary to the China-Tibet Conference.

As it was feared that there might be friction in future unless the boundary between India and Tibet is clearly defined, I submitted the map, which you sent to me in February last, to the Tibetan Government at Lhasa for orders. I have now received orders from Lhasa, and I accordingly agree to the boundary as marked in red in the two copies of the maps signed by you subject to the condition mentioned in your letter, dated 24th March, sent to me through Mr. Bell. I have signed and sealed the two copies of the maps. I have kept one copy here and return herewith the other.

Sent on the 29th day of the Ist month of the Wood-Tiger year (25th March 1914) by Lönchen Shatra, the Tibetan Plenipotentiary.

Seal of Lönchen Shatra.

16. *Convention between Great Britain, China, and Tibet. Simla 1914*

His Majesty the king of the United Kingdom of Great Britain and Ireland and of the British Dominions beyond the Seas, Emperor of India, His Excellency the President of the Republic of China, and His Holiness the Dalai Lama of Tibet, being sincerely desirous to settle by mutual agreement various questions concerning the interests of their several States on the Continent of Asia, and further to regulate the relations of their several Governments, have resolved to conclude a Convention on this subject and have nominated for this purpose their respective Plenipotentiaries, that is to say :

His Majesty the King of the United Kingdom of Great Britain and Ireland and of the British Dominions beyond the Seas, Emperor of India, Sir Arthur Henry McMahon, Knight Grand Cross of the Royal Victorian Order, Knight Commander of the Most Eminent Order of the Indian Empire, Companion of the Most Exalted Order of the Star of India, Secretary to the Government of India, Foreign and Political Department;

His Excellency the President of the Republic of China, Monsieur Ivan Chen, Officer of the Order of the Chia Ho ;

His Holiness the Dalai Lama of Tibet, Lönchen Ga-den Shara Pal-jor Dorje ; who having communicated to each other their respective full powers and finding them to be in good and due form have agreed upon and concluded the following Convention in eleven Articles :—

ARTICLE 1

The Conventions specified in the Schedule to the present Convention shall, except in so far as they may have been modified by, or may be inconsistent with or repugnant to, any of the provisions of the present Convention, continue to be binding upon the High Contracting Parties.

ARTICLE 2

The Governments of Great Britain and China recognising that Tibet is under the suzerainty of China, and recognising also the autonomy of Outer Tibet, engage to respect the territorial integrity of the country, and to abstain from interference in the administration of Outer Tibet (including the selection and installation of the Dalai Lama), which shall remain in the hands of the Tibetan Government at Lhasa.

The Government of China engages not to convert Tibet into a Chinese province. The Government of Great Britain engages not to annex Tibet or any portion of it.

ARTICLE 3

Recognising the special interest of Great Britain, in virtue of the geographical position of Tibet, in the existence of an effective Tibetan Government, and in the maintenance of peace and order in the neighbourhood of the frontiers of India and adjoining States, the Government of China engages, except as provided in Article 4 of this Convention, not to send troops into Outer Tibet, nor to station civil or military officers, nor to establish Chinese colonies in the country. Should any such troops or officials remain in Outer Tibet at the date of the signature of this Convention, they shall be withdrawn within a period not exceeding three months.

The Government of Great Britain engages not to station military or civil officers inTibet (except as provided in the Convention of September 7, 1904, between Great Britain and Tibet) nor troops (except the Agents' escorts), nor to establish colonies in that country.

ARTICLE 4

The foregoing Article shall not be held to preclude the continuance of the arrangement by which, in the past, a Chinese high official with suitable escort has been maintained at Lhasa, but it is hereby provided that the said escort shall in no circumstances exceed 300 men.

ARTICLE 5

The Governments of China and Tibet engage that they will not enter into any negotiations or agreements regarding Tibet with one another, or with any other Power, excepting such negotiations and agreements between Great Britain and Tibet as are provided for by the Convention of September 7, 1904, between Great Britain and Tibet and the Convention of April 27, 1906, between Great Britain and China.

ARTICLE 6

Article III of the Convention of April 27, 1906, between Great Britain and China is hereby cancelled, and it is understood that in Article IX (*d*) of the Convention of September 7, 1904, between Great Britain and Tibet the term 'Foreign Power' does not include China.

Not less favourable treatment shall be accorded to British commerce than to the commerce of China or the most favoured nation.

ARTICLE 7

(a) The Tibet Trade Regulations of 1893 and 1908 are hereby cancelled.

(b) The Tibetan Government engages to negotiate with the British Government new Trade Regulations for Outer Tibet to give effect to Articles II, IV and V of the Convention of September 7, 1904, between Great Britain and Tibet without delay; provided always that such Regulations shall in no way modify the present Convention except with the consent of the Chinese Government.

ARTICLE 8

The British Agent who resides at Gyantse may visit Lhasa with his escort whenever it is necessary to consult with the Tibetan Government regarding matters arising out of the Convention of September 7, 1904, between Great Britain and Tibet, which it has been found impossible to settle at Gyantse by correspondence or otherwise.

ARTICLE 9

For the purpose of the present Convention the borders of Tibet, and the boundary between Outer and Inner Tibet, shall be as shown in red and blue respectively on the map attached hereto.

Nothing in the present Convention shall be held to prejudice the existing rights of the Tibetan Government in Inner Tibet, which include the power to select and appoint the high priests of monasteries and to retain full control in all matters affecting religious institutions.

ARTICLE 10

The English, Chinese and Tibetan texts of the present Convention have been carefully examined and found to correspond, but in the event of there being any difference of meaning between them the English text shall be authoritative.

ARTICLE 11

The present Convention will take effect from the date of signature.

In token whereof the respective Plenipotentiaries have signed and sealed this Convention, three copies in English, three in Chinese and three in Tibetan.

Done at Simla this third day of July, A.D., one thousand nine hundred and fourteen, corresponding with the Chinese date, the third day of the seventh month of the third year of the Republic, and the Tibetan date, the tenth day of the fifth month of the Wood-Tiger year.

Initial of the Lönchen Shatra. (Initialled) A.H.M.
Seal of the Lönchen Shatra. Seal of the British Plenipotentiary.

Schedule

1. Convention between Great Britain and China relating to Sikkim and Tibet, signed at Calcutta the 17th March 1890.

2. Convention between Great Britain and Tibet, signed at Lhasa the 7th September 1904.

3. Convention between Great Britain and China respecting Tibet, signed at Peking the 27th April 1906.

The notes exchanged are to the following effect :—

1. It is understood by the High Contracting Parties that Tibet forms part of Chinese territory.

2. After the selection and installation of the Dalai Lama by the Tibetan Government, the latter will notify the installation to the Chinese Government whose representative at Lhasa will then formally communicate to His Holiness the titles consistent with his dignity, which have been conferred by the Chinese Government.

3. It is also understood that the selection and appointment of all officers in Outer Tibet will rest with the Tibetan Government.

4. Outer Tibet shall not be represented in the Chinese Parliament or in any other similar body.

5. It is understood that the escorts attached to the British Trade Agencies in Tibet shall not exceed seventy-five per centum of the escort of the Chinese Representative at Lhasa.

6. The Government of China is hereby released from its engagements under Article III of the Convention of March 17, 1890, between Great Britain and China to prevent acts of aggression from the Tibetan side of the Tibet-Sikkim frontier.

7. The Chinese high official referred to in Article 4 will be free to

enter Tibet as soon as the terms of Article 3 have been fulfilled to the satisfaction of representatives of the three signatories to this Convention, who will investigate and report without delay.

Initial of the Lönchen Shatra. (Initialled) A.H.M.
Seal of the Lönchen Shatra. Seal of the British Plenipotentiary.

About the withdrawal of the Chinese, a Declaration was signed by the Plenipotentiaries of Britain and Tibet declaring that the Convention was to be binding on the Governments of Britain and Tibet both of them also agreed that so long as the Chinese Government withheld its signature, it would be debarred from enjoying the privileges accruing thereunder.

17. *Anglo-Tibetan Trade Regulations—3rd of July 1914*

Whereas by Article 7 of the Convention concluded between the Governments of Great Britain, China and Tibet on the third day of July, A.D. 1914, the Trade Regulations of 1893 and 1908 were cancelled and the Tibetan Government engaged to negotiate with the British Government new Trade Regulations for Outer Tibet to give effect to Articles II, IV and V of the Convention of 1904 ;

His Majesty the King of the United Kingdom of Great Britain and Ireland, and of the British Dominions beyond the Seas, Emperor of India, and His Holiness the Dalai Lama of Tibet have for this purpose named as their Plenipotentiaries, that is to say :

His Majesty the King of Great Britain and Ireland and of the British Dominions beyond the Seas, Emperor of India, Sir A.H. McMahon, G.C.V.O., K.C.I.E., C.S.I. :

His Holiness the Dalai Lama of Tibet, Lönchen Ga-den Shatra Pal-jor Dorje ;

And whereas Sir A.H. McMahon and Lönchen Ga-den Shatra Pal-jor Dorje have communicated to each other since their respective full powers and have found them to be in good and true form, the following Regulations have been agreed upon :—

(I) The area falling within a radius of three miles from the British Trade Agency site will be considered as the area of such Trade Mart.

It is agreed that British subjects may lease lands for the building of houses and godowns at the Marts. This arrangement shall not be held to prejudice the right of British subjects to rent houses and godowns outside the Marts for their own accommodation and the storage of their goods. British subjects desiring to lease building sites shall apply through the British Trade Agent to the Tibetan Trade Agent. In consultation with the

British Trade Agent the Tibetan Trade Agent will assign such or other suitable building sites without unnecessary delay. They shall fix the terms of the leases in conformity with the existing laws and rates.

(II) The administration of the Trade Marts shall remain with the Tibetan Authorities, with the exception of the British Trade Agency sites and compounds of the rest-houses, which will be under the exclusive control of the British Trade Agents.

The Trade Agents at the Marts and Frontier Officers shall be of suitable rank, and shall hold personal intercourse and correspondence with one another on terms of mutual respect and friendly treatment.

(III) In the event of disputes arising at the Marts or on the routes to the Marts between British subjects and subjects of other nationalities, they shall be enquired into and settled in personal conference between the British and Tibetan Trade Agents at the nearest Mart. Where there is a divergence of view the law of the country to which the defendant belongs shall guide.

All questions in regard to rights, whether of property or person, arising between British subjects, shall be subject to the jurisdiction of the British Authorities.

British subjects, who may commit any crime at the Marts or on the routes to the Marts, shall be handed over by the Local Authorities to the British Trade Agent at the Mart nearest to the scene of the offence, to be tried and punished according to the laws of India, but such British subjects shall not be subjected by the Local Authorities to any ill-usage in excess of necessary restraint.

Tibetan subjects, who may be guilty of any criminal act towards British subjects, shall be arrested and punished by the Tibetan Authorities according to law.

Should it happen that a Tibetan subject or subjects bring a criminal complaint against a British subject or subjects before the British Trade Agent, the Tibetan Authorities shall have the right to send a representative or representatives of suitable rank to attend the trial in the British Trade Agent's Court. Similarly in cases in which a British subject or subjects have reason to complain against a Tibetan subject or subjects, the British Trade Agent shall have the right to send a representative or representatives to the Tibetan Trade Agent's Court to attend the trial.

(IV) The Government of India shall retain the right to maintain the telegraph lines from the Indian frontier to the Marts. Tibetan messages will be duly received and transmitted by these lines. The Tibetan Authorities shall be responsible for the due protection of the telegraph lines from the Marts to the Indian frontier, and it is agreed that all persons damaging the lines or interfering with them in any way or with the officials engaged in the inspection or maintenance thereof shall at once be severely punished.

(V) The British Trade Agents at the various Trade Marts now or hereafter to be established in Tibet may make arrangements for the carriage and transport of their posts to and from the frontier of India. The couriers employed in conveying these posts shall receive all possible assistance from the Local Authorities whose districts they traverse, and shall be accorded the same protection and facilities as the persons employed in carrying the despatches of the Tibetan Government.

No restrictions whatever shall be placed on the employment by British officers and traders of Tibetan subjects in any lawful capacity. The persons so employed shall not be exposed to any kind of molestation or suffer any loss of civil rights, to which they may be entitled as Tibetan subjects, but they shall not be exempted from lawful taxation. If they be guilty of any criminal act, they shall be dealt with by the Local Authorities according to law without any attempt on the part of their employer to screen them.

(VI) No rights of monopoly as regards commerce or industry shall be granted to any official or private company, institution, or individual in Tibet. It is of course understood that companies and individuals, who have already received such monopolies from the Tibetan Government previous to the conclusions of this agreement, shall retain their rights and privileges until the expiry of the period fixed.

(VII) British subjects shall be at liberty to deal in kind or in money, to sell their goods to whomsoever they please, to hire transport of any kind, and to conduct in general their business transactions in conformity with local usage and without any vexations, restrictions or oppressive exactions whatever. The Tibetan Authorities will not hinder the British Trade Agents or other British subjects from holding personal intercourse or correspondence with the inhabitants of the country.

It being the duty of the Police and the Local Authorities to afford efficient protection at all times to the persons and property of the British subjects at the Marts and along the routes to the Marts, Tibet engages to arrange effective Police measures at the Marts and along the routes to the Marts.

(VIII) Import and export in the following Articles :—

arms, ammunition, military stores, liquors and intoxicating or narcotic drugs.

may at the option of either Government be entirely prohibited, or permitted only on such conditions as either Government on their own side may think fit to impose.

(IX) The present Regulations shall be in force for a period of ten years reckoned from the date of signature by the two Plenipotentiaries ; but, if no demand for revision be made on either side within six months after the end of the first ten years the Regulations shall remain in force for another ten years from the end of the first ten years ; and so it shall be at the end of each successive ten years.

(X) The English and Tibetan texts of the present Regulations have been carefully compared, but in the event of there being any difference of meaning between them the English text shall be authoritative.

(XI) The present regulations shall come into force from the date of signature. Done at Simla this third day of July, A.D. one thousand nine hundred and fourteen, corresponding with the Tibetan date, the tenth day of the fifth month of the Wood-Tiger year.

Seal of the Dalai Lama.

A. HENRY McMAHON,
British Plenipotentiary.

Signature of the Lönchen Shatra.

Seal of the Lönchen Shatra.

Seal of the British Plenipotentiary

Seal of the Drepung Monastery

Seal of the Sera Monastery

Seal of the Gaden Monastery

Seal of the National Assembly

Negotiated and signed only by the British and Tibetan Plenipotentiaries.

18. *Agreement on Measures for the Peaceful Liberation of Tibet (17-point Agreement of May 23, 1951)*

The Tibetan nationality is one of the nationalities with a long history within the boundaries of China and, like many other nationalities, it has done its glorious duty in the course of the creation and development of the great Motherland. But, over the last 100 years or more, imperialist forces penetrated into China and in consequence also penetrated into the Tibetan region and carried out all kinds of deceptions and provocations. Like previous reactionary Governments, the Kuomintang reactionary Government continued to carry out a policy of oppression and sowing dissension among the nationalities, causing division and disunity among the Tibetan people. The local government of Tibet did not oppose the imperialist deception and provocation and adopted an unpatriotic attitude towards the great Motherland. Under such conditions the Tibetan nationality and people were plunged into the depths of enslavement and sufferings. In 1949 basic victory was achieved on a nation-wide scale in the Chinese people's war of liberation ; the common domestic enemy of all nationalities—the Kuomintang reactionary Government—was overthrown and the common foreign enemy of all nationalities—the aggressive imperialist forces—was driven out. On this basis the founding of the People's Republic of China (CPR) and of the Chinese People's Government (CPG) was announced.

In accordance with the Common Programme passed by the Chinese People's Political Consultative Conference (CPPCC), the CPG declared that all nationalities within the boundaries of the CPR are equal and that they shall establish unity and mutual aid and oppose imperialism and their own public enemies, so that the CPR will become a big family of fraternity and co-operation, composed of all its nationalities. Within the big family of all nationalities of the CPR, national regional autonomy shall be exercised in areas where national minorities are concentrated and all national minorities shall have freedom to develop their spoken and written languages and to preserve or reform thein customs, habits and religious beliefs, and the CPG shall assist all national minorities to develop their political, economic, cultural and educational construction work. Since then, all nationalities within the country—with the exception of those in the areas of Tibet and Taiwan—have gained liberation. Under the unified leadership of the CPG and the direct leadership of higher levels of people's governments, all national minorities have fully enjoyed the right of national equality and have exercised, or are exercising, national regional autonomy.

In order that the influences of aggressive imperialist forces in Tibet might be successfully eliminated, the unification of the territory and sovereignty of the CPR accomplished, and national defence safeguarded ; in order that the Tibetan nationality and people might be freed and return to the big family of the CPR to enjoy the same rights of national equality as all other nationalities in the country and develop their political, economic, cultural and educational work, the CPG, when it ordered the People's Liberation Army (PLA) to march into Tibet, notified the local government of Tibet to send delegates to the central authorities to conduct talks for the conclusion of an agreement on measures for the peaceful liberation of Tibet. In the latter part of April 1951 the delegates with full powers of the local government of Tibet arrived in Peking. The CPG appointed representatives with full powers to conduct talks on a friendly basis with the delegates with full powers of the local government of Tibet. As a result of the talks both parties agreed to establish this agreement and ensure that it be carried into effect.

(1) The Tibetan people shall unite and drive out imperialist aggressive forces from Tibet ; the Tibetan people shall return to the big family of the Motherland—the People's Republic of China.

(2) The local government of Tibet shall actively assist the PLA to enter Tibet and consolidate the national defences.

(3) In accordance with the policy towards nationalities laid down in the Common Programme of the CPPCC, the Tibetan people have the right of exercising national regional autonomy under the unified leadership of the CPG.

(4) The central authorities will not alter the existing political system in Tibet. The central authorities also will not alter the established status, functions and powers of the Dalai Lama. Officials of various ranks shall hold office as usual.

(5) The established status, functions and powers of the Panchen Ngoerhtehni shall be maintained.

(6) By the established status, functions and powers of the Dalai Lama and of the Panchen Ngoerhtehni are meant the status, functions and powers of the thirteenth Dalai Lama and of the ninth Panchen Ngoerhtehni when they were in friendly and amicable relations with each other.

(7) The policy of freedom of religious belief laid down in the Common Programme of the CPPCC shall be carried out. The religious beliefs, customs and habits of the Tibetan people shall be respected and lama monasteries shall be protected. The central authorities will not effect a change in the income of the monasteries.

(8) Tibetan troops shall be reorganised step by step into the PLA and become a part of the national defence forces of the CPR.

(9) The spoken and written language and school education of the Tibetan nationality shall be developed step by step in accordance with the actual conditions in Tibet.

(10) Tibetan agriculture, livestock—raising, industry and commerce shall be developed step by step and the people's livelihood shall be improved step by step in accordance with the actual conditions in Tibet.

(11) In matters related to various reforms in Tibet, there will be no compulsion on the part of the central authorities. The local government of Tibet should carry out reforms of its own accord, and, when the people raise demands for reform, they shall be settled by means of consultation with the leading personnel of Tibet.

(12) In so far as former pro-imperialist and pro-Kuomintang officials resolutely sever relations with imperialism and the Kuomintang and do not engage in sabotage or resistance, they may continue to hold office irrespective of their past.

(13) The PLA entering Tibet shall abide by all the above-mentioned policies and shall also be fair in all buying and selling and shall not arbitrarily take a needle or thread from the people.

(14) The CPG shall have centralised handling of all external affairs of the area of Tibet ; and there will be peaceful co-existence with neighbouring countries and establishment and development of fair commercial and trading relations with them on the basis of equality, mutual benefit and mutual respect for territory and sovereignty.

(15) In order to ensure the implementation of this agreement, the CPG shall set up a Military and Administrative Committee and a Military Area HQ in Tibet and—apart from the personnel sent there by the CPG—shall absorb as many local Tibetan personnel as possible to take part in the work. Local Tibetan personnel taking part in the Military and Administrative Committee may include patriotic elements from the local government of Tibet, various districts and various principal monasteries ; the name-list shall be set forth after consultation between the representatives designated by the CPG and various quarters concerned and shall be submitted to the CPG for appointment.

(16) Funds needed by the Military and Administrative Committee, the Military Area HQ and the PLA entering Tibet shall be provided by the CPG. The local government of Tibet should assist the PLA in the purchase and transport of food, fodder and other daily necessities.

(17) This agreement shall come into force immediately after signature and seals are affixed to it.

Signed and sealed by delegates of the CPG with full powers : Chief Delegate—Li Wei-Han (Chairman of the Commission of Nationalities Affairs) ; Delegates—Chang Ching-wu, Chang Kuo-hua, Sun Chih-yuan. Delegates with full powers of the local government of Tibet : Chief Delegate—Kaloon Ngabou Ngawang Jigme (Ngabo Shape) ; Delegates—Dazasak Khemey Sonam Wangdi,

Khentrung Thupten Tenthar, Khenchung Thupten Lekmuun, Rimshi Samposey Tenzin Thundup. Peking, 23rd May, 1951.

19. *Sino-Indian Agreement, 29th April 1954*

AGREEMENT

Between

THE REPUBLIC OF INDIA AND THE PEOPLE'S REPUBLIC OF CHINA ON TRADE AND INTERCOURSE

Between

TIBET REGION OF CHINA AND INDIA

The Government of the Republic of India and the Central People's Government of the People's Republic of China.

Being desirous of promoting trade and cultural intercourse between Tibet Region of China and India and of facilitating pilgrimage and travel by the peoples of China and India.

Have resolved to enter into the present Agreement based on the following principles :

(1) mutual respect for each other's territorial integrity and sovereignty,

(2) mutual non-aggression,

(3) mutual non-interference in each other's internal affairs,

(4) equality and mutual benefit, and

(5) peaceful co-existence.

And for this purpose have appointed as their respective Plenipotentiaries :

The Government of the Republic of India, H. E. Nedyam Raghavan, Ambassador Extraordinary and Plenipotentiary of India accredited to the People's Republic of China ; the Central People's Government of the People's Republic of China, H.E. Chang Han-fu, Vice-Minister of Foreign Affairs of the Central People's Government, who, having examined each other's credentials and finding them in good and due form, have agreed upon the following :—

ARTICLE I

The High Contracting Parties mutually agree to establish Trade Agencies :

(1) The Government of India agrees that the Government of China may establish Trade Agencies at New Delhi, Calcutta and Kalimpong.

(2) The Government of China agrees that the Government of India may establish Trade Agencies at Yatung, Gyantse and Gartok.

The Trade Agencies of both Parties shall be accorded the same status and same treatment. The Trade Agents of both Parties shall enjoy freedom from arrest while exercising their functions, and shall enjoy in respect of themselves, their wives and children who are dependent on them for livelihood freedom from search.

The Trade Agencies of both Parties shall enjoy the privileges and immunities for couriers, mail-bags and communications in code.

ARTICLE II

The High Contracting Parties agree that traders of both countries known to be customarily and specifically engaged in trade between Tibet Region of China and India may trade at the following places :

(1) The Government of China agrees to specify (1) Yatung, (2) Gyantse and (3) Phari as markets for trade. The Government of India agrees that trade may be carrried on in India, including places like (1) Kalimpong, (2) Siliguri and (3) Calcutta, according to customary practice.

(2) The Government of China agrees to specify (1) Gartok, (2) Pulanchung (Taklakot), (3) Gyanima-Khargo, (4) Gyanima-Chakra, (5) Ramura, (6) Dongbra ; (7) Puling-Sumdo, (8) Nabra, (9) Shangtse and (10) Tashigong as markets for trade ; the Government of India agrees that in future, when in accordance with the development and need of trade between the Ari District of Tibet Region of China and India, it has become necessary to specify markets for trade in the corresponding district in India adjacent to the Ari District of Tibet Region of China, it will be prepared to consider on the basis of equality and reciprocity to do so.

ARTICLE III

The High Contracting Parties agree that pilgrimage by religious believers of the two countries shall be carried on in accordance with the following provisions :—

(1) Pilgrims from India of Lamaist, Hindu and Buddhist faiths may visit Kang Rimpoche (Kailas) and Mavam Tso (Manasarovar) in Tibet Region of China in accordance with custom.

(2) Pilgrims from Tibet Region of China of Lamaist and Buddhist faiths may visit Banaras, Sarnath, Gaya and Sanchi in India in accordance with custom.

(3) Pilgrims customarily visiting Lhasa may continue to do so in accordance with custom.

ARTICLE IV

Traders and pilgrims of both countries may travel by the following passes and route :

(1) Shipki La pass, (2) Mana pass, (3) Niti pass, (4) Kungri Bingri pass, (5) Darma pass, and (6) Lipu Lekh pass.

Also, the customary route leading to Tashigong along the valley of the Shangatsangpu (Indus) River may continue to be traversed in accordance with custom.

ARTICLE V

For travelling across the border, the High Contracting Parties agree that diplomatic personnel, officials and nationals of the two countries shall hold passports issued by their own respective countries and visaed by the other Party except as provided in Paragraphs 1, 2, 3 and 4 of this Article.

(1) Traders of both countries known to be customarily and specifically engaged in trade between Tibet Region of China and India, their wives and children who are dependent on them for livelihood and their attendants will be allowed entry for purposes of trade into India or Tibet Region of China, as the case may be, in accordance with custom on the production of certificates duly issued by the local government of their own country or by its duly authorised agents and examined by the border check-posts of the other Party.

(2) Inhabitants of the border districts of the two countries who cross the border to carry on petty trade or to visit friends and relatives may proceed to the border districts of the other Party as they have customarily done heretofore and need not be restricted to the passes and route specified in Article IV above and shall not be required to hold passports, visas or permits.

(3) Porters and mule-team drivers of the two countries who cross the border to perform necessary transportation services need not hold passports issued by their own country, but shall only hold certificates good for a definite period of time (three months, half a year or one year) duly issued by the local government of their own country or by its duly authorised agents and produce them for registration at the border checkposts of the other Party.

(4) Pilgrims of both countries need not carry documents of certification but shall register at the border checkposts of the other Party and receive a permit for pilgrimage.

(5) Notwithstanding the provisions of the foregoing paragraphs of this Article, either Government may refuse entry to any particular person.

(6) Persons who enter the territory of the other Party in accordance with the foregoing paragraphs of this Article may stay within its territory only after complying with the procedures specified by the other Party.

ARTICLE VI

The present Agreement shall come into effect upon ratification by both Governments and shall remain in force for eight (8) years. Extension of the present Agreement may be negotiated by the two Parties if either Party requests for it six (6) months prior to the expiry of the Agreement and the request is agreed to by the other Party.

Done in duplicate in Peking on the twenty-ninth day of April, 1954, in the Hindi, Chinese and English languages, all texts being equally valid.

(Sd.) NEDYAM RAGHAVAN,	(Sd.) CHANG HAN-FU,
Plenipotentiary of the Government of the Republic of India.	Plenipotentiary of the Central People's Government, People's Republic of China.

Notes Exchanged

NOTE

Peking, April 29, 1954

YOUR EXCELLENCY MR. VICE-FOREIGN MINISTER,

In the course of our discussions regarding the Agreement on Trade and Intercourse Between the Tibet Region of China and India, which has been happily concluded today, the Delegation of the Government of the Republic of India and the Delegation of the Government of the People's Republic of China agreed that certain matters be regulated by an exchange of Notes. In pursuance of this understanding, it is hereby agreed between the two Governments as follows :—

(1) The Government of India will be pleased to withdraw completely within six (6) months from date of exchange of the present notes the military escorts now stationed at Yatung and Gyantse in Tibet Region of China. The Government of China will render facilities and assistance in such withdrawal.

(2) The Government of India will be pleased to hand over to the Government of China at a reasonable price the postal, telegraph and public telephone services together with their equipment operated by

the Government of India in Tibet Region of China. The concrete measures in this regard will be decided upon through further negotiations between the Indian Embassy in China and the Foreign Ministry of China, which shall start immediately after the exchange of the present notes.

(3) The Government of India will be pleased to hand over to the Government of China at a reasonable price the twelve (12) rest houses of the Government of India in Tibet Region of China. The concrete measures in this regard will be decided upon through further negotiations between the Indian Embassy in China and the Foreign Ministry of China, which shall start immediately after the exchange of the present notes. The Government of China agrees that they shall continue as rest houses.

(4) The Government of China agrees that all buildings within the compound walls of the Trade Agencies of the Government of India at Yatung and Gyantse in Tibet Region of China may be retained by the Government of India. The Government of India may continue to lease the land within its Agency compound walls from the Chinese side. And the Government of India agrees that the Trade Agencies of the Government of China at Kalimpong and Calcutta may lease lands from the Indian side for the use of the Agencies and construct buildings thereon. The Government of China will render every possible assistance for housing the Indian Trade Agency at Gartok. The Government of India will also render every possible assistance for housing the Chinese Trade Agency at New Delhi.

(5) The Government of India will be pleased to return to the Government of China all lands used or occupied by the Government of India other than the lands within its Trade Agency compound walls at Yatung.

If there are godowns and buildings of the Government of India on the above-mentioned lands used or occupied and to be returned by the Government of India and if Indian traders have stores, godowns or buildings on the above-mentioned lands so that there is a need to continue leasing lands, the Government of China agrees to sign contracts with the Government of India or Indian traders, as the case may be, for leasing to them those parts of the land occupied by the said godowns, buildings or stores and pertaining thereto.

(6) The Trade Agents of both Parties may, in accordance with the laws and regulations of the local governments, have access to their nationals involved in civil or criminal cases.

(7) The Trade Agents and traders of both countries may hire employees in the locality.

(8) The hospitals of the India Trade Agencies at Gyantse and Yatung will continue to serve personnel of the Indian Trade Agencies.

(9) Each Government shall protect the person and property of the traders and pilgrims of the other country.

(10) The Government of China agrees, so far as possible, to construct rest houses for the use of pilgrims along the route from Pulan-chung (Taklakot) to Kang Rimpoche (Kailas) and Mavam Tso (Manasarovar) ; and the Government of India agrees to place all possible facilities in India at the disposal of pilgrims.

(11) Traders and pilgrims of both countries shall have the facility of hiring means of transportation at normal and reasonable rates.

(12) The three Trade Agencies of each Party may function throughout the year.

(13) Traders of each country may rent buildings and godowns in accordance with local regulations in places under the jurisdiction of the other Party.

(14) Traders of both countries may carry on normal trade in accordance with local regulations at places as provided in Article II of the Agreement.

(15) Disputes between traders of both countries over debts and claims shall be handled in accordance with local laws and regulations.

On behalf of the Government of the Republic of India I hereby agree that the present Note along with Your Excellency's reply shall become an agreement between our two Governments which shall come into force upon the exchange of the present Notes.

I avail myself of this opportunity to express to Your Excellency Mr. Vice-Foreign Minister, the assurances of my highest consideration.

(Sd.) N. RAGHAVAN,
Ambassador Extraordinary and
Pleni-potentiary of the Republic of India.

His Excellency Mr. Chang Han-fu,
Vice-Minister of Foreign Affairs,
Central People's Government,
People's Republic of China.

20. *Trade Agreement (Agreement between the Republic of India and the People's Republic of China, 14 October 1954)*

The Government of the Republic of India and the Central People's Government of the People's Republic of China, animated by the common desire to develop trade between the two countries and to strengthen further the friendship that already exists between the Governments and the peoples of India and China have, on the basis of equality and mutual benefit, reached agreements as follows :—

ARTICLE I

The two contracting parties being desirous of adopting all appropriate measures for the expansion of trade between the two countries agree to give the fullest consideration to all suggestions for the promotion of such trade.

ARTICLE II

The two contracting parties agree that all commercial transactions between the two countries shall be carried out in accordance with the Import, Export and Foreign Exchange Regulations in force from time to time in their respective countries.

ARTICLE III

The two contracting parties agree to accord, subject to the laws and regulations of the two countries for the time being in force, facilities for the import and export of the commodities mentioned in the attached Schedules 'A' and 'B'.

ARTICLE IV

The present Agreement will not preclude the two contracting parties from facilitating trade in commodities not mentioned in the attached Schedules 'A' and 'B'.

ARTICLE V

The Trade between the Republic of India and the Tibet Region of the People's Republic of China will be conducted in accordance with the provisions of the Agreement between the Republic of India and the Tibet Region of China signed in Peking on the 29th April 1954.

ARTICLE VI

The Government of the Republic of India agree that on request by the Government of the People's Republic of China, they will subject to the regulations in force, accord reasonable facilities for the entry into the Port of Calcutta and subsequent movement to the Tibet Region of the People's Republic of China, of such commercial goods as cannot be obtained in India. These facilities will be accorded only to goods of Chinese origin.

ARTICLE VII

All commercial and non-commercial payments between the Republic of India and the People's Republic of China may be effected in Indian rupees or in pounds sterling as may be mutually convenient. For the purpose of facilitating such payments, the People's Bank of China will open one or more account(s) with one or more commercial bank(s) in India authorised to deal in Foreign Exchange to be called account(s) 'A'. In addition, the People's Bank of China will, if necessary, open another account with the Reserve Bank of India to be called account 'B'. All payments between the two countries will be made through account(s) 'A'. Account 'B' will be used only for replenishing the balance(s) in account(s) 'A' whenever necessary. Payments to be made by residents of India to residents of the People's Republic of China will be effected by crediting the amounts of such payments to the above-mentioned accounts(s) 'A'. Payments to be made to residents of India by residents of the People's Republic of China will be effected by debiting the said account(s) 'A'. The account(s) 'A' will be replenished as and when necessary by one of the following methods, namely :—

(i) by transfer of funds from another account 'A' of the People's Bank of China with another commercial bank, or from account 'B' with the Reserve Bank of India ;
(ii) by sale of sterling to the bank concerned. Account 'B' will be replenished by either sale of sterling to the Reserve Bank of India or by transfer of funds from account(s) 'A'.

2. Article VII of this Agreement covers the following payments :—
(i) Payments for the commodities imported or exported under the present Agreement ;
(ii) Payments connected with commercial transactions and covering insurance, freight (in case of shipments of goods by the ships of either country), port charges, storage and forwarding expenses and bunkering ;
(iii) Payments for distribution of films, for incomes and expenses of cultural performances and other exhibitions ;
(iv) Payments of expenses on account of tours of delegations of commercial, cultural, social or official nature ;
(v) Payments for the maintenance of the Embassy, Consulates and Trade Agencies of the Republic of India in China and for the maintenance of the Embassy, Consulates and Trade Agencies of the People's Republic of China in India ;
(vi) Other non-commercial payments on which agreement is reached between the Reserve Bank of India and the People's Bank of China.

3. Any balances on the credit side of the account(s) 'A' or account 'B' maintained by the People's Bank of China will be convertible on demand into sterling at any time at the usual Banks' selling rate for sterling as fixed from time to time by the Indian Exchange Banks' Association . The above mentioned balances will be convertible into sterling even after the expiry of this Agreement.

4. Payments for Border Trade between the Republic of India and the People's Republic of China, however, will be settled according to the customary practice.

ARTICLE VIII

The two contracting parties agree to consult with each other on questions that may arise in the course of the implementation of the present Agreement.

ARTICLE IX

This Agreement will come into force from the date of its signature and will remain valid for a period of two years.

This Agreement can be extended or renewed by negotiation between the two contracting parties to be commenced three months prior to its expiry.

Done in duplicate in New Delhi on the fourteenth Day of October 1954, in the Hindi, Chinese and English languages, all texts being equally authentic.

(Sd.) KUNG YUAN,
On behalf of the Government of
the People's Republic of China

(Sd.) H.V.R. IENGAR,
On behalf of the Government
of the Republic of India.

Schedules of Goods for Export not reproduced.

United Nations General Assembly

Fourteenth Session

Eight hundred and thirty-fourth Plenary Meeting
October 21st 1959

The Question of Tibet : Draft Resolution submitted by the Federation of Malaya and Ireland.

The General Assembly,

Recalling the principles regarding fundamental human rights and freedoms set out in the Charter of the United Nations and in the Universal Declaration of Human Rights adopted by the General Assembly on December 10th 1948,

Considering that the fundamental human rights and freedoms to which the Tibetan people, like all others, are entitled include the right to civil and religious liberty for all without distinction,

Mindful also of the distinctive cultural and religious heritage of the people of Tibet and of the autonomy which they have traditionally enjoyed,

Gravely concerned at reports, including the official statements of His Holiness the Dalai Lama, to the effect that the fundamental human rights and freedoms of the people of Tibet have been forcibly denied to them,

Deploring the effect of these events in increasing international tensions and embittering relations between peoples at a time when earnest and positive efforts are being made by responsible leaders to reduce tension and improve international relations,

1. Affirms its belief that respect for the principles of the Charter and of the Universal Declaration of Human Rights is essential for the evolution of a peaceful world order based on the rule of law,

2. Calls for respect for the fundamental human rights of the Tibetan people and for their distinctive cultural and religious life.

Voting by roll call :

In favour : Federation of Malaya, Greece, Guatemala, Haiti, Honduras, Iceland, Iran, Ireland, Israel, Italy, Japan, Jordan, Laos, Liberia, Luxembourg, Mexico, Netherlands, New Zealand, Nicaragua, Norway, Pakistan, Panama, Paraguay, Peru, Philippines, Sweden, Thailand,

	Tunisia, Turkey, United States of America, Uruguay, Venezuela Argentina, Australia, Austria, Bolivia, Brazil, Canada, Chile, China, Colombia, Cuba, Denmark, Ecuador, El Salvador.
Against :	Hungary, Poland, Romania, Ukrainian Soviet Socialist Republic, Union of Soviet Socialist Republics, Albania, Bulgaria, Byelorussian S.S.R., Czechoslovakia.
Abstaining :	Finland, France, Ghana, India, Indonesia, Iraq, Lebanon, Libya, Morocco, Nepal, Portugal, Saudi Arabia, Spain, Sudan, Union of South Africa, United Arab Republic, United Kingdom of Great Britain and Northern Ireland, Yemen, Yugoslavia, Afghanistan, Belgium, Burma, Cambodia, Ceylon, Dominican Republic, Ethiopia.

The draft resolution was adopted by 45 to 9 votes. 26 members abstained from voting. India was one amongst those abstaining.

Costa Rica, whose delegate was absent, at the time of voting later voted in favour of the resolution.

Index